One Ha...
suffragis... Th...
of women's rights at the turn of ... ...ill, personal experience of trade unionism and domestic struggle against poverty and hardship led to their demands for equal pay, educational opportunities, better birth control, child allowances, the right to work. Their strength was always at grassroots level and their demands reflected their painstaking, democratic approach. Opposed to the violence of the suffragettes, they felt that the vote was only the beginning of rights for women, and after the vote was won they continued to campaign for other reforms – many still demanded by women today.

This important book is based on a wealth of unpublished material – local newspaper accounts, unpublished diaries, handwritten minute books, forgotten biographies, as well as interviews with the people still alive who remember these remarkable women of seventy years ago. In telling their story, the history of the suffrage movement is placed in a broader and more accurate perspective.

Jill Liddington was born in Manchester in 1946 and lives in Halifax, West Yorkshire. She teaches at Leeds University Department of Adult Education and is author of *The Life and Times of a Respectable Rebel: Selina Cooper 1864-1946* (Virago Press 1984). Jill is a contributor to *Over Our Dead Bodies: Women against the Bomb* (Virago Press 1983), and is currently writing a history of the women's peace movement this century. Jill Norris was born in Newcastle in 1949, and died in 1985. She taught in Manchester primary schools and adult education for eight years. In 1979 she moved to Macclesfield where she lived with her two daughters. She was one of the founders of the Macclesfield Silk Museum, and at the time of her death was currently doing research on the lives of women workers in Macclesfield.

ONE HAND
TIED BEHIND US

The Rise of the Women's Suffrage Movement

JILL LIDDINGTON

JILL NORRIS

First published by VIRAGO PRESS Limited 1978
41 William IV Street, London WC2N 4DB

Reprinted 1984, 1985

British Library Cataloguing in Publication Data

Liddington, Jill
  One hand tied behind us.
  1. Women—Suffrage—England—Lancashire—History
  I. Title   II. Norris, Jill
  324′.3′094276   JN985.L/

  ISBN 0-86068-008-8

Printed in Great Britain by litho
at The Anchor Press, Tiptree, Essex

The illustration on the cover,
Women Weavers 1895, is reproduced by
kind permission of the City of
Salford Cultural Services

CONTENTS

ILLUSTRATIONS

Women's Suffrage leaflet, Rossendale Election 1910
(by kind permission of Andrew Bullen)

Lees and Wrigley Spinning Mill, Oldham, circa 1890.
(from the Oldham Chronicle)

Peterloo Veterans, 1884
(from a photograph by John Birch, September 27th 1884, reprinted in Percival, P., *Failsworth Folk and Failsworth Memories,* Manchester 1901.)

Sarah Dickenson
(by kind permission of Ruth and Eddie Frow)

Ada Nield and George Chew
(by kind permission of Doris Chew)

Selina Cooper with fellow suffragists on a campaign in the west country, circa 1910
(by kind permission of Mary Cooper, Herbert Morris, Colin Bean and Nelson Library)

Lancashire and Cheshire Delegates on the Women's Franchise Deputation to the Prime Minister, 1906
(by kind permission of Mary Cooper, F.R. Clark, Colin Bean and Nelson Library)

Lancashire winders, Droylsden: weekday working and Sunday best.
(City of Manchester Cultural Services: Local History Library)

Factory gate suffrage meeting, circa 1910.
(by kind permission of Mary Cooper, Harold Burkinshaw, Colin Bean and Nelson Library)

Ada Nield Chew campaigning at the Crewe by-election, 1912.
(by kind permission of Doris Chew)

CHRONOLOGY

THE LANCASHIRE SUFFRAGE CAMPAIGN

1867   J.S. Mill's women's suffrage amendment to Second Reform Bill. Regional suffrage societies formed: Lydia Becker becomes Secretary, Manchester Society.

1883   Women's Co-operative Guild formed.

1884   Northern Counties Amalgamated Association of Weavers formed. Trades Union Congress votes in favour of women's suffrage.

1886   Amalgamated Association of Card & Blowing Room Operatives formed.

1890   Death of Lydia Becker.

1891   First Labour Church formed, in Manchester.
Robert Blatchford starts the *Clarion.*

1893   Independent Labour Party founded.

1893   Special Appeal launched by Suffrage Societies.
Esther Roper becomes Secretary of Manchester Suffrage Society.

1894   Ada Nield's Crewe 'Factory Girl' campaign.

1895   Independent Labour Party votes to give the vote to both men and women.
Manchester & Salford Women's Trade Union Council formed.

1897   Eva Gore-Booth joins Esther Roper in Manchester.
National Union of Women's Suffrage Societies formed, with Mrs Fawcett as President.

1900   Textile workers' suffrage petition campaign launched.

1901   Deputation of Lancashire cotton workers takes petition to Westminster.
Helen Silcock raises women's suffrage at Trades Union Congress.
'Taff Vale No. 2': Blackburn Weavers liable for strike damages.

1902   Deputation of Yorkshire and Cheshire textile workers to Westminster.
David Shackleton elected at Clitheroe – third Labour MP.
Helen Silcock raises women's suffrage at Trades Union Congress again.

1903   Lancashire & Cheshire Women's Textile and other Workers' Representation Committee formed.
Women's Social and Political Union formed by Pankhursts.

1904   Burnley Weavers' suffrage motion passed by Labour Representation Committee.
Women's Co-operative Guild votes to support women's suffrage.

1905   Selina Cooper raises women's suffrage at Labour Representation Committee.
Adult Suffrage Society formed, with Margaret Bondfield as president.
Free Trade Hall incident: mass meeting organized in support.
Radical suffragists resign from North of England Society.

1906   General Election: Thorley Smith stands as suffrage-Labour candidate in Wigan.
Women's Social and Political Union moves down to London.
Selina Cooper employed by the National Union of Women's Suffrage Societies.

1907 Selina Cooper raises women's suffrage at Labour Party Conference.
Pankhursts resign from Independent Labour Party.
Women's Freedom League formed.

1908 Eva Gore-Booth raises women's suffrage at Labour Party Conference.

1909 People's Suffrage Federation formed.

1910 General Election: suffrage candidate stands at Rossendale.

1912 Labour Party votes to support women's suffrage.
National Union of Women's Suffrage Societies starts Election Fighting Fund
to support Labour candidates at by-elections.

1918 Women over 30 win the vote, at the end of First World War.

ABBREVIATIONS

NESWS	North of England Society for Women's Suffrage
MNSWS	Manchester National Society for Women's Suffrage
NUWSS	National Union of Women's Suffrage Societies
Textile Comm	Lancashire and Cheshire Women Textile and other Workers' Representation Committee
Ind & Prof	National Industrial and Professional Women's Suffrage Society
Lab Rep Comm	Labour Representation Committee
Trade & Lab	Manchester and Salford Women's Trade and Labour Council
W Co-op G	Women's Co-operative Guild
PLG	Poor Law Guardian
TUC	Trades Union Congress
ILP	Independent Labour Party
SDF	Social Democratic Federation
W Lab L	Women's Labour League
WTUL	Women's Trade Union League

ACKNOWLEDGEMENTS

For help and encouragement in writing this book, we would particularly like to thank:

Mary Cooper for the long conversations about her mother, and for giving us such generous access to her mother's papers; and Eddie Conway and Bessie Dickenson for originally introducing us to Mary; Doris Chew for telling us about her mother, and help in tracing her writings; Lenny Holden for talking to us about her mother, Ethel Derbyshire; Louisa Dearden, Evelyn Coop and many other ex-pupils from Bolton, for telling us about their elementary school teacher, Alice Collinge; Alice Hartley for information about her aunt, Margaret Aldersley; and Elizabeth Dean, Elsie Plant and Ethel Brierley for helping us to imagine what life was like when they were young; thanks are also due to the following; Ruth and Eddie Frow for so generously giving us access to their excellent collection of local history books in their Working Class Movement Library, and for help in discovering more about Sarah Dickenson; Bill Williams, Audrey Linkman and Dermot Healy in the Manchester Studies Unit at Manchester Polytechnic for access to their oral history archives; and Thea Vigne for access to the SSRC Oral History Project, *Family Life and Work Experience before 1918*, at Essex University: librarians throughout the north west, in particular Susan Byrne at Nelson, Richard Peroni and Julian Hunt at the Oldham Local Interest Centre, and R.G. Manders at the North West Museum of Science and Industry: North West Arts for a grant towards the expenses involved in research and writing; Catherine Vickers from Preston and Andrew Bullen from Rossendale for valuable local research; Catherine Leech and Susan Bryan for help on suffrage groups in Manchester; Mrs Tottle for discussions on the Women's Co-operative Guild; Sheila Rowbotham and Anna Davin for their generous encouragement; Gloden Dallas for all her wise and friendly advice when we were struggling to weld our research into a book; Michael Rose, Paul Thompson, Dermot Healy, Bill Williams, Sheila Rowbotham, Anna Davin and Judith Summers for all their comments on the final draft; and Chris and Peter for putting up with it all for so long as tolerantly as they did.

COPY OF LETTER TO

WOMEN'S SUFFRAGE CANDIDATE.

Liverpool Labour Representation Committee

Sec: ARTHUR W. SHORT.   Affiliated to the National Labour Party.

8, Brook Road, Bootle,

January 5th, 1910.

Dear Mr. BULLEY,

The above Committee learn with gratification that you are taking up the **Workers' battle in Rossendale.** We wish you every **success** and hope that **EVERY** Trade **Unionist** in the Constituency will give you their hearty support, knowing, as we do, how valuable an acquisition you would be to the cause we are working for, if **returned to Parliament.**

Yours faithfully,

ARTHUR W. SHORT.

Mr. A. K. BULLEY.

WORKERS! FOLLOW THIS ADVICE

By voting for BULLEY

Printed and Published by C. Hargreaves, Burnley Road, Waterfoot.

INTRODUCTION

We wrote this book because we felt that an important aspect of the women's suffrage story had never been told. Living in Lancashire, we had become increasingly aware that tens of thousands of working women in the cotton towns had supported a campaign to win the vote. Yet this vital contribution has been largely neglected by historians.

We knew that Lancashire women had been politically active throughout the nineteenth century, both in radical politics and in their local cotton trade unions. It seemed to us that when the focus was on the single demand for the vote, all the earlier developments were at their strongest, and made the most dramatic impact on national politics.

We suspected that there was far more to the suffrage movement than the picture presented in the conventional histories. They usually suggest that the genteel Manchester Suffrage Society, formed in 1867, quietly faded out during the 1890s; and that little important happened until Mrs Pankhurst formed her Women's Social and Political Union in 1903. It is implied that, two and a half years later when the Pankhursts moved down to London, Lancashire virtually disappeared from the political battle over giving votes to women. Yet even the orthodox accounts hint that the Pankhursts built their suffragette campaign on a strong local tradition of radicalism among women.

When we tried to follow up our hunch, we immediately ran into a fundamental problem. Virtually all the books on the subject told the suffrage story in terms of middle class, London-based leaders — especially the Pankhursts and the suffragettes. 'Suffrage' and 'Pankhurst' seemed to have become almost synonymous in most people's minds. It is easy to understand why. For the first two or three years, the Women's Social and Political Union consisted of a handful of little-known women, mainly friends of Mrs Pankhurst; it did not attract much notice until the first show of militancy, when Christabel Pankhurst and Annie Kenney were thrown out of the Free Trade Hall in 1905 for demanding votes for women. Militant actions like this not only took considerable courage and determination; they also attracted public attention, especially when boosted by a well orchestrated publicity campaign. Militancy seemed glamorous and began to interest Fleet Street. In January 1906 the *Daily Mail* coined the word 'suffragette' and two months later the *Daily Mirror* devoted its entire front page to these sensational women.

The Pankhursts were certainly brilliant publicists. From the beginning they interpreted the campaign exclusively in terms of themselves, dismissing all earlier efforts. 'The history of women's suffrage prior to 1906 forms a dreary record of disappointed hopes and trust betrayed,' Christabel wrote at the time, 'but a knowledge of it helps those who work for votes today to steer their course.'[1]

Their perspective on the suffrage movement coloured their subsequent written histories. The first, Sylvia Pankhurst's *The Suffragette*, was published in 1911 at the height of the militant campaign. It is a vivid but partisan account of the Pankhurst movement which dismisses any other groups in a few offhand sentences. Both Christabel and Mrs Pankhurst later wrote their own stories in a similar vein.[2]

The most important of the Pankhurst histories is Sylvia's carefully researched book, *The Suffragette Movement*, published thirteen years after the vote was won. In the preface she wrote that her account is 'largely made up of memories', and 'I have essayed to describe events and experiences as one felt them... In this effort I have often been thrown back upon my own experience.' The result is an immensely readable story, full of fascinating pen pictures of her contemporaries; but the historian has always to bear in mind that this would-be definitive account is in many ways based on partisan recollections. The few references she makes to the efforts of the 'old' suffrage societies in the 1900s tend to be coolly dismissive; their puny efforts, she wrote, went 'virtually unnoticed'. She describes the battles to get the Labour Party to take up women's suffrage solely in terms of her family and friends, ignoring the tremendous impact of campaigns led by working class women outside the Women's Social and Political Union.

The Pankhurst version was corroborated by other writers, notably Annie Kenney, virtually the only working class woman close to the decision-making leadership of the suffragettes. In *Memories of a Militant* she blithely dismisses the campaign that pre-dated the Pankhursts ('there was no living interest in the question') and interprets subsequent events largely in terms of her hero worship of Christabel, whose judgement she accepted unquestioningly. 'I had faith in Christabel. It was exactly the faith of a child.'

Books published in the last few years have added their weight to the growing emphasis on the Pankhursts' sensational campaign[3]. For instance, *Shoulder to Shoulder*, serialized by BBC TV and later published in paperback has continued the uncritical acceptance of the militant version.

The only available antidote is the lesser known story of Mrs Fawcett and her leadership of the giant non-militant National Union of Women's Suffrage Societies. Mrs Fawcett has tended to suffer by comparison with Mrs Pankhurst, for she had neither her gift of rousing oratory nor her compelling good looks. Her strengths were those of a quiet, dignified leader who could co-ordinate and conciliate, and these are the qualities that emerge in her books. Her accounts tactfully paper over the gaping cracks between militants and non-militants and are bland rather than revealing.[4] A few years later, Ray Strachey, one-time parliamentary secretary to the National Union, wrote an authoritative account of the development of the women's movement, *The Cause*, published in 1928. Although her descriptions of outstanding women like Josephine Butler, Elizabeth Garrett Anderson and Mrs Fawcett are still unmatched, she too had little understanding of groups like the Lancashire suffragists, which lay outside her own range of experience.[5]

So often, the published information is sadly marred by its too narrow perspective and lack of balance. For suffrage leaders, young and old, the campaign was an unforgettable experience; it was almost impossible to write neutrally about it afterwards. The result is that we inherit a particular version, with the emphasis constantly on the experience of the Pankhursts, and sometimes Mrs Fawcett and her circle – who constituted the national leaderships. Our minds are filled with the strong, dramatic images of the militant campaign. We are familiar with photographs of suffragettes being carried off by policemen, of arrests and trials, and of dignified women posing in their prison uniforms. And we are often reminded of the gallant work suffragettes did during the First World War, and the esteem in which the government held the Pankhursts.

It is only with extreme difficulty that historians can clear their minds of this powerful succession of images and see the early suffrage movement with new eyes. It is almost impossible to realize what it meant to be involved in the campaigns in the early 1900s before the slogan 'Votes for Women' captured the headlines.

We are told so much about the personalities of the national leaders, but so little about the tens of thousands of women in suffrage societies up and down the country who backed the demand for the vote. We know little about the working class women – other than Annie Kenney and her sisters – who were active in the campaign; we know even less about their reasons for wanting the vote. Even in Lancashire, where working women's independence was more firmly rooted than elsewhere few working class *women* have recorded their life-story.

A few historians had already hinted that there had been a thriving Manchester movement before the Pankhursts hit the headlines. Roger Fulford's excellent (though with a pro-Liberal bias) *Votes for Women*, published twenty years ago, devoted a few pages to 'two forgotten but devoted ladies – Miss Esther Roper and Miss Eva Gore-Booth' and their campaign among the disenfranchised women cotton workers, casually dismissed by Sylvia Pankhurst merely in terms of her sister's short-lived involvement with them.

Ten years later Marian Ramelson brought out *The Petticoat Rebellion*; her concerns as a socialist encouraged her to take the research further and see if there was more evidence of working women campaigning for the vote. She used material like a 1902 pamphlet called *Working Women on Women's Suffrage*, and the Labour Party Annual Reports which showed how working class women had demanded the vote for themselves. More recently Andrew Rosen in his scholarly account of the militant campaign *Rise Up, Women!* devoted some of his early pages to the women in the textile unions, even quoting from the essay Esther Roper wrote in 1902, 'The Cotton Trade Unions and the Enfranchisement of Women', before firmly turning his attention back to the Pankhursts.

This was the sum total of the references to Lancashire working women in the suffrage histories. (Labour histories were even less helpful, usually dismissing women's suffrage as an irrelevant issue.) It was not much to go on but at least it convinced us that our enthusiasm was not entirely misplaced. How could we find out more about the cotton workers' campaign?

The logical place to begin was the Archive Department of Manchester Central Reference Library which houses the annual reports of the local suffrage society. Each year Esther Roper as secretary had written up what had taken place, including an impressively long list of all meetings and speakers, with such typical entries as: 'Salford Women Weavers' T.U. Meeting in Public Hall; 'Nelson Women Weavers' T.U.

Meeting'; 'Clitheroe Women's Co-operative Guild'; 'Wigan Trades Council'; 'Blackpool Socialist Party'.

We became familiar with the names of the regular speakers — Mrs Dickenson, Mrs Cooper, Miss Reddish, Miss Silcock (at this point we did not even know their Christian names) — and began to realize what strong links all these women had with the working class organizations that flourished in each town, in particular the Women's Co-operative Guilds, Independent Labour Party branches and local groups of women textile trade unionists. We came across the names of these suffragists time and again in the reports of organizations like the Women's Trade Union League and the Manchester and Salford Women's Trade Union Council, and we coined a title — 'radical suffragists' to describe them. (There is a biographical list of leading radical suffragists on page 288.) They all seemed to share considerable industrial experience and a political radicalism that set them apart from many non-militants; together they appeared to have worked as an effective pressure group during the 1900s.

We found we could make connections between suffrage and labour organizations but we did not yet have any strong picture in our minds of the individual women who became radical suffragists. We only knew their public faces; we wanted to know about their families and how they had managed to cope on a day-to-day level with the demands the suffrage campaign must have made on their lives.

Again, we came back to the problems of sources. Nobody had thought it worthwhile to record the lives of women who did not achieve the national fame of an Annie Kenney or a Christabel Pankhurst. There are a few excellent autobiographies of local working class women of this generation, but sadly none throw any direct light on the radical suffragists. Alice Foley wrote a vivid, telling account of her early life called *A Bolton Childhood*; unfortunately she was too young to have been involved in the movement, though she did refer in passing to her elder sister Cissy being 'allied with the suffragettes'. We wondered whether Cissy, then a frustrated and ambitious jack-frame tenter in a cotton mill, might have been one of the women involved in the textile workers' campaign. Hannah Mitchell wrote an equally compelling autobiography, *The Hard Way Up*; unfortunately for us, she joined the Pankhursts (although she soon became disillusioned by their fanatical single-mindedness and left their group), and her account is of the early days of the Women's Social and Political Union. What we did learn from both books was something of the problems working class women faced when they became involved in political campaigns. 'No cause can be won between dinner and tea,' Hannah Mitchell wrote bitterly, 'and most of us who were married had to work with one hand tied behind us.'

Our search for original sources was made harder because we could find no newspaper or magazine in which the radical suffragists had recorded their day-to-day achievements. They attached less importance to publicity than other suffrage groups, and had nothing comparable to the suffragettes' monthly, *Votes for Women*. Lydia Becker, the energetic organizer of the old Manchester Suffrage Society, had edited the *Women's Suffrage Journal* which lovingly recorded all the 'two steps forward, one step back' progress during the late nineteenth century; but after her death in 1890 no one was brave enough to take on the task and the *Journal* disappeared. Nothing really filled the gap until Helena Swanwick, a Manchester suffragist, started the *Common Cause* in 1909. Those vital nineteen years went almost unrecorded[6] — another reason why so little is known about the radical suffragists.

Contemporary newspapers are not particularly helpful. It was a period when the new mass circulation dailies, like the *Daily Mail*, the *Daily News* and the *Daily Mirror*, were building up tremendous readerships. Local newspapers also flourished, pre-eminently the prestigious *Manchester Guardian*, and each small town boasted at least one paper, and often more. But of course non-militants seldom provided good copy; peaceful tactics seemed rather dull compared to slapping policemen on the face or being thrown out of Liberal party meetings, and unlike the suffragettes the radical suffragists seemed to fight shy of any kind of newspaper publicity. And although textile workers might contribute substantially to the country's wealth, Lancashire weavers, disenfranchised or not, had none of the sensation value of, say, the women in sweated industries exposed in the *Daily News* Exhibition of 1906.

Although we were certain that our original hunch was sound, we were constantly hampered by the anonymity of our radical suffragists. It was very difficult to find out what sort of women they were. They had been active so long ago; if any of them was still alive she would be at least ninety, and not necessarily living in Lancashire.

Then, unexpectedly, a friend put us in touch with Mrs Cooper's daughter who was still living in the family house in Nelson, just north of Burnley. Mary Cooper, now in her late seventies, had always been very close to her mother, and had reacted against the image of the

Pankhursts (particularly Christabel) as heroines. Although her mother admired many of the suffragettes for their courage, she totally disapproved of their violent tactics and elitism, and of the way they abandoned the campaign for women after the vote was won. Selina Cooper on the other hand 'continued after they got the vote . . . getting clinics going and welfare. . . She wanted allowances for children. . . She went speaking, all for nothing. . .all over Lancashire and Yorkshire.'[7] Mary told us a great deal about her mother — what a powerful speaker she was, how locally everybody looked up to her — and she could still remember clearly her impressions of the local suffrage society meetings in the front room: 'I thought I was in charge, 'cos I made coffee out there. . .It was all like a bit double-dutch to me, but I'd only be about ten.'[8]

We were also able to interview the daughter of another Lancashire suffragist, Ada Nield Chew. Doris Chew, the same age as Mary Cooper, was equally incensed that all the publicity showered on the Pankhursts and the suffragettes had obscured the enormous contribution made by non-militants like her mother. Like Selina Cooper, she saw women's suffrage as part of a much wider political campaign; but her contribution has been largely forgotten for she destroyed her autobiography shortly before she died.[9]

The excitement of taping these two interviews encouraged us to hunt for evidence of other Lancashire suffragists. Sometimes we seemed to be forever chasing down blind alleys. For instance, one of the most active women, Helen Silcock, a weavers' union leader from Wigan, seemed to disappear after 1902. We couldn't think why, until we came across a notice of 'congratulations to Miss Silcock on her marriage to Mr Fairhurst' in a little-known labour journal, the *Women's Trade Union Review*[10]. Even though we now knew her married name we still could not find out much more about her; she may possibly have resigned from her trade union job to bring up children. Whatever the reason, it was an object lesson for us in the difficulties of tracing women activists.

We wrote to all the local papers, asking people with information to get in touch with us. One of the few replies came from someone in Blackburn; her mother, an active suffragist and Independent Labour Party supporter, had died aged ninety seven only a few months previously. Other pieces of evidence turned up unexpectedly. For instance, we came across a 1911 list of radical suffragists and found that Cissy Foley was listed as a committee member. Our original idea had again been proved right.

We found that by balancing written and oral evidence we were gradually able to build up a detailed picture of who the radical suffragists were and what their campaigns were like. Written documents provided us with a precise chronology of events, and gave us a perspective on the various organizations and their stand on women's suffrage. Taped interviews gave us an idea of what individuals thought and did, and how their allegiances spilled over from one organization into another.

To arrive at a balanced picture of what took place, it is vital to compare oral sources with documentary evidence.[11] Written reports confirm that over sixty thousand women felt so incensed about their lack of political rights that they signed the textile workers' petition. The reports also confirm that in every cotton town, big and small, the radical suffragists held well-attended meetings during their campaign.

Memories, especially over a period of seventy years, retain some images more clearly than others. Political campaigns are less easy to remember than, say, details of childhood games or family relationships. It is probably true that even the radical suffragists, with their strong local contacts, found it virtually impossible to involve the majority of local working women. Nevertheless, the unique strength of their campaign was the degree to which it did touch the lives of women who had never before been concerned with politics. It was this backing that gave the radical suffragists so great an influence.

Careful use of oral history and local records has helped to challenge the Pankhursts' version of the suffrage movement. It has helped to bring to life the forgotten suffragists, and to show how their principles and tactics differed from those of the more celebrated national leaders. Used in a detailed local study, it has helped to challenge the view that women's suffrage was largely a middle class concern.

Our decision to concentrate on local rather than national history, and to use the research methods that we did has meant questioning the historians' habit of compartmentalizing everything neatly into 'suffrage history', 'labour history', 'political history' and 'social history'. The lives of the radical suffragists overlapped into all these categories. Their attitudes to winning the vote for women like themselves developed from their own personal experience of industrial life; their commitment to the labour movement was dovetailed into their experience of growing up in working class families. They emerge not only as a group who made an important local contribution to political history, but also as women who were not deterred by the perennial problems of combining political activity with their family commitments.

Jill Liddington
Jill Norris
1977

When we re-read what we wrote six years ago, we both felt that the new edition of the book should remain substantially unchanged. Little new source material has come to light to challenge the story of the radical suffragists. Where we have made alterations, these have been minor ones, to correct a date, to rephrase a sentence, or – on one or two occasions – to give a different emphasis.

In addition two new biographical accounts have come to light recently which substantially widened our understanding of the radical suffragists. *Ada Nield Chew: The Life & Writings of a Working Woman* (Virago 1982) was subsequently dramatised by Alan Plater in *The Clarion Van* (Granada TV 1983); and the story of Selina Cooper is told in *The Life & Times of a Respectable Rebel* (Virago 1984).

Jill Liddington
Jill Norris
1984

PART 1: WORKING WOMEN

I

Who were the radical suffragists?

> In the cotton districts during the summer months the workers spend their evenings out of doors, more after the fashion of Continental than English towns, and on certain nights in the week anyone going into the market-place can get an audience of interested and intelligent men and women, varying from 600 to 1,000 and even 1,500, who will stand for an hour or two to hear the question discussed.[1]

The question was women's suffrage, and the year was 1905. Several years before 'suffragette' became a household word, the cotton workers of Lancashire were debating the controversial issue of votes for women in meetings at their factory gates, street corners and in town squares. The speakers who addressed the crowds were not educated middle class ladies, but local women who had come to the suffrage movement through their experience of factory work and of organizing working women.

These women, the radical suffragists, knew at first hand the harsh conditions under which the majority of women lived and worked at the beginning of this century, and had the courage and determination to struggle for something better. They worked closely with the growing labour movement, wanting to change conditions rather than simply to alleviate them, and they used their influence to build a movement of working women who claimed not only the right to vote but to take part in politics for themselves.

It is impossible to guess how many women were involved in the radical suffragists' campaign. The names of only the most active are known; brief biographies of about three dozen of them are listed on page 288. The full life-stories of only a handful of leading suffragists have been recorded in any detail. One such woman was Selina Cooper, who had gone into one of the local mills when she was ten; she was the only working class woman with the confidence to stand up at Labour conferences and try to push through motions on women's suffrage. She came from Nelson in north-east Lancashire and by the 1890s was closely involved in the growing socialist movement there.

Because of her unique talents as a speaker she got drawn into the national suffrage movement, and was soon in great demand as a working woman on its platforms.

A resolute-looking and courageous woman, she could take in her stride a rowdy mob of Cambridge undergraduates who carried her shoulder-high through the streets singing 'She's a Lassie from Lancashire', or go down to Westminster to tell Members of Parliament that, as a mother, she believed working women needed the vote because 'we have to educate our children; if we are not ourselves interested in national life, how can we impart to our children a knowledge of true citizenship?'[2] Her own daughter Mary thoroughly enjoyed being brought up in an atmosphere of politics and meeting the Labour and suffrage speakers who visited her parents. Selina's husband Robert, a weaver, was equally active in labour politics and wholeheartedly supported her commitment to women's suffrage. The Cooper family always remained part of the Nelson community and Mary remembered the place Selina held in local esteem: 'They always worshipped her. It was the strange thing about my mother — she didn't just get admiration, she got worshipped. Because she never left the earth. Never left her roots. And always kept friendly with everybody.[3]

Another textile worker, Helen Silcock, carried the women's suffrage campaign into the male-dominated precincts of the TUC at the turn of the century. As president of the Wigan weavers' union she was in a unique position to carry the power of organized labour behind the claims of working women. Public speaking was nothing new to her; her first experience of the kind dated back to when she stood up, an unassuming little wisp of a woman, to address a Labour Day demonstration in Hyde Park in 1895, one of the first working class women to confront such a large crowd.[4]

Helen Silcock and Selina Cooper were only in their twenties when they first became involved in organizing working women. Both seem to

21

have been helped by·the wide experience of an older woman, Sarah Reddish. Born in 1850, she too had started work as a child and had spent much of her adult life working in mills and factories around Bolton. She never married, and decided to put all her energies into politics. By the time she was in her thirties, new opportunities were opening up for working women, and Sarah Reddish was one of the first to take advantage of them. She left her factory job and became a co-operative, and then a trade union (and later suffrage) organizer.

Because she left no children, it is difficult to find out much about her personal life. Photographs show her with her hair drawn severely back from a high forehead, a wide mouth, and a composed look upon her face, and her public pronouncements have the daunting air of Victorian earnestness. 'I believe that all physical, social and moral evils have their source for the most part in a bad economic and industrial system,' she declared, 'and, therefore, I would have society and the industry of the kingdom established and worked on new lines — on the lines of true and universal co-operation, or the principle of equal effort in producing and equal participation in results.'[5]

But as a successful trade union organizer Sarah Reddish could also make her points pithily and effectively. She made a meeting of MPs laugh with, 'These [women] cotton operatives...should have representation in the making of the laws of the country. I am sure that although men do their best, they would do a great deal better with the help of women.'[6] And we know that she carried her love of independence to the point of defying convention: in a photograph of forty radical suffragists Sarah Reddish stood out as the only woman who refused to wear the unwieldy hat that was then a badge of respectability.

While Selina Cooper, Helen Silcock and Sarah Reddish were championing women's suffrage at a national level, other radical suffragists concentrated their efforts on building up a local base. In Manchester Sarah Dickenson played a leading role in organizing women into trade unions. She had begun work in Salford in 1879, when she was eleven, and soon established her reputation as a strong-minded woman. On one occasion a factory inspector came round and insisted that the workers should be provided with stools to sit on; the firm grudgingly agreed, but retaliated by deducting 2d a week from their wages; Sarah Dickenson adamantly refused to accept this and she brought the girls she worked with out on strike.[7] From her own experience of low pay and bad conditions in factories, she went on to

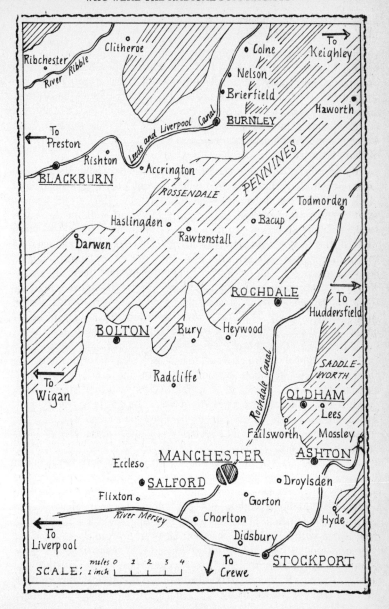

press for the vote, and was soon enrolling other working women into the suffrage campaign.

During the early 1900s the radical suffragists inspired other young women to join them, including two from Bolton, Cissy Foley and Alice Collinge. Cissy Foley, 'a small dumpy girl with a sallow, pimply complexion, but the face was distinguished by a pair of large tragic brown eyes', worked in the cardroom of a local spinning mill; she had taken an active interest in her trade union — a rare thing for mill women — and 'had tenaciously elbowed her way into the male precincts of that executive.'[8]

Alice Collinge was an elementary school teacher, remembered with great affection by her former pupils as a tall imposing woman with black hair, who astonished them all by being a vegetarian and wearing what seemed to them outlandish clothes — stout walking shoes and thick woollen stockings. Influenced by the wise counsel of Sarah Reddish she too became drawn to the radical suffragists' campaign, and she began to pay special attention to the kind of education girls received at school. One of her ex-pupils remembered how she always went out of her way to encourage them. 'She taught us more than the three Rs, especially the girls. She was always pushing the girls forward. And she used to say "You're as good as any of the boys, and better brains than these" — the girls'd be this side, the boys the other — she'd say "More brains than these".'[9]

As the radical suffragists' campaign gathered momentum in the 1900s, it drew in other women active in the labour movement. Outstanding among these was Ada Nield Chew, who had started work as a low-paid tailoress in Crewe. There, when she was only twenty four, she created a furore by writing to the local paper and exposing the appalling conditions in the sweated workshops where she and her fellows had to work.

She married George Chew, a weaver, who shared both her anger at the way most workers had to live and her commitment to labour. She had one daughter, Doris, and, like Selina Cooper, she managed to combine motherhood with a full programme of political work. Her daughter remembered how, 'between two and seven I trailed round everywhere with her . . . and she went all over, both to the lowlands of Scotland and all over the north of England.'[10] As a women's trade union organizer she would travel to remote groups of working women, trying to persuade them that joining a union was just as important as getting their housework done: she reported from one distant village,

24

Heptonstall in the West Riding, beyond Todmorden, on the kind of problems she came up against. 'The meeting here was entirely in the nature of an experiment; as it is almost impossible to get a meeting anywhere in these parts on a Friday night (cleaning night) it was gratifying to us we were able to get an audience, if small.'[11]

As well as a practised organizer, she was also a prolific writer and used the labour and suffrage papers as a platform for her beliefs. She thrived on controversy and even took on Christabel Pankhurst in an argument about suffrage. She was not afraid to tackle the thorny issue of married women's work, denouncing the 'tabby-cat' stay-at-home mentality put forward as 'the ideal to which all womanhood should aspire.'[12]

What brought women like these, with their wide experience in trade union and labour politics, into the women's suffrage movement? What made the vote so vitally important to them?

Certainly the radical suffragists wanted more than an abstract right; they were not merely interested in the possession of the vote as a symbol of equality. They wanted it in order to improve conditions for women like themselves. The majority of working class men had won the vote in the electoral reforms of 1867 and 1884, and by 1900 had begun to send their own representatives to Parliament. But working class women had no such rights. 'Even though women had joined the Lancashire cotton unions in their thousands, they lacked the men's extra bargaining power, as the radical suffragists complained in one of their earliest pamphlets, *Women Workers and Parliamentary Representation:*

> A vote is in itself a small thing, but the aggregate vote of a great Union is a very different matter. The Cotton Unions of Lancashire – some of the largest Trade Unions in the country – have a majority of women members – 96,000 women against 69,000 men. It will be seen then that this great industry is to a very large extent disfranchised. What wonder that the trade, except in the mule spinning department, where women are rarely employed, is considered a poor one for men?[13]

The cotton trade unions were the logical place for the radical suffragists to begin to build their campaign. But to demand the vote for working class women was positively revolutionary at the turn of the century. In all the demands for extending the existing franchise, working class women came at the bottom of the list every time.

The radical suffragists boldly rejected the aim of the traditional women's suffrage societies led by Mrs Fawcett, who asked only for the vote 'as it is, or may be, accorded to men' — that is, a property-based vote. Many working class men could meet the qualification as heads of households, but few women — only the better off — could claim to hold property in their own right.

The radical suffragists wanted the vote not just for a wealthy few, but for women like themselves. They formulated a demand for 'womanhood suffrage', to include *all* women over the age of twenty-one. Since it was inconceivable that any government would grant this demand without giving the vote to the small number of men who still lacked the right, it was basically a call for votes for all adults, but with the stress on the claims of women.

And just as they rejected the limited aims of the existing suffrage societies, so, by the late 1890s, the radical suffragists realized that womanhood suffrage could never be won by the traditional methods of drawing-room meetings and discreet lobbying of individual MPs adopted by the North of England Society for Women's Suffrage. The only way was to build a mass movement of working women, firmly based in the Lancashire cotton unions.

This rejection of the middle class suffrage groups only came about gradually, however. The radical suffragists were initially drawn together by a young Manchester graduate called Esther Roper, who became Secretary of the local suffrage society in 1893. With her friend, Eva Gore-Booth, she had the vision to appreciate the importance of working class support. By 1900 she was deliberately pursuing a policy of taking women's suffrage ideas out of the drawing-rooms and into the cotton towns of Lancashire. Sarah Reddish, Selina Cooper, Helen Silcock, Sarah Dickenson and other leaders of local working women's organizations were attracted by this new policy and enthusiastically added their efforts to hers.

Their contacts were invaluable, and the movement expanded rapidly during the early 1900s. Soon women's suffrage, which for so long had virtually been run by a handful of middle class women, was effectively taken over by enthusiastic and experienced working class women. Although they were still operating as a ginger group within the old North of England Society, their methods were those they had learned elsewhere: factory gate meetings, pushing suffrage motions through union branches, organizing through trades councils.

As the campaign expanded, tension between the old-fashioned suffrage women and the labour activists grew. The radical suffragists realized that they could work better through an organization of their own, no longer restricted by the traditional aims of the older society. And so, in the summer of 1903, they formed the first organization of working women for the vote, with the unwieldy but precise title of The Lancashire and Cheshire Women Textile and Other Workers' Representation Committee; this gave them greater leeway to operate independently of the staid North of England Society.

The Committee's first public statement was a manifesto to their fellow workers in the north-west, calling on them to lead the struggle for working women's rights. It argued that 'political enfranchisement must precede industrial emancipation' and reminded them how the lack of political power had weakened their bargaining position. And it ended defiantly: 'What Lancashire and Cheshire women think today England will do tomorrow.'[14]

From their base among the cotton workers the radical suffragists continued their attack upon the complacent attitude to women's suffrage adopted by most politicians. Friends in the labour movement were quick to realize their potential strength. Ramsay MacDonald, leader of the growing Labour Party and later the first Labour Prime Minister, wrote to Selina Cooper advising her how the radical suffragists could best use their influence to get women's suffrage backed by the Labour Party's national conference: 'You must strongly try and get a resolution in favour of women's enfranchisement put upon our next Agenda in the name of the Textile Operatives . . . I do not see much hope in doing it yet, unless the cotton operatives take the lead.'[15]

At that time it seemed to the radical suffragists that one of the best ways to win the vote for the majority of women was with the help of the growing Labour Party, since the Liberals and the Conservatives had shown little real interest over the past fifty years. But as MacDonald recognised, Labour supporters would not take kindly to feminist propaganda from anyone they did not regard as intrinsically part of their own movement. Organized textile workers could put their case where middle class women might be conveniently ignored, or even treated with hostility. The radical suffragists, with their political roots firmly in the working class movement in Lancashire, were the only suffrage group who could carry this demand through.

But even for radical suffragists like Selina Cooper working through the Labour Party (or Labour Representation Committee, as it was formally known until 1906) was not easy. For years women's suffrage had been a purely middle class demand, and to many of the trade union and socialist men who made up the bulk of the Party's support feminism was simply another name for increasing privileges of propertied women.

Still the radical suffragists continued their campaign to get womanhood suffrage accepted by the labour movement. They realized that Labour, with all its shortcomings and hesitations, was now becoming the Party of progress, and that if women's issues were not made an integral part of its programme now they would be neglected in the years to come.

In trying to build as wide a movement as possible the radical suffragists did not work only through the Labour Party. Equally important to their grass-roots campaign were their constant attempts to get the official backing of the local trades councils and trade unions, and their contacts with sympathetic women's organizations, especially local Women's Co-operative Guild branches. They still retained links with the old established North of England Society, valuing its ties with other women's suffrage societies throughout the country, even when their demands outgrew its limited aims. They also worked with the Pankhursts' Women's Social and Political Union (WSPU) in its early years in Manchester.

To begin with, the WSPU was just a small group of women brought together by the Pankhursts in 1903, and in its first few years co-existed quite peacefully with the radical suffragists. But by 1906, when the Pankhursts moved down to London, the differences between the two groups had become apparent. The radical suffragists continued to work closely with the local labour organizations, while the Pankhursts soon dropped their working class support, except for a few token speakers like Annie Kenney and her sisters, in favour of influential allies among upper and middle class women. Or, as Christabel Pankhurst blandly put it, 'All belonged to the aristocracy of the suffragettes.'[16]

Their tactics also diverged sharply. The radical suffragists had always opted for the painstaking methods of building support at a local level, while the Pankhursts increasingly relied on sensational actions by a few London-based militants in order to catch the headlines. At first such tactics were brilliantly successful because of their originality, but, after the novelty wore off, the WSPU leaders were forced to resort to more extreme actions, which the radical suffragists could only see as a downward spiral of violence that would inevitably alienate vital grass-roots support. Nor would the Pankhursts brook any criticism of their policies, from whatever quarter; Christabel in particular was quick to reject any ally who did not agree with her all along the line.

28

It is important to stress that while the radical suffragists did not court martyrdom or imprisonment, this was not from cowardice (they were after all well used to facing hostile crowds), but because they saw these tactics as ultimately self-destructive. Selina Cooper was horrified by the Pankhursts' eventual resort to arson, and in any case she and women like her did not believe that the elitist actions of a few militants could ever carry the weight of the demands of the mass of organized working women.

The radical suffragists also disagreed fundamentally with the Pankhursts' aims. To the militant leaders, the vote became virtually an end in itself. Mrs Pankhurst declared that 'Our members are absolutely single-minded; they concentrate all their forces on one object, political equality with men. No member of the WSPU divides her attention between suffrage and other social reforms.'[17]

To the radical suffragists, such an attitude was little short of ridiculous. What was the point of a vote without any idea of how it could be used? Without exception, they were all involved in wider campaigns for working women. As trade unionists they tried to improve women's wage levels and conditions at work. They campaigned for improved education for working class girls, and better facilities for working class mothers and their children. Selina Cooper summed up the position of the radical suffragists when she told an open air meeting in Wigan:

> [Women] do not want their political power to enable them to boast that they are on equal terms with the men. They want to use it for the same purpose as men — to get better conditions . . . Every woman in England is longing for her political freedom in order to make the lot of the worker pleasanter and to bring about reforms which are wanted. We do not want it as a mere plaything![18]

II

Daily life for working women

To understand the way in which the suffrage campaign took off it is
essential to be familiar with life in the Lancashire cotton towns in the
1880s and 90s. When the radical suffragists were growing up, large
families were the norm, each living in a cramped back-to-back terrace
house; schooling was harsh and uninspiring, and lasted only until a child
could enter the neighbourhood cotton mill; and opportunities for
working class women were still virtually non-existent. The radical
suffragists were only too familiar with the relentless drudgery of
working class women's daily lives: they had seen their mothers and
other women of that generation worn down by the long, wearisome
battle against poverty and dirt.[1]

Housework was laborious and exhausting. 'Oh, that Lancashire
cleanliness! That cleaning of the front step and flags! That scrubbing
down of the back-yard! Those steel fenders and fire irons! Those brass
candlesticks that had to be polished till you could see your face in
them!'[2] wrote Harry Pollitt, himself brought up in the little Lancashire
mill town of Droylsden in the 1890s. Housework still had to be tackled
without any of the labour-saving devices of today. Stoves had to be
blackleaded, bread had to be baked, clothes had to be handwashed with
a dolly stick in a tub, and steps had to be whitened with a
donkey-stone.

The work was not only heavy but extremely time-consuming.
Women like Mrs Pollitt who went out to work (she was a weaver in a

30

local mill) only managed to get through their housework by an almost superhuman effort. Even women who stayed at home found that their daily grind left them with virtually no leisure to call their own. One Lancashire housewife described her weekly routine:

> On Monday I clear up all the rooms after Sunday, brush and put away all Sunday clothes, and then separate and put to soak all soiled clothes for washing. On Tuesday, the washing is done, the clothes folded and mangled. After the washing, the scullery receives a thorough cleaning for the week. Wednesday is the day for starching and ironing, and stocking darning, as well as the usual week's mending. On Thursday, I bake the bread and clean the bedrooms. On Friday I clean the parlour, lobby and staircase, as well as the living-room. Saturday morning is left for all outside cleaning – windows and stonework – besides putting all the clean linen on the beds. I finish work on Saturday about 2 pm, the rest of the day being free.[3]

To the burden of housework was added that of continual childbearing. Birth control was still a subject shrouded in mystery, particularly among the working class, and the view of those in authority was that it should stay that way. Even as late as the 1890s, birth control advocates could still be prosecuted, and at least one was imprisoned with hard labour.[4] Certainly, most of the radical suffragists came from large families: Ada Nield Chew had three sisters and nine brothers, Helen Silcock was one of ten children, and Ethel Derbyshire one of fourteen.

At the turn of the century, working class couples still had to resort to the traditional, unreliable methods of contraception: abstinence, withdrawal, perhaps the use of a vaginal sponge. 'They wouldn't know birth control in those days,' the daughter of a Lancashire suffragist remembered. 'My mother and father always had separate beds in the same room. But in those days that was looked upon as heretical, to have separate beds.'[5] Although more reliable methods such as the sheath or cervical cap were gradually becoming available, birth control still remained an agonizing and unspoken problem for most married women; it was high praise to say of a husband that 'he doesn't bother me too often.'

For most women, the inevitable result of marriage was a succession of pregnancies culminating in births largely unaided by medical skill. With no health service, families had to pay for doctors and hospital beds themselves. A man might pay a weekly contribution to a friendly society to cover expenses when he was sick, but this would not help his wife, and many women in childbirth waited until too late before calling a doctor. Hannah Mitchell, from Ashton-under-Lyne, determined to

31

have no more children after her first experience of labour:

> One Friday, having done my weekend cleaning and baked a batch of bread during the day, I hoped for a good night's rest, but I scarcely had retired before my labour began. My baby was not born until the following evening, after twenty-four hours of intense suffering which an ignorant attendant did little to alleviate . . . My baby was brought into the world with instruments, and without an anaesthetic . . . Only one thing emerged clearly from much bitter thinking at that time, the fixed resolve to bring no more babies into the world. I felt it impossible to face again either the personal suffering, or the task of bringing a second child up in poverty.[6]

Her husband agreed with her decision, and they had no more children. But large families were still the norm rather than the exception, and it was the women who had to shoulder the major responsibility of making the limited family income stretch as far as was humanly possible.

Since for most families weekly wages, already at an inadequate level, were often depressed by seasonal or trade fluctuations, this was a daunting responsibility, and one that was gradually being recognized by middle class social investigators. One man, speaking before the Royal Statistical Society in 1893, referred to working men's wives as 'chancellors of the domestic exchequer', and stressed 'the importance of good housewifery, which is often sufficient to turn the balance of comfort in favour of one workman whose wages are much below those of another.' In the same way, Lady Bell, the wife of a Middlesborough employer, claimed from her local survey of working class families a few years later, that 'the husband's steadiness and capacity to earn are not more important than the wife's administration of the earnings.'[7]

In practice, however, the role of domestic chancellor was more exacting than exalted. A housewife depended on the wages of her husband and elder children. Husbands usually gave their wives the whole of their wages, except for a few shillings kept back for beer and tobacco; younger children, who knew their place in the family hierarchy, would 'tip up' their wages for the mother at the end of each week, and she would give them back a penny in the shilling for their own use. Older children on higher wages who were still living at home were allowed to do as Cissy Foley did, pay board and lodging and buy their clothes and other necessities out of the remainder. Few wives had sufficient housekeeping money left out of this to spend anything on themselves. Their first concern was to hold the family together, even though in the process their own health and needs were the first to go by the board.

So the women struggled on, many finding only a fine dividing-line between solvency and debt. Most relied heavily on the corner shop where they were known and could get credit. Cissy Foley's mother shopped 'at a higgledy-piggledy place kept by one of her old friends named Kitty. Neither mother nor Kitty could read or write, but they had their own symbols for reckoning up the score which later was chalked up on the door leading to the living room.' But Cissy, trying to raise her family above their squalid poverty, eventually persuaded her mother to shop at one of the Co-operative Stores, where 'thrift was the symbol and dividend the snare.'[8]

The 'Co-op' offered working people a guarantee of unadulterated food and a share of any profits that were made. From the 'Rochdale Pioneers' of the 1840s, the Co-op flourished, particularly in the industrial towns of the north of England. It expanded its services from food to funerals, from milk deliveries to insurance, reinvesting a considerable proportion of its profits into a wide variety of social, political and educational activities for the benefit of members.

The Co-op encouraged self-reliance and independence; the rule was that no credit could be given, and this had the effect of deterring many women from shopping there. The very poor could not keep up regular payments even at the local shop, and for them there were only two options open: they could visit the pawnbroker, and for families like the Foleys it became a regular weekly routine to pledge the Sunday clothes from one weekend to the next; or they could turn to the last desperate resort of the needy, the Board of Guardians. Established by the 1834 Poor Law, the Boards were usually reluctant to make adequate payments for 'outdoor relief', paid to those living at home, and many luckless families found they had nothing to fall back on but the Dickensian horrors of the workhouse.[9] Only the totally destitute made their way there, and few made their way out. The sexes were segregated and families were split up. The idea was to make indoor relief as unattractive as possible, to keep down the poor-rate. Hannah Mitchell, elected as a socialist to the Ashton Board, earned much disapproval by her battle to retain the Christmas treat of beer given by a local brewery: the demon drink was generally held to be one of the major causes of poverty.[10]

For poor families, then, every source of income, no matter how small, was vital. Large families, a liability when the children were young, became an asset as soon as they could leave school and start earning. They left school at the earliest possible moment, nominally at

33

thirteen; but, especially in the textile districts of Lancashire and the West Riding of Yorkshire, many left earlier under the 'half-time' system. This allowed children who had reached a certain educational standard to go to school in the morning and to work in the afternoon, or *vice versa*. The 'Labour Exam' which tested this standard was notorious for never failing anyone. As one half-timer bitterly remembered: 'The mill owners who controlled the educational bodies took precious good care that the biggest dunce in the school could pass it. What did they care? They wanted cheap labour, and intended to see that they got it.'[11] And another, J.R. Clynes, who rose from half-timer in the mill to membership of the first Labour Cabinet, later recalled, 'When I was a young man the term "to have been through the mill" had a grim meaning . . . it described a mill worker whose childhood had been ruined by hard labour and little sleep, and who in manhood looked shrunken and white-faced.'[12] Selina Cooper, Ethel Derbyshire and Sarah Dickenson — among others — had all 'been through the mill'; even in the early 1890s the half-time system was still the experience of half the child population over ten years old in Lancashire.

Children who spent long mornings in the mill were in no fit state to be taught in the afternoon. Progressive teachers thought the system appalling. One of Alice Collinge's ex-pupils in Bolton remembers:

> The half-timers used to get up at five o'clock. They started work in the mill at six. Then, of course, in the afternoon, they'd be like this [sleeping] . . . But she wouldn't wake them. Other teachers would have shook them and said, 'Come on, get on with your lessons.' But she said one day 'Let them sleep. It will do them more good than knowing what so-and-so mountains are.'[13]

Many parents too bitterly regretted this abrupt ending to their children's education, but the extra money made too great a difference to the overstretched family budget to resist. 'I will never forget,' one Lancashire mother said, 'the first time my daughter brought in her first week's wage. The 2s 4d seemed to go further than any sovereign had done previously.'[14] Feeling ran so high that the MP for Middleton and his wife were even spat upon by angry women in one village because he had supported the 1899 bill which raised the leaving age.[15]

Even for children who stayed on at school full-time as long as they could, educational opportunities were limited. Few working class children had the chance of secondary education; most spent their schooldays in one of the huge new brick Board Schools that towered over the neighbouring streets. The education dispensed there was of the most basic kind. Learning was by rote, largely because of the difficulties of teaching the enormous classes of the time. Years later, Cissy Foley's younger sister found that, 'Nothing remains . . . save the dim echo of monotonous chanting.'[16]

Girls often had even less chance than boys to benefit from their education. Teachers and School Board officials, who took a severe view of a boy's absence as 'truancy', were more likely to turn a blind eye when a girl was away, particularly on wash day; it could be considered as 'helping at home', an invaluable part of her training for later life. Much of the teaching that working class girls did receive was directed at their future role as mother and housewife. One Salford woman, who had started work in a cotton mill when she was nine, remembered the lessons the master's daughter gave the girls after they had finished their eleven-hour stint at the looms. One lecture, she recalled, enlightened them on 'three ways of stuffing a cod's head for a penny.'[17]

Parents and teachers colluded in believing that girls' academic education mattered less than boys. One girl who won a place at Cheetham Higher Grade School in Manchester said:

All the books had to be bought, and when the bill came, how much the books were going to cost, my father didn't think that, as a girl, he could spring to this. If it had been a boy it would have been different . . . So I had to leave the Higher Grade School at thirteen and go back to the elementary school till I was fourteen . . . So I missed out a lot on education.[18]

Even some libraries joined in the discrimination. Sir Neville Cardus the journalist recalled his boyhood in Manchester: 'After working all day in an insurance office, 9.30 to 5, I went home and had a quick tea. Then off to Dickenson Road Library: boys only; girls weren't allowed in.'[19]

The burden of housework and keeping a home together was a heavy one, but many women combined it with an outside job as well. Victorian wives were expected to stay in their 'place' at home, but many had no choice other than to try to augment their husbands' insufficient or unreliable wage themselves. In the many homes which lacked a male breadwinner women did their best to bring up their families without resorting to the dreaded Guardians. Unmarried working class women had to earn their own keep, and throughout the second half of the nineteenth century there were more than a million 'surplus women' — such unequal numbers made it unlikely that they would marry.

Although many households were dependent upon women's wages, the actual amounts earned were pitifully small. One trade union secretary reported at the turn of the century:

35

A man thinks himself badly off if he cannot earn more than 17s a week. It is no exaggeration to say that there are thousands of girls in Manchester who think themselves lucky if they bring home 7s at the weekend, and more older and skilled women who can never hope to earn more than 12s to the end of their lives . . . These are surely the wages of the poorest poor. These workers are living very near the subsistence level. Without any industrial or political defence, they are fully exposed to the crushing and numbing force of the bare struggle for life.[20]

The impact of low wages was made worse by the unreliability of work. A survey organized in the Manchester area in the mid 1890s of conditions in all-women industries such as shirt-making and umbrella-covering showed that out of the hundred and twenty workers questioned only three could always rely on a regular wage. The vast majority were on piece work, and, depending on how fast they worked, could earn anything between 3s and 20s; in slack periods few earned more than 5s. At these starvation rates, commented the organizers of the survey, a woman had 'to use the largest stitch that will stand the inspection of the giver out of work . . . '[21]

The climax of such investigations was the exhibition of work in the sweated industries, organized in 1906 by the *Daily News*. The public conscience was sufficiently roused by it for Trade Boards to be introduced in 1909, with the power to fix minimum wage rates in such trades as tailoring, box-making and chain-making.

The largest group of women workers, however, remained unprotected by any factory act or Trade Board investigation — domestic servants. They flocked into the kitchens of the upper and middle classes in such numbers that by the 1890s over one and a quarter million women were in service.

Like the working class housewife, the servant girl's life was one long battle against dirt and disorder. The draughty Victorian mansions, with their heavy furniture and proliferation of ornaments, required a continual onslaught of cleaning and polishing. Hours were long and pay was extremely low. Not for nothing were maids-of-all-work known as 'slaveys'.

In spite of its extreme exploitation, domestic service was considered very suitable work for girls, since it was a good preparation for the work every woman would have to tackle. Other jobs were regarded less favourably. During the nineteenth century, skilled men, organized into strong craft unions, adopted the view that it was unsuitable for married women to go out to work. Their husbands should earn enough to allow them to bring up the family and look after the house. It was an idea expressed forcibly at the Trade Union Congress of 1877, when Henry Broadhurst, secretary of the powerful Parliamentary Committee, declared:

> It was their duty as men and husbands to use their utmost efforts to bring about a condition of things, where their wives would be in their proper sphere at home, instead of being dragged into competition for livelihood against the great and strong men of the world.[22]

The million 'surplus' women and the families with no male breadwinner did not enter into his calculations. Instead, men like Broadhurst brought their considerable influence to bear on the industries considered particularly unsuitable for women. For instance, they argued fiercely against women working as chain-makers in the Black Country. One local trade unionist, a Mr Juggins, described how unsuitable this kind of work was for young girls: 'It is a disgrace to civilization and a disgrace to the country ... I wish to see [these girls] delivered from the thraldom in which they are placed, and set in a position that would make them good wives and daughters, and so help them to be useful in the sphere for which by nature they are intended.'

When Mr Juggins again tried to limit the women chain-makers' work in the Black Country at the 1887 Congress, he was opposed by Clementina Black, the secretary of the Women's Trade Union League, in a speech that exposed some of the fundamental issues about women's work. The horror stories from Cradley Heath and the surrounding area, she said, could be capped

> ... by a worse story of the sufferings of women employed in trades which no one dreams of forbidding, such as needlework and match-box making. But men never propose to interfere with these trades? Why not? There is no need to ask. Men do not work at these trades and suffer nothing from the competition of women. The real point to be complained of is the low rate of payment earned by the women; and the way to prevent the employment of women in any trade they are unfit for is for men to join in helping them to combine in order that they may receive the same wages for the same work. If employers have to pay women the same prices as men, there would be no temptation to them to employ women to do what they are less fit to do than men. But the women are not represented here to speak for themselves, and I protest against the attempt of one class of workers – especially a class whose interests are concerned – to impose restrictions upon another class of workers.[23]

The Women's Trade Union League, campaigning on issues which are still familiar today, was the earliest organization to fight for working women. It had begun in 1874 as the Women's Protective and Provident League, a name carefully chosen so as not to alienate the middle class support on which it initially depended. At the end of the century, as trade unionism grew stronger among women workers, it changed both its name and its approach. By the 1890s the League was a considerable force in organizing and co-ordinating small unions of women throughout the country. A system was introduced whereby unions could affiliate to the League for a small fee, in return for the services of an experienced, salaried organizer. These were mainly working class women who had personal experience of industrial conditions. Significantly several of them came from the north-west with its long tradition of unionization among women.

One of the League's first organizers was Annie Marland, who came from out of the cotton unions in east Lancashire. First appointed in 1892, she became full organizing secretary in 1894, on a wage of about 18s a week, travelling round the country to speak to women as far apart as Port Glasgow, the Potteries and the West Riding. It was uphill work for the handful of women organizers, and the League was always casting around for ways to supplement their efforts. Its *Review* published propaganda in the flowery language of popular fiction:

> 'Women have no sense of comradeship,' Fred Sewell spoke as one having authority. 'I shall vote against your appeal, Margaret.'
>
> Margaret Read flushed painfully. She had a delicate, sensitive face, which served as a faithful mirror to her emotion. 'Is that treating us quite fairly?' she enquired.
>
> Her tone was almost timid; but the clear grey eyes fixed upon her cousin, lolling in lordly fashion on the opposite side of the fireplace, were unflinching in their gaze . . .
>
> 'I deny', [he replied] 'that they can be trusted to stick to a *cause*. Therefore no women members of our union, say I, and so say all of us, as Margaret will find out next week. You might just as well withdraw that request for an equal membership, Margaret: it hasn't the ghost of a chance with our committee.'[24]

While the League tried to inspire and co-ordinate women's unionization nationally, much was still left to local initiative. Lady Dilke, the League's President, joined with the Manchester Trades Council to attempt to organize women there. In 1892 a woman organizer, whose name is unfortunately lost, was appointed, and she spent eleven weeks going from workshop to workshop distributing thousands of leaflets. But nothing came of her efforts, and there was little unionization among the unskilled and semi-skilled 'women's trades' until in 1895 the

Manchester and Salford Women's Trade Union Council was formed.

Like the League, the Council relied heavily on middle class patronage, though it did have the sponsorship of the Trades Council. The initial committee consisted of Liberal well-wishers and male trade unionists, but it did appoint two working class women as full-time organizers. One was Frances Ashwell, who conducted the survey of Manchester women's low and irregular wages; the other was Sarah Dickenson. She had been Secretary of the small Manchester and Salford Association of Machine, Electrical and Other Women Workers since 1889, and her experience in organizing women workers was to be invaluable to the radical suffragists.

It was hard going; but slowly some progress was made. In May 1896 the Women's Trades Council saw the formation of its first union, the 'Manchester and Salford Society of Women Employed in the Bookbinding and Printing Trades'; Isabel Forsyth, who had started work aged thirteen at a printing works on a wage of 3s 6d a week, became secretary. Other unions followed, among them tailoresses, cafe-workers, shirt-makers, weavers and others.

Although the Women's Trades Council always remained weak compared to the original men's Trades Council, it did manage, by careful negotiation rather than strikes, to raise and stabilize wages for its members. But Sarah Dickenson and Frances Ashwell found that they had to fight against the ignorance and apathy of the women as well as the tight-fistedness of employers. The Council's first Annual Report noted:

> The single women often look upon their work as merely a temporary necessity ... The married women find that home duties fill in such leisure time as they have when the day's work in the factory or workshop is over. Their estimate of their own position is a low one, and they seem to think ... that any display of independence on their part would oust them from the labour market entirely.[25]

While the Women's Trade Union League and local organizations like the Women's Trades Council were beginning to make some headway in improving the position of women at work, women at home had no one to stand up and speak for them. Isolated in their houses, weighed down by housework, they could only be reached by an organization which touched their responsibilities as housewives. It would have to appeal to their interests as provider and consumer, as manager of the household budget and treasurer of its limited income. In 1883 the Women's Co-operative Guild was formed, and for the next thirty years it remained the only group to represent women at home.

Women had a potentially strong position in the Co-operative movement. Since it was they who decided whether or not to shop at the Co-op, they found that they had considerable economic bargaining power. But at first they were slow to realize their strength. In January 1883 an article in the new 'Woman's Corner' of the *Co-operative News* complained about their lack of involvement. 'What are men always urged to do when there is a meeting held at any place to encourage or start co-operative institutions? — come! help! vote! criticize! act! What are women urged to do? — come and *buy*!' Instead, the writer, Alice Acland, suggested, why not start 'co-operative "mothers' meetings", where we may bring our work and sit together, one of us reading some co-operative or other book aloud, which may afterwards be discussed? Are we not as important as the men? Are we not more than half the nation?' So began the Women's League for the Spread of Co-operation, as it was then called.

Initially it was very small, limited in its discussions to domestic subjects, and regarded with some suspicion and even antagonism by male co-operators. But the Women's Co-operative Guild, as it became known within the first year, grew and prospered. As it won a place for itself among the co-operative institutions, the men's latent hostility gradually faded.[26] The Guild took women out of their kitchens and brought them together to discuss matters beyond the narrow confines of their homes. The women grew in their own esteem and in that of their families, as D. H. Lawrence perceptively described in his portrait of a Nottinghamshire mining family:

> When the children were old enough to be left, Mrs Morel joined the Women's Guild. It was a little club of women attached to the Co-operative Wholesale Society, which met on Monday night in the long room over the grocery shop of the Bestwood 'Co-op'. The women were supposed to discuss the benefits to be derived from co-operation, and other social questions. Sometimes Mrs Morel read a paper. It seemed queer to the children to see their mother, who was always busy about the house, sitting writing in her rapid fashion, thinking, referring to books, and writing again. They felt on such occasions the deepest respect.[27]

As the movement grew, the range of topics broadened out from domestic and co-operative matters to include such matters as political economy and rational dress. Single discussions led to series of lectures on subjects as diverse as nursing the sick and French. Social activities grew as well. During the summer, the Bury branch organized 'rambles and picnics, many interesting places having been visited, amongst others the CWS Works.'[28] There were entertainments for members and their children. Selina Cooper's daughter described the Nelson Guild where her mother was a member:

> Occasionally they'd have a social evening. All the women used to dance together ... with somebody playing the piano. I learned to dance at Co-op Guild! ... Oh, and I'll tell you what they did too. When times were bad, the Co-op organized ... activities during the holidays when we couldn't go away ... If it were wet we could come back to the Co-op Hall and play games.[29]

To begin with the Guild's main strength was in the south of England. Then, in the early 1890s, there was a rapid growth of Guild members among the mill workers of Lancashire and Yorkshire. In 1892 the number of branches reached one hundred, and, to celebrate, the Guild organized a 'festival' in Manchester, the headquarters of the Co-operative movement. It was held during three days in July, with delegates present from seventy seven of the branches. The Guild's secretary, Margaret Llewelyn Davies, described the impact this national gathering of women had on those who attended:

> How interesting an occasion this was to the delegates, some of whom had never left home for eight, twelve, or even eighteen years, may be imagined. 'The older women especially,' wrote a member afterwards, 'had had no outings of this kind, having experienced only "mothers' meetings" and treats; but this affair seemed to show them that they were of importance, and some of the older women marvelled at it.[30]

The success of this festival encouraged other national activities. Contact was established with the Women's Trade Union League, and the Guild even tried to improve the conditions of women as paid workers as well as housewives. Campaigns were mounted to encourage women to buy only goods made by unionized labour and to avoid sweated goods. And the Guild took an active concern in the question of the half-timers, where they found that their interests as mothers directly conflicted with their interests as managers of the inadequate household income.

For the first time working class women found in the Guild, the League, the local Women's Trades Council and similar groups a forum to express their grievances and work out their own ideas and campaigns. They also found, again for the first time, outlets for their talents of leadership and organization. The traditional weakness of such women becomes obvious when it is realized that none of the new groups was established without middle and upper class initiative; the majority of

41

the early leaders, such as Lady Dilke and Alice Acland, the wife of an Oxford don, came from outside the working class and could afford to work without a salary. But as such they could not easily reach the mass of ordinary women; the end of the nineteenth century thus saw the rise of a new phenomenon, the salaried working class woman organizer. It was from their numbers that many of the most active radical suffragists — including Sarah Reddish, Ada Nield Chew, Sarah Dickenson, and Helen Silcock — were drawn.

This rise in women's organization did not of course occur in a social vacuum. During this period there was an upsurge of unionization and political activity among unskilled and poorer workers generally. Until the 1880s only a small minority of the working class had been unionized and able to wield any significant political power. They were the skilled male workers, such as the engineers and the spinners, who had built up their unions on the basis of restricted entry to their trades, so ensuring demand for their labour, and a high rate of subscriptions to be paid out in sickness and unemployment benefit, which poorer workers simply could not afford.

Along with their craft unions and co-operative societies, their regard for thrift and for social respectability, they adopted great caution in industrial and political affairs. Marx's friend, Engels, saw what was happening and in 1892 commented bitterly:

> For more than fifteen years not only have their employers been with them, but they with their employers, upon exceedingly good terms. They form an aristocracy among the working class; they have succeeded in enforcing for themselves a relatively comfortable position, and they accept it as final.[31]

In the late 1880s there had been an upsurge among unskilled workers, both men and women. It began with the famous match-girls' strike in London in July 1888. Bryant and May's employees worked long hours in highly dangerous conditions, with their low wages often further reduced by fines. An article in the socialist paper *The Link* inspired them to strike, and, with the help of the editor, Annie Besant, they won significant improvements. The same year also saw strikes by blanket weavers in Yorkshire, women cigarmakers in Nottingham, cotton workers, and jute workers in Dundee. The following year the unrest continued; mill girls in Kilmarnock came out over the bad quality of yarn they had to work on, and at a woollen mill near Wakefield women weavers rejected reduced rates of pay and marched through the streets.[32] That summer there was the celebrated London

Dock Strike, when some of the poorest labourers in the country went on strike for a month to win the princely rate of 6d an hour.

As women had so rarely been union members earlier, it is not surprising that only one or two had ever attended the Trade Union Congresses, and that those who did found the men not unnaturally suspicious of middle class women championing working women's interests. The growth of female trade unionism at the end of the century did help to increase their numbers, but it was still difficult for them to act effectively. They had, for instance, no representation on the powerful TUC Parliamentary Committee which brought trade union pressure to bear on the government. And there were more mundane difficulties: when Annie Marland, representing her textile union, stood up to speak at the 1894 Congress, the *Women's Trade Union Review* reported proudly that she 'overcame the usual difficulties experienced by female delegates and made herself heard . . . a fact much commented on.'[33]

Politically, the 'labour aristocracy' of which Engels wrote had ignored the interests of the mass of working people, and had become happily absorbed into the two-party system of the nineteenth century. Its leaders had prospered under the patronage of the middle and upper classes. An extreme example was Henry Broadhurst, the powerful Parliamentary Secretary of the TUC from 1875. In 1880 he became a Liberal MP, and served the party so faithfully, even to the extent of supporting employers as candidates at elections, that he rose to become Under Secretary of State, and was invited to stay at the Palace, where the Prince of Wales did him the much appreciated honour of coming into his bedroom and poking his fire. Most other trade union leaders were Liberals like Broadhurst, but, a few, for instance James Mawdsley of the Spinners, gave their allegiance to the Conservative party instead.

But as the bulk of the working class developed industrial muscle it began to want to use it politically as well. From the beginnings of the new unionism, socialists had been encouraging the workers to struggle for more than just short-term gains, while helping them to organize their new societies. Karl Marx's daughter, Eleanor, who was involved in the formation of the Gasworkers' Union, which came to include many other unskilled workers, Annie Besant, who had sparked off the matchgirls' strike, and John Burns who had led the dockers' strike were all members of the marxist Social Democratic Federation. Founded in 1884, and led by H.M. Hyndman, a wealthy London businessman, it always remained small, rather isolated from other socialist groups, but with a certain amount of influence. Although it counted several active and articulate women among its early members its general attitude to feminism was unsympathetic. Hyndman himself said that he could not 'get up much enthusiasm for female suffrage'. And among the working class members, Harry Quelch, editor of *Justice*, the Federation's paper, was one of the most vigorous opponents of what he saw as the bourgeois fad of feminism.[34]

The Federation's main strength was in London, though in the 1890s it built up a considerable following in Salford, Wigan and in north east Lancashire. By 1893 the Burnley branch alone had eleven hundred members, and put forward Hyndman as its parliamentary candidate in 1895. Although he was unsuccessful, the Federation increased its influence among the cotton workers; by 1893 one of its members was elected vice-president of the Burnley Weavers' Association, and in nearby Nelson the Liberals had to work hard to get enough of their supporters to come along to union meetings to outvote the socialists. In Colne, a few miles further up the valley a weaver who was also a Federation member was even elected on to the town council in 1898.[35] Among the Federation's recruits from the mills were Helen Silcock and Selina Cooper, at that time both active members of the Weavers' Association.

But these isolated pockets of Lancashire marxism were exceptional. The Federation was too narrowly sectarian to have any real mass appeal, and many people turned instead to another new socialist group, the Independent Labour Party (ILP), whose strength often lay in its appeal to the emotions and day-to-day experiences, rather than elaborate political theory. It was led by Keir Hardie, the Ayrshire Miners' Secretary. His personal warmth and straight speaking converted thousands to the socialism he had come to through the hardships of his early life. He was a fervent teetotaller, and used to joke that when socialism arrived he would celebrate with a schooner of lager. He became a much loved figure when he came to visit Lancashire socialists; Mary Cooper as a child confused him with Father Christmas, because of his long white beard and kindly manner.

Men like Hardie made a strong appeal to the nonconformist working class of the north of England; the main strength of the early ILP came from the textile towns of the West Riding and Lancashire. Bradford ILP was the first, founded in 1891 after an unsuccessful strike by textile workers. Manchester followed a year later, after an immense May Day demonstration. The national ILP was not formed until 1893, and the local branches always retained a large degree of control over their own policies and activities.

But while branches varied in the details of their approach, the ILP as a whole stood for a 'co-operative commonwealth' that would radically improve the quality of everyday life, in place of the existing system of economic competition. It demanded direct parliamentary representation of working class interests, independent of both Liberal and Tory parties. To achieve this, it insisted on the necessity of a new parliamentary grouping that would be responsible to working people alone.

The ILP on its own was not large or rich enough to become the new party of Labour. The power of the big battalions, the trade unions, was needed to support and finance the attempt. But the old craft unions still preferred to back tried and trusted Liberals like Broadhurst or even Tories like Mawdsley. The TUC repeatedly rejected attempts by Keir Hardie and others to commit it to supporting independent candidates. When such a proposal was finally carried in 1899, two of the most powerful unions – the miners and the cotton workers – voted against it. Consequently the group of socialists and trade unionists who met in London in February 1900 to form the Labour Representation Committee had almost no money or influence. In order to keep trade union support, the secretary, James Ramsay MacDonald, had to play down socialist principles, settling instead for independence from the other political parties and the right of MPs to vote as they pleased on any issue that did not directly affect labour.

This meant that the new party had no agreed policy on women's issues; members were free to take the old Broadhurst line, or, like Keir Hardie, to support any measure that they felt would advance women's emancipation. Generally, ILP members were more likely to hold views favourable to women than the trade union representatives, but tended to be outvoted.

From the very start the ILP had a far better reputation for treating women as equals than other political groups. Women and men joined on the same basis; although a branch might have an informal women's group, there was no official section to which the women were automatically relegated. (Liberal and Tory women were kept firmly in their own ghetto organizations, the Women's Liberal Federation and the Primrose League.) Some branches went out of their way to welcome women. A Crewe socialist wrote to the local paper in 1894 to insist that 'The ILP is as much a women's party as a men's'[36] and his branch made considerable efforts to help women workers locally to improve their conditions.

Many women responded eagerly to the new Party's appeal; the Manchester elementary school teacher Teresa Billington wrote later; 'I was one of the idealists who saw as the hopeful dawn not the political Labour Party then coming to birth before our eyes but a great missionary movement for mental and moral uplift based on the solid foundation of an egalitarian economy.'[37]

But others found that they had to assert themselves if they were not to be treated just as women were in other political organizations, as unpaid canvassers, and fund raisers and caterers. There was often a wide gap between equality in theory and in practice, as Hannah Mitchell, an early ILP member, remembered:

> Even my Sunday leisure was gone [as a wife and mother] for I soon found that a lot of the Socialist talk about freedom was only talk and these Socialist young men expected Sunday dinners and huge teas with home-made cakes, potted meats and pies, exactly like their reactionary fellows.[38]

III

Nineteenth century Lancashire

Women's labour was essential to the textile industries; among the Nottinghamshire hosiery workers, the woollen workers of the West Riding and the cotton workers of Lancashire there was a strong tradition of women's employment. This was particularly true in the cotton towns where it was common, for instance, for the married woman to work a 'double shift', spending her days in the mill and her evenings and Sundays looking after her family.

One such Lancashire woman was Louisa Pollitt, Harry Pollitt's mother. Her husband worked as a blacksmith's striker and earned only 18s a week, while she could earn about 20s as a weaver at Benson's mill in Droylsden. Like thousands of other Lancashire children, Harry Pollitt's earliest memories of growing up in the 1890s were mostly of how his mother coped:

> My sister and I were carried out of our bed at 5.30 every working day to be left in the care of Granny Ford for 4s a week, until it was safe to leave us in bed to look after ourselves, and that wasn't very long. Mother came rushing home from Benson's in the breakfast half-hour to give us our breakfast, and my first actual recollection is of one such morning when I was sitting with my back to the fire and a cinder flew out and stuck on the back of my neck. But Benson's bell was ringing them back to work and a neighbour had to come in and make a fuss of me and stop my crying.[1]

The roots of this tradition of women's work extend back to the eighteenth century. Spinning had traditionally been the job of the women of the family — hence the word 'spinster', meaning simply a woman spinner. The spinster was a vital member of the domestic workforce, and her spindle transformed the loose cotton into yarn ready to be woven. Weaving was usually done by a man, and the Lancashire handloom weaver became noted for the pride he took in his work. The solidly built weavers' houses in the Pennine valleys testify to the stability of this domestic system of production. Wages were relatively high and work usually plentiful; often adolescent sons and daughters, or the weaver's wife, would supplement his earnings on a second or third loom.

Yet the days of this cottage industry were numbered. By the end of the eighteenth century, new inventions began to revolutionize the cotton industry. Crompton's 'mule' mechanized spinning, and the first mills mushroomed to accommodate the new machinery. Not long afterwards, Cartwright's power loom began to compete with the handloom, and steam-powered weaving factories began to cluster along the valleys as well. As cotton production was increasingly transferred to the factories during the early decades of the nineteenth century, handloom weavers found their wages beaten down to 9s, 7s, and even to 5s a week. The wives and daughters of these impoverished men saw that their only hope of survival lay in becoming 'power-loom slaves'. An Oldham ballad of this transitional period shows how the hand-weaver's pride began to falter in the face of women's enviable factory wages:

> I am a hand-weaver to my trade.
> I fell in love with a factory maid.
> And if I could but her favour win,
> I'd stand beside her and weave by steam.
>
> My father to me scornful said:
> How could you fancy a factory maid,
> When you could have girls fine and gay,
> And dressed up like the Queen of May?
>
> Where are the girls? I'll tell you plain.
> The girls have gone to weave by steam,
> And if you'd find 'em, you must rise at dawn,
> And trudge to the factory in the early morn.[2]

The number of women weaving in factories doubled, trebled and quadrupled and their wages crept up way beyond those of any diehard hand-weavers still hanging on to their old way of life. Factory owners preferred employing women to men: they were cheaper and more biddable. Marx noted in *Capital* that a cotton manufacturer who

employed females exclusively at his power-looms. . . gives a decided preference
to married females, especially those who have families at home dependent on
them for support; they are attentive, docile, more so than unmarried females,
and are compelled to use their utmost exertions to procure the necessaries of
life.[3]

Similarly children and adolescents were often preferred to grown men
for the same reasons. The job of helping an adult weaver could easily be
done by a ten-year old girl, and indeed, smaller children were more
adept at crawling under the looms and cleaning the machinery. Boys
whose labour could be bought for 5s a week cost a mill owner over 20s
a week once full grown; so unless they had particular skills, men could
often find themselves laid off by other workers who undercut their
wage levels.

But while factory owners were glad of a cheap labour force, some
observers began to protest that such work undermined the family,
deprived young children of any kind of education, and led to ill health.
During the mid-nineteenth century, arguments about the human cost of
factory work went back and forth. It did seem that mills were
unhealthy and often dangerous places to work in; the babies of working
mothers were less likely to survive or to grow up strong, and the long
hours of work reduced the lives of women and children to serf-like
misery. So, despite the opposition of certain Liberal manufacturers
(who disliked any interference in their affairs) and high-minded experts
(for whom women's low wages were Providence's way of keeping
women in their proper sphere at home), the result was a succession of
progressive Factory Acts, passed between 1832 and 1850, which
reduced the hours of work for women and young children.[4]

Far less easily resolved was the controversy over whether women
should be allowed to work in factories at all. The critics who opposed
women's work were more vocal than their opponents. Factory work,
they said, took the wives and mothers away from the home during the
day. It gave women wages that made them pert and cocky, and
encouraged them to neglect their homes in favour of their own clubs
and friendly societies. In the 1850s Mrs Gaskell described in *North and
South* how the girls leaving one Manchester mill 'came rushing along,
with bold, fearless faces, and loud laughs and jests, particularly aimed at
all those who appeared to be above them in rank or station.'[5] Another
novelist, Mrs Tonna, added her voice to protests about the
irresponsibility of girls like these once they became mothers; in her
book *The Forsaken Home* she wrote:

49

A man came into one of these clubrooms, with a child in his arms. 'Come, lass' said he, addressing one of the women, 'come home, for I cannot keep this bairn quiet, and the other I have left crying at home.' 'I won't go home, idle devil' she replied, 'I have thee to keep, and the bairns too, and if I can't have a pint of ale quietly, it is tiresome.'[6]

These protests against married women's work did have some reasonable basis behind them. The unhealthy conditions in the mill affected pregnant and nursing mothers and their babies. But the claim that married women workers lived wilfully independent lives was largely ill-founded. Mill owners did prefer employing women and children, but not to the extent of paying them wages comparable to those of adult men. Figures for wages in the 1830s show that it was virtually impossible for a woman to earn more than 10s a week, whilst men could earn at least twice that amount by their late twenties. A young unmarried girl could earn 7s or 8s a week and this might give her the kind of jaunty self-confidence that had struck Elizabeth Gaskell. But by the time a woman was thirty, with perhaps two or three children, her wages would have only increased by about a shilling, hardly sufficient to buy even an occasional pint of ale.

Men's rates, on the other hand, were usually over £1 a week. The highest wages, up to £2, were paid to the mule spinners.[7] Spinning was the key job in the mill, and from the beginning it became the province of highly paid skilled men, instead of the task of the domestic spinster.

The reasons for this change are complex. Once Crompton's mules, with their hundreds of spindles, were harnessed to steam-powered engines, the cotton spinning process demanded a high degree of technical skill on the part of their operators, which called for a long apprenticeship. And such 'craft' jobs, which included having authority over assistants, were increasingly considered to be outside women's province.

As industrialization progressed the differentiation between men's and women's roles increased. When the workplace was still in the home, women could combine spinning with household tasks. Now it had moved to the factory, and paid labour became separated from unpaid housework. Previously all the members of a family were expected to contribute to the total income; now, with wages paid to individual workers, there developed the concept of the 'family wage' paid to the male breadwinner, which would be sufficient for him to keep his family at home. Up to the end of the eighteenth century, only middle class families had been able to afford to rely exclusively on the income of the adult male. Now the idea began to percolate down the class structure.

In the poorest families — like the Pollitts — the question of relying on a single wage was academic: a wife would work as long as childbearing permitted, for without her wage the family would starve. In families of skilled workers the pressure on all members to earn was not so great. The manner in which this ideal of the family wage was taken up by skilled working class families is still the subject of great controversy, and it is difficult to disentangle economic motives from social ones. Yet it does seem certain that among the early nineteenth century cotton spinners the demand became widely adopted quite early on, and was one extra lever with which mule spinners managed to up their wages and exclude women from doing their work.

When the spinning machine first came into use, women complained about their exclusion. At Leicester in 1788, for instance, an informal union of hand-spinners, known as the 'sisterhood', got up a petition against the sinister machines that were taking away their livelihood. For the spinsters, their work was more than just a source of income, it was 'consistent with civil liberty, so full of domestic comfort and so favourable to a religious life'. But the cards were stacked against them. The male mule spinners, concentrated in a few mills in Oldham, Bolton and Manchester, enjoyed a strong sense of solidarity from the very beginning: many of them had been skilled handloom weavers or millwrights, conscious of their craft skills, and used to supervising younger assistants.[8]

Until the 1820s the exclusion of women was informal and piecemeal, but gradually the spinners came to the conclusion that local rulings were insufficient and that national organization was essential. So, in 1829, various local societies took part in a conference in the Isle of Man. Here the spinners agreed to form a general union to protect their interests. One penny a week levy was fixed, with 10s a week strike benefit. In addition they stipulated:

> That no person or persons be learned or allowed to spin, after the 5th of April 1830, except the son, brother, or orphan nephew of spinners, and the poor relations of the proprietors of the mills, and those only when they have attained the full age of fifteen years . . .
>
> That female spinners be urged to become members of an association to be formed exclusively for themselves, and that an entrance ceremony be prepared for them, suited to their circumstances; and that they pay into and receive from their own fund, such sum or sums as they may from time to time agree upon; and that they receive the aid of the whole confederation, in supporting

them to obtain men's prices, or such remuneration for their labour as may be deemed sufficient, under general or particular circumstances.[9]

The spinners' fear was of the very real threat that women's low wages would undercut their prices. A spinner from Bolton made this point inadvertently the following year, 1830. He wrote to the *United Trades Co-operative Journal* complaining he had been displaced by a woman spinner; she worked for 12-14s a week, while he was paid 25-30s. Spinning was unhealthy for women, commented the *Journal* editor sympathetically, and their employment was subversive to the natural order of things whereby a man should support his family.[10]

The Amalgamated Association of Operative Cotton Spinners, founded in 1837, kept to the Isle of Man policy. Entry to the trade was kept under the tightest control. All big and little piecers (assistants), women, and all people working on rival spinning processes (the water frame, jenny or throstle) were excluded. To keep numbers down by controlling the supply of workers, they even paid their members an emigration benefit to coax them to spin in some distant colony.

Throughout the nineteenth century the mule spinners were able to maintain their superiority above all other workers in the mill. They were excellently organized, with nine out of ten spinners joining the Association. Their wages were always far higher than those of other mill workers: 25s in the 1830s and over 30s by the 1870s. Union dues followed suit, with benefits covering not only strikes but also lock-outs, unemployment, accidents, funerals and breakdowns.

The women who flocked to the early mills were rarely the wives and daughters of these elite craftsmen; more commonly, their husbands and fathers were impoverished handloom weavers, farm labourers or lower-paid mill workers who lacked the bargaining power to claim a 'family wage'. These women badly needed their jobs to help support their families; but unlike the mule spinners, women workers had no strong union to defend their interests.

Excluded from the technical and supervisory jobs, and with their working lives interrupted by frequent childbirth, women were unable to impose a tight apprenticeship system. All that women cotton workers were able to organize in the mid-century was a series of local, usually short lived trade societies, such as the oddly-named Ancient Virgins, an Oldham card-room society from the 1830s.[11]

By the 1850s weaving was fully mechanized, and concentrated in the mills around Blackburn. The weavers, of whom the majority were women, tried to band together to maintain a standard list of rates at which their piecework wages could be calculated. A few local groups of men weavers did manage to maintain their own lists, but for the vast mass of women weavers there was no effective regional organization until the 1880s.

The wages of the male weavers were well below those of the spinners, and yet they too began to adopt the demand for the family wage by the middle of the century, and seem to have been supported by at least some of their wives in this. For instance, in 1853 a Mrs Fletcher of Preston addressed a meeting in Darwen, a weaving town not far from Blackburn, urging 'that every man should earn enough money to keep himself and his family without the necessity of sending his wife into the mill.' The main emphasis still seems to have been on men rather than women organizing into local trade associations; at another Darwen meeting a woman was reported 'advising girls present to repulse all their sweethearts who did not subscribe to the Preston Operatives'.[12]

The values attached to men's and women's work by the Preston weavers became more widespread in the 1850s and 1860s. Writers began to celebrate the Victorian 'cult of domesticity' and construct spiritual reasons for women to stay at home. John Ruskin's ideas found a particularly strong response among working class readers. 'The woman's power is not for rule, not for battle,' he said in his lecture 'Of Queen's Gardens' in 1868, 'and her intellect is not for invention or creation, but for sweet ordering, management and decision. She sees the quality of things, their class, their places.'[13]

Even in the cotton towns, where women flocked into the mills during the nineteenth century, women's work was increasingly seen as marginal and their status sank relative to men's. By the 1890s the separation into men's and women's rightful spheres of work had become so much part of the orthodoxy that even the *Cotton Factory Times* could with a straight face print:

> How sweet it is when toil is o'er
> To sit upon the hearth once more
> To whistle, sing, and sweet converse,
> With the sweetest queen in universe,
> In homely way[14]

Yet the position of women cotton workers in the late nineteenth century was, by comparison, far stronger than that of any other group of working women. Their wages were far higher, and they were far more likely to be organized into a local association. The demand for the family wage to be paid to a male breadwinner took a weaker hold in Lancashire than elsewhere.

Equally important, the Lancashire cotton industry's profitable exports to underdeveloped countries grew continuously until by the end of the century 90 per cent of production was exported, two-thirds of it to India, while the home market remained negligible.[15] Cotton production was growing at an average rate of 1¼ per cent a year and more and more women were drawn into the factory system to operate the mill machinery. Despite the popularity of the Victorian cult of domesticity, women still needed to go out to work to add their wages to the limited family budgets. By 1900 no fewer than a quarter of a million Lancashire women were employed in the cotton mills. It became the common expectation for a girl from a working class family in one of the cotton towns to work in a mill until she was married, and quite possibly afterwards as well.

Another of the dramatic aspects of the cotton trade was that it was so heavily concentrated in the eastern half of Lancashire and the northern tip of Cheshire. 'I cannot too strongly emphasize,' said one mill owner in the 1900s, 'the fact that the cotton trade is the mainstay of all who make their living within a radius of forty miles from Manchester, no matter what their occupation may be.'[16] Often the only other major employer in a cotton town was a textile engineering firm. Oldham, for instance, was dominated by spinning and engineering; Platt Brothers, which built textile machinery for export to Italy, Russia and Brazil, had almost twelve hundred employees by the turn of the century.[17]

The Lancashire cotton towns, often as tightly knit and as socially compact as mining communities, spread out in a series of concentric arcs from the industry's centre in Manchester. They ranged from tiny villages to great, sprawling towns. Mills still clung to their original Pennine hillsides and valleys, and many of the villages had scarcely changed since industrialization. 'Old Bacup remained unaltered along the bleak high hills,' wrote Beatrice Webb in the 1880s. 'The mills, now busily working overtime, nestled in the valley, long unpaved streets of two-storied cottages straggled irregularly up the hills. . . The monotony of its daily existence likens the hand-loom villages of a century ago.'[18]

What was life like in these tiny communities at the turn of the century? Mary Luty spent her childhood in an isolated hamlet in Rossendale, in the heart of the cotton region. Her home was a farmhouse, known as 'Back o'th Low', on the edge of the moors. The men of the family worked in the local stone quarries, while it was the woman's job to take the butter and eggs to market in baskets on the backs of recalcitrant donkeys. Mary and her brother were brought up by her mother after their parents separated, and Mrs Luty went to work as a weaver in a nearby mill to support the three of them. She was one of the Lancashire women for whom the double shift was the normal way of life. 'Around 1895 the cotton trade was very bad,' Mary wrote later, 'and wages extremely low, so my mother had to work all the time she could to earn sufficient for food. After the long day in the mill, she returned to her cottage and on a Monday evening would do the week's washing — another night she baked the bread which would last a full week.'[19]

Soon Mary's own time came to join her mother in the mill. When she was eleven she 'passed' her Labour Exam and ran home excitedly to pin the certificate up for her mother to see. Her enthusiasm was short lived; now she too joined the half-hour walk to the factory gate, and started as a half-timer tenter to her mother in return for three shillings a week.

As soon as I could start and stop looms properly and take up odd ends of twist which might break, and thread shuttles by drawing the weft up through the shuttle eye with my lips, my mother got six looms ... At thirteen years of age I left school and began as a full-time 'tenter' for my mother, altho' I used to pretend I really had two looms. The extra money meant much in the home, and we began to have little luxuries not known previously.[20]

Living in such an isolated area, neither Mrs Luty nor her daughter had much option but to go into the mill. Farming jobs for women had become increasingly scarce during the nineteenth century, and in any case the paltry wages compared very unfavourably with weaving rates.[21]

However, such isolation was rare: all through the nineteenth century villages had swollen into suburban sprawls as the cotton industry expanded further and further into the Lancashire countryside. Helen Bradley, a local painter, born in 1900, describes this mixture of town and country in terms of Lees, just outside Oldham:

The village had lost the few farms it once had. The cotton mills had spread out from Oldham, and rows of little back-to-back houses for working people filled the once open spaces ... Grandma's house was only on the other side of the High Street and as in those days there were only horses plodding slowly by with their lorry-loads of bales of cotton we could run across to see her without much fear of accident.[22]

Ethel Brierley also grew up in Lees, where her father had run the local Co-op since the 1880s. Her childhood memories were dominated by the mills.

> When we were young folks used to complain about the chimneys smoking...
> My father used to say, 'Give over grumbling about the chimneys smoking,
> because,' he said, 'if you worked where I do' – he was a grocer, you see – he
> says, 'they have the spending power when chimneys are smoking. They're
> earning money when chimneys are smoking.'[23]

She remembers counting at least fourteen working mills along a mile of road, each with its own mill pond. Over half were old stone built ones – Grotton Hollow Mill, Livingstone Mill, the two Springhead spinning mills known as Company Top and Company Bottom, Clough Mill, Woodend Mill, County End Mill, the Lees Union, Acorn Mill, and a very old one called Mary Broadbent's. Annie Kenney worked in the Woodend cardroom from 1889, the year of her tenth birthday, and her brother Rowland worked as a 'little piecer' for about four years in one of the Springhead spinning mills. With the exception of Woodend Mill, part of which is today still cotton, all the stone mills have either been converted to other uses or have been pulled down. The mill where Rowland Kenney used to work has long been a pile of forgotten rubble on the banks of the tiny clough.

The rest of the mills down this stretch of road were newer brick ones – Stanley Mill, Stamford Mill and Lees Brook – with bigger ones going up quite regularly. 'Rome wasn't built when I'm talking about now,' Ethel Brierley said. 'I could remember the Athens being built. It was a lovely modern mill.'[24] By the mid nineteenth century the stone mills began to be ousted by these new, harsh rectangular blocks of red Accrington brick, so familiar from the paintings of L.S. Lowry. They were given exotic titles – Cairo, Durban, Nile, Athens or Rome – and these names were built in white brick letters into the seven-storey high mill towers by ambitious owners with an eye to impressing shareholders.

Lees was still surrounded by fields at the turn of the century, and the new spinning mills loomed up above the green Pennine skyline. Yet there were large areas of Lancashire covered by densely populated towns, made up of long terraces of cheap insanitary brick houses, packing the spaces between the towering mills (see illus.). The half dozen major cotton towns – Preston, Blackburn and Burnley in the north, with Bolton, Rochdale and Oldham in the centre – repeated this pattern of sprawling, smoky gloom. H.M. Hyndman, leader of the

Marxist Social Democratic Federation, who stood as a parliamentary candidate in Burnley, shuddered at what he encountered in the northern cotton towns:

> Do you know Burnley? If not, don't . . . I shall never forget the first time, when, in quest of a little fresh air, I walked up to the top of the Manchester Road and looked down on Burnley from the hill-top. There it lay in the hollows, one hideous malebolge of carbon-laden fog and smoke, the factory chimneys rising above the mass of thick clouds like stakes upon which . . . successive generations of the workers and their children had been impaled.[25]

Yet beneath the similarities of grime and smoke, the Lancashire towns were proud of their individuality. Each had its own specialization in the cotton process, its own particular product that distinguished it from its neighbours.

In the early nineteenth century, weaving and spinning usually took place under the same cottage or factory roof. But gradually a geographical division developed. The northern towns began to concentrate on weaving and those to the south on spinning. This was by no means a rigid separation — most towns retained some weaving and some spinning — but it was one that became more and more marked. By the 1880s, the northern area had monopolized more than three-fifths of the looms, and the southern area three-quarters of the spindles. The giant spinning mills dominated the skyline of south Lancashire, while the single storey weaving sheds, with one side of the roof made out of glass to allow maximum light to fall on the looms, were characteristic of northern villages like Nelson, Darwen and Colne.

Girls in working class families living north of Rochdale would automatically go into the mill — usually into the weaving shed — when they left school. The pressure to earn mill wages as soon as possible was very strong and could often lead to fierce family arguments for and against weaving. Ethel Derbyshire was the youngest of fourteen children: all her sisters had become weavers and her brothers spinners in the various mills in Blackburn. When she was ten it was her turn. She had taught herself to sew and very much wanted to become a seamstress: her daughter described what actually happened:

> The boys of the family, they said, when she came to [start work], 'For goodness sake, let's keep youngest of the family out of the mill.' The sisters, they were weavers, but her sisters — probably a touch of jealousy, I don't know — said they'd been in the mill and she should go into the mill, even if she learned to weave. That was a big thing, they used to talk about, the cotton workers, 'You've a *trade* in your hands, a wonderful trade, a weaver. A trade

in your hands if you learned to weave.' So they said, 'Well she ought to go in and learn to weave, she'd always have something in her hands.' And the lads, the boys, the brothers, said, 'Nay, I think the youngest should be kept out.' Let her go to sewing.'[26]

Somehow her sisters' arguments prevailed and Ethel Derbyshire went to work in the mill. She worked for the next fourteen years, until she married in 1903, and even then continued until her second child was born.

In the three major weaving towns — Blackburn, Burnley and Preston — no less than three-quarters of the unmarried women worked, and about one third of the women continued working after they were married. In Burnley as many as 34 per cent of married women went out to work, and in the satellite villages and towns like Brierfield, Nelson, Barrowford and Colne which spread north of the town up the valley of the little River Calder, it may have been even higher.[27] Here the married women's 'double shift' was commonplace. Mary Cooper described how, when she was a child, none of the local mothers stayed at home as housewives, but each kept her job on in the nearby mill. [28]

In fact in 1891 a law had been passed requiring women to stay away from factory work for at least four weeks after giving birth. This was, of course, leave without pay, and it was unenforced and unenforceable.[29] Selina Cooper worked at a mill in Brierfield, probably typical among the weaving towns. 'I've heard my mother tell that they'd their babies at the looms . . .' Mary said. 'Because they stood in a rotten position . . . It did drop easily . . . But the mothers daren't get off their work, because they'd lose their job.'[30]

The mid century arguments about working mothers still carried on, although emotion now had to contend with more accurate statistics. Infant mortality rates were consistently higher in Burnley or Preston than in non-textile towns like Lancaster or Barrow: social scientists deduced from this that babies of working mothers were at greatest risk because it was difficult to fit their feeds in with the mill buzzer, and they were therefore more likely to come into contact with unhygienic feeding bottles.[31] Others argued that infant mortality rates in the weaving towns were no higher than in, for instance, the Potteries where the proportion of married women working was much lower;[32] they concluded that it was poor housing and unhealthy diet that increased infant mortality rather than working mothers.

Others backed this up by showing how local family networks ensured that few children were really neglected. The Women's Co-operative

Guild was particularly concerned about child care, and from 1894 Sarah Reddish forwarded monthly returns for the *Labour Gazette* entitled 'The State of Women's Employment', based on reports from fifty seven correspondents in different textile towns. Another Guildswoman, Mrs Ashworth from Burnley, herself a weaver for over twenty years, organized a local survey of the conditions under which children were left when their mothers went out to the mill. The results were also published in the *Labour Gazette* in 1894, and showed that out of 165 children, one in four was left with grand-parents, a further one in four with other relatives, nearly half with neighbours, and only in nine cases were children left with no one to take care of them.[33] Certainly Mary Cooper grew up surrounded by her father's extensive family and knew that there were always relatives in nearby houses she could go to if there was no one at home when she came back from school.

In the spinning towns south of Rochdale working mothers were less common. Husbands were more likely to be miners, mule spinners or engineers, and to earn sufficient to keep their wives at home, and the wages women could earn preparing the cotton for spinning were lower than those of the northern weavers. In Bolton, which specialized in fine spinning, and in Oldham, which concentrated on the coarser yarn, more than two-thirds of the unmarried women worked, but less than a fifth of the married ones. Here too, it was almost automatic that a working class girl would go into the mill when she left school. Cissy Foley went straight into the card-room; her sister Alice, after an abortive trial month as a shop assistant, was told by her mother, 'Well, tha'd better put thi' clogs on an' ger' a job in't mill.'[34] Another Bolton woman who left school in 1907 explained how few alternatives there were to going to work in the mill.

> I didn't know what on earth to do – all the children went in the mill . . . When I left school [my sister said to me] 'I don't know what I'll do with you.' I thought, 'Oh, I don't want to go in the mill.' I couldn't bear the machinery; you know, when you came out of the mill, you couldn't hear . . . 'You'll have to do something, you know.' So I said, 'I'd like to be a dressmaker.' 'You're not doing that,' she said, 'you have to pay to learn. You can't do that.' So I thought, oh, the mill it'll have to be.[35]

The majority of women in the spinning towns left the mill when they married or when the first child was due. Certainly Cissy Foley's mother had worked in the cardroom since she was ten or eleven, but she gave it up when she had children, although it was the only job she knew. 'She preferred being in the mill to being mithered to death by father hanging round the house,' Alice Foley recalled, but because there were no nurseries she had to stay at home, and the family was 'brought up mainly out of her wash-tub earnings'.[36]

Further west, there were the towns in the coal belt, like Wigan, where cotton was merely a secondary industry. The miners, whose relatively high wages were well protected by their union, seemed to adopt the demand for a family wage in the same way that the spinners had done. They seemed to accept that their daughters might go into the weaving sheds, but not their wives. Just over a thousand Lancashire women, most of them unmarried, worked as pit brow lasses, unloading and sorting the coal at the surface of the mines. Their small numbers, quaint trousers and low wages meant that the pit brow lasses' work was increasingly seen as marginal to that of the miners and there were repeated attempts to ban women from doing this work at all.[37] All these factors conspired to make the Wigan women cotton workers among the least organized, lowest paid in Lancashire.

The hub of the cotton industry was the twin cities of Manchester and Salford. Here raw cotton was brought into Lancashire (from the end of the nineteenth century by the new Manchester Ship Canal), and here woven cloth was brought back to be exported around the world. By the turn of the century, Manchester and Salford, as well as the smaller towns nearby, concentrated on finishing rather than on spinning and weaving, and from early on Manchester acted as a trading and commercial centre for the cotton towns. Even as early as the 1840s, Engels had noted that the surrounding towns were 'purely industrial and conduct all their business through Manchester upon which they are in every respect dependent'.[38]

As the tentacles of the Lancashire cotton trade extended out to India — as well as to Argentina, Brazil and other underdeveloped countries — so the Manchester Exchange became a solid symbol of Lancashire's prosperity. Built in 1809 and greatly extended in 1839 it was the 'largest Exchange room in Europe', and was seen as 'the parliament house of the lords of cotton'.[39] But while business men boasted of its commercial efficiency and architects marvelled at its Grecian columns, other inhabitants took a more jaundiced view of its magnificence. Not far from the Exchange were some of the worst slums in Europe. They had horrified Engels in the 1840s, and forty years later they still provoked outbursts of indignation:

One thing is certain, it is a sin and a shame that human beings should be permitted to exist in such misery, to live in such horrible dog-holes as do too many unfortunates within a quarter of an hour's walk of one of the wealthiest Exchanges in the world. Houses rotten and tumbling to pieces, rooms filthy, damp, mildewed, with great holes in the floors, great gaps in the walls, where the plaster should have been; people half-starving, and with scarcely a rag to cover their nakedness. [40]

There were still mills operating in Manchester and Salford at the turn of the century, though only a few; in the two cities there were under seven thousand women weavers compared to over twice that number in Blackburn. Even fewer men went to work in the mills there, and the status and wages of the local cotton workers was as low as in Wigan.[41] And all attempts to form a local trade union branch had failed; as late as 1901 Women's Trade Union Council noted how ill-organized and badly paid were the women weavers and card room workers in the city. Walter Greenwood grew up in Salford in the 1900s and recalled how his mother was offered her old job back in the weaving sheds where she had worked before she married. 'I have seen all I wish to see of weaving sheds,' she replied proudly to the overlooker. 'No thank you, Mr Wheelam. I would rather pick oakum.'[42] There was more choice for a working woman in Salford than in Rossendale, and Mrs Greenwood eventually found a job as a waitress.

Against the general current of Victorian England the majority of Lancashire mill women had developed a tradition of skilled, well paid work. They enjoyed limited independence which working women elsewhere could not match. It was an independence and security that varied from town to town and was considerably stronger in, say, Burnley or Nelson than in Wigan or Salford; and it was an independence that could really only be fully enjoyed by unmarried women whose domestic responsibilities were still comparatively light.

Women cotton weavers might have none of the mule spinners' national organization, but even their short-lived local associations and societies were better organized than those outside the textile area. Indeed, Lancashire women acquired something of a reputation for radicalism at work, however sporadic.

Early spinners' societies — Manchester, for instance — had had women members, and women took part in weavers' strikes early in the century. 'The women are, if possible, more turbulent and mischievous than the men,' *The Times* reported anxiously in 1808.[43] In 1834 two *Times* correspondents, covering the Eight Hours' riot in Oldham, noted that the trade union 'delegates are moving in all parts of the country, and a system of speedy and secret communication has been established. Even the women's lodges, the "Female Gardeners" and "Ancient Virgins", are said to be anyways rather than coy in their co-operation ...' Among the thirteen people arrested for rioting was one woman, Sally Whitehead, accused of stealing a soldier's bayonet, though she was eventually discharged 'after a very tedious examination.'[44]

Twenty years later, women cotton workers seem to have played an important role in the Preston strike.[45] Certainly women were active in the Blackburn riots of 1878 that followed a threat by mill owners of a ten per cent reduction in wages; the workers, four thousand strong, took to the streets in open defiance. They marched from mill to mill smashing windows, the women strikers carrying the ammunition for the men in their aprons, producing stones, pokers and other odds and ends when they were needed.[46]

Radicalism at work reflected wider political demands. It is usually thought that working women in the nineteenth century did not claim political rights for themselves; this is generally true, for most demands were for political rights for men, yet Lancashire women seem to have been exceptionally vocal. In 1818 and 1819 the first Female Reform Societies were formed in Bolton, Blackburn, Preston, Manchester, and Ashton-under-Lyne. In the Blackburn society, members pledged themselves 'to use our utmost endeavour to instil into the minds of our children a deep and rooted hatred of our corrupt and tyrannical rulers', and to this end invented 'The Bad Alphabet for the use of the Children of Female Reformers': B was for Bible, Bishop and Bigotry; K for King, King's evil, Knave and Kidnapper; W for Whig, Weakness, Wavering and Wicked.[47]

At the great Reform meeting of Peterloo, several banners were inscribed 'Universal Suffrage' and many were carried by women - the banner from Failsworth near Oldham by twenty girls.[48] Sixty five years later when local radicals organized a demonstration against the House of Lords at the time of the Third Reform Bill, ten of the Peterloo survivors accompanied them, with their banner. Four of the elderly contingent were women, Mary Collins, Catherine McMurdo, Susannah Whittaker and Alice Schofield.[49]

By the 1830s the Chartist demands included 'universal suffrage' and much of their support came from women in the cotton towns. For instance, there was an active Female Political Union in Ashton, whose members in 1839 wrote an open letter to the women of Great Britain and Ireland:

> Dear Sisters, We the females of Ashton-under-Lyne, venture to address you in
> a spirit of love and kindness . . . Join with us, dear Sisters, in pointing out to
> our husbands and friends, the necessity of uniting in the strictest bond of
> unity, to wrest from those merciless villains those privileges, those political
> rights they have so long been deprived of, and we do not despair of yet seeing
> intelligence, the necessary qualification for voting, and then, Sisters, we shall
> be placed in our proper position in society, and enjoy the elective franchise as
> well as our Kinsmen . . .[50]

The Ashton sisters' hopes for enfranchisement were soon dashed to the
ground. 'Universal suffrage' was replaced by 'manhood suffrage', since
asking for votes for women was thought so dangerously incautious that
it would alienate valuable support. By 1850 there was no longer any
demand for universal suffrage. The Chartists' demand, revolutionary in
its conception, was to abolish the property qualification for voting —
but now only for men.

Thus Lancashire working women were as politically disadvantaged as
all other Victorian women. Neither the 1867 nor the 1884 Reform Act
paid any attention to the valuable contribution women cotton workers
made to Britain's economic prosperity. They might be in heavy demand
by factory owners, but this neither gave them equal pay with men nor
the parliamentary vote, nor did it release them from the full weight of
their domestic responsibilities.

Yet despite this, women workers in the cotton towns were always in
a considerably stronger position to demand the vote than women
elsewhere. They were better organized and better paid; they could call
upon a tradition, however localized and sporadic, to strengthen their
determination. It was no accident that the radical suffragists sprang
from the cotton towns. Women like Sarah Reddish came from the
tradition of the Female Reformers and the women who marched to
Peterloo. What working class women of her generation lacked was a
means of expressing their political grievances.

IV

Women's suffrage in Manchester

When Sarah Reddish was a young mill worker in the 1860s and 70s there was no suffrage movement that touched the interests of women like her. At that time, the demand for votes for women was exclusively the concern of a few highly educated middle class women, who wanted to share the political rights their brothers and husbands traditionally enjoyed.

Much of the mid nineteenth century debate on women's suffrage was conducted in terms of the restoration of ancient rights, rather than a progressive move towards equality. Under Tudor and Stuart law a woman who was recognized as a freeholder or a burgess was entitled to vote at parliamentary elections. During the eighteenth century, a period when woman's dependence on man was increasingly seen as natural and inevitable, this right fell into disuse and in the nineteenth century was completely swept away. Tidy minded lawyers, drafting the 1832 Reform Act, swept away such loose ends by expressly debarring women from the franchise in the newly-created constituencies. Voters were now exclusively referred to as 'male persons'.

These changes in constitutional law were a microcosm of larger changes in women's status. Women had traditionally exercised a wide range of freedoms in their own right: they had been able to operate as independent producers and traders, sign contracts and be legally responsible for their own financial transactions and property. Now many of these rights became hedged in by the Victorian urge to formalize and codify the haphazard system of common law.

Nowhere was this seen more dramatically than in the position of married women. Under the convention of 'coverture' married women lost the right even to a legal existence independent of their husbands. Like children in the care of their parents, wives were assumed to be completely under the protection of their husbands. Until 1839 a woman had no right of access to her own young children, however small — her husband was entitled to take them from her as soon as they were born, even while she was breastfeeding. [1] As late as 1891 a husband could still obtain a legal decree to force his wife to concede his conjugal rights.[2]

But with all its restrictions and potential degradations, marriage was the only real option for middle class Victorian girls. A wife's legal subjection was far more tolerable than the social derision and pity heaped on the shoulders of the thousands of luckless spinsters unable to find a husband-protector.

While waiting for the longed for proposal, a girl was expected to fill her time acquiring a futile smattering of accomplishments — embroidery, piano-playing, a little French — rather than any more systematic form of education which might scare away potential suitors. Medical experts even suggested that if a young woman 'overloaded her brain' it might have dire physical consequences, and popular opinion still held that 'nice girls' had no business knowing too much. A verse in *Punch* published in the 1880s reflected this consensus:

> Oh pedants of these later days, who go on undiscerning,
> To overload a woman's brain and cram our girls with learning,
> You'll make a woman half a man, the souls of parents vexing,
> To find that all the gentle sex this process is unsexing.
> Leave one or two nice girls before the sex your system smothers,
> Or what on earth will poor men do for sweethearts, wives and mothers?[3]

Florence Nightingale was among those only too familiar with the enforced triviality and self-denying vacuity that middle class girls endured at home, and she railed bitterly against these petty tyrannies:

> [The] family boasts that it has performed its mission well, in as far as it has enabled the individual to say, 'I have *no* peculiar work, nothing but what the moment brings me, nothing that I cannot throw up at once at anybody's claim'; in as far, that is, as it has *destroyed* the individual life . . . Marriage is the only chance (and it is but a chance) offered to women for escape from this death; and how eagerly and how ignorantly it is embraced![4]

Some spinsters were fortunate enough to be able to live off a private income that ensured them at least a degree of respectability. By the accepted standards, Victorian ladies simply did not work. For the ones forced by economic necessity to earn their own living, the respectable occupations available were severely limited. They turned to dressmaking, with its long hours and low pay, or to private teaching, where governesses, poised unhappily between the family and the servants' hall, suffered constant humiliation.

By 1850 there were over twenty one thousand governesses. Their wages were pitiably small — Jane Eyre was paid £30 a year, considered a good wage — and their work often hard and unrewarding. Its main advantage was that it carried none of the dreaded social stigma of factory work; Charlotte Brontë wrote bitterly of 'governess drudgery' and protested that this was all she could do, although she would gladly have exchanged it for 'work in a mill'.[5]

Governesses themselves were seldom properly trained for their job as teachers, and it was often a case of the blind leading the blind. Only gradually was it realized that the only way to improve such women's status was to provide them with a proper education. A series of lectures for governesses and other young women was started in London, and led to the opening of Queen's College for Women in 1848 and Bedford College in 1849. (Though both were called colleges, they were more comparable to secondary schools, and took girls over twelve as well as governesses with years of teaching experience.)[6]

This was a step, but only a small one. Women who shared the bitter dissatisfaction of Florence Nightingale and Charlotte Brontë began to think of other ways to widen the extraordinarily narrow range of options open to them. In the 1850s and 60s the seemingly tranquil surface of middle class family life began to be ruffled by the stirrings of a larger revolt.

Three women, Emily Davies, Elizabeth Garrett and her younger sister Millicent stand out among the early pioneers. Emily Davies, the oldest, led a campaign to open the universities to women and finally succeeded in founding Girton College, Cambridge in 1873. Elizabeth Garrett's ambition was to become a doctor, but British medical schools consistently refused to accept women students. She only managed to qualify after many years' persistence and entered the profession through the back door by passing the examination of the Society of Apothecaries in 1865; this gave her the necessary licence to practice as a doctor.

Elizabeth Garrett's younger sister, Millicent, later married Henry

Fawcett, one of Gladstone's cabinet ministers. He took an advanced line on women's rights, and she soon became involved in the campaign for political emancipation, which she took up with characteristic quiet efficiency. [7] Mrs Fawcett developed into an experienced and effective suffrage leader, and was one of the handful of women who saw the campaign from its earliest days through the partial success of 1918 right up to victory in 1928.

Before her marriage in 1867, there was no organized movement for women's suffrage, and the uncompromising demands of the early Chartists had slipped away into history. The campaign for women's rights was still in its infancy, and existed only among small enclaves of educated middle class women. Of these, the most important was the Ladies' Discussion Society, formed in Kensington in 1865, where the quarterly meetings were attended by Emily Davies and Elizabeth Garrett; among the other fifty members was Barbara Bodichon, who had studied at the new Bedford College and became the guiding inspiration behind the *Englishwoman's Journal* (later the *Englishwoman's Review*) which was founded in 1857 as a women's rights magazine. The first meeting of the Kensington society discussed the highly pertinent problem of the limits of parental authority, and the second, 'Should women take part in public affairs?'. Barbara Bodichon read a paper on suffrage and virtually all the members voted in favour. Encouraged by this support, she wanted to form a Women's Suffrage Committee right away, but Emily Davies restrained her, thinking it would be premature and ill-advised.[8]

In 1865 a new champion of women's suffrage came to their attention, John Stuart Mill. Mill was already a formidable exponent of women's rights. His friendship with Harriet Taylor, a highly intellectual feminist, was disparaged by many who did not believe that men and women could enjoy a genuinely equal relationship. Yet, when they married, Mill signed a document divesting himself of the traditional rights of Victorian husbands, and when he wrote *The Subjection of Women* in 1861, two years after his wife's death, he was obviously greatly influenced in his criticisms of the existing system by Harriet Taylor.

Mill stood successfully in the 1865 General Election and attracted the notice of the Kensington women by including a plea for women's suffrage in his election address. They seized the opportunity, and in April 1866 Barbara Bodichon organized a women's suffrage petition for

Mill to present in Parliament. Over one and a half thousand signatures were collected within a fortnight, and, in June, Emily Davies and Elizabeth Garrett set out for Westminster Hall with their great scroll of names.[9]

The specific legislation Mill hoped to influence was the Second Reform Bill, then being debated in Parliament. The debate still took place within the property-based framework established in the 1830s, and hinged on how much property male copyholders, leaseholders and lodgers needed in order to qualify for the vote. Mill bravely introduced his amendment to the Bill, 'to leave out the word man, in order to insert the word person thereof'. Young Mrs Fawcett, whose husband spoke in support of the amendment, listened to Mill's speech from the Ladies' Gallery and later praised it as 'a masterpiece of close reasoning, tinged here and there by deep emotion'.[10]

Predictably, Mill's amendment was soundly defeated. It was in practical terms a very cautious proposal as the number of women who would satisfy the property qualifications in their own right was severely limited to a few well-to-do widows and spinsters. But in the mid-century the very notion of even a few propertied women voting in parliamentary elections seemed to threaten the very fabric of Victorian society. At a time when the institution of 'coverture' still prevailed (the first Act giving married women some rights over their own property was not passed until 1870), the demand for women's rights could easily be dismissed as the silly preoccupation of a few vinegary spinsters who needed votes as compensation for their lack of husbands.

Despite the ribaldry and derision, the women's suffrage campaign emerged from its defeat in Parliament with renewed vigour. In the late sixties a pattern of regional suffrage societies was set up that survived for fifty years until the vote was won. The first group, formed in January 1867, about four months before Mill introduced his historic amendment, was based in Manchester.[11] The following November it affiliated to the societies in London and Edinburgh, and together formed a loose federation, the National Society for Women's Suffrage, which was later joined by the Bristol Society, formed in 1868.

In many ways mid nineteenth century Manchester was the logical place for a women's suffrage movement to flourish. It was the hub of Victorian commercialism, with its emphasis on Liberalism and the rights of the individual. 'Dissent, Free Trade, popular enfranchisement; all that was comprised in Radicalism and Chartism had their stronghold there,' summarized Sylvia Pankhurst.[12] The Anti-Corn Law League, which campaigned against existing import duties on foreign food, was founded in Manchester in 1839 and led by two local businessmen, Richard Cobden and John Bright.[13]

Run by local millowners and industrialists, the League was never directly concerned with wider social reform (although it could always draw considerable support from local progressives of all classes), and women's suffrage certainly found no place in its programme. Wives and daughters of League members were, it is true, welcomed as organizers of bazaars to raise funds. But when League ladies presided at the tables of a vast tea party in the Corn Exchange in 1841, there was no hint that they might break out of their restricted role as unspeaking hostesses.[14]

The League was dissolved in 1846, but left behind a wake of progressive political thought which soon became recognized as the 'Manchester School'. It was in this tradition that the Manchester National Society for Women's Suffrage held its small first meeting on 11 January 1867. The backgrounds of these early members tell us much about the stern middle class ideals upheld by the School. The debt to the League was immediately apparent: Jacob Bright, John Bright's younger brother and an MP for Manchester, was, along with his wife Ursula, a valuable supporter. The connections with Non-conformism were also strong: the Reverend Steinthal, one of the society's longest serving members, was minister, under Elizabeth Gaskell's husband, of the Unitarian Cross Street Chapel. Elizabeth Wolstenholme, a school mistress who pioneered girls' education and the rights of married women, was the daughter of a Methodist minister at Eccles.

Equally important were the Society's links with progressive Liberalism, which became personified by the best known member of this group, Dr Richard Pankhurst, an able barrister, a member of the city's Chamber of Commerce, founder member of the Manchester Liberal Association, and champion of all progressive causes from Mechanics' Institutes to recodifying the law.[15] Lydia Becker, who came along to the second meeting and took on the demanding job of secretary, had none of these formal connections with the progressive causes of the day.[16] Yet because of her own deep-felt personal commitment to women's suffrage, she, more than anyone, kept both the Manchester Society and the national campaign going over the next twenty three years.

Born in Manchester in 1827, she lived quietly as a comfortably-off, plain-looking spinster. But underneath her respectable exterior, she experienced frustrations as intensely as Charlotte Brontë or Florence

Nightingale. She once wrote with some feeling that, while women like herself had few opportunities to work, 'women of the lower classes have nearly as good a chance of maintaining themselves in an independent position as men, at least in the manufacturing districts.[17] Her primary interests were scientific, and she studied astronomy and botany within the limits imposed on a mid Victorian lady, even writing two short books, *Botany for Novices* and *Elementary Astronomy*. She corresponded with Charles Darwin and persuaded him to send a paper to the small Manchester Ladies' Literary Society she had initiated.

But at the age of almost forty Lydia Becker had not yet found a satisfactory outlet for her considerable energy and organizing talent. Then, in October 1866, she attended a local meeting organized by the National Association for the Promotion of Social Science, and listened to Barbara Bodichon reading a paper on 'Reasons for the Enfranchisement of Women'. There was 'no reason why the single ladies and widows. . .' she was told, 'should not form as sensible opinions on the merits of candidates' as male voters.[18] She was immediately converted to the new cause. It was a campaign that gave meaning to her restricted life.

She became particularly interested in the quality of education girls received and, once she was elected to the first Manchester School Board, used her influence as best she could to improve it. In 1877 when she laid the foundation stone of the fifth school built by the Manchester Board, she discovered to her horror that the school, for girls and infants, was to specialize in cookery. In her speech she fiercely criticized this narrow domestic training and said that if she had her way every boy in Manchester would be taught to mend his own socks and cook his own chops. 'No true man,' she said later, 'should want to be the husband of a domestic slave.'[19]

Lydia Becker devoted the rest of her life to women's suffrage, painstakingly canvassing MPs, persuading them into introducing women's suffrage bills, and mustering sympathizers to vote for them. Her campaign concentrated on these Parliamentary private members' bills; but, without the support of either of the main political parties, her reliance on sympathetic individual MPs severely limited the effectiveness of her campaign.

The results of her patient lobbying were detailed in the monthly issues of the *Women's Suffrage Journal*, which she edited from 1870 till her death in 1890. In addition to its careful record of parliamentary progress, and its laborious instructions on how to prepare a petition, the *Journal* was also a fascinating collection of snippets about the condition of women's lives, from information on newsworthy achievements ('A Woman Astronomer in Japan') to complaints about the unhealthiness of current fashions.

The new Manchester Suffrage Society began with a great burst of energy. Lydia Becker kept an eagle eye out for any incident to strengthen the campaign, and managed to find one within a few months. In 1867, the name of Lily Maxwell had accidentally appeared on the electoral roll in Manchester. She was a widow who ran her own small shop selling kitchen crockery: as a rate-payer she was just the sort of person the suffragists needed for a test case. Lydia Becker hurried round to see her and accompanied her to the polling station, where the Returning Officer had to accept her vote for Jacob Bright. Encouraged by this unexpected success, Lydia Becker organized other women householders in the north-west (there were five thousand in Manchester alone) to ensure that their names were on the 1868 electoral roll.

Their claims were not recognized in Manchester, but were allowed in various other places in south Lancashire, including the nearby townships of Gorton, Levenshulme and Denton. Appeals against the claims that had been dismissed were taken to the High Court; in the celebrated Chorlton *v.* Lings case, Richard Pankhurst, then only thirty two, appeared as the junior defence barrister, and brought his impressive knowledge of judicial history to support the women's claims. In spite of the detailed arguments he put for women's historic right to vote, the case was brusquely dismissed. 'In modern and more civilized times, out of respect for women and by way of decorum. . .' one of the judges explained, 'they are excluded from taking any part in popular assemblies, or in the election of Members of Parliament.'

Although the activities of the Manchester Suffrage Society now seem rather pedestrian and small scale, such incidents were startling and sometimes even shocking for their time. In April 1868 the Society held the first ever public women's suffrage meeting. The Assembly Room of the magnificent new Free Trade Hall was chosen as the venue, the Mayor of Salford took the chair, and Lydia Becker (who later admitted that even she had been 'unnerved') moved the resolution. It was the first meeting in this country to be addressed by women. (What Manchester thinks today London thinks tomorrow: the following year the London Society organized its first public meeting. John Stuart Mill and Henry Fawcett went along, and Millicent Fawcett, aged only twenty two, made the first public speech of her life.)[20]

71

From then on, women speakers at public meetings became more usual, even if still something of an oddity. One of the Bristol Suffrage Society's leading members described her experience of speaking tours in 1871-2:

> It was evident that the audiences always came expecting to see curious masculine objects walking on to the platform, and when we appeared, with our quiet black dresses, the whole expression of the faces of the audiences would instantly change. I shall never forget the thrill which passed through us when, on one occasion, a Non-conformist minister assured the audience in his speech from the chair that we 'were quite respectable'.[21]

Indeed, the early suffragists were possibly *too* respectable. With the franchise still based on a narrow property qualification, the number of women they envisaged getting the vote was extremely small indeed. Only occasionally did the suffragists try to widen the appeal of their campaign. In October 1879 the Manchester Society tried to organize all the women who had the right to vote in the municipal elections to demand the same right in the parliamentary elections, and decided to hold a meeting in a working class area of Manchester. They were amazed by the numbers they attracted, and agreed to hold another meeting the following night. So many women came along – 'all seeming electors – all poor working women' – that Lydia Becker, delighted by the surprising turn of events decided to organize a 'grand demonstration of women citizens' in the Free Trade Hall four months later. She was apprehensive that they might not fill the Hall, but fill it they did – almost entirely with women. The secretary to the London Society described the occasion: 'The largest hall in the city, packed from floor to ceiling with women of all ranks and occupations, working women in very large proportions. Men were only present as spectators, and that in the galleries by payment of half-a-crown.'[22] This unusual meeting was not, however, thought worthy of reporting in the *Manchester Guardian*, and after it the impetus fizzled out.

A few years later, the *Women's Suffrage Journal* devoted page after page to reporting the TUC debate on Broadhurst's proposal to limit the jobs of the Cradley Heath chain-makers, and on a similar debate about the pit-brow lasses who sorted coal at the surface of the mines. Yet this concern with working women always stemmed from a middle class belief in the rights and freedoms of the individual, in a way that inevitably antagonized trade unionists. This certainly seemed to be Lydia Becker's logic when she travelled up to Whitehaven in the

Cumberland coal-field and made an impassioned speech defending the traditional right to work of the hundred and fifty pit-brow lasses there. 'Why is this attack made now upon the labour of women? . . . I believe the root of the matter is that the working women whose labour is threatened have not the protection of the Parliamentary vote. . .The Labour of the working woman is her capital; and Parliament has no right to take away existing rights without giving compensation.'[23]

Yet Lydia Becker's sporadic attempts to enlist working women's support were not based on any real understanding of industrial conditions and did not form part of any sustained campaign. The suffrage societies in Manchester and other cities were predominantly composed of middle class women. There were of course exceptions; women like Isabella Ford (a prosperous Quaker suffragist whom Sylvia Pankhurst always respected for her ready kindliness) recruited local mill girls into the Leeds suffrage society and was an active supporter of the Women's Trade Union League, later writing a pamphlet on 'Industrial Women and How to Help Them'. But such commitment to involving working class women was very rare.[24] The vast majority of suffragists merely wanted to share the privilege of a limited franchise based on narrow property qualifications.

The methods of the suffrage societies were equally narrow. They never drew on the populist tactics of earlier working class movements like Chartism.[25] Instead of mass demonstrations and processions the Manchester Society relied on the more discreet methods the Anti-Corn Law League had found successful. 'We cannot hope for immediate, perhaps not even for speedy, success,' Lydia Becker wrote to Jacob Bright. '. . .We have to tread the path that the other causes of progress have done before us — the Anti-Corn Law League, the Reform Movement. . .'[26]

Their limited approach and genteel tactics caused the early suffragists to lose ground after a while. This process was accelerated by the Corrupt Practices Act of 1883, an attempt to clean up elections and reduce bribery, which made it illegal to pay canvassers. Since the foot-slogging and door-knocking was now voluntary work, the parties turned to women to do it for them. So when the Conservatives formed the Primrose League in 1885 and Mrs Gladstone established the Women's Liberal Federation a year later 'to help our husbands' the suffragists lost the support of many politically minded women.[27]

The suffrage societies not only lost the support of party women in the 1880s but also the commitment of their more progressive members, who felt increasingly dissatisfied with the line Lydia Becker and her associates took on married women. She felt that women with husbands had a smaller claim to the vote than unprotected spinsters and widows, and that the rights of married women were a deviation from the central issue of enfranchisement. Suffragists like her also feared that too wide a claim would lose them precious support. Such a limited view was not really surprising from a woman in Lydia Becker's situation; it is remarkable how far she managed to see beyond the restricted horizons of her class and generation. However, her influence narrowed the appeal of the suffrage societies, and made them prey to the barbs of journalists and cartoonists, who had malicious fun with images of frustrated spinsters; Lydia Becker, plump, bespectacled and bookish was a particularly easy target for their humour.[28]

One of the women who joined the progressive wing was the young Mrs Emmeline Pankhurst, who, after her marriage in 1879 to the talented Manchester barrister was drawn into the suffrage campaign.

Emmeline Goulden was born in Manchester in 1858, the daughter of a prosperous self-made manufacturer and ardent Liberal, whose own parents had been keen supporters of the Anti-Corn Law League in the 1840s. Emmeline's mother was a Manxwoman, who often took her children to the Isle of Man for holidays. In the 1880s women householders there were given the vote, and the island became the example quoted by suffragists like Lydia Becker and Mrs Fawcett to show that a limited women's franchise did not lead to constitutional chaos. The atmosphere in the Goulden home was one of Liberalism and discussion ranged over all the advanced causes of the day. As a child, Emmeline was taken to meetings in support of the abolition of slavery in America, and when she was only twelve she accompanied her mother to a women's suffrage meeting where she heard Lydia Becker speak. Within a year or two of her marriage to Richard Pankhurst she was co-opted, out of respect to her husband, onto the Married Women's Property Committee, 'finding herself the youngest and least informed of its members.'[29]

The Committee's main target was the legal convention of coverture, dismissed as irrelevant by the more traditional suffragists. The controversy over married women's rights grew so heated in the 1880s that some women felt they had no option but to break away from what they condemned as the betrayal by the existing societies. Led by Mrs Pankhurst, Ursula Bright and Elizabeth Wolstenhome-Elmy (as she became known after her marriage), they formed a breakaway group called the Women's Franchise League in 1889.

The Pankhurst family was at that time living in London, in Russell Square, where their house became the centre for many of the advanced political thinkers of the day, such as Annie Besant and William Morris. (Morris, Mrs Pankhurst declared, was 'prejudiced against her because she was wearing a dress from Paris when they first met.'[30]) Here too the Franchise League held its meetings. While it purported to break from the 'timidities' of Mrs Fawcett and Lydia Becker, the League's methods were in fact very much those of the older societies — drawing room meetings and lobbying Parliament — although its style may have had a little extra panache; Sylvia described how her mother used to take 'infinite pains for the Franchise League functions, arranging elaborate teas, music by celebrated artists, speeches by famous people; Women's Suffrage had grown dowdy and dull; it must come forward in a new guise, surrounded by all that was elegent and *recherché.*'[31] But the League only managed a brief flowering and lacked the stamina of the older regional societies.

The sporadic efforts of Lydia Becker to link the suffrage campaign with the interests of working women, and of Mrs Pankhurst to give the movement a fresher image had no lasting impact. The struggle seemed to be losing ground. After 1884, when the franchise was extended to most working class men, suffrage ceased to be an immediate political issue to all but a handful of dedicated suffragists. With Lydia Becker's death in 1890, the Manchester Society lost its valuable Secretary, and its stop-gap appointment of a timid woman, Miss Atkinson, who was overawed at having to follow such an indomitable leader, did little to stop the downhill slide of the Society's affairs.[32] The efficient membership machine that Lydia Becker had built up was allowed to get rusty; there had been nearly a thousand names in the Society's account book, but they drifted away until fewer than two hundred remained.

Without Lydia Becker's conscientious editorship, the *Women's Suffrage Journal* ceased to appear, and the national movement lost its most effective co-ordinator. Luckily Mrs Fawcett, by now an experienced organizer in her forties, was able to take on much of the responsibility. When the various suffrage societies were reorganized and the umbrella National Union of Women's Suffrage Societies was formed in 1897, Mrs Fawcett was the obvious choice for President.

Mrs Fawcett, who had been widowed since 1884, looked the perfect Victorian lady. Neatly dressed, always dignified, her qualities were those of quiet and gentle good sense rather than rousing platform oratory. One suffragist later described her leadership of the suffrage movement as 'thoughtful, persistent and dogged', but it was never passionate.[33] For Mrs Fawcett passion suggested an unreasonable lack of balance. Another of her many followers, the Manchester suffragist Helena Swanwick, for whom Mrs Fawcett was always 'our most remarkable woman', tells a story that bears this out. 'Once in Committee,' she wrote, 'when Mrs Fawcett was presented with a declaration drawn up by someone else, for her signature, in which she was supposed to describe herself as "passionately desiring" the enfranchisement of women, she looked up whimsically and asked, "*Must* I be passionate? Oh, very well! . . . " [34]

About 1890 the suffrage campaign seemed to have reached its lowest ebb. Again and again, Private Members' Bills had sunk without trace. Then in April 1892 there came a flutter of hopeful excitement. A cautious bill, introduced by Sir Arthur Rollitt, designed to enfranchise the widows and spinsters already entitled to vote in local government elections was lost by merely twenty three votes.

Despite defeat, the amount of support it received in the Commons debate heartened the organizers, and they looked about for ways to build on this strength. On 1 June 1893 they convened a meeting in Westminster Town Hall, attended by Isabella Ford, Mrs Fawcett, and other devoted suffragists. The meeting agreed that Rollitt's Bill might have had more success if grass-roots support for it had been more visible. So they decided to organize a Special Appeal with the object of removing this 'common but ignorant objection to the extension of the franchise — that women do not care about the suffrage.'

Even the practised constitutionalists who filled the Town Hall that day admitted that by then petitions had become fairly mechanical and that politicians seldom took much notice of them any more. But this Appeal was to be different; it was to be signed only by women, and by as many women as possible. 'An Appeal from Women of all Parties and All Classes' was drawn up, which for the very first time included a reference to women's industrial position: 'in the factory and workshop [the exclusion of women from the franchise] places power to restrict women's work in the hands of men who are working alongside of women whom they too often treat as rivals rather than as fellow-workers.'[35]

On this new wave of energy, an Appeal Committee with a temporary office of its own was set up: a secretary was appointed specifically for the campaign, and small books for collecting the signatures were issued to women up and down the country. Altogether three to four thousand people helped, a hundred and forty meetings were held in drawing rooms, cottages and public halls, and, within a year, over quarter of a million signatures had been collected.[36]

There was a simultaneous increase in activity in Manchester. Two months after the Westminster meeting, the Manchester Society found a replacement for the timorous Miss Atkinson. A young woman called Esther Roper took on the job, and under her guidance during the following twelve years, the moribund Society experienced an exciting and important renaissance. She managed to replace its middle class gentility with a much more forceful campaign based on the growing industrial strength of local working women.

Esther Roper became Secretary when she was only twenty five. Till then she had lived the conventional life of a middle class girl. She was born in 1868 in Wilmslow, then a pleasant Cheshire retreat for cotton merchants and stockbrokers who commuted each day to Manchester. Her family later moved to Victoria Park in Manchester, near to the house the Pankhursts took when they returned from London in 1893-4. Sylvia Pankhurst described the area as 'a residential park of houses surrounded by substantial gardens with fine old trees.'[37] Esther shared the house in this pleasant suburb with her brother Reginald, seven years younger than her; he read Classics at Owens College (later Manchester University), got his MA and subsequently became a master at Eton. She herself graduated from Owens with a BA in 1891, at a time when it was still fairly unusual for a girl, even from a middle class family, to go to university.[38]

She seems to have enjoyed the years she spent as a student and she kept in close contact with the University, only half a mile away from her home, for the rest of her life. In 1895 she became a committee member of the University Settlement, a charitable organization based in the slums of Ancoats, which tried to establish links between the University and the industrial areas.[39] She kept an active interest in the Owens College Women's Debating Society and in 1899 presided at a debate led by Mrs Fawcett on women's suffrage. A few months later she proposed the motion that 'Women should have equal rights with men.' In 1902 she spoke at a deputation of women graduates to Westminster, as well as standing as the only woman candidate in the election of the Owens governors; she was only narrowly beaten in the voting.[40]

All this would be orthodox behaviour for a serious-minded

unmarried woman graduate who never had to earn a penny in her life. Even taking on the secretaryship of a suffrage society was treading a path well marked by Lydia Becker and Mrs Fawcett. What marks Esther Roper out from her fellow secretaries in the other regional societies is the way she directed her efforts towards working class women, beginning immediately with her approach to the Special Appeal.

The Westminster meeting had decided to appeal to 'Women of All Classes'. For most suffragists, this seems to have been merely a nod of recognition towards women's growing industrial strength and little else. Esther Roper was one of the few who took it seriously.

Her plan was, in her own words, 'to bring the Special Appeal under the notice of the factory women of Lancashire and Cheshire'. To this end, she adopted tactics that must have seemed positively revolutionary to the old stalwarts of the Manchester Society. 'The women were visited in their homes as well as at factory gates,' she wrote, 'and a large quantity of women's suffrage literature was given away.'[41] Meetings were held wherever there were large numbers of women workers, and so the major cotton towns became her most immediate target. She soon realized what an immense amount of work needed to be done, far too much for her to undertake by herself.

Esther Roper decided to deal with the problem in an unprecedented way. Within a few months of taking over as Secretary, she appointed two working class women from the cotton towns to join her in organizing the campaign. Mrs Winbolt came from the Stockport area, and had been originally won over to the women's suffrage movement by Lydia Becker in the 1880s. She had worked as a handloom weaver in the local silk industry for over twenty years, and soon after she was appointed was addressing meetings of working women in the southern half of the area. Annie Heaton, was a Burnley mill worker, and, although less active than Mrs Winbolt, was a useful organizer in the northern weaving towns.[42]

The campaign kept them very busy. During 1894 at least fourteen meetings were arranged and during one week in the summer, open air meetings were held every night in different parts of Manchester, with speakers including Dr and Mrs Pankhurst and Mrs Winbolt. The finale was 'A Great Demonstration' of over five thousand people in the Free Trade Hall, with Mrs Fawcett and Dr Pankhurst on the platform.[43] The following year was even busier and an additional secretary had to be employed for six months to cope with the extra work. The Special Appeal already had over 250,000 signatures and was being so widely promoted in Lancashire that Esther Roper decided to form two local sub-committees, one in Gorton, an industrial district on the outskirts of Manchester, and the other in Rochdale, a typical cotton town.

How had Esther Roper, coming from a similar background to Lydia Becker, managed to make these connections across the rigid class lines in so short a space of time? It is difficult to give a precise account of the development of her political beliefs, or of the people she was influenced by, for Esther Roper was an extremely reticent woman, with a marked distaste for personal exposure. She remains almost anonymous behind the organizations through which she worked, and seems to have preferred the role of *eminence grise* to that of platform personality.

Unlike Isabella Ford from Leeds she never joined the Independent Labour Party, although by the time she became Secretary of the Manchester Society, a Manchester ILP branch had been established for about a year and had attracted two local suffragists, Dr and Mrs Pankhurst, away from the Liberal Party. Nor was she ever directly involved in the new Manchester and Salford Women's Trade Council, although many of the most loyal members of the Manchester Suffrage Society were among the Council's middle class supporters — for instance, the Reverend Steinthal, Bertha Mason, daughter of a local Liberal MP, and Margaret Ashton, a wealthy Liberal.

Esther Roper must have realized the urgency of widening the suffrage campaign to include working women by noting the momentous political and industrial changes that were taking place in the 1890s. Although she had no formal connections with the Women's Co-operative Guild she could surely see how branches began to flourish in the cotton towns after the 1892 Guild festival in Manchester. Most importantly, she must have taken note of the work being done by the Women's Trade Union League. For instance, in 1893 Annie Marland as a League organizer had addressed a meeting of a thousand people in Manchester; the same year she spent two weeks in Todmorden, only a few miles away, organizing the women working in the ready-made clothing trade. When she went there, she took Annie Heaton along to assist her.[44]

It seems highly likely that Esther Roper knew about the League's practice of appointing working class women as organizers by the time she approached Mrs Winbolt and Annie Heaton. She may well have been influenced by conversations with Isabella Ford, who still managed to combine suffrage work with, for instance, helping the League to organize the Leeds Tailoresses' Society, (It may even have been Isabella Ford who introduced Esther Roper to Annie Heaton.) Despite her reserve, Esther Roper seemed to share this ability to bridge the chasm between Mrs Fawcett's world of Liberal respectability and the harsher life of the mill workers. She even managed to double the subscriptions from middle class supporters, in order, ironically, to fund her campaign to enlist the support of working women.[45]

After four years as Secretary, Esther Roper's personal life underwent a sudden and radical change. In 1896 she went on holiday to Italy, to Bordighera on the French-Italian border, the home of George Macdonald, an expatriate novelist who had spent part of his life in Manchester. Here she met the Irish poet, Eva Gore-Booth, who was recuperating from illness. The two young women, the reserved suffragist and the striking Art Nouveau poet, immediately found each other's company irresistible. 'For months illness kept us in the south,' Esther Roper wrote later, 'and we spent the days walking and talking on the hillside by the sea. Each was attracted to the work and thoughts of the other, and we became friends and companions for life. Very soon [Eva] made up her mind to join me in the work in Manchester.'[46]

In fact Eva Gore-Booth thought she was dying of tuberculosis and, with this threat hanging over her, decided to devote the remainder of her life to the working women of Lancashire. Her diagnosis turned out to be too pessimistic, and she lived for another thirty years during many of which she was actively involved in Esther Roper's campaigns. Her arrival in Victoria Park in 1897 brought a new and important vigour to the local suffrage campaign, and a lasting friendship to Esther Roper.

Eva Gore-Booth came from County Sligo, the daughter of one of the largest landowners in the west of Ireland. The Gore-Booths were philanthropic, fox-hunting gentry with a taste for literature who for generations had owned land in England, including parts of Salford. Eva was an avid reader of Greek and Roman history (she had taught herself Greek) and poetry, and in 1897 she published her first book of poems which established her reputation as a minor *fin de siècle* literary figure. Her rather ethereal appearance matched the spiritual tone of her verse. Sylvia Pankhurst, who came to know her about 1901, summed Eva up as 'tall and excessively slender, intensely short-sighted, with a mass of golden hair, worn like a great ball at the nape of her long neck, bespectacled, bending forward, short of breath with high-pitched voice and gasping speech, she was nevertheless a personality of great charm.'[47]

Even before her first book of poetry was published, Eva Gore-Booth began to consider other activities. In 1896 she formed a local suffrage committee in Sligo with her famous sister Constance, later, as Countess Markievicz, the first woman elected to Parliament. These early meetings, at which both women made impassioned speeches received with both heckling and frenzied cheering, must often have seemed to their Sligo tenants both bizarre, and, in the light of the bitter struggle for Home Rule, patronizing and irrelevant.[48]

Once settled in Manchester Eva Gore-Booth soon revealed her rare ability of inspiring enthusiasm and commitment in other people. Teresa Billington, then a young teacher who later became involved in the Pankhursts' suffrage campaign, was never one to give a kinder obituary than was strictly deserved; yet she wrote much later that 'talking of rebels. . . some people could be lighted like candles, some needed hammer blows to bring out a spark, and some like Eva Gore-Booth were liquid pools of spontaneous combustion.' She summed her up as a woman 'who missed greatness only by external accident of time and place.'[49]

Eva Gore-Booth enhanced Esther Roper's skill of working with women from very different backgrounds, and acted as a vital catalyst who could inspire affection among working women. One of the first people she met in Manchester when she arrived was Sarah Dickenson, who later recalled:

> My first impression of her was her charming and interesting personality. When I knew her better I found how very genuine she was in all her dealings and discovered all the beautiful traits in her character. The friendly way that she treated all the women Trade Unionists endeared her to them. If she was approached for advice or help she never failed.[50]

Other working women bore out this glowing testimonial. Mrs Green, deputy chairman of the Gorton suffrage sub-committee and active Guildswoman told Esther Roper years later how 'one dark and stormy night we had been holding a meeting in a poor and rather squalid street. When [Eva Gore-Booth's] speech was over a woman suddenly rushed out of the darkness, seized her hand and kissed it, vanishing without a word.'[51] Louisa Smith, later an active suffragist, was one of the sixteen girls ('we were all machinists and we *were* rough') who went along to the dramatic society Eva Gore-Booth formed through the University Settlement. 'We thought she was a being from another world,' she recalled. 'I don't think I exaggerate when I say we worshipped her, but she never knew it, she was so utterly selfless.'[52]

Eva Gore-Booth used her gifts to very practical, specific ends. The old Manchester National Society had been renamed, more appropriately, the North of England Society for Women's Suffrage, in the reorganization that accompanied the formation of Mrs Fawcett's National Union. Eva Gore-Booth joined the Society's Executive Committee, and, with Esther Roper and a new energetic London secretary, Edith Palliser, was soon involved in running the National Union as well. By 1898 Eva Gore-Booth was addressing ILP and Guild branches on women's suffrage. 'In the interests of wage-earning women,' she declared, 'it is necessary that women should possess the vote, for it is like fighting without bayonets to try to get many reforms through Parliament at the present time — reforms which, of course, deal with the conditions under which many women and children have to work.'

Most importantly, she was appointed as Co-Secretary of the Manchester and Salford Women's Trade Union Council in 1900, when Frances Ashwell left to get married. Three years later she was co-opted from the Council onto the city's Education Committee, and was placed on the Technical Instruction Committee. Because of pressure from her, a strongly worded protest was made against the exclusion of girls from scholarships at the Municipal College for Technology.[53] In addition, she edited a paper called *The Women's Labour News*, a women's suffrage quarterly, which aimed to provide 'fellowship . . . coherency and free discussion, and the ventilating of pressing grievances' for 'those of us who are working for the betterment of political and industrial conditions of women'. 'The next ten years,' Esther Roper summed up modestly, 'were full to overflowing.'[54]

By the turn of the century Esther Roper and Eva Gore-Booth had taken the local suffrage movement a considerable distance from its moribund condition at Lydia Becker's death. Yet in some ways the similarities between the three women are more striking than the differences. All came from middle or upper class families, and all had, in one way or another, acquired an education far above the level of most Victorian women. Similarly, the local suffrage movement that they led hardly changed from the 1860s in that it was still possible for one skilful, efficient woman to direct the organization in her own way. This was not at all surprising: there was still no real alternative to this tradition of individualistic middle class leadership.

Yet there were beginning to be significant signs of change. The appointment of Mrs Winbolt and Annie Heaton already hinted that there might be something in the air. By the late 1890s the right of a handful of privileged women to speak for women's suffrage began to be challenged by a new generation of working class women who were emerging through the growing labour movement.

V

Weavers and winders

The factory workers of Lancashire and Cheshire were the obvious source of support for Esther Roper to turn to. Women working in the cotton mills could call on an unusually long tradition of both radicalism and feminism, and by the 1890s had become by far the best organized group of women workers in the country. The 1896 *Report on Trade Unions* showed that the 90,000 or more women members of the cotton unions represented no less than five sixths of all organized women workers.[1]

Esther Roper drew heavily on these established groups of women trade unionists to campaign for women's suffrage. In each of the cotton towns suffrage speakers could find a ready audience of union members whose interest could easily be aroused and who would listen eagerly to an appeal for their rights.

Yet the cotton workers were far more than a pool of passive support for the middle class suffragists. The cotton mills also provided a political education for the new generation of suffragists. The majority of the leading radical suffragists 'went through the mill', and countless others whose names are lost were drawn into the local suffrage campaign through their experience of mill work.

Whether they were drawn in or not often depended on the kind of work they did in the mill. Jobs varied considerably within a fairly rigid hierarchical structure. Since mule spinning had long been monopolized by skilled men, women were left to prepare the loose cotton for the spinners and to weave the spun yarn into cloth. Yet even within these broad categories, there were significant distinctions between the workers employed in the different processes. It is important to appreciate the complexity of mill jobs in order to understand the kind of woman who joined the Lancashire suffrage campaign.

When the cotton first arrived at the mill, the bales were broken open by men swinging axes against them, and the raw cotton was fed into a series of machines that opened, cleaned and blended the fibres. It emerged as a 'lap' (a thick loose blanket) which the men then carried to the carding machines. Here women card 'tenters' fed the laps through rotating cylinders, covered in wire spikes, which removed any remaining tangles or dirt and turned out the cotton as a 'sliver', or a thick rope of loose cotton. Skilled men, working as strippers and grinders, removed odd bits of cotton from the spikes and ground the wires so that they were all precisely the same height.

The sliver then went through a drawframe, speed frames and a jack frame — all minded by a woman 'tenter' — until it emerged as a manageable yarn known as a 'roving', still thick and soft, but with a little bit of twist. The cotton was now ready for the spinners.[2]

Men and women's work, then, was segregated in the card and blowing rooms. The men's jobs, slightly more skilled than those of the women, were hard and sometimes dangerous, the women's often monotonous, and all workers were susceptible to byssinosis, or cardroom asthma, as it was known, caused by inhaling too much of the cotton fluff in the air. 'There's many a one as works in a carding-room, that falls into a waste, coughing and spitting blood, because they're just poisoned by the fluff,' explained one of the mill girls in *North and South*.[3]

Diagram of a Lancashire mill

Card and Blowing Room
20 men : strippers & grinders: 25s
70 women: card frame tenters: 18s

Spinning Room
40 pairs of mules
40 men: mule spinners: 41s
20 men: big piecers: 18s
60 boys: little piecers: 12s
2 men: overlookers: 43s

Weaving shed
800 looms
100 men: weavers: 25s
160 women: weavers: 21s
10 boys: tenters: from 4s
15 girls: tenters: from 3s
10 men: tacklers: 42s

Sizing Room
3 men: tapesizers:
    : 44s

Beaming & Winding Room
40 women: winders: 19s
10 men: beamers: 30s

Minding the frames could also lead to dangerous accidents. Sylvia Pankhurst mentioned that Annie Kenney, as a half-timer, 'learned to fit into place the big bobbins covered with fleecy strands of soft, raw cotton; and to piece these same fleecy strands when they broke, as they did so often, while they were being spun out thinner and stronger. Once, as she seized the broken thread in her tiny fingers, one of them was caught somehow and torn off by the whirling bobbins.'[4]

The cardroom women came low in the mill hierarchy and had the reputation of being among the toughest in the mill. When Harry Pollitt started work as a half-timer:

> The usual tricks played on a learner were played on me, but the weavers, being a cut above the cardroom operatives (as they thought) played only polite, lady-like tricks on me. It was left to the buxom girls and women in the cardroom to break me in by taking my trousers down and daubing my unmentionable parts with oil and packing me up with cotton waste.[5]

The only two women cardroom workers who are known to have been involved in the suffrage movement coped with the harshness and monotony of their work in very different ways. Annie Kenney spent her adolescence in escapist fantasies, playing with dolls like a little girl and going shares in a weekly girls' paper 'full of wild romance, centred around titles, wealth, Mayfair, dukes, and factory girls'.[6] Cissy Foley's reaction was quite the opposite. She was employed as a jack-frame tenter in one of the Bolton spinning mills, and could not shut her eyes to the depressing conditions in which she worked. Alice wrote that she understood a little of what the cardroom meant to her ambitious elder sister when she began to take Cissy's dinners to the mill, past the other workers in fluff-covered shawls, clutching a hot-pot in a basin tied up with a towel and some tea in a billy can:

> Between walking and running I managed to reach the mill by 12.30 and find my way among the now silent machinery to Cissy's frames. Here she sat on an upturned carding can, neatly washed and reading the day's news in a narrow alley-way amid a sickening smell of warm, oily cotton-waste. We spoke little to each other; she hated the deadly routine of factory life and had nothing to say in its praise.[7]

Cissy Foley started work about 1892. In a sense, women of her generation were more fortunate than their predecessors. There was by then an organization through which they could work to change their conditions. A cardroom union, which welcomed women members, had existed for six years. Until the 1880s only a few local associations, mainly groups of skilled stripper and grinder men, had survived for any length of time. Then in 1886 the Amalgamated Association of Card and Blowing Room Operatives was formed — two years before the London matchgirls' strike. Composed largely of unskilled workers, the great majority of whom were young women (like Cissy Foley and Annie Kenney), it was typical of the new unionism of the later 1880s; like the Gas Workers' Union, formed in 1889, it had no membership restrictions and aimed at recruiting tens of thousands of poorly paid workers whose interests the craft unions had never protected.

Women immediately joined the union in great numbers. By 1891 more than one in three of the cardroom workers had become members of whom three quarters were women; so, within six years the union had enrolled 18,500 women. Most of them came from Oldham, still the biggest spinning town, where the association had 90 per cent female membership by the 1890s; but some came from Bolton and the other mill towns around Manchester. Cissy in Bolton 'had to join the trade union the first day she went to work. Father was an ardent unionist and made us join,' according to her sister,[8] though probably Cissy's thoughts were already turning in that direction.

Like the other new unions, the Cardroom Association was strong in numbers but weak in all other respects. Its members' wages were relatively low for mill workers. The male strippers and grinders averaged about 25s a week, but it was rare for a woman in the cardroom to earn more than 20s.[9] Tenters who were on a flat rate averaged 16s and those on piece-work, 19s 6d; young girls would be paid half this rate, and half-timers only 2s 6d or 3s a week. Yet these were enviable rates compared to women in other industries, where wages averaged only 13s or 14s. But they were low for cotton workers; for instance, a mule spinner in Bolton, the centre of fine spun Egyptian cotton, could be paid 45s 9d a week, and male workers as a whole averaged 29s 6d.[10]

On wages of under a pound a week, the cardroom tenters could only afford a small weekly payment to the Association. Their dues averaged a mere 1½d a week compared to the 1s to 2s contributions paid by the spinners or engineers. It was little wonder that spinners' leaders like Thomas Ashton, then Secretary of the Oldham Trades Council, could cock a snook at these puny unskilled upstarts. He predicted that 'we shall find they will ultimately go down as rapidly as they have sprung up. A society based on 1d or 2d subscription per week cannot continue, in as much as when disputes arise, they have to appeal to the public for support.'[11] His feeling of superiority was soundly based. When it came to industrial bargaining the Card Room Association was at a disadvantage.

Its members' jobs demanded such minimal levels of skill that it was difficult for them to insist on long apprenticeships to control entry to their trade in the way the spinners had done. If they went on strike an employer could easily replace them with blackleg workers. Also they could easily find themselves on the losing end of the spinners' strikes, as for instance in 1889 when members of the large Oldham Cardroom Association were thrown out of work. They were unemployed for over three months, their meagre funds were soon exhausted and the Oldham Board of Guardians, always keen to keep down the poor rate, refused them relief. Four years later the cotton trade was temporarily depressed; mill owners ordered a ten per cent reduction in wages and the workers refused to accept it. There was a twenty week lock-out. J.R. Clynes remembered:

> The familiar Oldham streets were filled with sullen loungers. In poorer homes, children wailing for bread grew so feeble that they no longer disturbed nature's serenity with their cries. They died: and collarless men in clogs, who had pawned their overcoats and jackets to get food, begged and borrowed to get them out of pawn again, so as to follow respectfully clad at the funerals.[12]

The cardroom workers felt the impact of such times more harshly than any other group. On this occasion their Association funds were fully stretched, and they had to look to local sympathizers to bail them out: the Amalgamated Society of Engineers, which had a strong base in Oldham because of textile machinery firms like Platts, levied its members and raised £1,300.[13]

The Cardroom Association had to struggle to survive. The fight against constant insecurity and the threat of unemployment and for a uniform list of wages took up most of the union's energies. There was little time left to do anything about the grievances specific to women members. The Association was run by the strippers and grinders, often fathers of girl members, and they exercised an influence out of all proportion to their numbers. There were no women officials and very few women represented above local committee level. Cissy Foley was extremely unusual, for she was active locally from the 1890s, having succeeded in making her way onto her local executive. Such union experience provided the ideal training ground for her later suffrage campaigning.

She was not entirely alone. Annie Marland, from Mossley, an isolated textile village in the Tame valley, beyond Ashton, was even sent by her union as a delegate to the 1894 TUC, and so was the first woman to represent the cotton workers nationally. She worked for the women's Trade Union League from 1892, married in 1898 and reappears in the League reports as Mrs Marland-Brodie. But with her increased domestic responsibilities and League work, she seems to have had little time to get involved in the textile workers' suffrage campaign.

Cissy Foley and Annie Marland were the only women known to be active in the Cardroom Association in its early years. Annie Kenney, who started working in the cardroom in 1889, probably joined the Oldham Association when she was in her teens, but does not seem to have played any active role in union affair until she came under the influence of the Pankhursts in about 1905. Then she put herself up for election to the Lees branch of the Association, was voted in, and attended the local meetings. In fact, her contact with the Association was short lived, for she led the suffragette exodus down to London early in 1906.[14]

It is no surprise, then, that the Cardroom Association only produced two known suffrage workers, Cissy Foley and Annie Kenney. Segregated from the cardroom men, poorly paid, doing monotonous jobs, absent from the union leadership, cardroom women were low down the mill hierarchy. Their thousands of union members had little political muscle, though, because they were already organized into local branches; nevertheless they provided a ready base for suffrage speakers who visited the spinning towns.

From the next process, spinning, women were still totally excluded. The cotton left the cardroom as a 'roving', or thick, soft yarn that was still quite fragile. It then went through a spinning mule which pulled the roving thinner and thinner, and added a twist to make it stronger. The spun yarn was then wound onto a mule cop, which looked rather like an elongated cotton reel with pointed ends.

Mule spinners, paid about 41s in most mills, earned 13s a week more than the average man. Part of the reason for their high wages was that they still excluded their assistants, known as piecers, from union membership. The piecers were paid out of the spinner's own wages, and usually earned about a third of his rate, at the most about 18s, but it could be far less. Rowland Kenney started work as a half-time little piecer on 6d a week. He loathed the 'devil's roar' of eight pairs of mules, and the heat and danger in the spinning room where he was expected to run about barefoot on the oily floor, keeping the spinner supplied with rovings, mending the broken threads and removing the full cops of spun yarn.[15]

The spinners were aware of piecers as possible strike breakers: it was

89

in their interest to keep piecers as disorganized and subservient as possible. No piecer, however long his experience of working with mules, could guarantee that he would get one of the coveted spinners' jobs. Any attempts to form a special trade union were firmly squashed by spinner fathers telling their piecer sons to go home immediately and drop such fanciful ideas.

There had always been a few women piecers, particularly in Bolton, where men were attracted away from mill jobs by the high wages offered in the mines and foundries. Some of them even joined the short lived unions. To the mule spinners, women piecers were a great nuisance. This resentment built up into an explosion in the 1880s. Three women piecers at the Lockstock mill in Bolton started operating mules on their own. In protest, the spinners came out on strike and the local Spinners' Association upheld their decision.[16] A few weeks later, an Association meeting, convened to discuss the one hundred and seventy Lokstock men on strike, finally decided to take a hard line on women's work. They resolved that 'no member of this association shall in future teach or cause to be taught the trade of a piecer to any female child.' This ruling did not affect the three women concerned, 'the association preferring to allow the evil to gradually die out'.[17]

The threat to the spinners was not over. It reappeared under the guise of a new technology, ring spinning. This proved a far greater problem than ever a few truculent piecers or uppity women could be. Ring spinning had been invented in America and, because it was so much faster, simpler and less dangerous, had proved extremely popular there. The new technique was introduced into Lancashire in about 1880-1 and proved to be a great boon to mill owners who could now employ unskilled operators at 15s a week rather than 'craftsmen' demanding over 40s. The Spinners Association washed its hands of this new-fangled machine and relegated it to women's work. (Mule spinners still tuned their own machines: ring spinners did not need technical skill, and if adjustments were required a male ring jobber could be called in.)

Women ring spinners, growing in numbers, were among the lowest paid and most downtrodden adults in the mills and had none of the prestige of the mule spinner. Robert Roberts, who grew up in Salford in the 1900s, described their status there:

> They lacked social standing on several counts; first, the trade contained a strong Irish Catholic element, and wages generally were lower than in other sections. Again, because of the heat and slippery floors, women worked

barefoot, dressed in little more than calico shifts. These garments, the respectable believed, induced in female spinners a certain moral carelessness. They came home, too, covered in dust and fluff; all things which combined to depress their social prestige.[18]

After twenty years of ring spinning in Lancashire, the women were admitted to the lowly Cardroom Association; however, they remained badly paid, even below the level of women frame tenters (15s compared to 18s). But in the argument of rings over mules the new technology eventually prevailed; the number of ring spindles crept up on the number of mule spindles and after the First World War the mule began to die out.

Excluded from the Spinners' Association, frustrated as piecers, poorly paid as ring spinners, it is not surprising that women spinners were inactive both in industrial and in suffrage politics. They were the only group of women workers in the cotton mills who showed no interest in Esther Roper's suffrage campaign, and who never invited a suffrage speaker to come and address them.[19] Their own level of self-esteem was too low to encourage the thought of votes for themselves, and they had little energy left at the end of their working day to concern themselves with political campaigns.

The women workers who handled the cotton up to this point in the mill process — frame tenters, piecers, ring spinners — were poorly organized compared with other women mill workers. After the cotton yarn left the spinning room the situation was very different.

The spun yarn went through various intermediate stages before it was ready to be woven. It was first wound from the mule cop or ring bobbin onto a much larger cone by a woman winder, who removed all the lumps and irregularities. The cones were then divided into two groups: half became the weft thread that would go across the loom and half became the warp thread that would go right down the length of the material. The weft threads were wound onto weft pirns (as the small bobbins were known) ready to go into the shuttle for the weaver. The remaining warp threads went to the beamer, a man who drew the ends of cotton from five or six hundred of the winders' cones onto a long, cylindrical beam. When each beam was fully wound with warp threads, it was passed through a solution known as sizing and wound onto a second beam; the skilled men who were in charge of this operation were known as warp-sizers, and each was master of a secret formula to mix his sizing just right.

The number of women winders was small: one winder could keep about half a dozen weavers busy. Yet there seems to have been something rather distinctive about the women in the winding room. It was generally considered that they formed a select group (although their wages were usually lower than those of women weavers) because their winding room was far quieter than the weaving shed, and they did not have to resort to lip reading above the din of hundreds of looms. Selina Cooper worked in one of the winding rooms at Tunstill's mill in Brierfield and impressed this point on her daughter. 'In the winding room they talked a lot, did winders, because it wasn't noisy like the mill. Used to talk, used to chat all the time they were working... It wasn't particularly hard... but it was very dusty. The floors were constantly thick with this dust.'[20]

Alice Foley tells the same story: the winding room was relatively quiet, even though it was a basement and the atmosphere was unhealthy.[21] Gracie Fields, then a half-time winder in Rochdale, was even able to sing in her winding room. The other girls would say, 'C'mon, Grace, give us a song and we'll mind your frames.'[22] Ethel Derbyshire, after the arguments about her future between her brothers and her sisters were settled, went into the winding room of one of the Blackburn mills. Her daughter described how the women there had 'a little more liberty than what you had in the weaving shed. It wasn't as noisy... And it wasn't as dirty, neither. It was supposed to be nicer, cleaner... of mill life it was the most select.'[23]

Alice Foley also noted that the winders 'were a smaller and more homogenous group than in the weaving shed and accepted each other in varying degrees of good will or toleration.' She thoroughly enjoyed it when

> the monotonous drudgery of machine-tending was occasionally broken by our traditional 'footings' when a work-mate announced her approaching marriage... the elder ones offering ribald jokes, the younger girls giggling to hide their embarrassment. Later we were regaled with pop, pies and eccles cakes in a community mood of hearty fellowship.[24]

The feelings of community and fellowship in the winding rooms showed themselves in other ways. Winders belonged to the giant weavers' union, the Northern Counties Amalgamated Association of Weavers, Winders and Warpers. But within the Association, the winders seem to have stuck together and retained some degree of autonomy. For instance, a place was reserved on the Blackburn Weavers' Association executive committee for a winder, which implies that the winders had their own meetings at which they could elect delegates. Selina Cooper's daughter remembered how her mother joined the local winders' committee in Brierfield when she was very young, within the large Weavers' Association itself. However, she cannot remember what her mother did on the committee (it was before she was born), but from Selina Cooper's later life, it is highly unlikely that she was an inactive member. Certainly Ethel Derbyshire, who became a union member in 1891, made her mark on mill life. According to her daughter,

> she walked out and half the weavers followed her, over something – the manager – they were terrible in those days, the managers and tacklers, you know. And something had gone wrong and it wasn't her fault. . . it was the fault of the machinery or something. Nevertheless, she was brought up in the warehouse and she had to pay for it. And she said she won't do it. If it had been her fault she would. But she wouldn't do it. 'It's tha does it or tha goes home.' 'Well, I'll go home.' And she went and a few walked out with her. She lost one or two jobs, speaking up. She was a rebel.[25]

The list of winders who went on to become active suffragists is impressively long, and disproportionate to their numbers among other women mill workers. Selina Cooper and Ethel Derbyshire were two of the most outstanding. Others include Violet Grundy, Secretary of the Ancoats Winders' Union formed with the help of Eva Gore-Booth and Sarah Dickenson in the 1900s, and Annie Heaton, a Burnley mill worker, active in the Women's Trade Union League from 1893 and one of Esther Roper's earliest suffrage organizers. One of the most dedicated radical suffragists, Sarah Reddish, worked as a winder when she was young. (Her first job, when she left school at the age of eleven in 1861 was to wind the silk at home that her mother and neighbours then wove on handlooms. She worked as a winder and later as a 'roll-coverer' in a cotton mill and her responsibilities included giving first aid to the women who had suffered from the frequent machine accidents.) However, because of their small numbers, winders were never a particularly important source of support in the suffrage campaign: that was the role of the weavers.

From the winding rooms the cotton was taken to the weaving sheds. Women weavers comprised by far the largest group in the mill: nearly a third of all employees and certainly two thirds of all women workers.[26] In all they totalled over a hundred and fifty thousand strong. The typical Lancashire mill girls were weavers, in shawls, clogs, and 'laps', pieces of cloth from cut ends to protect clothing from loom friction, all and grease, while from their leather belts hung the tools of their craft, scissors, comb and reed-hook.[27]

In the northern weaving towns women weavers could be counted in five figures; there were over twelve thousand in Blackburn, Burnley and Preston. Rochdale, with as many spinning as weaving mills, had about 4,000 women weavers. Even a spinning town like Oldham had over 4,000 women weavers; a local journalist who was reporting the Eight Hours demonstration in 1893 could not help noticing them among the procession of male spinners and engineers, carpenters and tailors:

> . . . a change came over the scene, and instead of four-deep men marching along with a dignified air, and trying to prove oblivious to the vast crowds lining the streets, came a laughing and merry-making throng of women and girls, and the change proved to be a wholesome one. With their appearance, the spectators became more lively, and jokes between weavers and spectators were freely exchanged.[28]

A common sight in weaving towns was the rush when the dinner buzzer went. Women would hurry out of the sheds to get home to feed their children; they would pass people, often children, going the opposite way carrying tiny babies to be fed.[29]

One of these children was Walter Greenwood; when he was seven he owned a rickety vehicle cobbled together out of soap boxes and buckled pram wheels. An older boy, Nobby, used to rent it for collecting, delivering and returning four 'squallers' each dinner time. One day Walter went along with Nobby: as soon as the buzzer sounded, they were allowed into the weaving shed, as the weavers threw the belt driving their looms onto the idler pulley. 'The mothers claimed their screaming offspring, sat on the floor by their looms and began to suckle their infants while friends put steaming pints of tea at their sides and whatever it was they had brought to eat.'[30] But as the looms started up again, Walter found the deafening clatter so intolerable that, without waiting for Nobby, he dashed straight for the door and ran away.

Alice Foley, who worked as a weavers' tenter for a short while before she went to the winding room, had the same reaction. 'At first I was highly terrified by the noise and the proximity of clashing machinery. . . It was a vast, unexplored region, stifling, deafening and incredibly dirty.'[31] It was dangerous as well. A weaver would be in charge of two to four looms, and each minute of the working day the shuttle would be thrown by the picking-stick across each loom no fewer than two hundred times a minute. Accidents — including scalpings and amputations — often happened, and were reported in the local newspapers. One typical report about the death of a fifteen year old girl in Oldham read, 'Whilst doing something at her loom her hair was caught in the working and her neck dislocated. She was not missed until the works had been closed, and when search was made about 7 o'clock her dead body was found under the loom.'[32]

For Alice Foley the long hours and hateful work were 'redeemed solely by the day-to-day fellowship of countless other toilers'. It was this fellowship when organized into the massive weaving unions that gave the tens of thousands of women weavers their political muscle.

In 1884 the local grouping of weavers, especially strong in Blackburn and Burnley, joined together to form one united union, the Northern Counties Amalgamated Association of Cotton Weavers. Although this was four or five years before the wave of new unionism began, the Association grew at a great rate. Within four years there were forty thousand members, representing one in four weavers. Three years later, in 1891, this had grown to 65,000, of whom two out of three were women. Even the successful Cardroom union was far smaller and could only boast under 20,000 members. In terms of numbers no other textile union could compete with the giant Weavers' Association, and no other trade union anywhere had anything like its massive number of organized women workers.

Naturally, one of the Association's main concerns was the amount of money its members took home at the end of the week. The Lancashire weavers were paid according to a piecework 'list', by which payments were calculated according to loom widths, numbers of weft threads, and so on, in minute detail right down to fractions of a penny; and theoretically at least men and women were paid at the same rate. No distinction was made by age or sex, and both men and women weavers working on four looms could earn about 25s a week, (unlike the woollen weavers in the Huddersfield area, where the women suffered from a differential of 10 per cent less than the men).

However, the situation was complex, and there was considerable controversy over whether equal pay really existed in the Lancashire weaving sheds.[33] Men's wages seemed to work out about 4s higher than women's, largely because men usually worked four or six-loom machines, and women only three or four-looms and these were often the narrower looms which paid a low rate. Alice Foley noticed that it was only men who did the highly paid, heavy work of weaving counterpanes on very large wide looms.[34]

95

So completely equal pay in the weaving sheds was a myth. Nevertheless women could earn far more by weaving than they could doing any other job open to working class women, and the men and women weavers were paid at much nearer equal rates than in any other trade. Women were also much more likely to have a voice in the Weavers' Association than in any of the other big unions. In Oldham and Wigan nearly 90 per cent of the local union members were women: in the other cotton towns it was usually well over half. The effect of this was that in a few towns women inevitably did contribute more than just their dues to the union: there were only a handful of men members. One way in which women were active in the unions was working as house-to-house collectors, taking the members' weekly dues. In a town like Oldham there were at least five full or part-time women collectors employed by the local union. The union was a women's affair to such an extent that there were even instances of women collectors reprimanding men for not encouraging the women in their families to join:

> 19 October 1904: That the secretary and the assistant along with the Hollinwood collector Miss Dunkerley be instructed to have a personal interview with Mr Walter Brierley, Hollinwood re the case of his daughters being non members of this association. . .
>
> 5 September 1905: That the canvassers shall give a written report with the names and addresses of such individuals they have been successful or unsuccessful with: also if possible the names and Trades of the fathers or husbands of those they have not succeeded in making members of this society.[35]

The pressure to join a union did not come exclusively from husbands and fathers, as has often been suggested.[36] When a girl left school and started work in one of the cotton mills she usually had an elder sister, an aunt or a cousin working in the mill who would put pressure on her to follow her example and join the union. Cissy Foley was pressured to join by her father, but Ethel Brierley joined the Lees branch because of the example set by other women in her family: 'It was as well to be in a union, you know. . . my sisters worked in the mill then; Betty's mother was a twiner-piecer, and my other sister, she was a reeler. . . I joined because they were in, you see. This collector used to come, and my mother put me in. . . We'd find him the card and the money.'[37]

Yet, despite a huge female membership and the women employed as lowly collectors, the great majority of women in the Weavers' Association just paid their dues and left union organization to the men. Few of them ever went along to a union meeting. Moor Mill, where

Alice Foley worked, was probably typical; the well-paid men in the old 'Counterpane Association' had been organized long before the Amalgamation was formed:

> These men controlled a virile 'shop committee' keeping a sharp eye on their own special problems whilst prodding the female section, always slower to discriminate and complain than the men, to 'Tak' their grievances down tu't club'. It was never an easy task persuading women and young girls to officially voice their discontents for the fear of victimization loomed large and there were devious methods of isolating and 'picking-out' the so-called culprits. . .
>
> . . .[At shop meetings] time was a main factor, for if talks dragged on married women grew restless about possible irate husbands awaiting their delayed evening meal.[38]

Even so, the Victorian expectations about women's domestic priorities had a far weaker hold in the Weavers' Association than in any other major union. It even included one branch, Wigan, that was virtually run by women, and another, Oldham, where women were not only collectors, but sat on the committee.

In Wigan, where men were attracted away from the mills by the higher wages in the coal mines, the weavers' union had become a weak, virtually all-woman society. It was unable to maintain a wages list comparable to those of the other local unions, and soon the notoriously low rates of pay came to the attention of the Women's Trade Union League. In the mid 1890s Annie Marland visited Wigan and reported in the League *Review* how bad the local situation was and how she had 'tried to force home the great truth that if trades unionism is good for the miners it must be good for factory workers'.[39] The League took stock of the depressing situation and decided to employ a special salaried organizer just for Wigan to get the demoralized women weavers into better shape. They chose Helen Silcock for the job.

It was a good choice. Born in 1866, she was one of ten children of a Newcastle collier, himself a strong trade unionist. They moved to Lancashire, where at fifteen she started working in one of the local mills, joining the Wigan and District Association of Weavers and Winders in 1890, as soon as it was founded. Two years later, when she was twenty six, she was elected onto the committee, and after another two years was unanimously elected union President. In 1897 she was approached by the League and asked if she would give up her job in the weaving sheds and become full-time president-organizer at its expense.

It must have been a welcome offer. It was about this time that Helen Silcock joined the Social Democratic Federation and this kind of challenge complemented her political commitment. She had spoken for the first time at a large public meeting in Hyde Park during the 1895 Labour Day demonstration. Later that year, she was joined by Annie Marland and by Harry Quelch, editor of the Social Democratic Federation's paper, *Justice*; together the three of them campaigned to raise the level of the Wigan weavers' list.[40]

She took on the job for the League with great energy and dedication. To begin with, it was an uphill struggle, but Helen Silcock seems to have used both her political contacts and her determination to get what she wanted. She was on the Executive of the Wigan Trades Council, still a rare position for a woman. And, like Annie Marland before her, she was delegated to attend various Trade Union Congresses, including one in 1898 where she made a 'short forcible speech' against the hated steam jets that were injected into the weaving sheds supposedly to prevent the yarn from becoming brittle.[41]

Although some men in the Federation, like Quelch and Hyndman, had no time for women's suffrage, Helen Silcock did not share their views. At the turn of the century she joined Esther Roper's suffrage campaign with great enthusiasm; visiting suffrage speakers were always welcomed by her when they came to Wigan, and her local base became a valuable asset.

The Oldham union did not have to contend with such notoriously low wages and its officials were by no means all women. There were usually about four women on the committee of fifteen or sixteen (though two of them, Nellie Devine and Emma Turner, were committee members for at least ten years and were frequently delegated to attend regional weavers' meetings.[42]) Oldham also elected a woman president, Mary Callaghan, in the 1890s. Much of her work was like Helen Silcock's, inevitably concerned with the fight to maintain uniform list prices for her members. Even this must have been a difficult task for a woman. About 1897 Mary Callaghan retired from the presidency, apparently finding it too difficult to operate within the male-dominated world of the cotton trade unions. Certainly, she became part of the local mythology and, twenty years later, the *Cotton Factory Times* was still citing her unhappy presidency as one more reason why women should not meddle in trade union affairs. 'Th' next time tha comes to eawr place,' an Oldham employer is supposed to have advised the male secretary of the union, 'don't bring that woman president o' yores wi' thi. Aw couldn't put my side o' th' case in gradely language wi' her in th' office.'[43]

But throughout the cotton towns women were gaining valuable experience as members of their local weavers' union that later stood them in good stead when the suffrage campaign got under way. It taught them how to arrange an agenda, publicize a meeting, take minutes, keep accounts and handle an organization's money. For instance in Burnley, another weaver, Margaret Aldersley, like Helen Silcock the daughter of a miner, joined the suffrage campaign.[44] In Salford Nellie Keenan became Treasurer (and later Secretary) of a new Association of Power-Loom Weavers formed in 1902 with the encouragement of Sarah Dickenson and Eva Gore-Booth. In Brierfield Emily Murgatroyd, who had started work as a ten-year-old in about 1887, was a weaver at Wilkinson's Laurel Bank Mill and an active trade unionist. These three women, along with Helen Silcock and countless others whose names are lost and forgotten, became active suffragists, largely through their experiences in the weaving sheds and union branches. The only surviving record of their activities is the hundreds of meetings in the North of England Society reports.

The Lancashire cotton unions, however, were still run by men who were neither socialist agitators nor idealistic visionaries. They were hard-headed men whose skills were those of rapid calculation to fractions of a penny to assess a member's earnings from his or her looms, rings, frames or mules. They were not overtly political, and, along with the miners, tended to drag their feet over the cause of independent labour representation in Parliament. 'So far as the textile trades are concerned,' said the *Cotton Factory Times*, mill workers 'have not yet got to the point where they are willing to sink their difference and concentrate on labour.'[45] In 1901 the only cotton union affiliated to the Labour Representation Committee was the tiny Colne Weavers' Association, already well known for its unusual socialist tendencies.

The conservatism of the Liberal weavers and Tory spinners is the great irony of Lancashire politics at the turn of the century. These men worked alongside women whose claims to the vote were increasingly strongly felt and whose hopes for enfranchisement lay in support from the labour movement — both the trade unions and the new Labour Representation Committee. Yet local labour leaders were, on the whole, satisfied with the status quo and gave only limited support to the radical suffragists. (A further irony was that on the other side of the Pennines labour leaders had long campaigned for women's suffrage; though a Yorkshire-based campaign was hampered by the low wages and poor organization of the women wool workers.)

Women in Lancashire took great pride in their work and were conscious of their vital importance to the national economy. England's bread did hang by the thread woven by women in the mills around Blackburn, Preston and Burnley. But without a vote they were politically powerless:

> 'My opinion should have some weight,' said the Weavers' Secretary at a Lancashire Trade Council meeting, 'for I represent by far the biggest Union in the town.'
>
> 'What's the good of your Union?' said the Engineers' Secretary, 'why, it's all women; mine mayn't be large, but, at all events, they're voters.'[46]

The logic of arguments like these was beginning to be recognized by politically minded women in the cotton towns. Selina Cooper, for instance, had originally thought that the trade union movement itself gave sufficient protection to its women members; but now she said:

> I carefully watched the proceedings and the policy pursued by such great unions as the Miners, Cotton Spinners, and Engineers, who all pressed for state interference with the object of improving their industrial conditions. I was compelled to recognize the power of Parliament – a power that can and ought to be utilized for the public good. Those well-organized industries had the ballot box as a lever to raise their standard of life, but the women workers, however well they combined, had no such lever to help them in their demand for the redressing of their grievances.[47]

For Selina Cooper and others like her there was no option but to join together and campaign for the vote for themselves.

VI

Jobs outside the mill

To women from the cotton unions like Selina Cooper, who noticed how weak they were politically compared with the enfranchised men in the same unions, Esther Roper's Special Appeal campaign made a ready appeal. Less well organized working women were in no position to draw the same conclusion. They were also outside the network of union meetings through which the suffragists were able to contact the cotton workers: women working in shops or small isolated workshops were far less likely to belong to a union or to experience the robust cameraderie of the mill.

Mill work paid far higher wages than any of the other available jobs. Girls like Ethel Derbyshire found to their cost that the more genteel trades like sewing entailed a protracted learning period on little or no pay, while a job in one of the Blackburn mills had the overwhelming advantage of offering relatively high wages immediately a girl started work. Domestic service might be cleaner and less dangerous than mill work, but few Lancashire girls opted for its low wages, long hours and restrictions on their freedom when they could earn so much more in a nearby mill. Middle class families often had to import domestic servants from outside the cotton area. Helena Swanwick, the wife of a university lecturer, complained:

> Servants in Manchester were very hard to get and for the most part incompetent ... In the first sixteen years of my housekeeping, eighteen 'generals' floated in and out of my employment, and very few of these were fit

to be left in charge when we were absent ... At least four proved themselves abnormally weak-witted, almost idiotic. One ... was an irredeemable drunkard ... One suffered from melancholia ... Two turned out to be professional prostitutes ... Two others became pregnant while in my service, and had to be helped away from the men who had misled them.[1]

This restricted range of job opportunities began to expand towards the end of the century. While the number of mill jobs declined slightly, there was a dramatic boom in white-collar openings. Firms needed women clerks — lower paid than their male equivalents — to handle the growing volume of paperwork; new department stores and shops needed an army of shop assistants; successive Victorian governments had passed statute after statute, each of which needed day to day administration; and the new Education Acts, by making schooling compulsory, created a massive demand for elementary teachers.

Lancashire women[2]

	1891	1901	change
Commercial and business clerks:	1,800	5,600	205% increase
General/local government:	1,300	2,300	86% increase
School teachers:	16,000	21,000	30% increase
Tailoresses:	71,000	77,000	8% increase
Cotton workers:	282,000	274,000	3% decrease

These new openings attracted both the middle class girls for whom previously no job had seemed 'suitable', and some of the more ambitious, 'refined' working class girls who hated the noise and dirt of the mill and the social stigma of clogs and shawls. Many of them were in for a shock. Hours were long and working conditions unprotected by the Factory and Workshop Acts which governed conditions in the mill; and — again unlike the mills — the number of jobs were still limited.

Shop workers, for instance, who 'lived in' found that their working day started early and finished late, with only poor quality food at their rushed meal breaks, and as they were receiving 'board' their wages were substantially lowered. The newly formed National Amalgamated Union of Shop Assistants had great difficulty recruiting members in a trade still riddled with archaic practices, and it had a long battle to introduce even an early closing day bill. One local woman described how her seventeen year old sister, a shop assistant at Lewis's in Manchester, used to work from 8.30 am to 8 pm, and on Saturday until about 10 pm:

My sister Florrie would arrive home at nearly midnight, having walked the mile from the tram to our house and after having been on her feet all the long day (shop assistants were not allowed to sit down in view of customers) exhausted to breaking point. She would weep with weariness and though hungry be too tired to eat her supper. She would perk up a little on Sunday but obviously dreaded the return to work on Monday morning.[3]

Other white collar workers told similar stories. One girl, born in Manchester in 1890 whose father was a respectable pawnbroker left school at fourteen and decided to try office work. Her parents sent her to the Remington School for a three month shorthand and typing course. She found a job with a shipping firm in Oxford Street, and started at a wage of 15s 6d, considered an unusually good wage for a young girl:

> I soon found out why — because two nights a week, Tuesdays and Fridays, were shipping nights to China and India. And those nights there were no hours. My ordinary hours were half-past eight to six o'clock, but on shipping nights you just worked till you finished, which was very seldom before eight o'clock, sometimes after. No extra pay, just a tea, your tea in the warehouse, and that was all.[4]

It is no surprise, then, that none of the known radical suffragists came from the growing army of clerical workers. Their aspirations to middle class gentility prevented them from identifying with the problems of the mill workers, and their experiences in their jobs did nothing to give them a sense of wider political rights of which they were being deprived. They shared none of the solidarity to be found among mill workers; their work was often isolated and solitary. They probably felt that becoming involved in a textile workers' suffrage campaign would threaten their newly-acquired respectability.

The other booming career, elementary school teaching, did produce two of the most active of the women in the suffrage movement, Alice Collinge, as well as Teresa Billington, one of the Pankhursts' earliest recruits. Significantly, they both became politicized despite rather than because of their experience at work.

Like thousands of other girls from working or lower middle class families, they trained through the pupil teacher system, operated by the government since the 1840s, which allowed able pupils to stay on at school, usually from fourteen to eighteen, on an apprenticeship system, helping with the younger children in return for a small salary. Their training was somewhat haphazard, usually given before or after school by the headmaster, but the system had the very practical advantage of cheapness, and by the 1880s had attracted over twenty thousand women (and ten thousand men).

Teresa Billington came from an impoverished middle class family in Blackburn, which, despite its down-at-heel shabbiness, would never permit a daughter to enter one of the weaving mills. 'Six to eight loom weavers — went to work in clogs and shawls,' Teresa Billington wrote later, 'walked out on Sunday in the smart new fashionable clothes — much better than the penurious survivals of middle class non-working "ladies".' For her, the pupil teacher system was a boon; although her first teaching post paid her a meagre annual salary of £26, only half as much as a mill worker, she described herself as 'shabby, happy and absorbed', and was soon studying for a B.Sc. from London University, which would ensure bigger increments and satisfy her passion for learning. 'I loved all this education so much,' she wrote, 'I fell upon the feast with such delight, that commonplace everyday interests seemed to have little meaning for me.'[5]

Alice Collinge similarly set great store by education for which she had had to work so hard. She came from Rawtenstall in Rossendale, in the heart of the cotton region. She left school when she was twelve, in about 1885, and travelled down the valley each day to Newchurch, where she trained as a pupil teacher for six years, later becoming an elementary teacher at St Matthew's School in Bolton.[6]

Alice Collinge never read much when she was a child, but began to make up for it as a teacher. Poetry particularly appealed to her, especially that of Walt Whitman, Keats, Byron, Alice Meynell and Emily Dickenson.[7] Like Whitman she had a fervent passion for the countryside and lived in a cottage in the hills above Bolton, intriguing her pupils by walking through the fields to school each day, and transmitting some of her enthusiasm to them during nature and English lessons.

Unlike the mill workers who became active in the radical suffragist campaign, Alice Collinge was hardly influenced by trade union activity. The National Union of Teachers, heavily dominated by the minority of men, had little interest in the particular grievances of its women members. It saw no reason to campaign against the differentials between men's and women's wages (men earned about 30 per cent more) and had little interest in fighting the ruling which allowed local authorities to dismiss women teachers who got married. A Ladies' Committee was established on the union executive, but this token gesture had little effect on pay structures. In the 1900s an Equal Pay League was formed, and Teresa Billington became secretary of its vigorous Manchester branch from its formation until she left in 1905.

(The union only finally accepted the principle of equal pay in 1919, and even then the women were accused of rushing the issue through while men teachers were in the Forces.)[8]

Women teachers acted timidly over the question of the vote; although some teachers did eventually form their own Franchise Union, individual branches of the National Union of Teachers were often opposed to this kind of feminist campaign. In the Wigan branch, for instance, a resolution on women's suffrage was debated but 'despite the fact that three fourths of the members present were ladies, not a single supporter of the resolution was to be found.'[9] For women like Alice Collinge union meetings must have been a constant source of frustration, and at the turn of the century she seemed to have been looking round for out-of-school interests.

After mill work, the most common job for a Lancashire girl to take up was dressmaking or tailoring. The wages were extremely low, the hours long, and tailoresses had much to envy the lucky mill girls who came streaming out of the mill as soon as the afternoon buzzer sounded. There were various local attempts to form trade unions and two or three of the most active radical suffragists were drawn to the campaign from this kind of industrial experience.

Tailoring was organized rather like spinning. At the top of the hierarchy were the craft tailors, who belonged to the exclusive Amalgamated Society of Tailors, formed in 1866; such men averaged 33s 6d, but top fitters and cutters could earn up to 60s or 70s, wages at least comparable to the mule spinners. At the bottom end were the unskilled or semi-skilled workers, the vast majority of them women, who worked at home or in the fast growing machining factories; like the ring spinners, they were excluded from the Tailors' Society, which opposed not only subcontracting and mechanization but also competition from women workers. In 1891 the Southport and Liverpool union branches even went on strike against employing women and outworkers. Tailoresses' wages were among the lowest in the country, and undercutting was rife. Skilled women working in dress or millinery workshops might earn over 30s but the average wage was under 14s. Even this figure is deceptive as many tailoresses, especially those working irregularly at home, or in the back street sweated workshops, were invisible to official data collectors from the Board of Trade.

Tailoresses and dressmakers had made some attempts to organize, and a handful of isolated local associations had been formed, mainly in

Leeds and Bristol. For instance, in 1893 the Women's Trade Union League sponsored Annie Marland's visits to assist the Leeds Tailoresses' Society and to Todmorden to help organize the women in the ready-made clothing trade.

For women outside the major centres there was little protection against exploitation by unscrupulous employers. Yet a champion of the downtrodden tailoresses emerged in the least expected of places: Crewe, an isolated railway town in Cheshire, about twenty five miles to the south of the Lancashire cotton towns. Ada Nield, a twenty-four-year-old tailoress working in one of the local clothing factories, dared to take on the system single-handed in 1894. Later, she became one of the leading radical suffragists, and for this reason it is worth discussing her first campaign in some detail.

Ada Nield was born in North Staffordshire near the Potteries in 1870. She was one of thirteen children and had to leave school at eleven and take on the heavy responsibility of looking after her seven younger brothers, combining this with various odd jobs. Her father, a poor farmer, had to give up his farm for lack of capital, and moved his family to Crewe where he could more easily find another job.[10]

When she was nineteen or twenty she took her first job in one of the Crewe clothing factories, but only stayed there three weeks. Like so many other employers, they had a policy of not paying learners any wages during their first three months, and she could not live for so long without money. She applied for another sewing job in Crewe, at Compton Brothers, a firm which had been making uniforms for soldiers, policemen and railway workers on contract from the government since the 1860s. Ada Nield managed to persuade the firm to reduce her unpaid 'apprenticeship' to a week, and she took her place beside an older tailoress, Mrs Tanner, who patiently introduced her to the mysteries of sewing in tunic linings and sleeves, and of button-holing.

Her wages were 8s, well below average, but better than many other tailoresses received. Ada Nield found much else to disturb her at Compton's. To begin with, wages were paid on a piece-work basis per garment, and workers' earnings could fluctuate between 1d and 4d an hour. Also, out of the 8s they had to pay 2d or 3d for tea and hot water, especially aggravating for her as she did not drink tea. (Sarah Dickenson met the same petty meanness when she started work in a Salford mill at the age of eleven. A penny a week was docked from her wages to pay for hot water which she did not use as she went home for dinner. Her fellow workers must have supported her since, young as she was, she continued to agitate until the penny was restored to her pay. [11]) There were fines for lateness, and extortionate charges for the needles and thread they had to use. Favouritism was rife, and the men who handed out the work and inspected the finished clothes seemed to encourage bitter jealousies among the women. Particularly in the slack season, women were pitted against one another, each fighting for work:

Imagine the scene. . . A table with at least fifty girls on and round it. Lay a dozen garments, probably not worth more than 7s in all to us. These girls all clamouring, with arms outstretched, for a share of it, say a shilling's worth. . . When the season was very slack indeed I have seen the youngest hands literally fight and scramble for garments, for which 2d each is paid. [12]

Among the five hundred workers there was an elite of a hundred tailors who worked in aristocratic seclusion at one end of the room; the government had stipulated that the sewing-in of tunic sleeves should be done by these skilled men. In fact, this was normally done by the women, but when the Factory Inspector came round, the work was taken from them and given to the tailors. Ada Nield asked Mrs Tanner why this was:

Mrs Tanner looked at the girl, pityingly. 'You don't know much, child,' she said. 'How much do we get for sewing them in? Fivepence, isn't it? And it's skilled work, which cannot be scamped. But I, and you, since you've got so clever at it, can put in a pair in an hour, and that's not bad pay. But the men's price is 1s 5d. So you can easily understand why we get the job instead of them. [13]

Ada Nield saw no reason why the tailoresses should be humiliated and cheated in this way. With rare courage, she dared to do what no other working woman had done before. Solely on her own initiative she decided to stir up a public outcry against the appalling conditions in which she worked. She wrote anonymously to the local paper, *The Crewe Chronicle,* which published her letter:

Sir — Will you grant me space in your sensible and widely-read paper to complain of a great grievance of the class — that of the tailoresses in some of the Crewe factories — to which I belong?. . . . Though one cannot open a newspaper without seeing what all sorts and conditions of men are constantly agitating for and slowly but surely obtaining — as in the miners' eight hour bill — only very vague mention if ever is made of the underpaid, over-worked factory girl. . . The rates paid for the work done by us are so fearfully low as to be totally inadequate. . . 'A living wage!' Ours is a lingering dying wage. . . I am, sir, yours sincerely,

A CREWE FACTORY GIRL
Crewe May 1st 1894[14]

107

So began a protracted public correspondence — encouraged by the sympathetic *Chronicle* editor — which ran right into the autumn. Two weeks later another letter appeared which detailed the low wages and unjust fines:

> Home-work, then, is the only resource of the poor slave who has the misfortune to adopt 'finishing' as a means of earning a livelihood. I have myself, repeatedly, five nights a week. . . regularly taken four hours, at least, work home with me, and have done it . . .
>
> But we are not asking for pity, sir, we ask only for justice. . . . Our work is necessary (presumably) to our employers. Were we not employed others would have to be, and if of the opposite sex, I venture to say, sir, would have to be paid on a very different scale. Why, because we are weak women, without pluck and grit enough to stand up for our rights, should we be ground down to this miserable wage?[15]

At this point other readers took up the challenge. The Crewe branch of the Independent Labour Party had started in October 1893, and from the beginning was full of energy. The ILP secretary wrote to ask the 'Crewe Factory Girl' — whoever she was — to get in touch with him. She decided to remain anonymous, but wrote that if she ever revealed her identity in future, she would happily work with the ILP in order to improve the conditions, not only of factory girls, but of all other workers:

> The 'Crewe Factory Girl' would like to add that she watches the progress in the Independent Labour Party with deep interest; and is in perfect sympathy with them, especially in their efforts to have the working man (and woman) represented in Parliament by Labour candidates who understand their needs.[16]

The ILP secretary added that he raised his hat to 'The Factory Girl', and he quoted from a second anonymous letter-writer — 'A Crewe Dressmaker' — whose working conditions were even more intolerable; she herself had served a two year apprenticeship without pay and now worked ten hours a day for 10d a day, with no guarantee of regular work. 'I wonder there has not been some Dressmakers' Association or something started,' her letter ended, 'for I am sure there are enough dressmakers in Crewe to start one.'

There were already a few local branches of the new unions for unskilled workers — Post Office workers, for instance, and Co-op employees.[17] So the ILP took up 'Crewe Dressmaker's' challenge and promised to organize a public meeting for women workers as soon as possible. The next week a local minister, an ILP committee member, wrote in to offer his church hall for meetings for tailoresses, milliners, dressmakers and shop girls.[18]

By now Ada Nield had attracted attention further afield. The socialist weekly the *Clarion* had already reprinted her letters and reported that the women workers 'will now be able to combine, and can rely upon the ILP for help and redress of their grievances.'[19] A local member of the Tailors' Society joined in the debate. He admitted that nationally the Society was still divided about accepting women, but added that at a recent Crewe branch meeting there had been a definite majority in favour of admitting them. 'It is Folly for us to think of keeping women out of our trade,' he added.[20]

But by then such shows of solidarity were really too late. Events inside Compton's factory had taken over. Hardly surprisingly, the manager had been incensed by the constant public attacks on the company. At the end of July he had summoned a meeting of his workers at which he had denied that a farthing profit was made out of the tea money, and ordered as punishment that in future the tea room would be closed and late arrivals locked out of the factory. It was a shrewd move; understandably, resentment against the 'Factory Girl' welled up among workers, some of whom formed groups to try and find out who the traitor was so they could expel her.

A few days later, the owner, a well-fed man with an eye-glass, came up from London (normally he only put in an appearance at the annual entertainment) for a further meeting. 'I'm sure,' he said, turning to the girls, women and men who were listening, 'that I speak for all of you when I say that we are all very sorry for what this misguided girl has done. If she was dissatisfied she had a remedy — she could have left.' He asked them if anyone would admit to being dissatisfied with the conditions in his factory, and Ada Nield, feeling that this was the moment to abandon her anonymity, called out, 'Yes, I am.' The confrontation had finally come out into the open. A long argument followed, lasting well over an hour, in which the employer attacked her for her impudence while she defended her reasons for publicising bad conditions. No other worker dared to speak out; with absolutely no practice at public speaking, she managed, at the age of twenty four, to champion the workers' case from the shop floor against two powerful men.

As soon as both men had left the room, 'the stricken girl beside Mrs Tanner was nearly smothered by girls and women, who came to tell her that they loved her for not having "caved in", and that every word she said in the paper and out of it, was true.'[21]

The crisis came at the end of August. About a dozen tailoresses began to support Ada Nield's campaign. The Gasworkers' Union, which already had a branch in Crewe, admitted them as members. Compton's came to hear of this defiant behaviour and the women found themselves sacked on account of 'slackness of work'.

Local public opinion was now sufficiently aroused to mount a protest. A meeting was convened, supported by the ILP and the Gasworkers. Ada Nield made her first public appearance, and, with the backing of Eleanor Marx, long-time champion of the union, addressed the crowded audience. Compton's was publicly pilloried. The local MP championed the 'Crewe Factory Girl's' case, and Fleet Street and the Home Office were told of the conditions under which women sewed army uniforms. In the end the firm capitulated; the women who had been sacked were reinstated, the cost of materials they had to buy was reduced, and the fining system was overhauled. The wage rates, of course, were not increased.[22]

Ada Nield never went back to Compton's. She became an active member of Crewe ILP and was soon working with the local Trades Council. The next two years was a period of consolidating her political experience. Single-handed Ada Nield had carried out a shop-floor campaign against the tailoresses' atrocious wages and conditions, without even the help from middle class sympathizers that, for instance, the London match-girls had. At the risk of losing her own job, she took on her employer, although she had nothing like his education; her few years at dame school can hardly have trained her to be a fluent writer, yet she used her series of *Chronicle* letters to give a vivid account of the indignities the tailoresses had to suffer.

Other tailoresses who joined the suffrage campaign were introduced to politics in a less dramatic way, though they too suffered from low wages and poor organization. Louisa Smith worked in one of the Manchester machining factories, where, like Compton's in Crewe, there was no union organization. She came into contact with Eva Gore-Booth who 'was very keen on women's rights and trade unions. She persuaded me to join.'[23] This Manchester Tailoresses' Union, started in the late 1890s, joined the Manchester and Salford Women's Trades Council, and became a firm supporter of the suffrage campaign.[24]

In Nelson, Harriette Beanland, a close friend of Selina Cooper, was a skilled dressmaker in a position to command far higher wages than either Ada Nield or Louisa Smith. 'She was, I should imagine, better educated than my mother,' Mary Cooper explained. ' . . . She was exceedingly well-spoken and well dressed, of course. . . . She used to make my mother lovely things. My mother paid for them, but. . . . She [worked on] her own in the house, she was a tailoress, you see.'[25] She too became involved in the suffrage campaign.

But the few dressmakers and teachers were exceptional among the radical suffragists. Except for an outstanding woman like Ada Nield, the experience of working in factories, offices or schools lacked the political impact of mill jobs. So it was that for these women, as well as some of the cotton workers, political awakening often came through the wide range of socialist groups that sprang up in the 1890s and 1900s.

VII

Political Apprenticeship

During the 1890s a generation of ambitious but frustrated young women was growing up, dissatisfied with their work and its humiliating pay and conditions. It often took virtually all their waking hours to earn a living wage. 'Cultivation of the mind? How is it possible? Reading?' demanded Ada Nield bitterly in the *Chronicle*. 'Those of us who are determined to live like human beings and require food for mind as well as body, are obliged to take time from sleep to gratify this desire.'[1]

These feelings of pent-up frustration were shared by many other young women of that generation, born in the 1870s and early 1880s. 'I hated the factory,' Mary Luty wrote bitterly about the Rossendale mills, 'but could do weaving without giving much thought to it, and, better still, could forget it entirely once I was outside the gates.'[2]

Cissy Foley, born in 1879, echoed this resentment against the limits imposed on her life, and her feelings ran as deep as those of Ada Nield and Mary Luty. She longed for an opportunity to leave the hated cardroom and devote herself to something more rewarding. Eventually she became a nurse, but not until the great social upheaval of the First World War. Until then such options were always just out of the reach of girls like Cissy. Her father, who worked as a night caretaker for local foundries, was frequently out of work, and Cissy's regular weekly wages were much depended on at home.[3]

Her newspaper reading during dinner breaks at the mill and the practical experience she gained at the weekly union meetings gave her a sense of a wider world beyond the daily monotony of machine-tending. But the local Cardroom Association, with its sights narrowly focused on day-to-day wage list negotiations, provided little positive inspiration for a woman as politically minded as Cissy.

The path Cissy Foley followed from the 1890s to the mid 1900s when she joined with Sarah Reddish and other local suffragists, is typical of other restless young women of her generation, isolated among their contemporaries who had resigned themselves to the monotony of working life. Luckily for us, her intellectual, political and emotional development has been recorded by her sister Alice, twelve years younger, who in looking back on her childhood, recognized Cissy as the major influence in how she herself grew up.

Alice remembered how Cissy, then about fifteen, 'often acted as "little mother" in the home'. As she gave her younger sisters their bath on Friday evenings, Cissy 'scarcely spoke to us, . . . but her luminous brown eyes . . . invariably wore a far-a-way look as if exploring worlds other than our humble kitchen with its presence of two damp, lithe bodies curling on the rug before a glowing fire.'[4]

While grievances about pay and conditions at work were common to men and women alike, working class girls like Ada Nield and Cissy Foley who came from large families had an added source of resentment: as they grew up they were expected to shoulder many of their mothers' soul-destroying family responsibilities. While girls of an earlier generation had become resigned to this, young women were growing up who felt that this heavy domestic burden should no longer be tolerated. One of the more personal reasons that drove Cissy Foley (and others like her) into the suffrage campaign, was a heartfelt reaction against her mother's hopeless drudgery.

Mrs Foley's father had died when she was seven, and she was put out to work on a farm in return for a shilling a week and her keep, and later worked in the cardroom until her marriage. A kindly, forebearing woman, she never learned to read and write, but developed all the practical skills necessary to survive living with her irascible and drunken husband. Alice describes how he would follow her mother 'persistently round the kitchen whining monotonously, "lend us a penny, Meg; lend us a penny; I'm choking." At length, in a fit of desperation, a penny was flung on to the table, whilst mother snatched up her shawl and vanished into the street to find temporary refuge in a neighbour's home.'[5]

Alice loved her mother passionately, but Cissy was already developing into a rebellious critic of a system which permitted so much suffering. Once Mr Foley broke into Cissy's money-box and stole her precious savings to pay debts or buy drink. She never forgave this and developed a 'black, implacable hatred' towards him, which also coloured her attitude to her long-suffering mother 'whom she considered a poor fool for tolerating such an unsatisfactory husband.'[6]

Cissy's reforming zeal made her equally impatient of her mother's haphazard domestic management. In the same way that she had cajoled her into giving up her visits to the corner shop in favour of the Co-op, Cissy 'now insisted on various refinements in the home; the sanded kitchen was no more; the floor sported bright coloured linoleum; cups and saucers replaced the old blue and white-rimmed basins and the oil lamp was ousted by the incandescent gas-jet.'[7] She even conceived a passion for early morning cold baths, which entailed laboriously lugging the zinc tub and buckets of water upstairs. Against this onslaught from her progressive and intelligent daughter, Mrs Foley grew nervous and uneasy. She gave way on many things, but dug in her heels against reforms she dismissed as mere social pretensions, such as introducing a new-fangled egg-timer.

Cissy Foley's attitude to her family was not based on snobbery or genteel aspirations. It was the first adolescent stirrings of a wider political discontent, experienced by so many thoughtful girls of her generation. For instance Elizabeth Dean recalled bitterly how much she resented her father's callousness about the way her mother's constant pregnancies undermined her health: 'I always had it against him. My mother died when she was thirty-eight; she'd had eight children and she died with the last one . . . I always said my father turned me into a suffragette.'[8] Teresa Billington pitied but resented her ill-matched parents, and rejected her family's demands upon her. She wrote to her sister: 'The family is like a chain-gang. Its members may be kind to one another, may share experiences and the feelings they arouse, but the chain forces a unity and agreement based on force.' Later she noted 'I abolished all my relatives at seventeen retaining only those whom I love as friends.'[9]

Unlike Teresa Billington, Cissy Foley had no opportunity to stay on at school or to become a pupil teacher. Her rudimentary education at the nearby St Peter and Paul's Catholic School, where 'the lessons were as dull as the surroundings' was probably fairly typical. Very few working class girls were able to go on to the 'higher grade schools' that had developed in the late 1890s. For them the new adult education movement offered what the state elementary system patently failed to provide: teaching that extended a little beyond rote learning and plain sewing.

In 1886 Manchester University adopted the University Extension scheme, designed for people who had already left school but who wanted to continue their education in their spare time. It proved very popular, although it inevitably catered mainly for middle class rather than working class students. (There were some exceptions: Hudson Shaw, a popular extension lecturer from Balliol College, Oxford held working class audiences at the Oldham Co-operative Society which averaged six hundred and fifty but rose to over a thousand by 1896.)[10] Technical colleges also began to offer evening classes for people who worked during the day, and in 1903 the Workers' Educational Association was formed which tried to give working class students a broader understanding of the workings of society, with classes in politics, economics and local government.

Cissy Foley grasped these new opportunities enthusiastically. She and her friends attended a course on the poetry of Robert Browning organized through the Oxford University Extension Scheme. They then graduated to discussing, however cursorily, Marx's *Capital*, which may have helped Cissy understand more clearly the complex mechanics of the cotton industry.

Other young women took up new opportunities in different ways. Selina Cooper took practical courses in laundry, hygiene and first aid, and was invited onto the local St John's Ambulance Committee in 1895. 'She started the ambulance in Brierfield,' her daughter explained. 'In those days people daren't go to the doctor, and she used to set arms, and that sort of thing.'[11] Like her, Mary Luty preferred practical classes. She attended the local Rossendale night school to supplement her meagre four years of full-time education, studying commercial subjects. [12]

Other women who joined adult classes organized by socialist groups found themselves discussing subjects far too controversial for elementary school. Elizabeth Dean, by now a committed socialist, described the classes on Marxism she used to attend:' . . . we had a chap from South Salford . . . he used to walk up and down telling us, you know, what's a commodity, what's this and what's the other . . . He wouldn't take anything from us, you know, and he never got vexed with us and some of us asked some damned silly questions. Really.

Struggling with economics.'[13] Another Manchester woman, Elsie Plant, used to go along to an adult class in Pankhurst Hall, built by the ILP in Salford as a memorial to Dr Pankhurst: 'There was a big upsurge in the theory of evolution, just about that time. So this is what the adult class was tackling quite a lot. And to me, the revelation of the evolution of man, which I had never heard of before, it opened a whole new world to me.'[14]

Lancashire had long sustained a strong tradition of self-education and self-improvement, which still flourished at the turn of the century. Those who were beginning to question the inevitability of the Victorian social structure often coupled this with a great thirst for information about all aspects of the world they lived in. Doris Chew described how her father worked as 'a weaver, which he hated ... He used to put a book up at the end of the loom'; he managed to educate himself by walking from Rishton to Blackburn to attend evening classes and was given a copy of Shakespeare as a prize.[15] Cissy Foley was equally keen to seize any opportunity to extend her own horizons beyond the formal classes she attended. One of the first things she did was to persuade her family to join the Co-op library, and to borrow its books to take home, despite her mother's complaint that 'I met as weel goo eaut, for this place is nowt bur a deaf an dumb schoo'.'[16]

Other women shared her great enthusiasm for reading. Elizabeth Dean went to her local library in Sale, near Manchester, though she had little idea of what to ask for.

'Now, my father didn't like us reading, like, such as novels or anything like that ... I used to go into the library, and there was a young lady there, I should think she'd be about eighteen ... Well, I didn't know what to ask for, and she said, "Would you like such an author—" so I said, "Yes, anything to read, yes." So she would get me one and I would go home with it up my jumper, upstairs and into the bedroom so he wouldn't listen.'[17]

Many read with enthusiasm anything that came their way; one Manchester member of the Women's Co-operative Guild listed among books she had enjoyed 'in time stolen from my sleeping hours' a wide range from Ethel Snowdon's *The Feminist Movement* and a translation of Bebel's *Woman* to popular novels of the day, including *The Forsyte Saga* and 'all of Sheila Kaye-Smith's.'[18]

Cissy and her friends used to read and debate the books coming out of the new socialist movement — for instance William Morris's *Dream of John Ball*. In a house dominated by a Catholic father, this was provocation indeed. To Alice, still drinking in the stories regaled by the

116

nuns at school, full of hell and purgatory, 'it seemed the height of profanity and immediately Cissy's name was added to my prayer list as being in urgent need of spiritual solicitude.'[19]

Up in Blackburn, Teresa Billington, who had been sent by her strict Catholic family to convent school, was also beginning to try out 'pagan' ideas that would eventually lead to socialism and feminism. Before Benediction and Sunday high tea, Teresa and her friends set out on ritual walks on which she recalled, 'I became the critic, the questioner, the flyer of wild kites of free thought.' Eventually the group became her 'gaggle of girls' who described their afternoon as 'a nice walk round the Park . . . . while Teresa talked.'[20]

Teresa Billington was packed off to the family of an old friend of her mother's to become a millinery apprentice. She hated it, and fled to Manchester to become a pupil teacher. By now Cissy Foley too had drifted apart from the women who worked alongside her in the cardroom, and had found new friends, 'a group of sedate young ladies from shops and offices, all sedulously imbibing socialist ethics and culture'. When they came to Sunday tea Mrs Foley diplomatically shooed her husband and sons into the back regions of the house, while she sat at the head of the table 'mostly silent, but anxiously watching the disappearing piles of home-made currant bread whilst discussion ranged round politics, men, votes for women and culture'.[21]

The focus for Cissy Foley's progressive ideas was the Bolton Labour Church. The first Labour Church had been founded in Manchester in 1891 by John Trevor, a Unitarian minister who had become dissatisfied with the hypocrisy and humbug of conventional religion. The Labour Churches retained all the fellowship and music of a chapel service, but rejected, among other things, the usual Christian practice of relegating women to a subordinate role. The Bolton Labour Church encouraged young women like Cissy Foley and her friends to argue out the advanced ideas of the day in a comradely atmosphere. By the turn of the century it was also regularly inviting speakers like Esther Roper and Eva Gore-Booth to talk about women's suffrage.[22]

For Cissy Foley this talk of votes for women made absolute sense. It helped her understand why, in the cardroom, her wages were so much lower than men's, and why her mother was so subject to her father's fitful domination. Another Bolton woman who found the Labour Church experience equally influential was Alice Collinge, only a few years older than Cissy. Converted by the rousing, religious oratory of Philip Snowden, Labour candidate for Blackburn and famous for his

117

emotional appeals to join the socialist movement, she became organist at the Labour Church. Her account of these early years conveys something of their infectious enthusiasm:

> Coming into contact with the virile Labour Church, social proclivities which had been lying dormant wakened, and the socialism of *that* day claimed me. What days those were, and how privileged I was, in my humble role at the piano, to hear such people as Mrs Despard, Miss Margaret Macmillan, Mrs Bruce Glasier, Edward Carpenter, people who more or less gave time and service to the Movement and desired nothing in return but the good of the country. Idealists they were, putting their ideals into practice. Needless to say, I carried out my then political faith as far as I could, sometimes on political platforms, but mainly on orange-boxes, placed in various parts of the town.[23]

Under Cissy's guidance, the younger Foleys joined the Labour Church's offshoot, the Socialist Sunday School, where they learned to recite the Socialist Ten Commandments, including:

> Remember that all good things of the earth are produced by labour. Whoever enjoys them without working for them is stealing the bread of the workers. . .
> . . .Look forward to the day when all men and women will be free citizens of one community, and live together as equals in peace and righteousness.[24]

'In those days we were inordinately proud of our positive affirmations of faith as compared with the orthodox religious negatives,' Alice Foley wrote later. The service opened with a hymn usually set to a martial air, no doubt played by Alice Collinge; 'We seemed forever to be marching somewhere, even if we often failed to reach our destination.'[25]

The Labour Churches and Socialist Sunday Schools, however, only whetted the appetites of young women like Cissy Foley. For a more sustained socialist programme they turned to the new weekly paper, the *Clarion*, one of the greatest influences on many of the working class women who joined the suffrage campaign. Ironically its founder and editor, Robert Blatchford, was no feminist, but a boisterous Manchester journalist who had the rare knack of synthesizing and popularizing the socialist theories of the 1890s. He had been a sergeant in the regular army, and later described his role (quite accurately) as 'a recruiting sergeant . . . for the Socialist Army.'[26]

As a reporter on the *Sunday Chronicle*, Blatchford became converted to socialism after investigating conditions in the Manchester slums for a series of articles. When he was sacked from the paper he started his own weekly, the *Clarion*, in 1891. Rowland Kenney used to read the *Sunday Chronicle* articles to his grandmother:

> They brought to both of us a sense of beauty and betterment. The man who

could write such things was not of common clay ... Numquam [Blatchford's pen-name] was the God of our idolatory.

A Sunday came when there was no article by Numquam, and both my grandmother and I felt as if the sun had dissolved into a grey mist. But then it rose in greater splendour ... Instead of an article a week we got a whole newspaper ...

And I was a Socialist! I was a Socialist definitely and decidedly, Robert Blatchford had seen to that. His articles in the *Clarion* were so simple and vivid that even a half-timer in a cotton factory, eager to understand something of the world in which he lived, could understand them.[27]

Blatchford's socialism was based on ethics, not economics. He had a clear view of the injustices of nineteenth century conditions, and saw socialism as the way to achieve happiness and equality in everyday life. But he had no very clear idea of how it was to be brought about. He believed that people could be converted to his point of view by argument and persuasion, and that when the majority were socialists, socialism would somehow automatically follow.

The keys to the *Clarion's* success were its clarity and wit. Particularly in the north, where socialism was fast gaining ground among the industrial working class, people bought it in sufficient numbers to make it the first radical paper since the Chartists' *Northern Star* to pay its own way. It spoke to them in their own language, and, above all, it was entertainingly written and professionally produced.

It carried serious labour news and, at a time when national organization was weak and groups fragmented, acted as an open forum for the different socialist sects. The *Clarion* was accessible to all its readers, even to advocates of women's suffrage, and during the 1890s the weekly pages became the most widely read platform for arguing the pros and cons of the rights of working women.

Blatchford himself tended to take a rather cavalier attitude to women's suffrage. His own marriage was extremely conventional; his wife Sally stayed at home, looked after the children and took no part at all in political life. He argued that all women were, like her, uninterested in politics. 'Why do women take so little interest in the affairs of the world? It is not because they are denied votes,' he later wrote in the *Clarion*. 'It is because they do not understand. I would give them votes if I could. But I would a thousand times rather they should learn and understand.'[28]

For readers like Cissy Foley the most influential part of the paper was probably the section called 'Our Woman's Letter', written by Julia Dawson.[29] Like Blatchford, she had scant patience for the

119

old-established suffrage societies. Her concerns were far more immediate and practical: hints about more efficient housekeeping, propaganda for rational dress, appeals to women to join their nearest ILP branch, and contacts for isolated readers. Yet among the ILP women that Blatchford and Julia Dawson encouraged to write for the *Clarion* were some outstanding feminists and suffragists, — for instance Margaret McMillan, a member of the Bradford School Board, already emerging as a champion of the rights of needy schoolchildren. 'Women work in mills, workshops, homes, and therefore the question of Social Reform concerns them . . .' she wrote. 'The wage-struggle has taught woman that she even more than man is influenced by all that takes place in the economic and industrial world.'[30]

Enid Stacy, a socialist from Bristol, also joined the debate. She carried on a running argument with one of the *Clarion*'s more bigoted male correspondents, who had argued that a woman's 'gentle sympathy and loving care should wait the breadwinner's return from toil to kiss the cloud of weariness from his brow,' and that 'a wife should stay at home and accept her husband's chivalry . . . tender homage, and faithful service'. In her reply in the next issue, Enid Stacy retorted that 'it is always highly amusing to listen to an ordinary man discourse upon women', and denounced his conventional views. 'If you would have us "feminine" (I will not misuse the grand word "womanly") i.e. weak physically and mentally, given to alternate fits of frivolity and parson-adoration, with no wide interests or any aspirations towards citizenship, be it so; but in that case have the grace and common sense not to blame us for being what we are.'[31] From then on it was a small step for the *Clarion* to publish the arguments for and against women's suffrage.

Such knockabout arguments were typical of the *Clarion*'s casual, eclectic approach to the questions of the day. However, Blatchford did also try to present a coherent view of socialism, and in 1892 and 1893 the *Clarion* serialized his *Merrie England*. It was then produced as a shilling booklet later in 1893, and reprinted in 1894 in a penny edition which immediately became an outstanding success. 'A wave of enthusiasm swept through the young socialist movement,' wrote Rowland Kenney. 'The Press and the Liberal and Tory politicians and public speakers thundered denunciations.'[32] Within a few months over 700,000 had been sold. 'For every convert made by *Das Kapital*' it was said, 'there were a hundred made by *Merrie England*.'

Merrie England was 'addressed to John Smith, of Oldham, a

120

hard-headed workman, fond of facts'. Blatchford imagined John Smith as a staunch Liberal, hostile to socialism without knowing what it meant. He explained the ugliness and brutality of capitalism, and how it was possible for society to be ordered differently. His language was simple and direct:

> You live in Oldham and you are a spinner. If I ask you why you live in Oldham, and why you work in the factory, you will say that you do it in order to 'get a living'.
>
> I think also that you will agree with me on three points:- Firstly, that Oldham is not a nice place to live in; secondly, that the factory is not a nice place to work in; thirdly, that you don't get as good a living as you desire.[33]

Merrie England was not just concerned with economics; it also considered domestic life and the situation of women:

> Poor Mrs John Smith, her life is one long slavery. Cooking, cleaning, managing, mending, washing clothes, waiting on husband and children, her work is never done. And amid it all she suffers the pains and anxieties of child-bearing, and the suckling of children. There are no servants, and few workers, so hard wrought and so ill-paid as the wife of a British artisan. What are her *hours of labour*, my trade union friend? What pleasure has she, what rest, what prospect?[34]

His solution lay in communal living, though with housework still the woman's responsibility:

> We set up one laundry, with all the best machinery; we set up one big drying field; we set up one great kitchen, one general dining hall, and one pleasant tea garden. Then we buy all the provisions and other things in large quantities, and we appoint certain wives as cooks and laundresses, or . . . . we let the wives take the duties in turn. Don't you see how much better and how much cheaper the meals would be? Don't you see how much easier the lives of our poor women would be? Don't you see how much more comfortable our homes would be? Don't you see how much more sociable and friendly we should become?[35]

Blatchford's dismissive attitudes — 'we let the wives take the duties in turn' — provoked continual protests from women readers and correspondents. Yet the irony remained: Blatchford provided an excellent introduction to feminism and women's suffrage for young women of Cissy Foley's generation.

The only other writer who tackled the problem of women's role was Edward Carpenter, an idealistic socialist who lived near Sheffield. His pamphlets, published by the Manchester Labour Press, were gathered in 1896 into his major book, *Love's Coming of Age*, an attack on conventional marriage and 'our whole commercial system, with its barter and sale of human labour and human love for gains'. His ideas on women were far more radical than Blatchford's (he even suggested men should share domestic responsibilities) but he lacked Blatchford's popular tub-thumping appeal.

The *Clarion* was eagerly awaited each week in thousands of working class homes. Both Selina Cooper and Ada Nield became keen readers. In the Foley household the *Clarion*, *Merrie England*, and Blatchford's later *God and My Neighbour* were regularly read and discussed. Even Annie Kenney, never a great reader, later described how, when she was touring Lancashire and Yorkshire to drum up support for women's suffrage, she stayed with mill workers and discussed politics with them: 'Many, many are the happy evenings I have spent in some lonely cottage on the edge of the moors . . . The fire would have been lit . . . the lamp would be burning, and we would talk about politics, Labour questions, Emerson, Ruskin, Edward Carpenter, right into the night. None of these conversations ended without thanks for Blatchford and Hardie.'[36]

Around Blatchford and his writings there grew a host of other activities. The best known was the Clarion Cycling Club, a happy adaptation of the great craze of the 1890s to political propaganda. Cycling advertisements appeared in the *Clarion* at the beginning of 1893, and from then on its columns were dotted with paragraphs extolling the virtues of different machines. It was a sport that appealed to women as well as men, though not everyone approved of this sudden emancipation, as one contributor to the Manchester Co-operative Society *Monthly Herald* made clear:

Rock-a-bye, baby, for father is near,
Mother is 'biking' she never is here!
Out in the park she's scorching all day
Or at some meeting is talking away!
She's the king-pin at the women's rights show,
Teaching poor husbands the way they should go!
Close then, your eyes; there's dishes to do.
Rock-a-bye, baby; 'tis pa sings to you.[37]

It was perhaps inevitable that cycling was coupled with 'women's rights'. For a Victorian lady to propel herself along at speed, on her own, still shocked many of the social conventions. Working girls were less hampered, but still had to be quite daring to make such a definite bid for independence. Cissy Foley does not seem to have been swept up in the cycling mania, though her younger sister Alice, who was so greatly influenced by her, did take up the craze. She managed to save up 6d a week, until she had 25s, enough for a second-hand bicycle, which she learned to ride while the mill was on short time. 'As I returned home, wheeling the bike,' she wrote, 'mother greeted me with "Well, tha' art a seet, thee an' that crazy thing." '[38]

Once she could ride, she joined the local Clarion Cycling Club. The first of these had been formed in Birmingham, and launched with a tour of the West Midlands over the Easter weekend of 1894. The idea spread and clubs soon formed throughout the country. The organization was loose and friendly. 'Rules and riding disciplines were few and simple,' wrote Alice Foley; 'no passing the Captain; obedience to his whistle; cycling in pairs on busy roads, and all hands to the pump in case of punctures, breakdowns or accidents.'[39]

For the Clarionettes, as Blatchford's readers came to be known, the cycling clubs provided a much needed escape from the ugliness of the smoky industrial towns. The Manchester groups tended to head south for rural Cheshire and Derbyshire, while those from the northern towns made for the Ribble valley and the hills beyond. These outings were often the only holidays they could afford, and soon it became essential to organize the excursions on a more regular basis.

So in the summer of 1895 a few Manchester Clarionettes borrowed a van and a horse to pull it (reputedly 'quiet as a lamb, but a devil to go') and set off for Tabley in Cheshire, where they met up with eighty *Clarion* supporters who pitched their tents alongside the van. The camp was a great success, and was repeated the following year, although this time it was reported glumly that 'we were six weeks under canvas – and not one fine weekend!'[40] There was obviously a demand for something more permanent, and this was provided the following year. On Queen Victoria's Jubilee Day the first Clarion Club House was opened near Knutsford, funded through a committee of wealthier supporters, including Blatchford and Mrs Pankhurst.[41]

Another Clarion Club House was opened in the north west, at Clayton-le-Dale in the Ribble valley near Ribchester, and three others, in Yorkshire, Warwickshire, and the Home Counties. Members paid 5s a year and were offered friendship and the chance of a holiday on moderate terms that were well within the reach of most working people. For Ethel Derbyshire, the Ribchester Clarion House became a focal point for her family and their friends in the Blackburn ILP. Her daughter described how, 'we always had what you call a field day there. It was an outing – you took your own food, and you made your tea, and we had races, you know, winning the races at the Clarion.'[42]

Clarionettes did not just enjoy themselves and get out into the country. The Cycling Clubs combined exercise with taking socialist propaganda out to the remote country districts. Alice Foley described how the groups of cyclists dismounted in a village, formed the nucleus of an audience for a speaker, distributed literature, and 'on village greens disturbed the sabbath quiet with our socialist hustings'.[43]

The Clarionettes' unique mixture of fun and politics was effective but limited. It had a tremendous appeal to young people like Cissy Foley, and inspired a whole generation with socialism. However, it lacked a consistent political creed: groups of individuals were bonded together by friendship rather than by party discipline and organization. Sporadic trips to the countryside to distribute pamphlets often merely aroused antagonism, and, unlike a more sustained campaign, could leave little lasting impression.

For younger women, in their twenties at the turn of the century, the *Clarion*, along with the adult education movement, the Labour Churches, books borrowed from the Co-op Libraries, had a tremendous impact. For someone as isolated as Cissy Foley it opened a whole new world of possibilities that had been closed to women of her mother's generation.

But the Clarion activities' main appeal was to the young and energetic; older more experienced socialists had reservations about it. Both Christabel and Sylvia Pankhurst joined the Clarion Cycling Club, even though their father obviously took a dim view of the craze which drew them away from the serious political interests so dear to him.[44] Similarly, older women, like Sarah Reddish and Sarah Dickenson, had formed their political ideas through hard experience in the labour movement, and did not need the stimulus of the *Clarion* groups.

VIII

Women and socialism

The early radical suffragists came to the campaign by a different route from the women of Cissy Foley's generation. The oldest of them, Sarah Reddish, had many years of industrial experience behind her before the *Clarion* ever appeared, as had Sarah Dickenson. For them, and for all the radical suffragists of her generation, politicization began in the workplace and in the experience of organizing around it. Sarah Reddish moved from the mill and factory to the Women's Trade Union League and the Co-operative Guild. Others, including Selina Cooper, Ethel Derbyshire and Ada Nield Chew, went from the cotton mill or sweatshop to the new Independent Labour Party.

Here they learned to see their experience of work in a wider context and to relate their industrial struggles to political change. In particular they were able to develop their ideas about women's position, for the ILP, more than any other party, was sympathetic to the aspirations of feminism.

Yet even the ILP was ambivalent on the question of women's suffrage. In 1895 its Annual Conference had voted that the party 'is in favour of every proposal for extending electoral rights to both men and women'.[1] Some members, like Keir Hardie, believed wholeheartedly in this commitment. Others were content to agree with it in principle, but preferred to concentrate their energies into the more immediate problems of poverty, unemployment and electing labour MPs; still others found the very idea threatening and distasteful. Suffragists within the ILP recognized this ambivalence from the beginning. Enid Stacy complained in the pages of the *Clarion* in 1896: 'The Labour Party inscribes Adult Suffrage on its political programme; but in the mind of several of its masculine members there is a curious half-defined antipathy to it — an antipathy often but half conscious of its own entity, which nevertheless picks up and exhibits any item of news which is supposed to tell against the "New Woman".'[2]

The immediate problem the ILP faced in the 1890s was to co-ordinate existing socialist groups into one national organization. Allegiances varied from region to region, and even within one local group they could stretch from alliances with Liberalism to the extremes of utopian socialism. In Leeds, William Morris's Socialist League had a strong base and so the local ILP always had a noticeable leaning to atheism and anarchism. In the Lancashire cotton towns and the West Riding wool villages on either side of the Pennines the traditions of Non-conformism and temperance were particularly strong, and gave their ILP branches an atmosphere of self disciplined 'high thinking and low living'. Sectarian labels, to which precise meanings were attached in London, became less important further away from the big cities. Isolated socialist groups in an outlying mill town tended to blur the doctrinal lines; certainly in Nelson Selina Cooper managed to be a member of both the ILP and the Social Democratic Federation, and in Blackburn Philip Snowden was adopted as a joint ILP-SDF Parliamentary candidate.

Local ILP branches had considerable autonomy, and so there was scope for a wide range of opinion, both among the leadership and the local branch members. This revealed itself most clearly in the bargains and compromises that the national leadership had to make with the Lib-Lab trade union supporters in order to forge the basis for the Labour Representation Committee. Men like the Committee's Secretary, Ramsay MacDonald, were prepared to conciliate to a greater extent than purists like Hardie, and certainly far more than many of the branch members for whom socialism was a way of life, almost a religion. Other disagreements were not so fundamental but, as Enid Stacy had discovered, a few of the national leaders opposed Hardie's advocacy of women's suffrage, some with vehemence, some merely with a reluctance to take any action.

Philip Snowden, for instance, paid little attention to women's suffrage till the mid 1900s. Born in 1864 at Cowling, a small West Riding textile village on the Lancashire border, he brought to the early ILP a fine intelligence and cutting wit, and was soon elected on to its executive. His speeches, which always had a strong religious and emotional tinge, were full of references to 'the shame of injured manhood and womanhood', but at'the turn of the century he devoted little energy to improving women's injured lot by helping them to get the vote.

A far stronger opponent was Bruce Glasier, whose experience of the poverty and squalor of Glasgow had, he declared, made him a socialist. Like Snowden and many other ILP members in the 1890s, his politics were bound up with a strong sense of morality, even of religion. Sylvia Pankhurst described how, as a child, she 'loved to hear him speak of the beautiful life of Socialism, which was surely coming. For him... the future of his ideal was grounded in the Middle Ages, which his mind invested with a golden radiance.'[3] To him the issue of women's suffrage was an irrelevance. It did not matter, he argued, whether everybody was enfranchised, so long as the division was along sex, not class lines. Voteless women would be adequately represented by men of their own class, whose interests were the same as theirs. Women, he suggested helpfully, could specialize in areas other than politics.

With the exception of a few committed supporters, such as Dr Pankhurst and Enid Stacy, Keir Hardie was the only advocate of women's suffrage at a national level in the ILP until Isabella Ford was elected to the executive in the early 1900s. (The only woman on the first ILP executive, Katharine St John Conway, had had no particular interest in the question.) These divisions among the ILP executive had an influence when it came to resolutions, motions, voting and party conferences. However, although women were rare among the policy makers, they were strongly represented in the branches. From the beginning the ILP accepted men and women as members on an equal basis, and unlike other political parties did not relegate women to support organizations. Branches welcomed them and encouraged them to take an active part in local politics, not necessarily only on women's issues. Mrs Pankhurst was an early member of Manchester ILP, founded in 1892, and made her name at the free speech demonstrations at Boggart Hole Clough in the north of the city in 1896; here she defied the authorities in their attempt to ban socialist meetings from the area. She was fully prepared, she told magistrates, 'to take all the consequences of my own act in speaking at the meeting. I will pay no fine which there is no law to impose, will not be bound over to keep a peace which I have not broken'.[4]

Women speakers were always particularly welcome: Elsie Plant, a later member of Manchester ILP, remembered how she made her debut:

> The corner of Tib Street, Manchester, was our favourite spot and every week there, every Sunday night there were outdoor meetings there, and being young and a woman, you know, in the heat of youth, I volunteered for outdoor speaking. . . . A man called Sam Robinson used to be in charge of them and of course he was always anxious to get hold of a woman speaker because you always got a crowd pretty quick. . .
> . . . I always thought, 'Well, I can't speak', but if you were called upon outdoor, you'd find out you could. You'd carry on, and as soon as you got a bit tongue-tied, somebody'd throw something at you and you'd be off again.[5]

Such a rough-and-ready experience of public speaking provided a valuable training for women members of the ILP.

A year and a half after Manchester, Crewe started holding fortnightly committee meetings. The following May, Ada Nield launched her 'Crewe Factory Girl' campaign and within two weeks of her first letter the branch offered her its backing. A fortnight later a local socialist minister, a member of the branch committee, wrote in to assert that 'It has been agreed at [ILP] meetings that the rights of women workers must be recognized, that common cause must be made with these our sisters, and that something definite must be done sooner or later — and the sooner the better.'[6] The ILP continued to back Ada Nield's fight and after she had revealed her identity she joined the branch and became one of its most active members, finding among them the congenial atmosphere she had so lacked during her lonely time as a tailoress.

About the same time, a Blackburn winder called Billy Derbyshire joined his local ILP branch; he married Ethel in 1903 and she would have become a member too, but they could not afford two subscriptions. Even so, she took an active part in branch activities, and must have heard the speakers, including Selina Cooper, who addressed the branch on women's suffrage in the 1900s.[7]

The ILP may have been keen to recruit women members, but even so those who joined really had to assert themselves if they wanted to do more than make the tea and run fund-raising bazaars as their mothers had done in earlier organizations. 'The capable women sit by with folded hands,' complained Hannah Mitchell from her experience of Ashton ILP, 'until a social or tea party is needed, when they are entrusted with the hard work of getting it ready, while the men occupy themselves in electing a chairman to preside over the evening's

1. Lees and Wrigley Spinning Mill, Oldham, *circa* 1890. The Greenbank Mills were built between 1804 and 1887 and undertook everything from spinning and doubling to beaming and winding. The mills were closed down in the 1950s and are now virtually derelict.

2. Peterloo Veterans, 1884.
The four women, left to right,
Susannah Whittaker (81), Mary
Collins (83), Catherine McMurdo
(88) and Alice Schofield (79).

3. *below*: Sarah Dickenson.

4. *opposite above*: Ada Nield and
George Chew.

5. *opposite below*: Selina Cooper,
far left, and fellow suffragists on
a campaign in the west country,
circa 1910.

6. Lancashire and Cheshire Delegates on the Women's Franchise Deputation to the Prime Minister, 1906.
Seated: Eva Gore-Booth, Sarah Reddish, unknown, Selina Cooper; it is difficult to identify the others, even though they are forty of the most active radical suffragists. The banners,

left to right: Manchester, Salford and District Women's Trade and Labour Council; unknown; Union of Patent Cop Winders, Hank and Bobbin Winders, Gassers, Doublers and Reelers; Lancashire and Cheshire Women Textile and other Workers' Representation Committee.

9. Ada Nield Chew campaigning at the Crewe by-election, 1913.

entertainment.'[8] She realized that 'if women did not bestir themselves the Socialists would be quite content to accept Manhood Suffrage in spite of all their talk about equality'. Yet as soon as women started putting pressure on Labour candidates for support, they were told very grandly 'I am an adult suffragist'. 'We heard a lot about adult suffrage. ...from men who never seemed to have thought about it before,' she commented bitterly.[9]

In their uphill struggle for something more than token equality women in the local ILP branches had the support of a small band of highly educated middle class women who became itinerant ILP lecturers. They were socialists first and foremost, but they were all keenly interested in women's rights. One was Caroline Martyn, whose intensely religious vision of socialism made her one of the most popular visiting speakers. She was a firm believer in rational dress, and once proclaimed to the *Clarion's* Julia Dawson that 'She would never have had the strength to become a public speaker had she not discarded those instruments of torture used to compress the waists of women.'[10]

Another was Enid Stacy, the woman who had spoken out against male prejudice in the *Clarion*. An exceptionally good speaker, she was probably the greatest single influence in drawing together the two strands of feminism and socialism. Sylvia Pankhurst remembered her as a big handsome woman whose early death was contributed to by the exhausting routine of open-air speaking, constant travelling, hurried meals and uncomfortable beds.[11]

Although she had had an education far superior to the majority of ILP women, Enid Stacy never lost the ability to identify with those women who were expected to get on with their housework and take no part in political experiences while their husbands became enthusiastic, active socialists. In 1894 the *Labour Prophet,* the monthly paper of the Labour Churches, published an article by her written as a dialogue between two male socialists:

> B: Since I've joined this movement I've not cared much for home. Wife scolds at me so, and goes on about my being away so much, not caring for her, neglecting the children... Why, the very name 'Labour Movement', or 'Socialism', is enough to send her into a regular tantrum. You would think me one of the worst men going, and yet I never fail to give her nearly all my wage on Fridays, and she certainly cannot say that she ever saw *me* drunk in all her life. What more she can expect I don't know!
>
> A: Well, it strikes me she may *perhaps* expect such things as affection and your companionship — you don't mind me speaking straight?

B: No, of course, not... Only how can you talk of companionship? Why, what have we in common?... You can't expect women to take any interest, as a whole, on those matters. They aren't capable of it. They are too conventional and afraid of the parson, and —

A: Stop, stop. Don't go on so fast... You have been talking of your troubles, and have put your side of the question forward. Perhaps it doesn't strike you there *are* two sides?[12]

About this time Enid Stacy was drawn into the women's suffrage movement and became friends with Esther Roper.[13] Although the ILP Annual Conference had recently passed its resolution in favour of extending the suffrage to both men and women, little had been done to define what this declaration involved. Enid Stacy was one of the few able to fill that gap, and she developed some of the vital theoretical framework to bring socialist and feminist ideas together for the first time.

Her essay, 'A Century of Women's Rights', was part of an influential anthology of socialist writings collected together by Edward Carpenter and published in *Forecasts of the Coming Century* by the Manchester Labour Press in 1897. Here she was able to take the arguments she had been developing in her *Clarion* articles to their logical conclusion. She traced the movement for women's emancipation from its middle class origins in 'Manchester Radicalism', the doctrine of Free Trade and free competition. 'The movement was thus in this earlier stage both middle class and individualistic, its chief strength lying in the claim of the individual woman to the right of fighting her way in life and supporting herself by her own exertions.'

Although not unsympathetic to the women who agitated for their narrow legal rights, she showed how they represented only one phase of the movement — a phase that was inevitably left behind as social conditions changed. As the 'gospel of individual rights' lost its supremacy and ideas about the state's responsibility for its citizens' welfare grew, so the women's movement changed as well.

> The question had been placed upon a broader basis, not woman's *rights*, as a middle class spinster, with a livelihood to fight for, against hostile male forces, but woman's *duties*, not only as a spinster, but also as a wife and mother, and, in order that she amply fulfil these duties, her freedom as an individual and her equality as a citizen.[14]

A large part of this change, she argued, was due to the influence of socialism, whose leaders were 'believers in equality between men and women *at least in theory*.'

Enid Stacy discussed the importance of women's work, and the need for protective legislation, which had been such anathema to earlier feminists like Lydia Becker.[15] Women increasingly saw themselves as citizens, and realized 'how untenable is any position which claims the citizen's status without fulfilling citizen's duties'. Women's position had improved:

> Public opinion has largely altered for the better; education for women has progressed, and is steadily progressing; women have obtained entrance into many eminently suitable callings, chiefly by their own brave efforts; they have gained a strong footing in Local Self-Government; they now, as married women, control and administer their own property or results of their earnings; and are even recognized as legal guardians of their children!

But, she added, 'much remains to be done'. Enid Stacy ended her essay by listing the developments she saw necessary for the complete emancipation of women: the right to choose whether or not to have children; equality within marriage and fairer divorce laws; the right of mothers to guardianship of their children; full legal and political rights, including the vote in both local and parliamentary elections; and freedom as workers, so that as much protective legislation as possible applied to men as well as women workers. Only then would men and women achieve the socialist goal of a true 'co-operative commonwealth'.

'A Century of Women's Rights' remained the most comprehensive statement of women's claims within the ILP and labour movement for many years. Like Esther Roper in the North of England Society, Enid Stacy as a middle class woman had a vital role to play during a period when working class women's organizations were only just beginning to provide their own experienced and capable leaders.

Enid Stacy never ignored the gap between theory and practice in the stand the ILP took on women's suffrage. Although it remained the most sympathetic and helpful of all political parties, its support for women's claims could never be relied on without question. 'The Independent Labour Party was not formed to champion women,' Margaret McMillan commented. 'It took that battle in its stride, and might drop it in its ardour. It was born to make war on capitalism and competition.'[16] This definite order of political priorities might explain why only a few of the radical suffragists came from the ILP, among them Ada Nield, Selina Cooper, Alice Collinge and Ethel Derbyshire;

and why the relationship between the suffrage campaign and local ILP leaders was not as close as it might have been.[17]

Others seem to have had little contact with ILP groups, apart from speaking occasionally about the suffrage campaign to branches in the cotton towns. Sarah Reddish, Cissy Foley and others turned instead to the wide range of labour organizations which flourished outside the framework of party politics. Of these, the Clarion Van, the Women's Trade Union League and the Women's Co-operative Guild were tremendously important in providing a strong local base from which the suffrage campaign could be mounted; they also provided essential experience in public speaking and organizing for the suffragists. And because they were essentially practical organizations without an official line on political questions, they could accommodate the competing claims of feminism and socialism more easily than could the ILP or Labour Representation Committee.

There was however considerable overlap between the various Labour organizations. Blatchford's *Clarion* had from the beginning given its backing to independent labour representation, and it was from an idea put forward by the paper's woman editor Julia Dawson that the Clarion Van came into existence. Like many others, she realized the limitations of the cycling clubs in taking propaganda to the countryside, and early in 1896 used her 'Woman's Letter' to suggest that a caravan, staffed by women readers, should take the socialist message into 'the small market towns and country districts' in a more systematic way.[18] She was offered the use of the van that had taken the Manchester Clarionettes camping the previous summer, as well as a tent for male companions who would look after the horse, light fires and wash dishes. Her request for volunteers was quickly answered, and preparations went ahead. The van was refurbished, and by June, Julia Dawson was able to give her readers a rapturous description:

> The heart of woman could not wish for a prettier room to live in than the interior of the Van. The 'walls' are painted a delicate cream, the ceiling striped with cream and red. There are tricky little cupboards fixed up in the corners for china, and what not, all likewise painted cream... The windows are draped with pretty spotted muslin curtains, edged with 'bobbed' fringe; and the comfortable beds form nice wide cushioned seats by day. There is plenty of room for four to sleep in the Van at once, if they do not bring too much luggage with them.[19]

The names of the 'Vanners' were published in the *Clarion* along with their route for the benefit of supporters. The majority were women, and included Ada Nield, who by now had two more years' experience of labour politics since her dramatic confrontation with her Crewe employer. During this period she had met through the Crewe ILP her future husband, George Chew. Like her, he was critical of factory life and full of enthusiasm for the new party; he had given up the job he hated as a weaver to help organize new ILP branches. Although she knew little of her father's early life, Doris Chew was able to describe how he accompanied her mother when the Clarion Van set out. The expedition, she explained, included 'one or two young men to look after the horses and so on. I think he must have been very much in love because nothing else would have persuaded him to look after a horse.'[20] They were married the next year, and Ada Nield Chew seems to have given up travelling with the van at about this point.

The van set off from Chester on its first journey on June 18th 1896. The expedition turned out to be hard work: Julia Dawson wrote that 'The Vanners assure me that every mile travelled by the horse they themselves covered more than a mile on foot.'[21] But they were well received as they moved through Shropshire and Cheshire to Manchester. They continued on to Stockport where on 18 July they spoke to a crowd of five hundred, and sang Edward Carpenter's socialist hymn, 'England Arise':

England Arise, the long, long night is over,
Faint in the east behold the dawn appears;
Out of your evil dream of toil and sorrow
Arise, O England, for the day is here.

The van moved on through Yorkshire into Durham and Northumberland, where it spent the rest of the summer. Ada Nield joined the team at the end of August, and took on the job of writing the weekly reports to Julia Dawson. 'Miss Nield is so much encouraged by the Vanners' reception that she is never going to feel despondent again,' ran one cryptic message in the *Clarion*.[22] The tour finally ended on September 23rd, after fifteen weeks' hard work. It had been a great success, and there was a warm response to Julia Dawson's appeal for funds for a second, larger van to join it on the road the following summer.

Soon the van became an institution, keenly welcomed by local socialists wherever it went. Hannah Mitchell, then living in a mining village in Derbyshire, remembered the tremendous enthusiasm that the Clarion Van generated when it arrived in an isolated community, despite some doubts about 'the propriety of . . . two girls travelling about in the van with . . . two men.' She described the Sunday meetings:

. . . when scores of *Clarion* cyclists . . . descended on Newhall to support the Van . . . We were young and full of hope, thinking we had only to broadcast the Socialist message and the workers would flock to our banner. We followed the Van all week, through the surrounding villages, and when it moved on to Lichfield at the weekend, we hired a wagonette and twenty of us drove to Lichfield for the Sunday meetings.[23]

Although the principle idea behind the expedition was to bring socialism to country districts beyond the reach of other propaganda, the van incidentally provided a valuable training ground in open air speaking for working class women. It gave them the experience of arriving somewhere new, setting up a makeshift platform and trying to collect a sympathetic crowd. Certainly this was how Ada Nield Chew came to enjoy speaking and gained experience that later stood her in good stead in the suffrage movement.

Other pioneer Clarion Vanners included the much-loved Caroline Martyn (after her early death in 1896 a second van was named after her as a memorial), Miss Mayo, an organizer for the Women's Co-operative Guild, and Sarah Reddish. She too, although by now well used to arguing out her ideas in the course of her work for the Guild, found that the experience of speaking in the open air to a crowd that might be friendly, amused, indifferent or even hostile, stood her in good stead when she joined the suffrage campaign soon afterwards.

For the Vanners, the speaking tours could be little more than a working holiday. Ada Nield Chew and Sarah Reddish were both sufficiently committed to improving the lot of working women like themselves to look for something more permanent. The Women's Trade Union League provided such a structure, and they both followed the example of Annie Marland and Helen Silcock and became League organizers; their wages were paid from the fees of affiliated trade unions. The League, which had been complaining how it was handicapped by the difficulty of obtaining competent organizers,[24] welcomed them with open arms.

Sarah Reddish was appointed as a part-time organizer in 1899, and the League *Review* noted with relief that she was able to address Lancashire meetings which no regular League officials could manage to attend.[25] She travelled all over the north of England, and the reports she sent to the *Review* include a brief account of the Wigan Weavers' annual tea party, at which Helen Silcock presided, and where discussion of the low wages was always much to the fore.

A year after Ada Nield Chew's marriage in 1898 her daughter was born, and she gave up political activity until Doris was two. The League, already familiar with her as 'a well-known speaker on labour questions' appointed her in 1900. She was soon travelling up to Scotland from her home in Rochdale once or twice a year and regularly visiting the Potteries (she even went to live down there for a while) as part of the League's campaign to improve the pottery workers' appalling record of industrial accidents and diseases. Like Sarah Reddish before her, Ada Nield Chew spent some time in Wigan with Helen Silcock, and the reports she wrote from there for the *Review* make dispiriting reading. 'A meeting was advertised, but was a failure . . . Canvassed again, together and separately. Our week's work (one of the hardest I have put in for some time) met with discouraging results . . . Past difficulties have caused much bitterness of feeling which needs sympathetic but resolute handling.'[26]

Much more rewarding was her campaign among the women workers in Crewe in 1905. She was no longer a lone voice but now, eleven years later, had the full force of the League behind her. She sent back a triumphant report of a large meeting of the Crewe Women's Co-operative Guild at which she spoke on 'Should Women Join Trade Unions?' At the end of the debate her motion was 'carried with much enthusiasm', and it was agreed 'that the Guild should take steps to organize the factory girls of Crewe (tailoresses).' A few months later she travelled down to Crewe again, and organized a successful public meeting under the auspices of the League and Crewe Trades Council. Speakers included herself and none other than the General Secretary of the Society of Tailors, which had by now softened its attitude to women members. It must have been with mixed feelings of resentment of the past and triumph at the present that she heard over forty tailoresses give in their names saying that they wanted to join the union.[27]

At the turn of the century an informal network of women like Ada Nield Chew, Sarah Reddish and Helen Silcock had developed, linked together by the League and by Julia Dawson who regularly bludgeoned *Clarion* readers into supporting their efforts. On the whole they tended to work in the north west, but kept in close touch with national figures like Margaret McMillan in Bradford, Isabella Ford in Leeds, and, in London, Gertrude Tuckwell, the League's Honorary Secretary. But although several of the League's northern organizers moved from a commitment to women's industrial rights to a conviction that votes were essential for women workers, the League itself was in no sense a suffrage organization. It was too concerned with the everyday difficulties of organizing and sustaining small isolated unions, and too dependent on gaining and keeping the support of male unions to widen its brief and include votes for women.

The Women's Co-operative Guild had no such reservation about supporting women's suffrage. Unlike the League, it did not have to retain the good will of the big trade unions: it could form its own policy solely on the basis of its members' opinions. The majority were the wives of working class men enfranchised under the 1867 and 1884 Acts, and from the 1890s onwards the Guild provided one of the most important sources of support for women's suffrage.

Since the festival held in Manchester in 1892 the Guild had developed strongly in the cotton towns. It attracted women like Mrs Ashworth, who conducted the survey of child care in Burnley. She joined the Burnley Guild and in 1894 presided at the national congress. Another was Mrs Bury, a mill worker from Darwen. She attended her first Guild Conference at Leicester in 1893 and described how 'It was a revelation . . . At the close of the meetings I felt as I imagine a war-horse must feel when he hears the beat of drums. What I saw and heard at Leicester changed the whole course of my life for the next few years.'[28]

Selina Cooper had joined her local Guild by 1898,[29] and soon became one of the most popular speakers at meetings in the weaving towns. She spoke on a variety of subjects, from the more obvious, like first aid and personal hygiene, to the ones of particular interest to local working wives and mothers. 'I know she once exhibited a haybox,' her daughter remembered. '. . . It was very practical for weavers in those days . . . there was hay in, and then the pan was put right down into it, and lid on, and it cooked itself.'[30]

By far the most important Guildswoman from the cotton towns was Sarah Reddish.[31] The Guild was her major public commitment, and meant more to her than her work with the Clarion Van or the League. Like children from other skilled working class families in the industrial north, she grew up in an atmosphere where Co-operation was almost a way of life.[32] Her mother had urged her father to join the movement as early as 1866. Mr Reddish became an active member of the Bolton Co-operative education committee, and later became foreman in the

Society's warehouse. Sarah joined the Society in 1879,[33] and over the next few years her dedication and reliability earned her a respected place in the local, and later national hierarchy.

She became president of the Bolton Guild in 1886 and held the position for the next fifteen years. She was elected to the Guild's Central Committee in 1889, and was Guild President for 1897. As a regional Guild organizer from 1893-95 she succeeded in increasing membership and activity through northern England. Yet Sarah Reddish did more than just oil the wheels of Guild administration. Through her the Bolton Guild became a meeting place where suffrage speakers were always certain of a sympathetic audience. She also contributed to the development of Guild ideas, and read papers at annual conferences on subjects as diverse as 'Surplus Capital' (whether Co-op shop profits should be paid out in dividends or used for educational or other purposes), on 'Citizenship' and on 'Women on Borough Councils'.[34]

To Guild members like Sarah Reddish, it seemed vital for women to take up their opportunities, to stand for local elections, both in their own right and as valuable political experience. If women could prove themselves capable of sitting on local School and Poor Law Boards, surely it strengthened their claims to the parliamentary franchise.

At first women candidates met with prejudice and some hostility. 'Men bitterly resented this advent of women in their special preserves,' one Lancashire Guildswoman and Poor Law Guardian remembered.[35] When Sarah Reddish came top of the defeated candidates in the Bolton School Board elections in 1897, it was expected that she would be co-opted on to it, as was usually the case. But because she was a woman, the Board refused to consider her. Happily, the Bolton electorate voted her in at the next election.[36]

Slowly women candidates became accepted. Mrs Pankhurst was nominated by Manchester ILP as one of three candidates put up by a progressive alliance, formed in 1894, and which included in its programme free education, free pre-school breakfasts and 'equal pay for equal work, irrespective of sex.'[37]

Middle class women became eligible to sit on the Boards of Guardians that administered the Poor Law from 1875, and the 1894 Local Government Act extended these rights to many working class women.[38] Ada Nield was elected to the Crewe Board of Guardians in that very year, and must have been one of the first working class women guardians in the country. Others were not slow to follow, backed by the full encouragement of the Women's Co-operative Guild.

At its 1894 conference a paper was read urging Guild members to stand for election. Forty five Guildswomen stood in the local Guardian elections that December, and no fewer than twenty two were successful.

Such women had considerable effect in humanizing the administration of the harsh Poor Laws, particularly in working class areas where previously few women had been eligible. Mrs Bury found that 'before women sat on our Board all girls with sad histories had to come alone before a large body of men. Now, after I had pleaded with the Board and got a resolution passed, the women Guardians and matrons dealt with the cases in a separate room.'[39] Mrs Pankhurst, who was elected to the Chorlton Board of Guardians in 1894, found equally intolerable conditions: the girls working in the workhouse were not provided with nightdresses or underwear because the matron had not liked to mention such indelicate matters in front of the men on the Board.[40]

Many women still lacked the confidence to put themselves forward. The Bolton Association for the Return of Women as Poor Law Guardians, formed in 1897, sadly recorded that the Secretary 'had received refusals from all the ladies' who had been written to. Although its elaborate title does not specifically say so, the Association seems to have been particularly interested in the return of working class women; it worked closely with the local Women's Co-operative Guild, whose president Sarah Reddish was on the Association's committee from the start. Because of all her other commitments she did not herself stand for election until 1905 — but when she did she was immediately elected.[41]

Many of these women stood for election to the Boards both as women and as representatives of working class political groups. Hannah Mitchell, already known locally as a feminist speaker, was nominated as an ILP candidate for the Ashton Board of Guardians in 1904. Her election manifesto proclaimed her to be both a socialist and feminist: 'Out of 971 inmates of the workhouse, 371 are women, with 81 children. Show your sympathy with these by sending a woman to look after them . . . Vote for Mrs Mitchell The Workers' Candidate.'[42]

In Nelson, Selina Cooper was elected to the Nelson Committee of the Burnley Board of Guardians in 1901. As a Guardian she tried to improve the unappetizing meals the twenty five workhouse children were given; she was particularly concerned about their diet and managed to double their meagre butter allowance of two ounces per child per week. By 1902 she was demanding that the patronizing system of outdoor relief (in Nelson confined to the aged poor over sixty three) should be abolished and replaced by a small pension which at least got rid of the taint of pauperism. In her attacks on the Board's patronizing attitude to its clients, Selina Cooper was supported by two fellow socialists, both members of the Social Democratic Federation. The Board dealt with its troublesome left wing by occasionally holding meetings without Selina Cooper and the others ever being notified.

Despite this, she decided to put up for election again in 1904. This time she was joined by her friend Harriette Beanland from the Nelson ILP; they both stood as Labour Representation Candidates and wrote their election manifesto together. The manifesto is extremely interesting because it makes plain the very strong connection between Labour representation and women's participation in local politics, and, by implication, women's suffrage.

FELLOW CITIZENS,

At the request of the *Nelson Labour Representation Committee*, and a large number of *Ratepayers* in the *Town*, we offer ourselves as *Candidates* at the forthcoming *Guardians Election.*

The *Poor Law* was established to relieve and succour the distressed, and as the bulk of the recipients of *Poor Law Relief* are of the *Labouring Classes*, we are of the opinion that it is to the best interest of the *Poor* to be directly represented by people who can *realise* their *sufferings* and *privations* to the full extent.

We would also remind you that a large number of applicants for relief are *women* and *children*, and from past experience, we have no hesitation in saying, that it is almost imperative that *women* should be on the *Board* in order to administer acts and receive confidences that could not be extended to men in the same capacity.

It will be our aim to see that the *Lives* of the *aged* and *infirm* are made as bright as it is possible to make them. The *Children* shall have our special attention in order that their *Lives* and characters may be fully developed and that they may grow up to be useful *Citizens* and go out into the world without the taint of *Pauperism*.

We would welcome a system of extending *Out Door Relief* to deserving cases in preference to *forcing* them into the *Workhouse*.

We are in favour of the *Public* being admitted to the meetings of the *Board of Guardians*.

Recent Strikes in Burnley and District show that our Guardians are ever ready to advise Applicants for Relief to act the part of 'Blacklegs' and thus help to defeat those working men and women who resist injustice or seek to better their conditions of employment, but if elected, we shall oppose any method that has a tendency to use the weakness of poor people by forcing them into the undesirable position of 'Blacklegs.'

Other means will be adopted to place before you reasons why you should support the return of *Labour Candidates*, and, if you will use your *Votes* to this end you will have done your *Share* towards making the lives of the unfortunate *Poor* brighter and happier than they have been up to the present.

We remain,

Your Obedient Servants,

SELINA JANE COOPER,

HARRIETTE MARY BEANLAND.

March 9th, 1904.[43]

The two women, and Hannah Mitchell were elected. It was the kind of work that suited women like Selina Cooper and Hannah Mitchell who had young children. The meetings were always local, and were held regularly in a way to which a housework routine could be adapted. Hannah Mitchell's son was by now seven or eight and could be left at home while a kind neighbour came in to cook the midday dinner. Mary Cooper was only a baby when her mother first became a Guardian; she has dim memories of those early years:

> She would take me with her to the office and I wasn't of school age. I was only about three, and the office [people] used to look after me while she was in the meeting. They told me about it because I went into local government, and I met some of these people and they could remember giving me toffees and keeping me quiet.[44]

Another of Selina Cooper's· friends, Margaret Aldersley, had four children, but still somehow managed to fit in the various meetings of the Burnley Board of Guardians.

Yet however many of its members the Guild might encourage to stand for Board elections, suffragist Guildswomen found it was no compensation for the lack of the parliamentary vote. From the 1890s, when the relative success of Rollitt's Bill had encouraged the old established suffrage societies to renew their efforts, the Guild had actively campaigned for women's franchise. In this it was guided from 1889 by its formidably energetic General Secretary, Margaret Llewelyn Davies. She had grown up in a family where women's suffrage was given the highest importance: Emily Davies was her aunt and one of her uncles an equally active suffragist and friend of John Stuart Mill.[45] She had had direct contact with the lives of working women to an extent unusual for someone of her background, and was extraordinarily beloved and respected by Guild members during her long years as General Secretary. This, coupled with her ability to persuade anybody to do anything (Virginia Woolf claimed she 'could compel a steam roller to waltz') made her a valuable ally of the suffrage campaign.

In 1893 the London-based Special Appeal Secretary contacted the

Guild immediately after the Westminster Town Hall meeting, and within a few months the Guild's Executive Committee 'recommended the Appeal to the attention of the local Secretaries of the Guild in their winter circular.' The question was then discussed at meetings in the local branches. Altogether, one Guildswoman in four signed the Appeal and a total of 2,225 signatures were sent down to London.[46]

Guild support for women's suffrage continued through the 1890s. In 1897 one more women's suffrage bill passed its second reading — though as usual got little further. During the debates, the Guild branches were issued with papers on 'Why Working Women Need the Vote' which were then discussed at their sectional Conferences. 'Women's Corner' in *Co-operative News* ran this report of one such meeting:

> After this month let us hear no more of 'Working women do not want the vote.' The tone throughout the meeting was most practical and sensible. Working women want to make themselves felt in public life for definite purposes — to improve the social laws and administration, and particularly to watch over the lives of women and children. To reject from the electorate public-spirited workers like these is a folly which nothing but voluntary ignorance can account for.[47]

The Guild's interest in women's suffrage did not stop here. A few months later, in 1897, Henry Broadhurst MP spoke at a National Liberal Federation meeting in support of manhood suffrage. He was scathing on the subject of the women's suffrage amendment, which he derided as 'meaningless' and 'mischievous'. An incensed Guildswoman wrote in to 'Woman's Corner' strongly condemning this dismissive attitude, and twenty three Guild branches passed resolutions of protest. Complaints were also sent to another Liberal MP 'concerning his remark ... that the only women who wanted votes were idlers and Tory bigots, and we wish to know under which head to place the thousands of our Co-operative women who desire to be voters.'[48]

At the same time the *Englishwoman's Review* published letters in support of women's suffrage from three Guildswomen, two from Lancashire and one from London. They echoed the arguments put forward by Enid Stacy in her essay. Ada Slack, treasurer of the Accrington Guild, wrote that she wanted the vote for working class women.

> On the ground that wifehood and motherhood imply the most important social and civic duties and responsibilities, and to carry out such functions properly for the good of the community, as well as in the name of the individual, the State needs thoughtful, capable women, and that such women

141

cannot be obtained under the present social conditions, which tend to foster dolls, mere machines and drudges.[49]

The second Lancashire letter was from Mrs Bury from the Darwen Guild who argued that 'there are industries composed largely or wholly of women, and they ought to have a vote in making the laws and regulations of these industries'.

From this time on the Guilds in the cotton towns became among the strongest supporters of Esther Roper's suffrage campaign. For instance in 1898 Eva Gore-Booth went to speak on women's suffrage to the Manchester, Openshaw and Levenshulme Guilds. By now the Guild lecture lists included a paper entitled 'The Citizenship of Women, and its Responsibilities', and many Guild lecturers were impressing on members the importance of abolishing 'the political disqualification of sex, so that a vote shall no longer be denied solely on the ground of womanhood'.[50] The following year the Levenshulme Guild discussed — and passed — the motion that the vote should be extended to all women who paid taxes. By 1900 all Guildswomen were alert to the question of women's suffrage. Through the strengthening of the textile unions, the new Labour and Clarion groups, the League and the Guild, the ground was now well prepared for the radicals within the North of England Society to launch their suffrage campaign among the Lancashire textile workers.

PART 2: THE CAMPAIGN

IX

Textile workers and the suffrage campaign

The campaign Esther Roper had launched in 1893 'to bring the Special Appeal under the notice of the factory women of Lancashire and Cheshire' gathered momentum. By 1900 it had attracted the support of local Guild branches and influential women trade union organizers like Sarah Reddish and Sarah Dickenson. These women, along with Eva Gore-Booth, formed a radical group within the North of England Society. Their policy and tactics soon attracted the support of Helen Silcock, Selina Cooper, Nellie Keenan and many others, and the group as a whole took on a distinctive identity. From early 1900 until 1906 the radical suffragists ran an impressively successful suffrage campaign among the Lancashire textile workers, which had considerable impact on the older suffrage societies, the TUC, the growing Labour Representation Committee, and eventually on Parliament. It is interesting to trace the influence of this group which began as merely a handful of activists working through the North of England Society and the local Guilds.

It was during the late 1890s that Esther Roper and Eva Gore-Booth had become increasingly impressed by the growing support for women's suffrage in the cotton towns and in local Guild branches. Then, when Eva Gore-Booth was appointed Co-secretary of the Women's Trades Union Council in 1900, she began to work closely with Sarah Dickenson.[1] She also came into contact with Sarah Reddish, one of the earliest supporters of the Council, whose enthusiasm for women's

143

suffrage had crystallized during the 1890s through her close connections with the Guild.

These women formed an unusual quartet. The two younger ones were educated, well-to-do women, for whom women's suffrage was their primary political commitment. The two older women had between them nearly forty years of solid industrial experience in both mills and factories: during the 1880s and 1890s their first allegiance was to trade unionism, to the Guild, the Women's Trade Union Council and the Women's Trade Union League, and until recently women's suffrage had been low on their list of political priorities.

Now the two strands — suffrage and labour — were fused together. The problems of low pay and apathy that the League and Council organizers constantly confronted among women workers now appeared inseparable from women's lack of votes. While women workers remained disenfranchised they would always be subject to laws passed by governments which need take no account of their interests. Every Factory Act passed by Parliament, complained Eva Gore-Booth, became 'more and more fraught with consequences to the industrial lives of women; we have seen indeed the gradual widening of the social chasm between the men who have emerged into political power and position, and their women comrades.'[2]

The excellent response Esther Roper, Annie Heaton and Mrs Winbolt had met when they took the Special Appeal into the cotton towns in 1894 confirmed them in their views. Tens of thousands of women cotton workers *were* concerned about their lack of political rights, and yet critics still dismissed the women's suffrage as the preoccupation of middle class ladies with time on their hands. The demand for the vote by textile workers had somehow to be organized and made public to counteract this.

Esther Roper, Eva Gore-Booth, Sarah Reddish and Sarah Dickenson along with other activists in the North of England Society, decided to launch a petition to be signed exclusively by women working in the Lancashire cotton mills. This would show the rest of the country how powerful the demand for the vote really was among industrial women. It was a radically new tactic for a regional suffrage society to adopt, and one that the diehards in the North of England Society and National Union must have looked at askance. But the petition was unequivocal:

> To the Right Honourable the Commons of Great Britain and Ireland, in Parliament assembled. The HUMBLE PETITION of the undersigned women workers in the cotton factories of Lancashire.

Sheweth:

That in the opinion of your petitioners the continued denial of the franchise to women is unjust and inexpedient.

In the home, their position is lowered by such an exclusion from the responsibilities of national life.

In the factory, their unrepresented condition places the regulation of their work in the hands of men who are often their rivals as well as their fellow workers. . .[3]

The petition was launched with maximum impact on 1 May 1900 with an open air meeting in Blackburn. Both the time and place were chosen with considerable care. May Day, when traditionally Labour demonstrations were held, was selected as a fitting occasion for the first meeting. Blackburn too seemed the obvious place; with no fewer than sixteen thousand women working in its weaving mills, it had a stronger tradition of women's work than anywhere else in Lancashire. The earliest weavers' unions had been established there, and women members had early acquired a reputation for militancy after the part they played in the 1878 strike.

The first meeting took place in glorious sunshine,[4] and the crowd who came to listen was so enthusiastic that two further meetings were arranged for the 2nd and 3rd. All three were addressed by Mrs Hodgson Bayfield, a Guildswoman from Manchester, already working for the North of England Society and now its busiest speaker.[5] She was experienced at coping with the open-air meetings where suffragists had to handle persistent hecklers or make their voices heard above jeering crowds. During a by-election in Oldham the previous July she had spoken at no fewer than seven outdoor meetings within the space of twelve days.[6]

To get the petition everywhere, even the smallest cotton mill in the county, the North of England Society appointed four other women to help out, paying them expenses and a small salary for the work they did.[7] Sarah Reddish, by now an experienced organizer, was an obvious choice; the work dovetailed easily with the local organizing she was doing for the League. The others were Mrs Ramsbottom, Katherine Rowton, a Poor Law Guardian from Manchester and Mrs Green from Gorton, a leading member of the Beswick Co-operative Guild and on the Guild Central Committee.[8] Together with Eva Gore-Booth and Esther Roper these five women took the petition round to every group of women cotton workers they could possibly contact.

The North of England Society did not yet possess a car, and the petition workers had to rely on the network of trains provided by the various railway companies. Fortunately they were amply provided for: almost every little town had its own station, and larger towns like Oldham and Preston had three or four. The visiting speaker would get down from the train and, if lucky, be met by a local sympathizer like Mrs Winbolt or Annie Heaton, who would preside at the meeting or introduce her to women likely to sign the petition. Or, lacking a local contact, the petition worker would have to make her own way to the nearest mill, to the part of the town traditionally used by other open-air speakers, or to the room where the weavers or cardroom workers always held their branch meetings.

The petition workers arranged meetings among most of the local weavers' union branches in the northern towns, and among the cardroom union branches in the spinning towns further south. They had little idea what response to expect when they started their campaign. Although they could rely on existing groups of union members to provide the nucleus of a petition meeting, they could not automatically assume they would get a sympathetic response: the cotton unions were essentially apolitical organizations, concerned with practical day-to-day issues.

In the event, the petition workers' faith was justified. The summer of 1900, reported the *Englishwoman's Review*, was 'quite an experience':

> ...Canvassers in fifty places – one, two, three or four in each, according to the numbers of the factory population – were soon at work.
>
> The method of canvassing has been chiefly that of going to the homes of the workers in the evening, after factory hours... Some employers allowed petition sheets in the mills, and others allowed canvassers to stand in the mill yards with sheets spread on tables so that the signatures could be got as the women were leaving or returning to work.[9]

Union branches responded very sympathetically too. They might be run by men, but, certainly at a local level women were members in such numbers they could easily fill a meeting. The Preston weavers, for instance, supported at least five petition meetings, and in Wigan Helen Silcock, no doubt contacted through her recent League work with Sarah Reddish,[10] officially endorsed the meeting in June when Mrs Bayfield came to speak. About three dozen major open-air meetings were held, along with numerous smaller gatherings organized through local Guilds, Labour Churches and ILP branches.

The work was painstakingly slow. It involved much patient trudging down the cobbled back streets of the cotton towns, going from house

146

to house in the evenings to collect signatures from women who had just come home from work exhausted and were preparing the family meal. At times the petition workers must have despaired at the work involved in adding even an extra hundred signatures. But despite the enormity of the task, Esther Roper was able to tell the Annual Meeting of the North of England Society in November with triumph that:

> All our workers report themselves convinced that the women feel a real interest in the subject, many of them, particularly those who are rate-payers, keenly resent their exclusion from the franchise. There is no difficulty in obtaining signatures – only a very small proportion have refused to sign. . . One encouraging fact in the work has been the number of men who have shown themselves in sympathy with the women's claims.[11]

By this time the petition workers had collected 15,000 signatures, all from women cotton workers. Yet, in a sense, the importance of the meetings held during the summer and autumn was not only the thousands of signatures, but also the fact that the active interest of working women was aroused by the campaign, many of whom accompanied the petition down to Westminster the following spring. One was Mrs Pearce, whom Sarah Reddish knew from the Bolton ILP; another was Annie Heaton from Burnley who had worked as a Special Appeal organizer six years previously.

The most valuable recruit, though, was beyond doubt Selina Cooper, now in her early thirties. It is not certain how she was drawn into the campaign. She already had an active interest in labour politics, and would be likely to go along to listen to visiting speakers, so she may well have heard Mrs Bayfield speak at an open-air meeting in July in Nelson, or to the local Guild in November. She became one of the keenest supporters and was soon providing a strong north Lancashire base for the textile workers' campaign.

In 1900 she was largely devoted to caring for her new baby, Mary, and to looking after her mother, immobilised with rheumatism, whom she had to lift in and out of bed. The following year, much of her free time was taken up with her new duties as a local Poor Law Guardian. Yet during this period, she kept up an annual subscription of one shilling to the North of England Society funds, collected subscriptions from other local sympathizers, and even managed to go on two deputations to Westminster. By 1903 she was able to make time to do some local speaking for the Society, and the following year became founder-secretary of a Nelson and Colne suffrage committee, one of the most active of the Society's local groups. A year later she was speaking as far afield as Blackburn, Halifax and Stockport.

By the following spring, 1901, the total number of signatures on the petition had risen to 29,359, and the radical suffragists were ready to confront Westminster with the results of their campaign. On 18 March a deputation of fifteen Lancashire cotton workers took the petition down to London, accompanied by two 'deputation secretaries', Katherine Rowton and Esther Roper, who, as they had no personal connection with the cotton industry, remained firmly in the background and did not speak. The petition was so large, that, according to the *Englishwoman's Review*, it 'looked like a garden roller in dimensions'. Mr Taylor, MP for Radcliffe, who was among the small group of sympathizers who met them in Westminster, confessed that he had heard of larger petitions but had never seen one larger.

Sarah Reddish, as the senior and most influential woman, introduced the deputation, emphasizing that it consisted entirely of past or present working women, some of them, like herself, trade union officials. Although only disenfranchised women wage earners had signed the petition she warned the small gathering of MPs that 'there are many men in the homes of these workers who felt very strongly indeed the injustice cast upon women by the continual denial of the franchise'.[12]

Her speech was followed by strong contributions from Annie Heaton, Sarah Dickenson, Helen Silcock, Selina Cooper and Mrs Pearce. Helen Silcock explained: 'I represent the Association of Weavers at Wigan, which comprises between 800 and 900 women, all of whom are in sympathy with the movement. I consider it unjust that five millions of working women in this country are denied the right of assisting to make the laws which they have to obey.'[13] Sarah Dickenson spoke bitterly of her six years' experience of organizing women's trade unions, whose members' self-confidence was sapped by their political powerlessness:

> Many Lancashire women are keeping on homes, and even worthless husbands, and yet the latter when it becomes a matter of voting have the only voice in the affairs of the nation. The children are led by this to think little of their mothers and much of their fathers. . . . It is said that women have their trade unions and can be represented through them. Well, I know a union in Manchester into which the women pay a penny or twopence per week and are not allowed to attend the meetings, while if a male member tells a woman member what went on he is fined 2s 6d.[14]

That evening Millicent Fawcett, as National Union President, entertained the women to dinner, and the following day Mr Taylor presented the giant petition in the House, where 'the honourable member was cheered as he carried it with difficulty to the table'.

Fired by this success the North of England Society activists decided to cast their net more widely and to adapt the Lancashire petition tactics to the wool workers in Yorkshire and the cotton and silk workers in north Cheshire. Within the three counties, Esther Roper pointed out, 311,000 women (compared with only 217,000 men) worked in textiles, all without the parliamentary vote to protect their interests.

Meetings to collect the signatures from these textiles workers, especially those from the wool areas of the West Riding, began in earnest in June 1901. Mrs Green from Beswick spoke at no fewer than eighteen meetings during the next two months in the sprawling Colne Valley constituency, stretching from Saddleworth right over the Pennines and down towards Huddersfield. Petition workers made their way up to tiny hillside villages with just a handful of mills, as well as into the bigger industrial towns. Again they were met by tremendous enthusiasm. 'The canvasser at Batley reported,' wrote Sarah Reddish, 'that "whole streets of women engaged as rag-pickers wanted to sign," and in many other towns dressmakers, launderesses, and others were disappointed that they must not add their names'.[15]

Meanwhile Helen Silcock, inspired by the success of the Lancashire deputation, immediately followed it up with a large and successful public meeting in Wigan, at which she spoke alongside Eva Gore-Booth and Esther Roper. Local support for women's suffrage was assured, she could see. How could she harness it most effectively?

Gradually she evolved a strategy. Women might not be able to sit in Parliament but at least they could legitimately take part in the working man's parliament – the annual Trade Union Congress. So far the radical suffragists had not taken this up. In 1900 only two women delegates had attended, neither from the textile unions. 'The whole phalanx of Lancashire representatives were men,' Julia Dawson had complained in the *Clarion*, 'and yet there are more women than men in the weavers' union. It is a thousand pities that women hold back'.[16]

Helen Silcock decided to hold back no longer, but to take action at the 1901 Congress. As the President of the Wigan Weavers, she was in a unique position to demand the parliamentary vote on behalf of her notoriously ill-paid women members. With their support, and presumably with the full knowledge of the League which paid her salary, she was elected delegate to the Congress and mandated to introduce a women's suffrage motion: 'That, in view of the unsatisfactory state of legislation for women, especially those employed in our mills and workshops, the Parliamentary Franchise should be extended to women on the same terms as men'.[17]

The TUC's position on women's suffrage had ranged from benign indifference to outright hostility. In 1884 Jeanette Gaury Wilkinson, the delegate from the London Upholsteresses, had introduced the motion 'that this Congress is strongly of the opinion that the franchise ought to be extended to women on the same conditions as men'.[18] One opponent had argued that the resolution merely extended the property qualification, and that he would only support an adult suffrage motion, but the Wilkinson proposal was passed by an overwhelming majority. However, the Third Reform Act, passed the same year, meant that most TUC delegates were now enfranchised, and the suffrage question was forgotten until Helen Silcock raised it again seventeen years later.

Her resolution to enfranchise women on the same terms as men (on a property-based qualification) once again raised the old bogey of well-to-do women swamping the electorate and undermining the influence of trade union voters. So, when Helen Silcock was allotted one of the coveted places on the TUC Franchise Committee,[19] she found that her resolution was in direct competition with a rival motion, quickly cobbled together, demanding nothing less than adult suffrage. In the end the men on the Committee took the less threatening option and settled for adult suffrage, but as compensation they allowed Helen Silcock to present the agreed resolution to Congress: that the time was ripe to extend the franchise to all adult men and women and that the Parliamentary Committee be instructed to make this a test question at the next election.

Having done her duty by the Franchise Committee in outlining their motion, Helen Silcock continued her speech on heartfelt lines. Thinking of her own poorly-paid members, she told the Congress that in the weaving industry the 'tyranny might be somewhat lessened' if women weavers had the protection of the vote to improve their wages and conditions. She appealed to the men in the audience to stop their opposition (which is how she saw their sudden concern for adult suffrage). As an independent woman breadwinner herself she had a direct personal claim to the vote:

It is said that women are sufficiently protected by their husbands. I would point out that all women are not wives. There are in fact five million working women in this country who have to earn their livelihood, and some protection should be extended to them, so that by means of the vote they may assist in bringing about legislation which will enable them to live as well as exist.[20]

Cheering broke out as she finished speaking, but the TUC delegates were not persuaded by her impassioned speech and resolutely clung to the adult suffrage motion, which was carried by acclamation.

Helen Silcock had to accept the result of the TUC debate but her heart was still in *women's* suffrage, even though that entailed working for a property-based vote as the first step. The following February she accompanied the Yorkshire and Cheshire petition down to Westminster and was again one of the speakers from the deputation, threatening that the women members of the textile unions would give the men no peace until they helped to secure the vote for women. The following autumn she was back at the TUC, this time not as Miss Silcock but as Mrs Fairhurst, trying once more to persuade the delegates to give their valuable backing to women's suffrage. This time she played her hand more cautiously. Rather than introducing the motion herself, she was content with seconding it, and was fortunate enough to find an influential proposer among the textile trade unionists. He was Allan Gee from Huddersfield, who was not only secretary of the wool workers' union, but also, most importantly, on the Executive of the Labour Representation Committee. Like other members of his union, he was a long-standing sympathizer with women's suffrage, and as long ago as the 1884 Congress had argued in favour of the Wilkinson motion.[21] Yet, despite his influential support the resolution was narrowly defeated after stormy discussion. No wonder, commented Julia Dawson, caustically; there were only four women among the vast mass of male delegates.[22]

Although there was obviously a certain amount of support for women's suffrage within the TUC in the early 1900s in the end the Congress had come down on the side of full adult suffrage or nothing. Helen Silcock, twice defeated, now took the TUC decision to heart and began to entertain her own doubts about whether women *should* be given first priority in the battle for the vote. Certainly, she felt she could no longer continue working with the radical suffragists, and she cut herself off from all contact with their campaign.

The TUC's adamant rejection of the women's cause was a severe blow to the radical suffragists. Their campaign among the textile workers was badly hampered while the national trade union body would not support their claims. Yet, despite this setback, 1902 turned out to be an extremely encouraging year for them.

To begin with, the Yorkshire and Cheshire deputation in February attracted considerably more national attention than the Lancashire deputation had done the previous year. The radical suffragists organized wider newspaper coverage and arranged a special celebratory send-off for the sixteen delegates at the Grand Hotel in Manchester on the 17th February, the evening before they left for London.

The next day they went straight to the House of Commons. Two women carried the Yorkshire petition triumphantly into the House, followed by Mrs Winbolt with the smaller Cheshire one. Ten MPs were there to greet them, speeches were made, the petitions were presented, and Keir Hardie, one of the most ardent champions of women's suffrage, took the women on a tour around the House — rather a surreal experience in the circumstances. After tea, they drove to Chelsea Town Hall to a public meeting presided over by Richard Bell, Hardie's fellow MP from the Labour Representation Committee, and a member of the Railway Servants' Union.

At Chelsea, Hardie contributed one of the strongest speeches ever made in support of women's suffrage. Many of his points were not new: Enid Stacy had already asserted the importance of the vote to working women, Sarah Dickenson had pointed out how vital it was for mothers to be enfranchised, and Helen Silcock had pleaded for the vote to improve women's industrial conditions. But now these arguments were put by the first working man elected independently to Parliament, with immense personal influence in both the ILP and the Labour Representation Committee:

> Mr Bell was speaking about the way in which women are used to bring down wages. How far are men responsible for that fact? Treat the woman as an inferior and she will play the part, if only in self-defence. . . By treating women — I am speaking now from the working class point of view — as equals, by conceding to them every concession which men claim for themselves, the woman will play the part of an equal, not only in regard to wages, but in all other matters appertaining to industrial life. So the question of the Franchise is as much a man's question as a woman's question. . .

From his masculine point of view, women needed the vote as much in the interests of their husbands and sons as for themselves:

> The woman who is a drudge only, will produce sons unworthy of the fathers who have gone before them, but the woman who is not a drudge, and who

respects herself, will, though perhaps unconsciously, exert a noble and inspiring influence upon her children. Therefore the question is a national question.[23]

His speech continued along lines close to the radical suffragists' ideas. Like them, he valued the zeal of middle and upper class suffragists, but felt that 'without the active support and co-operation of working women they will have no chance whatever of being successful'. Much of his speech was devoted to countering the arguments against women's suffrage he had come across on the Labour Representation Committee. Socialists were fearful of the influence of the priest and the parson if women got the vote: Hardie said he preferred that to the influence on men voters of the publican (usually Tory) and the bookmaker. Trade unionists sometimes argued that votes for women could lead to domestic discord: what sort of domestic peace is it, Hardie asked, if it is based on the wife being treated as an 'inferior domestic animal?'

Hardie was just the champion the radical suffragists needed to counter the opposition to votes for women in the labour movement. Other speakers followed him, eagerly confirming Hardie's assertion: suffrage *was* important to working women. Agnes Close from Leeds described how she stood on an orange box in the market and had persuaded 2,800 out of the city's 3,000 women textile workers to sign. Miss Higginbotham from Hyde explained how she had worked in a cotton mill for twenty five years and had not had the slightest difficulty in getting women to sign. Finally the deputation, representing over 66,000 women textile workers, passed a resolution urging MPs and trade unions 'to take immediate steps' to obtain the vote for women workers, who 'are suffering under a disability which inevitably keeps down wages and lowers their position in the labour market'.[24]

But while the campaign among the textile workers was gathering this valuable support, women's existing political rights came under attack; ironically the threat gained the radical suffragists even more support. The Tory Government's Education Bill proposed to abolish local School Boards and to replace them by Education Committees, to which women could not be elected. Groups which had been half-hearted about women's parliamentary votes now created a storm of protest to defend their right to take part in local administration. The Secretary of the Women's Trade Union League registered her protest with the TUC. Julia Dawson took an uncompromising stand: 'It will be a bad day for Bradford if Miss McMillan ceases to serve on the School Board,' she warned, 'and a bad day for Bolton if Miss Reddish receives her dismissal'.[25]

The greatest anger, however, came from the Women's Co-operative Guild, which was not appeased by a loophole in the law which allowed women to be co-opted onto the new Committees. Several branches had helped to collect signatures for the two petitions on an unofficial basis, and on both deputations about half the women had been Guild members; but until now the Guild policy-making Central Committee had always decided against bringing women's suffrage up at the Annual Conference, as it was thought to be outside the Guild's parish.[26] Now the Guild officials could no longer ignore the fact that Parliamentary legislation affected housewives as well as wage earners. The government could just as casually prohibit women from serving as Poor Law Guardians. Under these threats, Lancashire Guildswomen began to take a far keener interest in the radical suffragists' campaign

The greatest boost to the campaign during 1902 came from a completely different direction: the election of the third Labour Representation MP. This time the contest was at Clitheroe, a constituency in the heart of the cotton weaving belt, where women mill workers were strongest. Before his election, it had been possible to dismiss the textile workers' petitions and deputations as the powerless pleading of the disenfranchised. Now a Labour MP was in Parliament largely supported by the contributions of these same disenfranchised women trade unionists. It was an argument which few could ignore. It hit right at the centre of the issue of independent working class representation in Parliament.

The radical suffragists found themselves in the middle of a very complex situation which had been coming to the boil over a period of several years. When the TUC finally committed itself to supporting Keir Hardie's plan for independent Parliamentary candidates in 1899, the majority of unions were unenthusiastic; only a few affiliated to the Labour Representation Committee, until the Amalgamated Society of Railway Servants went on strike against the Taff Vale Railway Company. The Company sued the union for £20,000 worth of damages, and finally won their case with a House of Lords decision in July 1901. This convinced many of the unions which had been dragging their feet over the need for independent labour representation to protect their interests, including their right to strike, in Parliament. Yet the big cotton unions still held themselves aloof. They had developed a system of lobbying the government directly, through a federation called the

United Textile Factory Workers' Association, and felt that this had served them adequately so far. Also, they were divided in their traditional political allegiances between weavers who supported the Liberals and the spinners who supported the Tories.

The cotton unions' complacency was not finally shattered until they had to confront the same problem on their own doorstep. At the end of 1901 — a few months after the Taff Vale judgement — the Blackburn Weavers' Association suddenly found itself liable for damages for picketing during a strike, even though the picketing had, as usual, been peaceful and had not involved threats or intimidation. The big Northern Counties Weavers' Amalgamation asked the TUC for support but in the spring of 1902 found that it would still have to pay £11,000. Attitudes began to harden. By the end of the year the *Cotton Factory Times* was calling the case 'Taff Vale Number Two' and 'a flagrant wrong', and in January 1903 the United Textile Factory Workers Association finally voted in favour of affiliation to the Labour Representation Committee.

By then these manoeuvres had been overtaken by other events. In June 1902, a vacancy occurred in the traditionally Liberal Clitheroe seat. The constituency included not only Clitheroe itself, but also Nelson and Colne, where socialist-inclined weavers' unions had been among the first to affiliate independently to the Labour Representation Committee. Distrustful of the Liberals, Selina Cooper's husband Robert, himself a weaver and a keen trade unionist, wrote to the local paper to urge putting up a Labour candidate.[27]

In July, just a matter of weeks since the vacancy originally appeared, David Shackleton, the secretary of the Darwen Weavers, was chosen as candidate. Shackleton, who had started work as a nine-year-old half-timer in Rossendale and worked his way up through the union to become a town councillor and magistrate, was an obvious compromise candidate. A giant of a man, weighing over sixteen stone, he was like many weavers a Liberal at heart, and the United Textile Factory Workers' Association, still hesitant about labour representation, could officially endorse him, confident that few Liberals would vote against him.[28]

As soon as the seat fell vacant, the radical suffragists seized their opportunity. They immediately drew public attention to the glaring anomaly of Shackleton's salary. Besides the normal levies exacted by the Labour Representation Committee of 10s per 1,000 members (both men and women), it also levied 4d a year from each member, of which 1d went to a fund to maintain Labour MPs in Parliament. As the final straw, the disenfranchised Clitheroe women trade unionists paid 6d each into a special fund to maintain their MP.[29]

Such blatant injustice was useful ammunition to the radical suffragists' campaign. Eva Gore-Booth drafted an angry letter to the *Manchester Guardian*, pointing out that no less than 60 per cent of the members of the local weavers' unions were women and girls. Julia Dawson noted the injustice in the *Clarion*, but was content to shrug it off: 'Twas ever thus.'[30]

The radical suffragists were not content to be so passive; they quickly formed a local deputation to urge Shackleton, as a prospective MP, 'if elected, to actively work for the enfranchisement of women who form a large majority of workers in the textile trade'. Shackleton agreed to their demands and 'pledged himself to seek the immediate enfranchisement of women on the same terms as men'.[31]

At the same time the radical suffragists within the North of England Society mounted a special propaganda effort. Katherine Rowton and Sarah Reddish travelled up to the constituency to inaugurate a great four week pre-election campaign. Two large public meetings were held in Nelson where Selina Cooper, now beginning to emerge as a talented speaker, presided; speakers included Sarah Reddish, Eva Gore-Booth, Esther Roper, Mrs Pankhurst and her daughter Christabel. Esther Roper dealt smartly with a persistent heckler, and the resolution was carried with only one vote against — presumably the heckler.[32]

Other meetings were held around the constituency, and a few days later Shackleton was elected unopposed. The implications of the election were not lost upon socialists. Even Julia Dawson, never an enthusiastic supporter of women's suffrage, but now prodded into action by the radical suffragists' campaign, used her column in the *Clarion* to publicise the voteless textile workers' cause:

> So Shackleton is the Labour Member for Clitheroe. . .
> Women, methinks, have waited long enough, without standing aside until the men get more than they appear to have been contented with for so many years. Women are the most downtrodden and sweated workers in all the industrial world. Taxation without representation has been their lot for so long that they are sick of it; and on the score that half a loaf is better than no bread, they are trying — and especially are the textile workers trying in Clitheroe — to get full political freedom by degrees, as the men are doing.[33]

This was excellent publicity. Not only did the radical suffragists appear to have acquired the support of the three Labour MPs, but a popular socialist weekly like the *Clarion* was beginning to take their ideas seriously. Esther Roper, loath to let any opportunity slip away, drafted the radical suffragists' propaganda leaflet, 'The Cotton Trade Unions and the Enfranchisement of Women'. It was a direct attack on a system of labour representation which excluded women, and was a rallying call to all women in the cotton unions.

> If it is as necessary, as the men say it is, for men to be directly represented in Parliament, how much more necessary must it be to women, the only entirely unrepresented workers, to have the protection and power of a vote.
>
> The women's best chance of winning their own enfranchisement is through the Cotton Trade Unions of the North. Here they have the power because they are more numerous than the men. . .
>
> The Trade Unions will become more and more a power in politics. . .
>
> Therefore, let all women having the great power of the Cotton Unions in their hands, help themselves, and the millions of women workers who are poorer and less able to help themselves than they, by making Women's Suffrage a Trade Union Question. The Cotton Trade Unions can and must secure the enfranchisement of the women workers.[34]

As Secretary, Esther Roper managed to publish the leaflet in the North of England Society's 1902 Report, no doubt to the consternation of the bulk of her subscribers, for whom labour representation smelt suspiciously of encroaching socialism. However, backed by the other radical suffragists on the Society's Committee she somehow managed to placate any unease and to bulldoze her way past any opposition.

The radical suffragists now calculated that their best strategy was to consolidate their existing gains. They might have failed to get the backing of the TUC, but at least they had a Lancashire MP on whom they could exert considerable public pressure. This advantage was confirmed the following January, 1903, when the United Textile Factory Workers' Association officially affiliated to the Labour Representation Committee. Within a few weeks David Shackleton received a deputation from local women trade unionists at the Nelson Weavers' Institute. They presented him with a petition from 5,500 of the women members of the cotton unions in his constituency, reminding him of the levy they each paid towards his salary, and asking him to introduce into the Commons that session a measure to secure votes for women on the same terms as men. Shackleton 'expressed his sympathy' with the women's position, and agreed to ballot for a place in the queue of backbenchers to introduce a Private Member's bill in the coming session.[35] Shackleton knew he had little option but to concede their demands, for they had attracted so much attention to the anomaly of his salary. Yet even at this point it must have been apparent to the radical suffragists that he felt closer to the progressive Liberals than to the tiny Labour group of MPs — (certainly he lacked Hardie's commitment either to socialism or to women's suffrage) — and that even if he did manage to introduce a Bill it would probably fall by the wayside like all earlier private members' bills.

While they waited for Shackleton to find an opportunity in Parliament, the radical suffragists turned their attention to another source of potential support: local trade union branches. Perhaps, they thought, they had been premature in their attempt at the TUC; they might do better starting with the solid backing of local support. The male-dominated Congress had rejected women's suffrage, but in the Lancashire cotton unions where women constituted such a majority of members there might be a better chance of approval. Perhaps another local constituency might even fall vacant, and the Shackleton campaign could be repeated elsewhere in Lancashire with a more promising candidate. The potential for local support must have seemed almost unlimited.

The radical suffragists addressed dozens of union meetings throughout Lancashire during 1903. Selina Cooper spoke on three occasions to the women weavers in Nelson, sometimes taking her little daughter with her. Sarah Reddish, still doing some work for the Women's Trade Union League, and Katherine Rowton (they were both paid a small salary by the North of England Society) did most of the speaking, and, helped by Esther Roper and Eva Gore-Booth, managed to cover most of the major cotton towns. Wherever they went, they asked the trade unionists at the meeting if they would arrange for their members to be balloted on the issue of making women's suffrage a trade union question, in the same way that affiliation to the Labour Representation Committee had been decided by individual trade unions. Since the strategy had worked for one political issue, the radical suffragists argued, might it not work for another?

By the end of the year, the results of the ballots were coming in. The signs were favourable: the weavers' unions in Bolton, Clitheroe, Colne, Nelson, Hyde and Haslingden all voted 'yes'. In addition, the influential Burnley union, with 11,500 members, instructed its Committee to bring women's suffrage once more before the TUC, and urged all Labour candidates supported by textile unions to introduce a women's suffrage bill once they were elected — obviously with an eye on the precedent set in Clitheroe. These seven unions, with support from some trades councils, presented David Shackleton with a petition at

Westminster representing 100,000 trade unionists. Yet Shackleton, only lukewarm himself, must have realized that even the enthusiasm of these Lancashire trades unions was little match for the solid opposition met by every women's suffrage proposal both in the TUC and in the Commons. Certainly he never introduced the bill he had repeatedly been asked to. Shackleton's dilatory behaviour must have been a sad disappointment to the radical suffragists, who had orchestrated so promising a campaign around him over the previous eighteen months. Once again, success in Lancashire had turned to failure when translated into terms of national politics.

Then, as so often seemed to happen, another champion turned up to help them: William Henry Wilkinson from Burnley. He was Secretary of the Northern Counties Amalgamated Association of Weavers, with over 80,000 members, and also Secretary of the even larger United Textile Factory Workers' Association. His first contact with the radical suffragists was in Salford. All previous attempts to organize weavers in the town had proved unsuccessful and their wages were notoriously low. Eventually, in April 1902, with encouragement from Sarah Dickenson and Eva Gore-Booth as secretaries of the Women's Trades Council, the Salford and District Association of Power-Loom Weavers was formed. Local women weavers leapt at this new opportunity and the union soon had about a thousand members. Nellie Keenan was appointed treasurer, and the Women's Trades Council report for that year noted that 'a strong interest in current politics, and a realization of the need for the Franchise to protect the interest of working women has been characteristic of this Union since its formation'. Here was a real vindication of the radical suffragists' strategy over the last few years.

This thriving new union soon came to the notice of William Wilkinson, and he came to address the five hundred women weavers who attended its bi-annual meeting in October.[36] His aim was to persuade them to affiliate to his Northern Counties Amalgamation, but the women, proud of their success, decided to remain independent; their dues were only 2d a week, compared with the Amalgamation's 3d, and included sickness benefit, a luxury unheard of outside the elite Spinners' Association.[37]

However, Wilkinson was not disheartened by this rebuff, and he became friendly with Eva Gore-Booth and Sarah Dickenson. Their suffrage views, combined with the strong support of the Burnley

Weavers, persuaded him to champion women's suffrage at the 1904 Labour Representation Committee Conference, the first at which the cotton trade unions had appeared in full force.

It was a mark of the success of the campaign among the textile workers that it was a cotton trade unionist, the Burnley Weavers' delegate, who proposed the motion. He asked that the conference should agree in principle that women should be given the vote on the same basis as they had it for parochial elections, and that the Labour MPs should introduce a bill to deal with this. Isabella Ford, an ILP delegate from Leeds and now a parish councillor, seconded his proposal which was carried by a large majority. This was the greatest triumph the radical suffragists had yet experienced. Labour now gave its full support to the idea of women's suffrage. Encouraged by this success, they determined to attend next year's Conference in person, this time armed with an even stronger women's suffrage motion.

This boost to their campaign was mirrored by widespread support at a local level too. Increasingly local working class women were drawn into the campaign, and began to come along to meetings addressed by the radical suffragists. Ten local suffrage committees, offshoots of the big North of England Society, were established in the major cotton towns, with a further seven committees in Yorkshire. For instance in Manchester Sarah Dickenson took on the job of committee secretary, in Nelson and Colne it was Selina Cooper, in Bolton Clara Staton, and in Oldham Ruth Dewhurst.

Sadly no reports or minute books of these local groups have survived from this early period. The only available document is the account book kept by Robert Cooper of the suffrage committee co-ordinated by his wife; but unfortunately the book only begins in 1912 and membership may well have changed over those eight years. However the group used to meet each week in the Coopers' front room, and Mary, curious about the odd things adults got up to, was an eye-witness to many of the meetings. Her earliest memories are of a few years later, but her account gives some picture of what one suffrage society in a northern weaving village was like.

> I can remember making the coffee. And I thought I was doing great. But I mustn't have been — I was about eight, and there was a great crowd of women in here. . .
> They used to stick to business. Then they'd have, you know, any other business and coffee and a chat. . .' Cos I remember listening at the keyhole, you know what I mean, listening at the door. I was puzzled by it, couldn't

understand it. But — there was always some resolution going before a trade union, or they were going to go and march somewhere, or go and help — they used to help candidates that were suffrage.[38]

Precisely how local women were recruited into the groups is not known. Certainly Selina Cooper must have been a central figure in mustering support in Nelson and Colne; by 1904 she had built up an extensive friendship network. She was in touch with the local Social Democratic Federation branch and may well have suggested to some of the members that they should challenge the Federation's line on women's suffrage. For some years she had been an active member of the Nelson Women's Co-operative Guild which had recently invited Sarah Reddish, Mrs Bayfield and Katherine Rowton to come and speak; a few of the local Guildswomen must have agreed that it was necessary to form a separate local suffrage committee. She had also made useful contacts with other socialists as a local Guardian. But probably the best source of support was the Nelson ILP; at least three of its members — Harriette Beanland, her sister Emily and Florence Shuttleworth — joined the suffrage committee.[39]

Selina Cooper's other interest was in the local trade union movement; although she no longer worked as a winder, she still kept up with her old friends — and her husband still worked in the mill. Mary Cooper recalled that at least two of the most active of the committee members — Emily Murgatroyd and Miss Shimbles — were both trade unionists. Emily Murgatroyd, Mary explained, 'fought the battles at the mill, both trade-union-wise and suffrage-wise'.

Nelson and Colne Suffrage Committee was a wholly working class group. No members subscribed more than a shilling a year (in contrast to, say, Eva Gore-Booth's donation of £20 to the North of England Society's fund for organizers' salaries), most paid 3d or 6d a year, and some not even that. 'Some of them, they were so poor, they didn't — that's only a record of payments. . . whether or no. Ones who just paid their way, you know what I mean. They just managed to pay for the coffee — that sort of thing'.[40]

It is difficult to assess how typical the Nelson and Colne committee was; it probably had a higher proportion of women textile workers among its members than groups in other cotton towns. Yet if working women joined the nine other Lancashire suffrage committees in comparable numbers the combined impact must have been colossal.[41]

Soon the North of England Society began to be recognized nationally for the unique way in which its radical activists were able to recruit so many working class women previously untouched by the suffrage debate. It struck a bargain with the Central Suffrage Society: Lancashire would provide experienced speakers to work in other industrial areas, if London would pay the costs involved. During 1903-4 Katherine Rowton, Mrs Green,[42] Eva Gore-Booth and Esther Roper addressed over a hundred meetings of women workers in the Potteries and hosiery workers in Leicestershire, while Sarah Reddish managed to collect nearly five thousand signatures from the women working in textiles in East Scotland. [43] Early in 1904 they accompanied the deputations from the Midlands down to London. But even then they must have realized that the tactics which had paid such dividends in Lancashire would not work when transferred to ill-organized, poorly paid women workers elsewhere.

A pattern of success and failure began to emerge. The radical suffragists came up against heavy opposition when they tried to influence politics on a national scale, whether it was the TUC or the House of Commons. (The only exception was their success with the Labour Representation Committee.) They got spectacular support from women in the cotton towns, but they kept on finding that their campaign did not travel well outside Lancashire. No other group of women could match the cotton workers' power.[44]

The very success of their local grassroots campaign brought its own problems. The respectable Liberals who still provided the bulk of the North of England Society's funds were becoming increasingly concerned over the emphasis the radical suffragists placed on labour. Many of them must have blanched when Esther Roper began sending copies of the Society's report to Keir Hardie, and disturbed by the approving comments he made in *Labour Leader*.[45] Although a few of them looked benevolently on the Women's Trades Union Council, many others still saw trade unions as dangerous societies, operating on the verge of illegality with unruly picketing during strikes.

For them, the very existence of Labour MPs was a threat to the traditional two-party political equilibrium. Since the suffrage movement had been run so smoothly since Lydia Becker's day on careful non-party lines, they could see no advantage in courting the rawest, least influential of political parties. Yet the list of meetings Esther Roper drew up for her Annual Reports demonstrated only too clearly where the Society was channelling its resources. Virtually all activity was directed towards working class women, with only a sprinkling of the traditional drawing room, debating society and Liberal Association meetings.

The radical suffragists wanted to avoid any possible resignations from any of the old stalwarts, for their influence was always useful, and their subscriptions and donations were vital to the Society's survival. On the other hand they found that the dead hand of the Society increasingly hampered their more ambitious plans. Eventually they compromised by retaining their membership of the North of England Society (with Esther Roper still as Secretary), but forming a separate, independent pressure group through which they could plan their most ambitious campaign.[46]

Sarah Reddish, Selina Cooper, Sarah Dickenson, Esther Roper and Eva Gore-Booth formed a new group sometime in the summer of 1903; it was known as the Lancashire and Cheshire Women Textile and other Workers' Representation Committee. Its cumbersome title suggests how the radical suffragists had noted the Labour Representation Committee's rapid growth during the last three years. If working class men could get their own representatives elected to Parliament, perhaps working class women could also persuade voters to elect *their* own candidate?

Unfortunately virtually nothing was recorded of the Committee's first half dozen years.[47] No minute books or annual reports (if they ever kept them) have been preserved, and it is unknown how often they met, how wide their discussions ranged and how quickly they attracted members. Some years later Sarah Reddish, the Committee's Treasurer, referred in a vague but affectionate way to the 'sisterly sociability of all the members, all meeting on one common ground and working for and aiming at one common good'.[48] Otherwise all that remains of its early years is its public statements. The first of these was the manifesto, dated July 1904:

Fellow Workers — During the last few years the need of real political power for the defence of the workers has been felt by every section of the Labour world. Among the men the growing sense of the importance of this question has resulted in the formation of the Labour Representation Committee. . . Meanwhile the position of the unenfranchised working women, who are by their voteless condition shut out from all political influence, is becoming daily more precarious. They cannot hope to hold their own in industrial matters, where their interests may clash with those of their enfranchised fellow-workers or employers. . .

The conclusion has been forced on those of the textile workers who have been working unceasingly in past years to secure the vote for women, that what is urgently needed is that they should send their own nominee to the House of Commons, pledged to. . . secure the enfranchisement of the women workers of the country.

A Committee has been formed. . . to select a suitable and zealous candidate, and. . . to collect and be responsible for the spending of £500, which is the amount absolutely necessary for one candidate's election expenses. . .

What Lancashire and Cheshire women think today England will do tomorrow. Yours fraternally,

THE COMMITTEE

The Committee immediately plumped for Wigan. It was a sensible choice in many ways. Their greatest hope of electoral and parliamentary success lay in aligning themselves with Labour, and Wigan was one of the few cotton constituencies without a Labour candidate waiting in the wings. It was traditionally a Tory seat held by the same MP since 1885; but the radical suffragists hoped that a combination of railwaymen, miners and cotton workers might lead a swing towards Labour in the next election. After all, a Wigan Labour Representation Committee had just been formed and the Trades Council had affiliated to it. Their choice of candidate — though possibly very zealous — was hardly so suitable. Hubert Sweeney taught in one of the London Board Schools and was training to be a barrister; unfortunately he had no known connections with Wigan, with the cotton industry or with trade unionism. Despite this unpromising start, the radical suffragists sent out an appeal for help to 'the Trade Unions and Working Men of Wigan':

Fellow Workers,

We appeal to you to support our Candidate, and to vote for him at the next Parliamentary Election.

The Candidate is pledged, if returned to Parliament, to work in season and out of season to secure the Enfranchisement of the Women Workers of the country, and to put this question before all others.

On all questions concerned with Women's Labour the Candidate undertakes to represent the opinions of the above Committee.

On all general questions he will vote in the interests of Labour.

. . .There is no Progressive Candidate for Wigan, and the present Conservative Member has voted against the Enfranchisement of Women in the House of Commons. Therefore, we urge upon you not to let this opportunity pass of securing the enfranchisement of over half the members of the Textile Trades. . .

Yours fraternally,
THE COMMITTEE[49]

The Committee's immediate problem was collecting the £500 to run the campaign, since they could no longer tap the funds of the North of England Society. Unfortunately 1903 was a bad year in that respect: supplies of raw cotton from America were blocked, and mills either closed down or went on short time; some families, it was reported, were even reduced to boiling potato peelings.[50]. Esther Roper appealed as widely as she could, even writing to all the women who had signed the graduates' suffrage petition the year before.

> The difficulties in the cotton trade have developed into a crisis, causing wide-spread and deep distress. Many of the keenest suffragists have been reduced from a position of comfort to one of acute poverty. Some of them, accustomed to earn 24s or 25s a week, now only draw 6s or 7s. . . The women are working hard, but find that, under these circumstances, a collection of a large sum of money from cotton workers is well-nigh impossible.[51]

Apart from appealing for funds and organizing occasional meetings in Wigan there was little the Committee could do. They just had to sit tight and wait for the Tory Government to admit it had no option but to resign and call a General Election. During this hiatus the radical suffragists' support did not stop growing. The Lancashire Women Textile Workers' Representation Committee now had twenty nine members, including among its recruits Cissy Foley[52] and Nellie Keenan. Of the other twenty seven, thirteen were Guildswomen, largely converted by the good counsel of Sarah Reddish who undertook the bulk of the responsibility for addressing Guild meetings. She attended the Guild's Annual Congress in Gloucester in July 1904, where, for the first time in its history, women's suffrage had been placed on the agenda.

The Guild debate focused on the wording of Will Crooks' suffrage bill which proposed the traditional demand: that women should be given the vote on the same terms as men. Many Guildswomen found it hard to swallow that they had to pay 4s a week rent to qualify. 'Many working women take objection to the Bill,' a Manchester woman explained afterwards, 'because they, as married women, are denied a vote because they are not paying this rent.' Still, in the end most Guildswomen decided that 'it will pave the way to other things in the future,' and the Congress voted emphatically in favour of women's suffrage.[53] This was another great triumph for the radical suffragists — and came only five months after their victory at the Labour Representation Conference. They now had the support of the only two organizations that could speak on the one hand for working class married women, and on the other for working class enfranchised men.

165

This invaluable backing was accompanied by other signs of growing popularity. During the winter 1904-5 a Liverpool Women Textile Workers' Committee held a large public meeting, addressed by Keir Hardie, Esther Roper, Isabella Ford, Eva Gore-Booth, Mrs Pankhurst and others. At the same time Campbell-Bannerman, leader of the Liberals (and so tipped as next Prime Minister) sympathetically received a deputation of women textile workers when he came to Manchester. Not long afterwards a suffrage meeting held in the Free Trade Hall attracted no fewer than 4,000 people and stirring speeches were made by socialists and feminists — Keir Hardie and the recently converted Philip Snowden, Sarah Dickenson, Eva Gore-Booth and Sarah Reddish. Up in Blackburn, Selina Cooper, Philip Snowden and Sarah Reddish addressed a packed meeting in the Exchange Hall.

If this momentum could be sustained elsewhere in Lancashire, the radical suffragists felt confident that their candidates would be elected at Wigan, and the campaign could be waged from a more powerful base at Westminster. Given these encouraging signs Esther Roper felt justified in ending her North of England Society Report for 1905 on an optimistic note:

> Such a stir has been made during the last twelve months, and the question has become so prominent amongst labour people of all shades of opinion, that there is no doubt that the pressure of working class feeling, and especially of the claims of the women cotton workers, are beginning to force the attentions of practical politicians. . .
> The popularity of our movement gives us great hopes. . .[54]

X

The Pankhursts in Manchester

During the 1890s Mrs Pankhurst had taken little interest in women's suffrage. In June 1894 she had spoken alongside her husband and Mrs Winbolt at open-air meetings organized by the North of England Society to promote the Special Appeal. But this was an isolated event and by the turn of the century her only link with the Society was a 10s subscription to its funds.

Instead she devoted her energies to the ILP. In 1894 the Pankhursts had moved back to the north west from London and taken a house in Victoria Park, not far from the Roper household. Both she and her husband, who had known Keir Hardie well for several years, responded to the visionary appeal of the new ILP with the fervour of converts. At the end of the year she was elected as ILP candidate to the Chorlton Board of Guardians, and the following year campaigned for her husband, ILP candidate for Gorton in the General Election. She appealed from her soapbox for people to vote for him thus: 'You put me at the top of the poll; will you not vote for the man who has taught me all I know?'[1] A few months later she was again in the thick of local ILP struggles, this time over the issue of free speech in Boggart Hole Clough; she emerged from the incident with her local reputation considerably strengthened.

H.M. Hyndman, of the Social Democratic Federation, wrote perceptively of Mrs Pankhurst's politics at this period. 'At the time I knew her best she was a socialist first and a suffragist afterwards . . . Active, well-read, pleasant, and very good-looking, Mrs Pankhurst was at this time a valuable "asset" . . . of the Independent Labour Party.'[2]

The family suffered an abrupt change in fortune in 1898 when Dr Pankhurst suddenly collapsed and died from stomach ulcers. The shock

167

his family experienced was not only emotional. He had little money to leave and the family had to move from Victoria Park to a smaller (though still elegant) house not far away, number 62 Nelson Street. Sylvia wrote that her mother 'could not endure a commonplace house in a row.'[3] To supplement her income she opened a small shop selling bric-a-brac, and accepted the part-time job as registrar of births and deaths offered her by a former colleague on the Board of Guardians. On her husband's death she had lost all heart for public work and had resigned from the Board.

She took no part in politics for the next two years, only renewing her interest when her old friend Keir Hardie was elected Labour MP for Merthyr Tydfil in 1900. Overjoyed at this news, she wrote to him that 'Parliament will be more interesting to us now.'[4] Under the auspices of the ILP, she was elected to the Manchester School Board; she also became one of the Manchester ILP delegates to the local Labour Representation Committee, where she found herself in the ironical position of helping to select candidates she could never vote for. Her reputation among socialists grew at a national level too, and in 1902 she proposed a strong women's suffrage resolution at the ILP's Annual Conference.

The ILP had done little about women's votes since it had agreed to support enfranchising 'both men and women' at its Conference seven years previously. Mrs Pankhurst had likewise let her earlier concern for women's suffrage lapse. Apart from her regular subscription to the North of England Society, she seemed to express little interest.

Yet her concern had not completely died away. Perhaps she had been impressed by the women textile workers' triumphant deputation down to Westminster in February 1902. Perhaps she was persuaded to raise the issue at the ILP Conference that Easter by suffragists like Isabella Ford and Keir Hardie. Whatever the reason, Mrs Pankhurst proposed the resolution at the 1902 ILP Conference:

> That in order to improve the economic and social condition of women, it is necessary to take immediate steps to secure the granting of the suffrage to women on the same terms which it is, or may be, granted to men.

Her resolution, seconded by an influential Bradford councillor, was passed unanimously. (Though its impact was somewhat muted by being followed by a second resolution – asking that Hardie should immediately introduce a bill to enfranchise *all* adults – which was also passed.)

Even after this success, Mrs Pankhurst's interest in women's suffrage apparently remained limited. She did travel up to the Clitheroe constituency and speak at two local meetings during Shackleton's campaign that summer; but her brief involvement in this was perhaps due as much to her interest in electing a third labour MP as to her commitment to Clitheroe's disenfranchised women mill workers. Rather, Mrs Pankhurst still seemed to put her influence and energies into routine ILP business rather than combining it with suffrage. She was a founder-member of a new local ILP branch, Manchester Central, formed in August 1902. Yet its minutes from this period make no mention of women's suffrage; at one meeting the following year, for instance, Mrs Pankhurst seconded a resolution in favour of general propaganda activity – but made no special reference to women.[6] She urged the branch to take action on unemployment and school meals, but never referred to women's suffrage. Until Christabel's interest was kindled it was just one of the many causes she approved of but gave little time to.

For Christabel, on the other hand, women's suffrage seemed always to have been the focus of her political beliefs. When she was later accused by her ILP branch of putting it above her support for Labour, she replied that it was 'the object of her political life'.[7] Certainly until she took up votes for women she seemed to have had only a limited interest in politics.

As the eldest Pankhurst child, Christabel had always been on at least the fringes of Labour. When she was fifteen she went with her parents to election meetings around Gorton and a year later witnessed the Boggart Hole Clough episode. Yet, unlike her sister Sylvia, she took no share in the drudgery of leafleting and selling pamphlets for the ILP, and confined her activities to carefree cycling trips with the Clarion club into the country on Sundays.

When she left Manchester High School she could find no obvious career to follow and no outlet for her considerable energies. She had entertained adolescent ambitions to be a ballet dancer, but they came to nothing. In the end she reluctantly helped her mother out in her shop. She found the work monotonous and restricting, her attendance was erratic and she absorbed herself in a constant succession of novels. 'Business was not good for me,' she later confessed 'and I was not good for business.'[8]

Helena Swanwick, the wife of a Manchester don, knew something of Christabel at this point and remembered her generally as a 'lonely person; with all her capacity for winning adorers (women and men) with all the brightness of her lips and cheeks and eyes, she was unlike her sisters, cynical and cold at heart. She gave me the impression of fitful and impulsive ambition and of quite ruthless love of domination.'[9]

Yet in 1901 Christabel was only twenty one and was more likely to conceive a passion for someone else, rather than inspire one. Her mother suggested that she follow a part-time course at Manchester University, and at a poetry lecture she came across Eva Gore-Booth and Esther Roper. Christabel soon fell under the sway of Eva Gore-Booth's infectious charm, started to attend her Poetry Circle, and became a frequent visitor to the Roper house in Victoria Park. 'Christabel adored her,' Sylvia wrote later, 'and when Eva suffered from neuralgia, as often happened, she would sit with her for hours, massaging her head. To all of us at home, this seemed remarkable indeed, for Christabel had never been willing to act the nurse for any other human being.'[10]

Esther Roper, impressed with Christabel's quick brain, suggested to Mrs Pankhurst that her eldest daughter should train as a lawyer. Such an idea could only have come from a committed feminist, for the legal profession remained closed to women until after the First World War. Christabel was not one to let Victorian prohibitions restrict her. Refused admittance to Lincoln's Inn where her father had studied, she began to read law at Manchester University; here she could receive a law degree even though she could not practise. She proved a brilliant student and in 1906 she (with one other person) graduated with first class honours.[11] Hyndman was probably not exaggerating when he called her 'one of the best-educated women in Great Britain'.[12]

Her schoolgirl passion for Eva Gore-Booth, and her moderate affection for Esther Roper now dominated her life: in 1902 the three of them went on holiday together to Venice. The relationship filled an important vacuum in Christabel's life and began to have other far-reaching consequences. Like Lydia Becker before her, Christabel now found that women's suffrage gave her life a new purpose. Her imagination was fired by what she recognized to be their 'woman's suffrage revival'. With her own personal experience of discrimination, she readily responded to their arguments that women workers could not rely on the automatic support of working men, but needed the vote in their own right. She became dissatisfied with what she saw as Labour's halfhearted support for women's demands; it seemed to her that 'to be in favour of women having the vote was the proper thing, but when it came to action there were many other matters that to men, even Labour men, seemed much more important'.[13]

Christabel joined the North of England Society in 1901 and the following year spoke at five public meetings in the Clitheroe constituency in the run-up to the Shackleton election. But she never became one of the Society's regular speakers, and during the next fifteen months she only addressed two meetings for the Society — Sheffield ILP and Glasgow ILP. Unlike the radical suffragists in the North of England Society, she did not address groups of Guildswomen, weavers, winders and cardroom workers, nor did she take part in laboriously collecting the signatures for the textile workers' petitions. Christabel's scant patience with the foot-slogging drudgery of grass roots politics suggests she never had much faith in building up an industrially-based campaign in Lancashire.

Despite her distaste for the daily grind of local politics, Christabel found much of her new commitment fascinating, and even joined the Women's Trade Union Council, where Eva Gore-Booth was co-secretary. 'The work outside the committee-room was of great political and human interest', she suggested later. 'Miss Roper, Miss Gore-Booth, Mrs Dickenson and I spoke indoors and outdoors, in Manchester and neighbouring places, urging the economic importance to women of abolishing their political outlawry.'[14]

Her involvement with the radical suffragists was such that, according to Sylvia, her mother became 'intensely jealous of her daughter's new friendship. She complained to me bitterly that Christabel was never at home now.'[15] At that time Christabel had no such reservations. 'This was a stage in my political apprenticeship of great and lasting value, and I owed much to the example of these two friends. . . Miss Roper and her friend Eva Gore-Booth . . . played an important part in the final phase of the Suffrage Movement.'[16]

Sylvia Pankhurst had more in common with her mother than with her elder sister in that her primary interest was the ILP; she became a member as soon as she was old enough, when she was sixteen. As a student at Manchester's Municipal School of Art she risked some unpopularity for her political opinions and after she won an art scholarship to study in London, Keir Hardie became her closest friend there. During one period at home, she joined the Manchester Central ILP and quickly became involved in the campaign to provide school meals. Similarly, she joined the Fulham branch of the ILP when she was in London. But generally Sylvia spent so little time in Manchester during the 1900s that she could be no more than an infrequent observer of the radical suffragists' campaign. Had she lived in the north west, events might conceivably have taken a slightly different turn. The radical suffragists' campaign would certainly have been better known, and they and the Pankhursts might have worked more closely together.

The younger Pankhursts, Adela and Harry, followed in the family footsteps as well. Both joined the ILP in their teens and worked for women's suffrage when they grew older.

At the beginning of 1903 Christabel was becoming increasingly impatient with Labour and the slow progress being made towards votes for women. Her mother still retained a great loyalty to the ILP, but Christabel began to quarrel with socialist friends of the family who believed that the interests of working women were adequately represented by their husbands. Her criticisms even extended to her mother, whose dormant suffrage sympathies began to be aroused. Sylvia recalled how 'she bitterly seconded Christabel's reproaches to her that she had allowed the cause of women to be effaced'. So Mrs Pankhurst took up the challenge with renewed enthusiasm, and, characteristically, allowed it to dominate all other issues. Sylvia remembered her refusing to give her usual donation to Keir Hardie's Parliamentary salary, saying that she 'would do no more for Labour representation till women's interests were considered'.

Now she too joined Christabel's attacks on visiting socialists, sometimes provoking anger that threatened to break old ties of friendship. Bruce Glasier, chairman of the ILP, recorded resentfully in his diary:

> A weary ordeal of chatter about women's suffrage from 10pm to 1.30am — Mrs and Christabel Pankhurst belabouring me as chairman of the party for its neglect of the question. At last get roused and speak with something like scorn of their miserable individualistic sexism, and virtually tell them that the ILP will not stir a finger more than it had done for all the women suffragists in creation.

And, he added waspishly:

> Really the pair are not seeking democratic freedom, but self-importance . . . Christabel paints her eyebrows grossly and looks selfish, lazy and wilful. They want to be ladies, not workers, and lack the humility of real heroism.[17]

Isabella Ford, now on the ILP executive, confirmed the Pankhursts' fears that this represented mainstream opinion, and that the party was only 'lukewarm' on votes for women, despite efforts of people like Hardie and herself. At this, Christabel, fired with zeal by Eva Gore-Booth and Esther Roper, began to lose faith in the ILP, though still working along with its supporters. She began to extend her criticisms of this shilly-shallying beyond family arguments and into the full glare of public debate.

In March 1903, just as the radical suffragists were planning to persuade local cotton unions to ballot their members on women's suffrage, Christabel launched her offensive. She circulated a letter to the *Clarion* and Hardie's *Labour Leader* both of which had expressed interest in the radical suffragists' campaign. Both published the letter, an angry criticism of the Labour Conference held the previous month in Newcastle, at which no mention of women's suffrage had been made. To make her point, Christabel adapted the arguments Esther Roper had developed six months earlier in her 'The Cotton Trade Unions and the Enfranchisement of Women', but used them to attack Labour rather than to construct a union-based campaign.

> It will be said, perhaps, that the interests of women will be safe in the hands of the men's Labour Party. Never in the history of the world have the interests of those without power to defend themselves been properly served by others . . . I hope the women of England will not have to say that neither Liberal, Conservative, nor Labour parties are their friends.[18]

Soon Christabel was attacking individual Labour candidates for their apathy over women's suffrage. In May, the Labour Representation Committee put up a candidate at the Preston by-election; his name was John Hodge, he was Secretary of the Steel Smelters' Union and, most importantly, a member of the Labour executive. He was not elected and afterwards he wrote to *Labour Leader* complaining of 'the efforts of Miss Pankhurst and her friends to damage my candidature by the poster they issued'. Christabel retaliated in the next issue, accusing him of neglecting the interests of working women, who comprised such a large proportion of the cotton trade unionists in Preston. Hodge, she alleged, had not mentioned the question of women's suffrage in his election address or at his first meeting, but, when pressed, had replied that he had supported it for a long time. His attitude acted as a red rag to Christabel. 'There is, after all, little to choose between an enemy and a friend who does nothing' she exploded angrily, and declared there had been little real difference between Labour and Tory candidates at Preston.[19]

By now Christabel had moved well away from the tactics adopted by the radical suffragists within the North of England Society. The previous year they had organized deputations to Shackleton to urge him to introduce a women's suffrage bill; but there is no suggestion that they disrupted meetings or antagonized candidates. They always tried to build up positive grass-roots support for their demands, rather than relying on the more negative strategy of attacks on particular 'opponents'. Yet Christabel stuck to her plan and a few months later followed the Preston incident with an uncompromising attack on what she saw as the timidity of the ILP which dared not 'offend the prejudices of the British working man'. The criticisms must have been widely read by socialists for they were published as the leading article in *ILP News*.[20]

The difference in approach between Christabel and her mother was becoming more apparent. Teresa Billington later perceptively summed up the distinction: 'I have always felt that Mrs Pankhurst believed there was hope for this Labour conversion policy, while Christabel only endured it till her time came.'[21] Mrs Pankhurst fully recognized that far greater pressure needed to be concentrated on the Labour Representation Committee; its support of women's suffrage became increasingly vital each year as more and more Labour candidates made their way to Westminster.[22] Although the ILP was just one small (though vocal) element within the Labour Representation Committee, she felt optimistic about relying on its influence to win Labour support. All that was lacking, she felt, was a small but effective pressure group that could niggle away at Labour until opposition was silenced and support guaranteed.[23]

In the autumn Mrs Pankhurst's deliberations began to take practical shape; she decided to form an organization parallel to, but independent from, the Labour Representation Committee. It was to be called the Women's Labour Representation Committee and its purpose was to agitate for votes for women.

Unlike Isabella Ford, Keir Hardie and other suffragists in the ILP, Mrs Pankhurst still attached little significance to the work being done by the radical suffragists. Yet Christabel remained intrigued by their activities and had recently seen the formation of their Lancashire Women Textile Workers' Representation Committee, though she took no active part in it.

According to Sylvia, Christabel came home from attending a meeting with Esther Roper and Eva Gore-Booth and, hearing of her mother's proposed new group, told her that the title would have to be changed because of its similarities to her friends' new committee. 'Christabel did not,' wrote Sylvia, 'at that time attach any importance to her mother's project: her interest lay with that of her friends.'[24] Mrs Pankhurst was hurt that her eldest daughter's first loyalties lay outside the family; but she acquiesced and chose instead to call her group the Women's Social and Political Union (WSPU).

Christabel immediately transferred her energies to the fledgling WSPU. She must have already experienced a certain disenchantment with the Lancashire Women Textile Workers' Representation Committee, presumably recognizing she could never play a leading role in a group largely run by past and present textile workers. Women like Sarah Reddish, Nellie Keenan or Selina Cooper would probably not have taken the sporadic involvement of an ambitious university student very kindly. Perhaps for this reason she began to think that the WSPU might provide greater scope for her considerable energy and talent.

According to Christabel, the beginnings of the WSPU were characteristically haphazard. ' "Women", said Mother on a memorable occasion, "we must do the work ourselves. We must have our own independent women's movement. Come to my house tomorrow and we will arrange it!" ' The next day, 10 October 1903, those summoned turned up. They were, according to Sylvia, 'a few obscure women members of the ILP' and, as the WSPU kept no records of this early period, only the names of a few have been recorded. One of the women was Helen Harker from Higher Broughton in Salford; she became treasurer, though no evidence of her work has survived. She was married to John Harker, a leading member of the Trades Council. Another was Rachel Scott from Flixton on the far side of Salford, who became secretary, largely a clerical job. She must have been comfortably off for her husband paid the rent for the room in Manchester Central ILP used for meetings, in order to qualify as a voter in the city. Both women were members of the Pankhursts' ILP branch, Central Manchester, as was another early recruit, Teresa Billington, who joined about Christmas time.[25]

Teresa Billington was a valuable addition to the tiny group. She had already come into contact with Mrs Pankhurst over her adamant refusal to teach religion in her elementary school, and had carved out a reputation for herself as strong-minded and rebellious through the University Settlement and the Manchester Teachers' Equal Pay League. A large, powerfully built woman with a pleasant, round face, she was, for Sylvia, 'one of the "new" young women, who refused to make any pretence of subordinating themselves to others, in thought or deed'.[26] She too joined the Pankhursts' ILP branch within two months of joining the WSPU.

None of the Pankhursts held formal office in the WSPU for, as

Christabel wrote later, they did not want 'the Union [to] be discounted as "just Mrs Pankhurst and Christabel" and dubbed a "family party".'[27]

Straight after the first meeting Rachel Scott was delegated to write to the *Labour Leader* to inform the readers that a new organization had just been formed:

Sir — It will be of interest to many of your readers to learn that we have in Manchester founded a Women's Social and Political Union, its objects being to secure for women complete equality with men, both social and political. As in the other political parties, so in the Labour party, the help of women is welcomed in the work of elections, but when our leaders and men members of the party are asked for efforts to be made to secure the enfranchisement of women, they express, at best, vague sympathy.

Every reform is considered more vital and more urgent than the removal of the unjust disability put on women. We ask you to publish this appeal to all women Socialists to join in this movement to press upon the party and the community the urgent need of giving to women the vote, in order that they may take their share in the work of social emancipation.[28]

During the winter 1903-4, differences began to emerge between the local suffrage groups. The radical suffragists, still operating within the old North of England Society, were mustering support from local unions like the Burnley Weavers', encouraging William Wilkinson to champion them at the forthcoming Labour Representation Conference, and widening their campaign beyond Lancashire to women pottery, hosiery and chain-making workers in the Midlands. On the other hand, the avowed aim of the WSPU was, from the outset, to influence Labour politics at a national level. Their strategy was to put sufficient public pressure on the ILP (still a standard-bearer for women's rights) for Labour to commit itself to supporting such legislation. What the WSPU thought of the success of the Wilkinson resolution, passed merely four months after their first meeting, can never be known; perhaps they realised how long it had taken the radical suffragists to become such an effective pressure group, or perhaps they felt inspired to follow this example.

The differing political priorities and practical strategies of the radical suffragists and the WSPU already emerge clearly: both aimed to influence Labour, one through a grass-roots industrial campaign and the other through a national political campaign. Yet the two groups, based so close to each other in central Manchester, seemed to be able to organize parallel activities that hardly touched the other group. Possibly because the WSPU was still tiny and virtually unknown, they seem to have co-existed peacefully over the next two years and, for instance, the North of England Society still welcomed Christabel to address its meetings. In fact as soon as the WSPU was founded Christabel suddenly became one of the Society's regular speakers, even though in the past she had only addressed a handful of meetings for them. Relying on the North of England Society's clout (in practical terms its ability to hire a hall, publicize a meeting and guarantee an audience) over the next few months she addressed ILP meetings in Leicester, Liverpool, Oldham and West Bromwich.

Although the WSPU was still only a handful of local women, it began to attract a certain amount of curiosity and support in socialist circles. 'Mrs Pankhurst, and a few other women in earnest, are starting a new crusade this year to force the Labour Party to work for women,' Julia Dawson noted approvingly in the New Year's Day *Clarion*. 'They feel that in the past women have been too apologetic for their existence, and too submissive .... That is good. I now look to women in other towns, and ask what they are doing?'[29]

At first the WSPU's approaches to ILP branches and candidates to pass resolutions calling on the ILP executive to take action made little headway. They could exert limited leverage compared to the radical suffragists and were still heavily dependent on local ILP sympathizers for publicity and support. The Pankhursts once again became restless before their policy had a chance to bear fruit, though this was, as Sylvia commented later, 'somewhat precipitate, following as it did, on a long period of inaction towards women's suffrage on Mrs Pankhurst's own part. Christabel, young and impetuous, was scarcely two years old in suffrage work; the rest of us younger still.'[30]

Christabel began to extend her attacks on Labour even further and to advocate an all-or-nothing attitude to male politicians. In November 1903 she spoke to the newly-formed Sheffield Women's Suffrage Society (which became affiliated to the North of England Society) and impatiently urged 'women not to be divided, but to belong to one party, to join together on one question — the vote'. She asked women to 'throw off "party", to stand together, and let their motto be — "He who is for us, for him are we." '[31]

The following February, irked by the lack of response, she decided to try to reach a wider public. She managed to get a good seat on the platform at a major meeting of the Free Trade League in the Free Trade Hall, and from this strategic position tried to move a women's suffrage amendment to the main resolution. The chairman refused to let Christabel disrupt the meeting, and after some argument she gave way.

Her interruption was given brief mention in the *Manchester Guardian*. Otherwise it was an isolated incident, quickly forgotten, with no further results. Casting around for other dramatic ways to make women's suffrage a subject that could no longer be ignored, Christabel focused on the Manchester and Salford Women's Trade Council. Since it was led by such outstanding suffragists as Sarah Dickenson and Nellie Keenan, she felt sure that she could rely on it not to vacillate — as the ILP did — but to come out in immediate support.

Christabel had taken little part in the Council's main work of organizing women into unions and during 1901 only spoke at three meetings. (Though she did help to provide 'entertainment' at two 'social evenings'). The following year she became a member of the small organizing sub-committee, but was never a member of the Council Executive. Over the next two years there is no record of her speaking at any trade union meetings, though in January 1903 she was one of the several speakers at the annual meeting of subscribers and friends at the Lord Mayor's Parlour. Christabel seems to have been one of the Council's sympathetic supporters, but not among those who provided much practical help and, for instance, she seems to have had nothing to do with setting up Nellie Keenan's Salford Power Loom Weavers. Her main interest in the Council, apart from its links with Eva Gore-Booth, was probably in its potential for propagating women's suffrage.

Towards the end of 1904 Christabel managed to bring the issue of the Council's attitude to women's suffrage to a head. A paragraph appeared in the *Daily News*, confusing the Council with the Lancashire Women Textile Workers' Representation Committee. Eva Gore-Booth, diplomatically wishing to distinguish the work of the two organizations, and Amy Bulley (Chairman of the Council and no suffragist) wrote to correct the mistake. Amy Bulley also wrote to the *Manchester Guardian* to make the Council's official position absolutely plain: the Council's purpose was to unionize and protect working women, not to conduct political propaganda of any sort.

Christabel immediately jumped into this opening with a rival letter to the *Manchester Guardian*, disassociating herself from Amy Bulley's views. By her precipitate action she left the Council with no option but to take a public stand on women's suffrage. She optimistically assumed it would come out in support. But she was wrong. At a special meeting called to discuss the affair, she was defeated. The Council wanted to retain its non-political status. 'By a large majority the Council decided that its special work, for which alone its subscribers' money was asked, was the organization of women's labour, and that the advocacy of Women's Suffrage, however desirable in itself, was outside its scope as a body.'

Forced into an untenable position on the Council, both Eva Gore-Booth and Sarah Dickenson resigned. The two of them formed a new organization called the Manchester and Salford Women's Trade and Labour Council; the 'Labour' in the title was significant, recalling how the same word had been added to the men's trades councils when it decided to support independent labour representation.

The original Council recorded the departures with considerable generosity considering that Eva Gore-Booth and Sarah Dickenson had taken with them no fewer than seven unions and two thousand members, including activists like Nellie Keenan, Louisa Smith, Violet Grundy and Isabel Forsyth. They were left virtually powerless, with a pitiful membership of only one hundred.[32]

Even at this stage, Christabel revealed sides to her character that were to emerge even more strongly as the WSPU policies developed. She was prepared to take action independently of suffragists with whom she had previously worked closely and considered her friends, even if this entailed the risk of wrecking nearly ten years of patient trade union effort. Christabel also demonstrated that, even by 1904, she was prepared to jeopardize every other political objective for the sake of this one demand. This was just the first in a long series of splits caused by the unswerving tenacity of her commitment to votes for women.

During 1904 Christabel developed into the fiercest critic of all Labour supporters who would not commit themselves to women's suffrage. She bitterly attacked Philip Snowden for writing a complacent article in *Labour Leader* on 'The ILP and Women's Franchise' which argued against any bill to enfranchise women on the same property qualifications as men. Socialists, he suggested, 'did not want to abolish class distinctions to raise distinctions of sex'.

'Sex distinctions exist however,' Christabel retorted with justifiable feeling the following week, 'and it is not by ignoring them, but by recognizing and attacking them, that we shall secure their abolition.'[33]

Christabel was presented with an even better opportunity to make her point six months later, towards the end of 1904, when discussion on proposed suffrage legislation brought the growing hostility between adult suffragists and women suffragists further into the open. At the annual ILP Conference the previous Easter, Mrs Pankhurst had been elected onto the Executive. Despite opposition she again introduced a successful resolution demanding the introduction of a private member's bill to enfranchise women. This was a great advance forward, but still one with only limited potential. First, private members' bills had little more chance of success than they had in Lydia Becker's day: without government backing they were doomed from the start. Second, the ILP was only one small constituent in the growing Labour Representation Committee, which itself had only five MPs. Nevertheless Keir Hardie and Will Crooks tried to find an opportunity for the bill, even though it was likely to be rejected without debate.

The bitter wrangling between the adult suffragists (who would support no measure unless it enfranchised all adults and totally abolished property qualifications) and women suffragists (who demanded limited enfranchisement of *some* women on a property basis as the first vital step towards the goal of adult suffrage) was extremely complex, and it persistently dogged events for over a decade. The debate partly hinged on the fact that neither Liberals nor Tories were likely to support complete adult suffrage which, even in the 1900s, still cast a shadow of mob rule in many people's minds. Also neither party was likely to support complete manhood suffrage (although they obviously found it less threatening than complete adult suffrage) because it smacked of Chartism and would destroy the property basis in the existing electorate. All suffragists found the prospect of a manhood suffrage bill extremely threatening: they knew that once it was passed, women's claims for the Parliamentary vote would be set back for decades. Here they were up against some socialists who argued that if complete manhood suffrage was easier to obtain than a limited women's suffrage bill, they should opt for the former rather than rejecting any attempt to widen the franchise.

There was also an extremely practical question to the controversy: what proportion of the women enfranchised by a limited suffrage bill would be working class? Keir Hardie, who championed the WSPU just as readily as he championed the radical suffragists, initiated a survey to be carried out by ILP branches to try and quantify this. At the same time the Lancashire Women's Textile Workers' Representation Committee, the new pro-suffrage Women's Trade and Labour Council, and the Women's Co-operative Guild, conducted a similar survey in Nelson and Bolton (no doubt master-minded by Selina Cooper and Sarah Reddish) and in three Yorkshire towns.[34] In each case the investigations failed to define precisely what they meant by the terms 'working class' and 'working women' and for this reason the results should be interpreted with great caution: still, they showed that at least 80 per cent of those who would be enfranchised were 'working class', and therefore a limited suffrage bill could no longer be contemptuously dismissed by Labour as a 'Ladies' Bill'.

Despite this flurry of woolly statistics[35] opposition to women's suffrage began to harden. Allegations flew about that to support such a limited suffrage bill would be treacherous disloyalty to Labour – and a great boost to the Tories. For instance, the influential Julia Dawson, previously a supporter of the radical suffragists' claims and scathing in her attack on Shackleton's behaviour in the House, began to reconsider her position. She reacted strongly to an article by Eva Gore-Booth in *Labour Leader* which had suggested that 'it would be easier and quicker to get a half-loaf than a whole one'. 'I don't think it would' retaliated Julia Dawson, and she went on to argue, inspite of her earlier support at the Clitheroe election, that

> even if it would, I think we should in justice wait for the whole loaf. But even if we take it for granted that it would be expedient to be content with half the loaf at first, why choose the top half? Should not the claims of the bottom crust come first, which, as everybody knows, supports the upper?[36]

Eva Gore-Booth had tried to argue that the many thousands of skilled women workers in the north of England could easily qualify for the lodger-franchise which demanded that a voter pay a minimum of £10 a year rent. Julia Dawson dismissed this peremptorily as wishful thinking: in Leeds women sewed knickers at 4½d a dozen and could not possibly afford the 4s a week rent to enfranchise themselves. The *Clarion*'s record was clean, she claimed, 'and we have no intention of staining it now by supporting any Bill in Parliament which leaves the oppressed and downtrodden out of the reckoning'.

Ada Nield Chew was one of the many *Clarion* readers who went along wholeheartedly with this adult suffrage line of argument. Ten years earlier in the *Crewe Chronicle* she had asked that working women should be represented in Parliament by Labour candidates, as well as working men, and she still held that position. But Julia Dawson's appeal on behalf of the oppressed and downtrodden must have struck a sympathetic note: that year she had been working with low-paid women workers in Scotland, the Midlands, the Potteries and Lancashire on behalf of the League, and must have recognized that the women she had closest contact with were highly unlikely to qualify for the vote on the lodger-franchise.

As an ILP member, she decided to throw her lot in with Bruce

Glasier and Philip Snowden, rather than with Hardie, Isabella Ford and Mrs Pankhurst. Just before Christmas 1904 she wrote an angry letter to the *Clarion* denouncing the ILP for backing a limited suffrage bill. If such a bill ever became law, she warned that

> the entire class of wealthy women would be enfranchised, that the great body of working women, married or single, would be voteless still, and that to give wealthy women a vote would mean that they, voting naturally in their own interests, would help to swamp the vote of the enlightened working man, who is trying to get Labour men into Parliament.[37]

The radical suffragists read this letter with some dismay. They had always supported any measure to enfranchise women and, in their survey of potential women electors in Nelson, Bolton and elsewhere, had tried to show that even under a limited suffrage bill the great majority of those enfranchised would be 'working women'. They had no greater wish to give privileges to wealthy women than had Ada Nield Chew, especially as they were nursing a suffrage-labour candidate in Wigan and knew that they would lose valuable votes if they became tarred with a 'privilege and property' brush.

Faced with this dilemma, the radical suffragists formulated a practical compromise — womanhood suffrage — that demanded the vote for all women over twenty one. (This in effect was a demand for adult suffrage, but it placed all its stress on the claims of women.) They sent the *Clarion* a considered statement of this policy, explaining why the present Bill was vital to the textile workers:

> Womanhood suffrage is the final aim of our franchise efforts; meanwhile, we welcome heartily every practical step in that direction... This we do, knowing that in England it is idle to expect revolutions, and that the most we can hope for at first is an instalment of justice — a measure that will include a large number of women wage-earners, especially in the more skilled trades, as the cotton trade. We think that until the franchise is given to these workers the trade unions will be hopelessly crippled in their efforts to protect the interests of their members; ... their wages will never rise above their present low level, and their whole industrial status will suffer. We are not responsible for, and we cannot dictate the terms of our own enfranchisement. The measure we want, and the measure we are working for, is simply the broadest measure it is possible to get.
>
> Signed on behalf of the Lancashire and Cheshire Women Textile and Other Workers' Representation Committee,
>
>   Secretaries
>   EVA GORE-BOOTH
>   ESTHER ROPER,
>   SARAH REDDISH, Treasurer
>
> On behalf of the Manchester and Salford Women's Trade and Labour Council,
>
>   SARAH DICKENSON, Co-Secretary.
>   NELLIE KEENAN, Treasurer.[38]

The other group which quickly responded to Ada Nield Chew's challenge was, of course, the Women's Co-operative Guild. Only five months previously (and partly dué to pressure from Sarah Reddish) its Annual Congress had, after heated debate, decided to support the limited franchise bill. They too had no wish to support wealthy women; Mrs Bury, the current Guild President from Darwen, and Margaret Llewelyn Davies, wrote to the *Clarion* on behalf of their 19,000 members, to make the Guild's position absolutely clear:

> The membership of the Guilds being composed mainly of married working women, the Guilds could only be satisfied with a measure which would enfranchise this class of women. But while womanhood (or adult) suffrage is their goal, the Guilds leave themselves free to support any measure which would be a step in the direction of this goal. By this is meant any Bill which would not disenfranchise married women, and which would include a large proportion of working women among those enfranchised.[39]

The radical suffragists and the Guild shared Ada Nield Chew's ultimate objective — to enfranchise all working women — but unlike her did not feel it made practical political sense to reject a measure merely because it only went half way to accomplishing this.

Christabel Pankhurst, on the other hand, was not prepared even to nod in the direction of Ada Nield Chew. By now her commitment to women's suffrage so heavily outweighed any other political consideration that she could only react to criticism of the Bill with an out-and-out attack. Increasingly for her, it was the principle of votes for women that counted rather than which class of women would benefit.

Christabel, who was familiar with the *Clarion*'s popular appeal (and had once cycled to Chester to attend the annual Clarion club gathering) realized that here was an excellent opportunity to publicize the WSPU point of view. Early in January 1905, she added her voice to the controversy. Ada Nield Chew had alleged that wealthy men would make sure that their wives, daughters and sisters had property enough to be enfranchised so that Labour voters were outnumbered. 'Some of us,' Christabel suggested acidly, 'are not at all so confident as is Mrs Chew of the average middle class man's anxiety to confer votes upon his female relatives.'[40] A week later Ada Nield Chew retorted angrily that she had 'suffered, ever since I began to think, from a keen sense of injustice of my sex politically', and had considered Christabel's answer, but still rejected the Bill in favour of 'the abolition of all existing anomalies . . . which would enable a man or woman to vote simply because they are man or woman, not because they are more fortunate financially than their fellow men and women'.[41]

The fiery exchange ran on through the spring and into March. The two women both relished confrontation, and neither was prepared to concede an inch. They had no sympathy for the other's views, and shared no common experiences that might help to bridge the chasm. Christabel, daughter of a barrister, had been educated at Manchester High School and was now a university student; despite her connections with women like Sarah Dickenson, she had little personal experience of working women's lives. Ada Nield Chew had known little else: from her *Crewe Chronicle* days to her current work with the League, her life had been a series of battles against women's low wages and appalling working conditions.

The class antagonism between the two women was never made explicit and was always channelled into arguments for and against the Bill. Tempers became frayed, especially when Christabel cooly 'invited' Ada Nield Chew to do a survey of her home town, Rochdale, so that she could see for herself that 90 per cent of those enfranchised would be working women. Ada Nield Chew retorted bitterly that she was far too busy and anyway, 'working women and the Labour Party have surely better work to do than to fight the battles of women rich enough and intelligent enough to do it for themselves'.[42]

This ill-tempered exchange eventually faded out, each side only more deeply entrenched in its prejudices, and neither taking time to consider the radical suffragists' practical compromise policy of womanhood suffrage.[43]

Anyway, by now the *Clarion* debate had to a certain extent been overtaken by political events. After the Wilkinson motion had been carried by a large majority by the Labour Representation Conference in 1904, ILP supporters and the radical suffragists decided to put forward an even stronger resolution at the 1905 Conference, to be held in Liverpool at the end of January. This time there was even greater reason to hope for success. The ILP was now much firmer in its support; Mrs Pankhurst was on the executive, and Philip Snowden, previously uninterested, had now become a fervent convert to the cause, largely due to the enthusiasm of his future wife, Ethel Annakin, whom he married in March.

The motion was to be proposed by a Scottish delegate from one of the most powerful unions, the Engineers; Selina Cooper, one of the ILP delegates, was chosen as seconder. This must have greatly cheered the radical suffragists. At the previous Conference, the speakers had either been union men (William Wilkinson) or middle class socialists (Isabella

Ford); now the policy of employing working class suffrage organizers and petition workers was really showing results. Not only had Helen Silcock spoken at the TUC, but now Selina Cooper, with her daughter four years old and able to be left with one of her relations for a day or two, had emerged as a gifted and effective public speaker, able to take on the hostility from trade union and trades council delegates.

The resolution, very carefully worded, proposed that 'this Conference heartily approves of adult suffrage and the complete enfranchisement of both sexes, and endorses the Women's Enfranchisement Bill introduced into Parliament last Session, believing it to be an important step towards adult suffrage.'[44]

The proposer gave way to the seconder. This was the moment Selina Cooper had been waiting for. If she could impress upon the great mass of adult suffragists in the audience that she spoke for working class women, and that to support the Bill was to *support* Labour, not to undermine it, the resolution might get the votes it desperately needed. She held the views that she did, she told them,

> because I am a working woman and because I recognize that it is only by the means mentioned in the resolution that we can take a practical step towards complete enfranchisement. I speak on behalf of thousands of women engaged in the textile trades, to whose class I belong. It is urged against those favouring the Enfranchisement Bill that we are asking for mere palliatives, but I would remind you that when the Conference dealt with the question of Unemployment on a previous day you were prepared to agitate for palliatives. Is not the feeding of children a palliative? Is not our very Trade Union Movement, of which we are all so justly proud, a palliative compared to the conditions we are working for when we will not need this protection? In the Clitheroe Division alone, 5,500 women have signed a petition in favour of women having the vote on the same terms as men, and I would impress upon you not to think that women want the vote merely as women. We are as keenly alive to the needs of the people as anyone, and if we have the vote we will be able to use it in the interests of reform.

No sooner had she sat down at the end of her passionate appeal than up rose Harry Quelch, delegate from the London Trades Council, a member of the Social Democratic Federation, and an implacable opponent of women's suffrage. Like other socialists from outside Lancashire, he had no direct experience of the radical suffragists' campaign among the textile workers, and his image of women's suffrage was limited to the genteel tactics of Mrs Fawcett and the well-to-do London suffragists.

Quelch reiterated the arguments against women's suffrage. Like Ada Nield Chew, he strongly believed that complete adult suffrage was the only franchise reform that should be supported by Labour MPs. 'Mrs Cooper has appealed to the sentiment of sex, but I repudiate that there is any sex antagonism,' he said. 'Mrs Cooper has placed sex first; but it is not the place of the [Labour Representation Committee] to place sex first; we have to put Labour first in every case;' and he moved an adult suffrage amendment that ran directly counter to the resolution.

Other speeches followed, evenly balanced for and against. The newly converted Philip Snowden admitted that the Bill would not give them everything but, he said, 'no sensible man can fail to realize that there is no likelihood in the imminent future of any House of Commons taking the important step of granting adult suffrage', and so the Bill should be strongly supported. Mrs Pankhurst backed up Selina Cooper, quoting the ILP surveys to prove that about 90 per cent of potential voters were working class women. 'I am appealing to you to discard sex prejudice' she said — for otherwise they would end up with manhood suffrage and votes for women would become a hopeless cause.

Quelch and those who supported him had resurrected the bogey of 'sex prejudice' versus 'class prejudice'. Selina Cooper had worked so carefully to build up a campaign that was guilty of neither extreme and was based on a practical compromise: womanhood suffrage as their aim, but support of all limited suffrage bills as the necessary first step to *all* women winning the vote. Yet Quelch's allegation that Selina Cooper 'placed sex first' was a phrase that immediately struck home to the listening trade union and trades council delegates. They had always been wary of women's suffrage, and Quelch's emotive rhetoric quelled any final doubts they might have had. His amendment was carried by 483 votes to 270, was put as a substantive motion and subsequently adopted. The triumphant adoption of the Wilkinson resolution the year before quickly faded from memory and became a forgotten achievement in suffrage history.

Selina Cooper returned from Liverpool to Nelson a bitterly disappointed woman. However much support local cotton unions and the ILP executive gave women's suffrage, there was always a solid wall of opposition from trade unionists outside the textile region. Every month, as the suffragists' stepped up their campaign, this opposition grew stronger. Two of the Conference speakers who opposed Selina Cooper were delegates from trades councils in Stockton and Bradford. Recently Bradford, London, Liverpool and Birkenhead Trades Councils had voted against women's suffrage.[45] A few weeks later an Adult Suffrage Society was formed to co-ordinate opposition to the limited suffrage bill: its president was Margaret Bondfield, a London-based organizer for the Shop Assistants' Union, and a woman of growing influence in the Labour movement.[46] In the face of this, radical suffragists had to fall back on their hopes of the Wigan election, trusting the voters would respond with the same enthusiasm as other cotton towns when it came to a General Election.

Since the Bill in question had never been properly debated in the Commons, Keir Hardie now determined to introduce a second ILP-backed women's suffrage bill. He was unlucky in the balloting and did not gain a place, but Mrs Pankhurst, who had come down to London to lobby MPs, was able to persuade Bamford Slack, holder of the fourteenth place, to take up the issue. Slack's Bill embodied the traditional demand shared by both the WSPU and the National Union: that women should be given the vote on the same property basis as men. It came before the Commons on 12 May 1905, only to be talked out by anti-suffragist MPs, who managed to use up all available debating time by an endless discussion of whether vehicles should carry a rear light as well as a front light.

Mrs Pankhurst, the other WSPU members, nearly two hundred Guildswomen, and suffragists like Isabella Ford, were all in the Commons Lobby for the debate and heard within minutes that the Bill had been talked out. 'This news reached the waiting, anxious women gathered in the lobby,' Christabel wrote later. '...Mother who... shared the indignation of the women at the news of the massacre, called upon them to follow her outside for a meeting of protest.' 'Our indignation was stronger and more burning than I for one have ever seen it before' Isabella Ford commented.[47]

In their fury at such treachery the WSPU members decided to stop lobbying Westminster for the moment, and to concentrate their energies once again on a campaign in the north of England to win Labour support there. Being Pankhursts they tended to prefer to work independently of other local suffragists, and there does not seem to have been much co-ordination between them and the meetings the radical suffragists organized in the open air or with Guild and ILP branches in the cotton towns; though the North of England Society still accepted Christabel as one of its regular speakers, and officially sponsored her when she addressed various trades councils, some as far away as Leicester and Sunderland, and others based in the larger cotton towns.[48]

Since its formation the WSPU roll-call of speakers had consisted entirely of the Pankhursts and Teresa Billington. Now their ranks were swollen by two important additions, Hannah Mitchell and Annie Kenney. Hannah Mitchell, on the Ashton Board of Guardians, had long felt deeply frustrated by the dismissive attitude of ILP men towards women members. Two years previously, three months before the WSPU was even formed, she had written to *Labour Leader* calling for a Woman's Party to tackle the problem, [49] and by summer 1905 she was helping the Pankhursts 'to fan into flame the smouldering fire of discontent lit by the older suffrage societies'.

Annie Kenney, an equally enthusiastic convert, was the first WSPU recruit who had no strong links with the ILP. An impressionable and childlike young woman, she was completely won over by the strength of Christabel's personality and enthusiasm. Sylvia later summed up her character with cruel candour. 'She was essentially a follower ... Her lack of perspective, her very intellectual limitations, lent her a certain directness of purpose when she became the instrument of a more powerful mind' — which was, of course, Christabel's. [50]

The early WSPU, now slightly enlarged, was heavily influenced by the campaign tactics developed over the previous five years by the radical suffragists, and by what they had learnt in the ILP. They too opted for the hurly-burly of street-corner and open-air meetings and at Annie Kenney's suggestion began speaking at the midsummer fairs, or wakes as they are called in Lancashire. Sylvia later described how they would travel round to the various cotton towns; she would take the chair and announce 'I have a young woman here to speak to you who has worked as a half-time hand in the cotton mill, and another young woman who wants to be a lawyer.' [51] Manchester Central ILP continued to give them the vital support they needed to survive and sponsored their Sunday evening meetings in Tib Street. In May, Keir Hardie's pamphlet 'The Citizenship of Women' was published, which quoted the earlier ILP survey of potential 'working women' electors, and this was sold at WSPU meetings.

Yet despite the summer's enthusiastic activity, Christabel was astute enough to realize that the opposition she encountered in the more distant trades councils, would never be dispelled merely by speaking at wakes' fairs or selling ILP pamphlets to the already converted. If the radical suffragists, with their firm base in cotton town Guilds, ILP branches and trade unions still encountered considerable opposition and apathy, how could a handful of women without the support of industrial workers expect to make any impact? They had no constituency; they represented no one but themselves; they could speak for no mass movement, and they could exert no pressure as trade unionists.

Christabel cast around for some new way to build up her suffrage campaign. In the summer of 1905 she was given a vivid example of how to make a real impact. She had noticed how local unemployment demonstrations were quickly followed by the desired government unemployment relief bill. She decided to attract government attention in an equally direct way.

Her opportunity arrived when Winston Churchill and Sir Edward Grey, two prominent Liberals who could reasonably expect Cabinet positions in the next election, were due to speak at a meeting of supporters at the Free Trade Hall on Friday 13 October. Christabel and a few hand-picked friends laid their plans very carefully, telling nobody else — not even Hannah Mitchell — what they intended to do.

Her daring strategy was to create such a disturbance that it would lead to arrest and imprisonment. Two seats were booked in the Hall, and Christabel and Annie Kenney sat through the packed meeting. They waited until question time to make their protest and then Annie Kenney jumped up and shouted out 'Will the Liberal Government give votes to women?' When she was ignored, Christabel stood up and joined in with her, and they unfurled their banner demanding 'Votes for Women'. In the end they were flung out of the meeting and marched off by policemen.

Christabel still felt sure that they had not done quite enough to guarantee imprisonment. So, unable to get her arms and hands free to strike out, she decided to commit a technical assault, and she spat at one of the policemen. This was sufficient provocation. The two women were quickly marched off to the police station and the following day the magistrate, ruling out of order Christabel's polemical speech in her own defence, sentenced her to seven days imprisonment and Annie Kenney to three in Strangeways Prison.[52]

The week in prison was merely the peg on which to hang a much larger campaign. Teresa Billington, one of the very few people party to the intrigue, had undertaken to arrange the publicity that was vital to success. It was essential to her plans that the two women remain in prison for their full sentences. In spite of Annie Kenney's rather unreliable memory of 'the very extremity of abuse, criticism and condemnation hurled at us by the morning Press' little notoriety was actually gained by the initial protest in the Free Trade Hall. The

Manchester Guardian, the most influential of the local papers, only gave their demonstration three short sentences in the middle of a long report of the meeting.[53] The court proceedings were reported at length, but without the protest meeting co-ordinated by Teresa Billington during their imprisonment, interest in the Free Trade Hall incident would quickly have faded away. After all, the WSPU had hardly been able to muster much public support over the last two years.

The first protest meeting was held on the night after the event in Stevenson Square, a favourite site for socialist groups. It was largely an ILP occasion and attracted a big crowd in spite of heavy rain. One of the members of Manchester Central ILP was in the chair and the main speaker was Teresa Billington: she described what had happened to Christabel and Annie Kenney the day before and demanded that 'from henceforth women and such men as were worthy of the name must wage war against the Liberal forces'. This martial rallying cry was followed by John Harker from the Trades Council, and Hannah Mitchell, who both condemned Liberal action. One of Annie Kenney's sisters and a representative from Oldham ILP also spoke, and Mrs Pankhurst declared herself 'proud to be the mother of one of the two young women who had gone to prison'.[54]

Teresa Billington used the following week to raise public support, especially from the ILP (which she was well placed to do as she was now employed as a party organizer on a small salary). At its Wednesday night meeting Manchester Central ILP passed a resolution of support for Christabel and Annie Kenney, and the two women were congratulated for 'their spirited and brave protest ... against the callousness of official Liberalism regarding the Enfranchisement of Women'. Teresa Billington then reported to the meeting that the ILP's national executive had met that week in Manchester and was planning a protest meeting to be held in the Free Trade Hall on 20 October, a week after the original demonstration.[55]

When Christabel came out of prison on Friday morning a crowd of about two hundred had gathered outside Strangeways. Members of the Women's Trade and Labour Council were there, as well as many ILP-WSPU supporters including Keir Hardie, Hannah Mitchell, Sam Robinson, and John and Helen Harker. Esther Roper and Eva Gore-Booth, who had been foremost in expressing solidarity with Mrs Pankhurst during the crisis, presented flowers. They had not been informed of Christabel's plans before the incident, and they must have had to swallow certain doubts about tactics which ran so directly counter to their own campaign. They knew Christabel only too well by now and had seen her attack Labour candidates, split the Women's Trades Council and spar with adult suffragists in the *Clarion*. While they had tried to build up positive local support for women's suffrage, she seemed to put her energies into wilful attacks on 'opponents'. Even so, Christabel was an old friend; they had been on holiday together and recently she had become one of the most energetic of North of England speakers. They owed her a certain loyalty, and they must have admired her courage. Also, Christabel's plan seemed to be having the desired effect: it attracted considerable local attention to the cause so dear to their hearts, and merited their valuable support. A few days later Esther Roper defended Christabel's actions at the Annual Convention of the National Union of Women's Suffrage Societies in Hull; her imprisonment, she stated 'had arisen out of an honest earnest effort' to ask a suffrage question, and the audience 'must not be led away by anything which happened outside the hall'.[56]

Esther Roper had straightened the record with the national suffrage movement. But the greatest contribution the radical suffragists could make to events that week was to lend their names to the protest meeting the ILP had planned for the 20th. This they did. A poster advertising the event was printed which listed thirteen star sponsors: the names included Bruce Glasier, Isabella Ford, Teresa Billington, Mrs Pankhurst and John Harker, but also Eva Gore-Booth, Esther Roper and Sarah Dickenson. In its first two years the WSPU depended very heavily on the local ILP for its survival, but it also had to lean on the radical suffragists when it came to drawing on support of local working women.[57]

The meeting was opened by Teresa Billington who read out letters of support from sympathizers, including one from Philip Snowden, then chairman of the ILP; he and his wife congratulated Mrs Pankhurst on her brave daughter. 'We are all proud of her and her friend Miss Kenney. Their action on this occasion has done more for the women's cause than all the continued work of such as Mrs Mills and Miss Ashton' (North of England Society members who pursued the traditional, respectable way of working for suffrage.) Another letter from Selina Cooper and her friends in the Nelson Women's Co-operative Guild, enclosed a strongly worded protest against the conduct of Sir Edward Grey and the Liberal leaders.[58]

The WSPU resolution demanding that the franchise 'shall be granted to women on the same terms as it is or may be granted to men' was moved by John Harker as President of the Manchester and Salford Trades and Labour Council, and seconded by Sarah Dickenson, as Co-Secretary of the Women's Trades and Labour Council. After Christabel and Annie Kenney spoke, and despite a great deal of heckling throughout, the meeting then passed a resolution proposed by Keir Hardie and seconded by Eva Gore-Booth, condemning Liberal behaviour at the previous week's meeting, and declared that it 'emphatically approves of their brave and determined protest against the persistent denial of citizenship to women'.

This Free Trade Hall protest meeting marked the high point of the cordiality between the ILP, the WSPU and the radical suffragists. Each benefited from the others' contribution: the WSPU provided the dramatic incident, the ILP provided political backing, and the radical suffragists came up with the valuable support of local working women. If this kind of co-operation could be maintained then it augured well for a successful election at Wigan, and for the wider campaign to win Labour support (and eventually government support) for women's suffrage.

Yet already difficulties began to loom. Co-operation was not in Christabel's nature. This temporary unity was never channelled into any campaign or alliance. The story of the suffrage movement over the next decade was one of growing bitter divisions and destructive splits which, in the end, seriously limited the effectiveness of the WSPU, the radical suffragists, and the overall suffrage campaign.

XI

The suffrage movements split

Even while the ILP, WSPU and the radical suffragists were co-ordinating plans to rouse public support after the Free Trade Hall incident, there were already signs that a rift between Christabel and the radical suffragists was imminent. Teresa Billington recalled how Christabel no longer attended Eva Gore-Booth's poetry classes, and that there was 'a cooling atmosphere'.

> I was in constant touch with the Gore-Booth—Roper household for some weeks during that emergency and found to my surprise that there was no direct communication then surviving between the parties, and second that it did not matter whether they showed their support or not. I was discouraged from approaching them.
>
> Some ILP friends said this was a very wise attitude for the Women's Trade Union Movement they sponsored was very unpopular with the male Trade Unionists.[1]

Since this was a time when Keir Hardie, Sarah Dickenson, John Harker and Eva Gore-Booth were all working closely together, this black and white view is probably a little exaggerated. Still, it marks the point from which Christabel — and hence the WSPU — began to separate themselves from other suffrage groups.

Eva Gore-Booth and Esther Roper had loyally supported Christabel during her imprisonment. Yet over the next few weeks they began to see that what had at first seemed a courageous gesture was, for Christabel, little more than a stunt that could later be manipulated to gain maximum credit and publicity. The episode over the Women's Trades Council was still fresh in their memories, and they could see no real value in resorting to gimmicks as a way of winning solid support for the campaign, especially at a time when they were hoping to consolidate their success at the forthcoming Wigan election. Teresa Billington described how,

> when Christabel and Annie Kenney were making their defensive speeches in the series of meetings we ran in nearby Lancashire after their release from Strangeways — Eva Gore-Booth was at one of those and one evening seized me dramatically as we left the platform and urged upon me that I should tell Christabel not to vary her defence from one meeting to another. Now she is out in the open, she said, she cannot fit her explanation to her audience. She either deliberately invited imprisonment or she was a victim; she either spat at the policeman or she did not. She can't tell one tale in Manchester and another in Oldham.[2]

At the time Eva Gore-Booth kept these reservations about Christabel fairly private. In fact, in many people's eyes the Pankhursts and the radical suffragists were still indistinguishable. This in itself carried its own potential for trouble: Esther Roper was still Secretary of the North of England Society, and Sarah Dickenson, Eva Gore-Booth, Sarah Reddish and Christabel Pankhurst were still on the Committee. The bulk of the Society's supporters had tolerated the textile workers' campaign and possibly even welcomed the formation of an independent Lancashire Women Textile Workers' Representation Committee. But the idea of the Society Secretary and Committee members endorsing rowdy interruptions at a Liberal Party meeting and then organizing a public meeting with the ILP was too much for them to swallow.

Margaret Ashton, by now an influential voice in Society affairs, was particularly incensed. As President of the Lancashire and Cheshire Union of Women's Liberal Association she took personal exception to what she saw as Labour attacks on Liberals in the name of women's suffrage. Philip Snowden's open sniping at the ineffectiveness of her work must have added fuel to the flames. She wrote to the *Manchester Guardian* to defend her party line and to point out curtly that Liberal women deplored 'the method used by the women of the Independent Labour Party . . . as calculated to retard rather than to hasten the extension of the franchise'.[3] She was equally angry a few months later when she read a letter from Mrs Fawcett, in her capacity as National Union President, making public her acceptance of the Free Trade Hall incident. Margaret Ashton immediately dispatched a protest letter bristling with indignation.

> Dear Madam — I have read your letter of the 11th Inst in the Daily News with

regret and I am sure you cannot have the facts of the case about these suffrage questions before you, or you together with the North of England Society and the Women's Liberal Association would have been compelled to condemn the actions of these few violent women . . .

The disturbances were not planned by the working women at all — as far as can be ascertained — but by a small clique calling themselves the Votes for Women Election Committee and including I believe Eva Gore-Booth, two Miss Pankhursts and other seceders from the North of England Society which disowns them . . .

It has been most deplorable from all points of view and has made it more difficult to approach the Government with dignity than ever before.[4]

Margaret Ashton represented the opinions of the great majority of Society members, all united in their condemnation. Esther Roper, Eva Gore-Booth, Sarah Dickenson and the other activists were equally adamant about the rightness of their campaign to win labour support; a head-on collision was inevitable.

It all exploded only a few weeks afterwards. On 24 November Esther Roper presented her report for 1905 to the North of England Society Annual Meeting. She confidently listed the year's activities, noting the support from Labour and working women. Prompted either by tact or embarrassment — or both — she never mentioned the Free Trade Hall affair, and apparently her report was accepted.

Yet when it was printed a few weeks later, a rather brusque note had been added. 'Since the Annual Meeting certain members of the Executive Committee have resigned, and have issued a circular to the subscribers asking them to leave this Society and transfer their support to a new Society which they have formed.' Those resigning, presumably unable to command a majority among the members, included Sarah Dickenson, Eva Gore-Booth, Nellie Keenan, Christabel Pankhurst, Sarah Reddish, Katherine Rowton, Esther Roper, and the faithful Reverend Steinthal, a member for nearly forty years. The Society was now rid of all its activists and speakers, and must have breathed a sigh of relief; the few remaining committee members noted that they 'wish to make it clear . . . that it continues to work on an entirely non-party basis without distinction of class'.

Christabel had resigned along with the radical suffragists, yet the days of co-operation between them were almost at an end. The dramatic break with the North of England Society seemed to have forced them to face up to the growing differences in tactics. By the end of 1905 the WSPU was persistently heckling and interrupting Liberal election meetings around Manchester. The radical suffragists had little time for what they saw as negative, unconstructive tactics, and certainly none of them joined the WSPU. At the same time, Christabel, according to Sylvia, 'lost all interest in . . . the activities of Eva Gore-Booth and Esther Roper, which had once been so important to her'.[5] She had never found a proper niche for herself with the radical suffragists in their Lancashire Women Textile Workers' Representation Committee. Over the next twelve months the WSPU maintained an uneasy truce with the radical suffragists, co-operating on one or two public occasions but each increasingly wary of the other group's tactics and support.

By the end of 1905 there were thus three distinct suffrage groups working in Manchester. First, there was the small WSPU, continuing its anti-Liberal propaganda campaign in the run-up to the Election. Second, there was the ultra-respectable North of England Society, now run by Margaret Ashton and rid of all radicals and 'trouble-makers'. The new committee immediately washed its hands of any contact with trade unionists, textile workers or Labour politicians, and settled down to a happy round of drawing room meetings and garden parties. 'A most successful little subscription dance was got up in Didsbury . . .' one report ran. 'Efforts of this sort might well be made in different parts of Manchester, for, besides bringing in money, they show people that an interest in politics does not divest women of their social taste and powers.'[6]

Typical of their new recruits at this time was Helena Swanwick, a Cambridge graduate and sister of the painter Walter Sickert. She had settled in Knutsford, the elegant Cheshire village that Mrs Gaskell used as the setting for *Cranford*. When she read in the paper of the Free Trade Hall incident 'my heart rose in support of their revolt . . . On reflection I decided, knowing a good deal about the Pankhursts, that I could not work with them.' Nor could she have worked with the radical suffragists, for the industrial orientation of their campaign would have seemed bizarre to her. But into the North of England Society, and Mrs Fawcett's National Union, she could — and did — put all her considerable effort, energy and feeling over the next decade.[7]

The third Manchester group was the radical suffragists. They now operated through three separate organizations — though the boundaries between the groups were never hard and fast, and women like Sarah Dickenson, Nellie Keenan and Eva Gore-Booth had a finger in all three pies. The first, the Lancashire and Cheshire Women Textile and other Workers' Representation Committee was now two and a half years old, and was run largely by Saran Reddish, Eva Gore-Booth and Esther Roper. The second, Manchester and Salford Women's Trades and Labour Council was a year old, and included union representatives of tailoresses, weavers, shirtmakers, cigar makers, ring spinners, winders, book-binders and printers, and electric and machine workers. It was led by Nellie Keenan, Sarah Dickenson and Eva Gore-Booth, and included Violet Grundy, Isabel Forsyth and Louisa Smith. The third and most recently formed was a group called the National Industrial and Professional Women's Suffrage Society. It had been set up to provide an outlet for middle class suffragists who wanted to resign from the North of England Society at the same period as the radical suffragists did, but who would have been uncomfortable aligning themselves with either trade unionists or textile workers. One of those was Mrs Alfred Haworth, MA, who had been on the graduates' deputation with Esther Roper a few years earlier; another was a wealthy woman called Mrs Thomasson, whose generosity gave a new lease of life to the radical suffragists: the Industrial and Professional Society's funds would have stood at a meagre £40 had she not donated £210.[8]

On 4 December 1905, the Conservative Government finally resigned, and the Liberals formed a new government under Campbell-Bannerman. A general election was fixed for January: here at last was the opportunity for the radical suffragists to field their candidate at Wigan.

What had seemed at first to be a sound choice of constituency now began to bristle with snags. To begin with their chosen candidate, Hubert Sweeney from London, withdrew at the eleventh hour, and they had to find a replacement as soon as possible. Then they had a stroke of good luck. A man called Thorley Smith stepped forward, who had all the advantages that Sweeney had so patently lacked. He came from Wigan and was well known in local Labour and trade union circles. Not only that, he was a local councillor and chairman of the local Labour Representation Committee and his candidature was supported by his union, the Stonemasons'. Equally important, he appealed to those people whose socialism came from a tradition of chapel-going and plain living: the Non-conformists and the Temperance Parties both published manifestos on his behalf. With the national swing already moving away from the Tories, Thorley Smith seemed to stand a sound chance at the polls.[9]

The Wigan Trades' Council refused to back the new candidate (despite the fact that it had affiliated to the local Labour Representation Committtee in 1903, of which Thorley Smith was

197

chairman.) The opposition seems to have come largely from the powerful miners on the Council. Like the cotton unions, they had dragged their feet over Labour Representation, preferring to keep their trust in the Liberals who had looked after their interests in the past. They also 'strongly objected to the suffragists coming in the field at the eleventh hour with a fresh candidate and expecting the trade unionists to accept their dictum without consultation.' However much Thorley Smith apologized, explaining there had not been time for consultation, the miners — and so the powerful Trades Council — remained adamant.[10]

Despite this, Thorley Smith opened his campaign on 3 January 1906 with a jovial speech that appealed directly to the Wigan electors:

> It is because I am a Labour man, a working man, a sober man, and a thrifty man, and I claim that I am an honest man [that I am standing for election]. (Hear, Hear.) ... The women's suffrage question is the first plank in my programme. The women who are paying the piper are entitled to call the tune ... If I am returned to Parliament I shall sit with the Labour group, and you may take it from me that no vote of mine will go astray. I am in favour of the eight hours day, of Home Rule, and I am a Temperance reformer ... I was the first working man to enter Wigan Town Council. (Hear, Hear.) I was the first to break down the opposition of the trades unions when they said it was wasting money to try and run a Labour candidate for the Council.[11]

Esther Roper seconded him. 'I wish every man in this room could be a woman for five minutes,' she said, 'and then they would understand the question.' The audience laughed, and at the end of her speech applauded her, and she was followed by Mrs Pankhurst and Eva Gore-Booth. (Mrs Pankhurst turned up at Wigan and took a guarded interest in the proceedings, but devoted most of her energy to Keir Hardie's election at Merthyr Tydfil. The major WSPU election effort was still concentrated against the Liberals — especially Winston Churchill — in Manchester.)

Two days later, Thorley Smith's election manifesto was published in the *Wigan Observer*, making a strong and impassioned plea for the tens of thousands of disenfranchised women textile workers whose union levies supported Labour candidates. The same day, Selina Cooper, introduced as a member of the Burnley Board of Guardians, made a powerful speech trying to counter the fear among many working class men that giving votes to women would hinder Labour's Parliamentary growth. It was this suspicion that, once again, posed the greatest problem for the radical suffragists and they went to great lengths to stress that the political interests of working men and women were identical. They even extended their 'womanhood suffrage' demand to accommodate the growing demand for complete adult suffrage now backed by Margaret Bondfield's Adult Suffrage Society. (Adult suffragists must have been particularly strong in Wigan where women cotton workers were poorly paid, where miners — whose wives tended not to work — were a large group, and where the Social Democratic Federation, which had no brief for women's suffrage, had a powerful base.) In answering questions after Selina Cooper's speech, Esther Roper made their sympathy with complete adult suffrage even more explicit. 'The committee wants all men and women over the age of twenty one to have the vote,' she said.

Thorley Smith had attracted widespread Labour backing. A letter of support from Keir Hardie was published in the paper, and Will Crooks and David Shackleton sent their apologies for not being able to come in person. Dora Montefiore, who had joined the Social Democratic Federation, even came up from London for the campaign and announced how delighted she was 'that in Wigan they had a Labour candidate who was standing for labour all round — for women and for men.'[12]

Despite the breadth of his appeal and the strength of his candidacy, Thorley Smith still found his campaign an uphill battle. With no financial support available from either the North of England Society or the Wigan Trades Council, funds were pitiably low. There was not even enough money to hire a regular hall. Despite the January weather most of the meetings had to be held out of doors and the *Wigan Observer* reported occasions when 'there was at one time a large attendance but the night was too cold for the majority to stay any length of time'. Eva Gore-Booth, who had never been strong, 'developed the capacity of withstanding hardships from which stronger people would shrink . . . and became hardened to open air meetings in the midst of winter snow and fog'.[13]

On polling day itself Thorley Smith, accompanied by six women, drove through Wigan in a large, gaily decorated carriage drawn by four horses and preceded by two outriders. Yet despite this final show of bravado, Thorley Smith did not win the seat. He was beaten by the Tory MP, Sir Francis Powell, though he did knock the Liberal into third place — a bitter pill for Margaret Ashton and Liberal suffragists to swallow. Thorley Smith won well over two thousand votes, despite powerful opposition from the miners. This success, although it did not achieve their goal, greatly encouraged the radical suffragists. They no doubt reflected on Labour's slow Parliamentary start and recalled how a candidate like Philip Snowden — now elected for Blackburn — had had to make several attempts before he was successful. They returned from Wigan determined to find another Lancashire constituency, without a sitting Labour candidate where they could rely on sufficient sympathetic cotton trade unionist electors to send their next suffrage candidate to Westminster.[14]

In contrast, the WSPU was taking its policy of attacking the Liberals to its logical conclusion: to move its headquarters down to London, so that it could put pressure more directly on Campbell-Bannerman and his new government. There were other advantages to be considered too. If they moved away from Lancashire, they would shed some of their dependence on the ILP, so strong in the northern textile towns. Their ILP image, which had once seemed an advantage, became increasingly a millstone round their necks. Another advantage of leaving Manchester was that they would then sever any remaining links with the radical suffragists; the two groups had now begun seriously to cramp each other's style.

In fact the WSPU already had a toe-hold in London: Sylvia Pankhurst was there as an art student. Annie Kenney, who by now had left her job at Woodend Mill and gone to live with the Pankhursts in Nelson Street, was sent down to join her soon after the general election. Mrs Pankhurst also asked Teresa Billington to give up her Manchester-based job as an ILP organizer, and help start the London campaign, which she did after a few months.[15]

A meeting was arranged in Caxton Hall for February, to which Annie Kenney brought three hundred women from the East End; (through Dora Montefiore she had made contact with groups such as the 'Unemployed Women of South West Ham.'[16]) The meeting was well attended: Mrs Pankhurst, Dora Montefiore and Annie Kenney all spoke and, when the news arrived that the new Government had not included women's suffrage in its programme, the meeting resolved itself into a lobbying committee and marched on Parliament.

The march attracted the attention of national journalists and photographers, and from then on the WSPU gained both Fleet Street coverage and many new supporters. The most important of the recruits were two wealthy socialists, Emmeline Pethwick-Lawrence and her husband who, on the recommendation of Keir Hardie, took on the job of putting the WSPU's affairs on a more business-like footing. Another valuable convert was an elderly and dignified Poor Law Guardian, Charlotte Despard, who, like Selina Cooper, was a member of both the ILP and the Social Democratic Federation. She had joined the Adult Suffrage Society but now rejected it in favour of fighting for women's suffrage.[17] At the same time, the South West Ham women voted to become the Canning Town Branch of the WSPU, and, with forty members, became the first London suffragette group.

During the first half of 1906 the WSPU's main support came from working class women and socialists in London. Much of their energy was devoted to persuading Campbell-Bannerman to give them an interview; in March two arrests in front of his house added to their growing notoriety and the term 'suffragette' began to catch on. At this point Mrs Pankhurst was still travelling up and down between Manchester and London, but when Christabel received her law degree in June they both arranged to base themselves permanently in London.

The non-militant suffragists were equally active. As soon as the General Election had been announced, Margaret Llewelyn Davies, the influential and persuasive Secretary of the Women's Co-operative Guild published a women's suffrage manifesto, which was signed by thirty six groups, including fourteen trade unions. Among the signatories were William Wilkinson's Northern Counties Weavers' Amalgamated Association, Allen Gee's union of Yorkshire wool workers, the Guild, the ILP and the radical suffragists.[18]

A few months later, Ben Turner, the other leader of the wool workers and as staunch a champion of women's suffrage as his friend Allen Gee, moved the women's suffrage resolution at the Labour Conference, only to have it rejected in favour of Harry Quelch's perennial appeal for adult suffrage. On this occasion the voting was extremely close — 435,000 to 432,000 — and the radical suffragists believed that with a little extra persuasion, Labour would finally put its weight behind women's suffrage next year. The initiative would have to come from them: they were the only group that represented a large number of wage-earning and trade union women. Ramsay MacDonald wrote to Selina Cooper to point out to her that the initiative now lay with the cotton operatives, and urging her to 'set about it at once, as time will soon fly. You should instruct your executive to place the resolution on our next agenda.'[19]

In the meantime the suffragists — like the WSPU — looked to the Prime Minister; he had already given a friendly reception to the deputation of women textile workers when he visited Manchester the year before, and he had a reputation for personal sympathy for women's suffrage. Plans for a massive deputation were drawn up between Mrs Fawcett's National Union, the Guild, Liberal and Temperance women's organizations and the radical suffragists. They wondered whether they should join forces with the suffragettes, or go ahead on their own. Esther Roper, a member of the organizing committee, felt dubious about the WSPU's ability to co-operate with others, and wrote to Dora Montefiore to suggest working separately. Her carefully worded letter reveals something of the uneasy truce between the suffragettes and the radical suffragists that dragged on through 1906.

> With regard to the Political and Social Union, there is no quarrel between us, but it seems undoubtedly better that the attack on the Government should come from as many quarters as possible, independently of one another, so that the Prime Minister may realize that he has numbers to deal with, and so cannot think he can tire us out. We therefore think it better that the first demonstration that we have, we should do without joining forces with the Union. There is plenty of room for both of us in London, and I do not think we should have any difficulty in getting a big demonstration.[20]

Esther Roper's feelings were not shared by other suffrage organizers, none of whom had so long an acquaintance with Christabel and the WSPU; a joint deputation of suffragists and suffragettes, representing over a quarter of a million women, was arranged for 19 May. The event was planned on a most impressive scale; four hundred women were present, representing fifty thousand textile workers, twenty two thousand Guildswomen, fifteen hundred graduates, and over fifty thousand members of the British Women's Temperance Association.

Eight women spoke to the Prime Minister; the first was the elderly Emily Davies, founder of Girton, whose commitment stretched back to the 1860s and the petition handed to John Stuart Mill. She was followed by Sarah Dickenson, speaking for 'Women Wage-Earners', who, according to Dora Montefiore, made one of the best speeches. Margaret Ashton spoke for the Women's Liberal Associations and Mrs Gasson, as current President, for the Guild. Mrs Pankhurst made an emotional appeal for the WSPU, urging the Liberal government to 'make time to deal with the gross injustice which is an outrage to women'.

Eva Gore-Booth then made a speech stressing the economic contribution of working women on behalf of the fifty radical suffragists who had come down from Lancashire with their banners:

The number of women who are engaged at this time in producing the wealth of this country is double the population of Ireland ... These women are all labouring under the gross disability and industrial disadvantage of an absolute want of political power. Every day we live this becomes a more grave disadvantage, because industrial questions are becoming political questions which are being fought out in Parliament.[21]

Her words were backed up by the presence of the women themselves. They captured public sympathy. In the *Clarion*, for instance, Julia Dawson commended the 'noisy suffragettes' for drawing attention to women's suffrage, but reserved her real praise for the northern working women:

The more I look on these brave women and their works, on the weavers and winders, shirt-makers, tailoresses, and other wage-slaves from Lancashire and Cheshire, who journeyed to London to help in the demonstration, the more I marvel that they should give so *much* and get so *little*.[22]

Campbell-Bannerman was not so easily persuaded. He himself approved of women getting the vote, but his Cabinet was generally opposed. He felt he could make no pledges, but only 'preach the virtue of patience'. Dissatisfied, the women marched to Trafalgar Square for a rally, the first of many such suffrage mass meetings to be held there.[23] Then they returned to their homes, deeply disappointed that they could not wring a promise out of the Government. Over the next few weeks radical suffragists like Selina Cooper tried to sway the Prime Minister be sending him the suffrage resolutions passed by their local Women's Textile Suffrage Societies, but he remained adamant.[24]

This deputation virtually marked the last occasion on which the WSPU and the radical suffragists co-operated. From summer 1906 the suffragettes' policy of militancy began to develop faster and faster, and was not to stop until the WSPU had become a small group of outlawed arsonists on the eve of the First World War. In June, infuriated by the Prime Minister's suggestion of the virtues of patience, they began heckling Asquith, then Chancellor of the Exchequer and one of the most anti-suffrage Cabinet Ministers. Their attempts to send deputations to his house led to clashes with the police, imprisonment and further publicity. Teresa Billington was arrested for trying to lead a group of women through police lines and slapping a policeman.

At the same time Christabel, now a law graduate, arrived in London. She decided that the London WSPU was too dependent on working class support and on women from the East End, and they began to be dropped.[25] Equally, working class organizations that had previously given support became increasingly alienated by the WSPU, and turned against it.

In June the Women's Co-operative Guild Congress discussed the rights and wrongs of militancy. Isabella Ford, who spoke as a visitor and had recently helped the WSPU with a loan, defended their tactics: the biggest reform in the country, she said, the right of free speech, was not accomplished till the men tore up the Hyde Park railings. Few Guildswomen went along with her views, for they saw no real value in 'the appeal to brute force made by a certain section of suffrage advocates, while fully appreciating the good faith and earnestness of this extreme enthusiasm'. Mrs Gasson, who had been on the Campbell-Bannerman deputation the month before, indicated Guild thinking at the time:

> The battle must be fought on our own hearths — (applause) — with our own menfolk — (applause) — so that they shall demand equal rights for us. (Applause). And more than that, we must steadfastly refuse to canvass for any candidate who will not pledge himself to work for our enfranchisement.[26]

Her speech hinted at the Guild's dissatisfaction with the women's suffrage campaign which two years earlier they had supported so strongly. Her reference to 'our menfolk' suggests that Guildswomen were beginning to consider adult suffrage; like Ada Nield Chew, they seemed to have doubts about supporting a bill that would not enfranchise many Guildswomen, certainly when it was supported by a few wealthy women who resorted to 'brute force'. The WSPU decided it did not need the backing of the sort of woman who joined the Guild, and the Guild decided it would no longer be party to WSPU campaigns.

Now doubts were also cast in the minds of many of the northern socialists who had previously supported the WSPU. This was partly a reaction against militancy; but also a dislike of their narrow franchise demands. The suffragettes had adopted the slogan 'Votes for Women', but in fact their demand had not changed from Lydia Becker's day — the vote 'as it is or may be granted to men'. Julia Dawson made this point quite clear in the *Clarion*; she wrote that her complaint about the suffragettes who had gone to prison was

> that they do not sufficiently explain in the public meetings what the 'cause' is. They have on their banners, 'Votes for Women', and the unthinking crowd who stand by to listen think that means votes for *all* women. Whereas, it really means votes for *some* women. Not for me, certainly; and not for you, perhaps, my gentle reader, but for some other women who have qualifications which we have not.[27]

Having forfeited the support of the Guild and of many of the *Clarion* readers, the WSPU finally lost almost all support from the radical suffragists. On 23 October 1906, Mrs Pankhurst led a demonstration to the opening of Parliament in protest against the omission of women's suffrage from the Government's programme. Scuffles broke out and ten women were arrested and imprisoned. Although most were ILP women, only one was a working class woman from the East End, one was Annie Kenney, and the rest were middle class suffragettes like Emmeline Pethwick-Lawrence, Adela Pankhurst and Anne Cobden Sanderson, daughter of Richard Cobden. That such women — especially the daughter of the man who gave Britain cheap bread — should be locked up in Holloway as common felons provoked an angry response among well-to-do sympathizers. Large donations began to roll in to the WSPU, and a flurry of letters was dispatched to the Editor of *The Times*. Mrs Fawcett, for instance, wrote to the paper to congratulate the suffragettes; she visited Anne Cobden Sanderson in prison, and later held a testimonial banquet at the Savoy Hotel in honour of the recently released prisoners.

Working class suffragists recoiled from such behaviour. They felt that they had little in common with people who could donate £100 to WSPU funds or whose response to a crisis was to write to *The Times*. There seemed few connections between the daily harshness of their own lives and what they saw as the self-indulgent behaviour of a few leisured women. The radical suffragists wrote to Mrs Fawcett to make this point: although they had supported the interruption of a Liberal meeting in the interests of free speech, militancy for its own sake merely alienated all the support they had so carefully built up among the textile workers. Their letter is phrased a little primly, but it does reveal the dramatic differences that now existed between the suffragettes and the radical suffragists:

> There is no class in the community who has such good reason for objecting and does so strongly object to shrieking and throwing yourself on the floor and struggling and kicking as the average working woman, whose human dignity is very real to her. We feel we must tell you this for this reason that we are in great difficulties because our members in all parts of the Country are so outraged at the idea of taking part in such proceedings, that everywhere for the first time they are shrinking from public demonstrations. It is not the fact of demonstrations or even violence that is offensive to them, it is being mixed up and held accountable as a class for educated and upper class women who kick, shriek, bite and spit. As far as importance in the eyes of the Government

goes where shall we be if working women do not support us?
... It is not the rioting but the *kind* of rioting. [28]

The radical suffragists could see the whole basis of their campaign crumbling before their eyes if the WSPU continued in this way. Already suffrage and militancy were linked in people's minds, which could only jeopardize attempts to build a mass-based campaign. The following month, November 1906, they were given an even more vivid instance of the bad impression the WSPU often seemed to have left behind.

The Lancashire Women Textile Workers' Representation Committee — which included tailoresses like Louisa Smith — had organized a special trade union meeting in London to discuss the proposed reduction of wages at the Royal Army Clothing Factory at Pimlico, where over a thousand women worked. Afterwards they wrote angrily to Edith Palliser, the London Suffrage Secretary:

> Miss Pankhurst and Miss Billington obtained permission to join the discussion pledging themselves to speak only of the present difficulty. Mr Butler complained bitterly that they broke their word and captured the meeting talking of nothing but 'the women in prison', and the next day announcing it as a 'Suffragette meeting on Pimlico Pier' at a moment when newspaper advertisement was absolutely necessary to the Trade Union. [29]

They had to persuade the irritated unionists that theirs was a 'Trade Union Committee and had no connection with the incident so much resented by the Union.'

After the experiences of the past few months the radical suffragists decided to distance themselves from the WSPU, [30] and the WSPU dropped all pretence of being an organization for working women. This change of emphasis suited Christabel whose attention was now firmly fixed on parliamentary politics. 'It was evident,' she wrote, 'that the House of Commons, and even its Labour members, were more impressed by the demonstrations of the feminine bourgeoisie than of the female proletariat.' [31] Working class women felt increasingly out of place in the WSPU; Alice Milne who had been left in charge of the Manchester end when the Pankhursts left for London, described her visit to the WSPU office at the end of October 1906. She found 'the place full of fashionable ladies in silks and satins. Tea and cakes were handed round and then the organizers each made a speech ... The ladies were much impressed and promised to return the following Monday with friends .... What a fever our Union Members in Manchester would have been in if such ladies made a descent on us.' [32] Working class women like Annie Kenney and her sisters were useful to give substance to the WSPU's claim to demand the vote for all women, but were never admitted to the WSPU's inner councils. All this had the effect of narrowing WSPU policy down to the one overriding demand; Teresa Billington described how 'the industrial evils which had formed the basis of much of our appeal were gradually pushed aside for the consideration of technical, legal and political grievances . . . the working class women were dropped without hesitation.'[33]

In 1906 the WSPU lost the support of most working class women. In 1907 it finally wore out the patience of the ILP. The signs of growing friction could be traced back four years to Christabel's attack on Hodge, the Labour candidate at the Preston by-election. More recently, conflict had broken out when, in August 1906, Robert Smillie, President of the Scottish Miners, stood as the Labour candidate at the Cockermouth by-election in Cumberland. Christabel, Teresa Billington, Mary Gawthorpe and Marion Coates-Hanson, all members both of the ILP and WSPU, went up for the campaign. They were given accommodation by local socialists, who expected them to speak on behalf of their candidate.[34] Instead, the WSPU not only attacked the Liberals but also refused to advise the men to vote for Smillie, an adult suffragist. The Conservatives won the election and Labour came a poor third.

The ILP was not slow to demand an explanation of this arrant disloyalty. The secretary of the Manchester and Salford ILP federation wrote to Manchester Central Branch demanding the resignations of Christabel and Teresa Billington. Christabel defended her actions at considerable length at a branch meeting in September, asserting that 'by their agitation they were promoting the highest interests of true labour representation'. After a long and stormy discussion the branch (always particularly helpful towards women's suffrage) voted by a large majority in support of the two women.[35]

Relations between the ILP and WSPU were temporarily patched up; many ILP women, including Margaret McMillan, Isabella Ford, Selina Cooper and Harriette Beanland signed a manifesto in support of the suffragettes who had gone to prison.[36] But the reconciliation was short lived. A few months later, the Cockermouth saga was repeated at the Huddersfield by-election. The WSPU slogan was 'Votes against the Government', but once again the suffragettes ignored the Labour candidate's complaints against their activities.

The ILP was furious. It seemed to them that the suffragettes, whom they had helped so substantially in the past, were deliberately provoking a show-down. Teresa Billington had even written in the *Clarion* that although she had been a socialist since she was nineteen and belonged to no fewer than three ILP branches, she was prepared to resign for the sake of 'true socialism'.[37] At the beginning of 1907 the ILP decided it had ignored these attempts to sabotage its election programme for too long. It put forward a resolution, to be debated at its national conference at Easter that the behaviour of 'certain members of the Party' at the two by-elections was 'detrimental to the Party, and that loyalty . . . to the Party is an essential condition of membership'. Manchester Central branch members, many of whom had known the Pankhurst family for years, were deeply divided over this. The majority still supported the WSPU. So the defeated minority decided that the only option open to it was to leave Manchester Central and form a second, rival city centre branch.[38]

At the Easter Conference, Keir Hardie made a passionate appeal in support of women's suffrage, which was carried by the majority. Then Charlotte Despard and others pledged themselves never to oppose Labour candidates at future elections. At this, Mrs Pankhurst leapt to her feet and publicly contradicted her. For Christabel and her mother, their all-or-nothing WSPU policy no longer accommodated the demands of broader organizations like the ILP. A split was inevitable. Mrs Pankhurst and Christabel resigned from the ILP, and the WSPU cut the last remaining links with its roots in northern socialism. For the majority of ILP members it must have been a great relief. For a few — Keir Hardie, Margaret McMillan, Selina Cooper, Isabella Ford — who had sought reconciliation for so long, it must have been a bitter blow.

The parting was certainly a relief to most of the WSPU members who — like Christabel — had long dismissed both Labour and the ILP as half-hearted about women's suffrage. To a few it was unacceptable that the ILP should be shrugged off so easily, and the Pankhursts' unilateral action merely highlighted the vexed question of who controlled the WSPU. Nominally it was run by a committee, but in fact it was dominated by the Pankhursts and Mrs Pethwick-Lawrence who together took all the major decisions and then publicized them to the membership. Teresa Billington-Greig (she added her husband's name to hers when she got married) had drafted a formal constitution which placed power in the hands of branch delegates (rather along the lines of National Union democracy) and this had been adopted by the WSPU conference in 1906. But Christabel and Mrs Pankhurst adamantly opposed her in this. In a letter to Sylvia, Christabel denounced her as 'a wrecker', and Mrs Pankhurst declared that 'as for the TBG affair, we have just to face her and put her in her place. She has gone too far this time.'[39]

They decided to pre-empt her. Mrs Pankhurst announced that the next WSPU conference, to be held in a month's time, was cancelled, along with the sections of the consitution relating to organization. This arbitrary decision was roundly rejected by several prominent WSPU members, among them Teresa Billington-Greig and Mrs Despard. They called a meeting of about seventy members to demand that the constitution be honoured and the conference take place as planned. To Teresa Billington-Greig the issue was one of principle, and she wrote later:

> I do not believe that a dictatorship can be right even if it is exercised by heroines, geniuses and benevolent reformers, not even a dictatorship of angels would win my approval ... The movement was certainly damaged by the absurdity of women demanding the vote in the community while accepting the denial of them in their own fighting society.[40]

Under such pressure the WSPU split in two. In 1907 about a fifth of suffragettes left to form the Women's Freedom League.

This was merely one in a long series of splits caused largely by Christabel's autocratic single mindedness. In all, she provoked no fewer than seven splits in the decade before war broke out — virtually one a year. The first was in 1904 when the Women's Trade Union Council had divided over its stand on women's suffrage. At the end of 1905, her heckling in the Free Trade Hall had precipitated the split between the Margaret Ashton faction and the radical suffragists in the North of England Society, when the activist minority had all resigned. The following year, the WSPU scuffles at Westminster and subsequent capitalizing on the imprisonments made the radical suffragists realize that it was time they too broke with the WSPU. About six months later, the WSPU anti-Labour election tactics caused such a furore in the Pankhursts' Manchester Central ILP branch that it divided into two rival camps over WSPU behaviour. A few weeks later, Christabel and her mother finally rejected the ILP; later in the year WSPU elitism — notably Christabel's — caused a major split within the ranks of the WSPU itself.

That was by no means the end. When Asquith replaced Campbell—Bannerman as Prime Minister in 1908, the WSPU intensified its militancy with window breaking and stone throwing; now even the conciliatory Mrs Fawcett and the National Union began to condemn the violence. The number of arrests went up and up and in 1909 suffragette prisoners began to go on hunger strike in protest against their treatment. Finally the Liberal Government responded to the potential political embarassment of having a suffragette's death on its hands with forced feeding, and with the cruel 'Cat and Mouse Act' which permitted prisoners to be temporarily discharged to recover their health and then readmitted to prison.

The WSPU operation became more and more military in character, with Christabel issuing orders for her troops to carry out. No dissent could be tolerated. Eventually she and her mother split off from everybody who would not unquestioningly accept their authority. The final show-down came in 1912 when first the Pethwick-Lawrences, and then Sylvia were told that they too must leave the WSPU.

Militancy, coupled with the attendant newspaper publicity, had begun as an inspired idea in Christabel's head in 1905. But it seemed to carry with it the seeds of its own destruction: each act had to be more violent than the previous one in order to hold public attention; and violence only attracted public interest, never mass support. In the end the WSPU resorted to arson, and in 1912 Christabel had to escape to Paris and the WSPU virtually became an underground organization of 'guerilla' fighters. As the WSPU membership was reduced down to an elite corps, so its politics correspondingly narrowed. Teresa Billington, one of its most informed critics, wrote bitterly of it at the time:

> Daring to advertise in an unconventional way the movement has dared nothing more. It has cut down its demand from one of sex equality to one of votes on a limited basis. It has suppressed free speech on fundamental issues. It has gradually edged the working class element out of the ranks. It has become socially exclusive, punctiliously correct, gracefully fashionable, ultra-respectable, and narrowly religious.[41]

XII

Working women as suffragists

From 1900 to 1906 the radical suffragists had run a tightly-knit campaign which had been remarkably effective. Through their textile workers' agitation they had made a significant impact on the Labour Representation Committee; they helped persuade the Women's Co-operative Guild to support women's suffrage; their candidate at the general election had confirmed how widespread was the backing in the cotton towns for 'womanhood suffrage'; and on the deputation to Campbell-Bannerman they had attracted considerable respect for their argument that working women needed — and deserved — the vote.

Support from women in the cotton towns was assured. But translating this to a national level had already proved difficult, because no other group of women could match the cotton workers' massive organization. From 1906 onwards, the radical suffragists began encountering additional problems. The rift between the WSPU and the ILP in the sour aftermath of the Cockermouth election meant that relationships beteeen Labour and other suffrage groups also deteriorated. Since the radical suffragists were hoping to build on their Wigan achievement with a second local Labour-suffrage candidate this further limited the effect they could have.

Similarly, suffragette militancy in London, especially since the Holloway imprisonments, monopolized so much of the public interest that 'suffrage' and 'suffragette' became synonymous, especially for readers of the popular dailies, with their regular supply of dramatic photographs. This meant that the debate about the finer points of suffrage got lost in the clamour of 'Votes for Women.' The radical suffragists' carefully considered call for 'womanhood suffrage' (with a limited suffrage bill merely as an expedient first step) became almost inaudible outside Lancashire, as the London suffragettes piled one daring exploit on another.

A further practical difficulty was lack of funds. The radical suffragists had forfeited access to the North of England Society's money. Local trades councils and trade unions might vote in favour of women's suffrage in principle, but their hard-headed committee men were hardly likely to make a donation to a group that gave them no immediate benefit. The little Industrial and Professional Women's Suffrage Society was still dependent on their sole wealthy benefactor Mrs Thomasson, while the Lancashire Women Textile Workers' Representation Committee had to rely on many small subscribers (the 1910 list opens with 'A Friend . . . 3s 6d') and local collections by Committee members. (Margaret Aldersiey collected 9s around Burnley; Mary Atkinson 5s in Brierfield; Alice Collinge 5s, Cissy Foley 10s and Clara Staton 4s 6d in Bolton. [1]

These practical difficulties, coupled with the intransigence of Asquith and the Liberals, posed real problems from the radical suffragists. How could they best sustain the momentum of their campaign? Once again, a champion appeared: Mrs Fawcett's National Union of Women's Suffrage Societies. It could provide the necessary funds and national organization, while Lancashire could offer energetic, experienced working class speakers. Within a few years the National Union had donated over £100 to their funds, Mrs Fawcett a further £20, and her eldest sister, Dr Elizabeth Garrett Anderson, ten guineas. As to the other side of the bargain, at least five Lancashire women — Selina Cooper, Margaret Aldersley, Sarah Reddish, Sarah Dickenson and, later, Ada Nield Chew — were employed by the National Union as salaried organizers, either on a full-time or part-time basis.

In this way the radical suffragists continued to fight their campaign over the next few years. They still formed a distinct group within the national suffrage movement, and still made a unique and vital contribution to suffrage politics; but they never regained the impact of their earlier years. For instance, the scale of textile workers' deputations to London of 1901, 1902 and 1906 was never repeated; instead, the radical suffragists tended to go down to London individually or in small groups to help co-ordinate National Union plans.

In 1907 the National Union — perhaps stung into action by the WSPU — adopted a new constitution, and formed an impressive new executive which included Ethel Snowden, wife of the Blackburn MP, Margaret Ashton, Isabella Ford, and the young Bertrand Russell. It also set up proper machinery whereby responsibility could 'devolve upon every Society in the Union', believing that 'it is from a truly democratic organization alone that satisfactory results can be expected'.[2] It also decided to set aside part of the National Union's swelling funds for regular suffrage organizers. In 1907 over £200 was allocated for wages, the following year this had doubled, and by 1910 organizers' salaries and expenses totalled no less than £1,000.

These organizers were, according to Mrs Fawcett, 'mostly highly intelligent young women of University Education'. Emilie Gardner was probably typical. Head girl of her school in 1900, she won a scholarship to Newnham College, Cambridge, where, like Esther Roper, she took a great interest in the College's Political Debating Society. In 1907 she became Secretary of the Birmingham Suffrage Society and the following year she helped Edith Palliser at a by-election in mid-Devon, and, by this time working as a National Union organizer, at a by-election in Peckham. A contemporary photograph shows her as a large, capable woman resplendent in ermine-trimmed gown and mortar board.[3]

Another of the National Union's most prolific speakers was Helena Swanwick, who had helped from a Knutsford branch. In 1908 she addressed no less than a hundred and fifty meetings, as well as attending committee meetings in London and Manchester. Yet although women like Emilie Gardner were employed as organizers elsewhere, in Lancashire it was different. Neither Helena Swanwick nor Esther Roper — two obvious candidates — was appointed. Instead, Lancashire organizers were chosen from among the many working class women who already had direct experience of mill or factory life, and who had good connections with the local ILP, Guild and trade unions. Since Mrs Fawcett had entertained the radical suffragists to dinner in 1901 when they brought their petition down to London, she seems to have kept an eye on what the Lancashire women were doing, and now she and her executive were able to ask local women whose abilities they respected to take on the job.

Their first recruit was Selina Cooper, a sound choice on many counts. She was already something of a national figure after her powerful speech at the Labour Representation Conference in 1905, and still had close links with the Nelson and Colne Suffrage Society — it met in her front room. Mary was now six years old and was able to be left at home with her father or a close relation if her mother were asked to go away speaking and organizing for a few days. In practical terms Selina Cooper could now afford to spread her wings a little.

The way in which the National Union contacted her is not recorded. Certainly by October 1906 Edith Palliser had been authorized by her committee to engage Ethel Snowden, Selina Cooper and Miss Rowlette (who had spoken for the textile workers' campaign in Yorkshire in 1904) to help the Miners' Federation candidate, who was standing for election in mid-Glamorgan.[4]

From then on, Selina Cooper was always in great demand. From autumn 1906 to spring 1907 she ran a special election campaign in Liverpool to arouse interest in women's suffrage. Eleanor Rathbone, Secretary of the Liverpool Suffrage Society and a cousin of Margaret Ashton, sometimes accompanied her as she addressed thirty five meetings, canvassed from house to house and distributed thousands of leaflets. In the midst of all this activity she kept in as close touch with Mary as she could. One of the postcards she sent, a picture of Lime Street and St George's Hall, said 'Dear Mary, I hope you have been a good girl. I am sending you a picture of a big Hall in Liverpool and there are lots of little children sat on the steps without any stockings on. I am coming home this week. S. Cooper.'[5]

A few months later, the National Union noted that 'an experienced canvasser was engaged and sent to Wimbledon', where Bertrand Russell was standing as a pro-suffrage Liberal candidate in the forthcoming by-election. Selina Cooper was dispatched south, and although Russell was unsuccessful at the polls, he did not forget to send her a note to thank her for the 'kind and valuable help you so willingly rendered during the election campaign'.[6]

The following year she helped in a Manchester by-election[7], and not long afterwards she was campaigning with other suffragists in the west of England. On one of her trips to this part of the country she became caught up in helping at a Welsh pit disaster. She was always conscious of what such commitments would mean to a small girl, as her daughter remembers:

My mother'd fetch me a frock back or something like that when she'd been away. You know, she used to go looking in her bags to see what she could fetch me back. But I pined for her. I always wanted her to come — and she had one bad spell away . . . at the famous . . . Welsh mine, where they were

214

buried alive. And my mother's ambulance [training] came in handy. Well, she was working for suffrage down there. There was some election pending, and she was living in a miner's cottage . . . and my mother wrote and asked if she could do her ambulance work and help . . . Oh, it was terrible. And she'd been away six weeks. And she wrote to say — my father . . . had to go to work the morning after — and she wrote to say she might get back — there was a train that got in to Nelson at midnight, a London train, and she might get back on it, but she wasn't sure, and we must go to bed . . . My father shooed me off to bed and' he went to bed, because he had to get up at six in the morning. I slipped out. I went up to station . . . And the porters got to know me . . . And my father was wild, because he was right vexed with me. And my mother wasn't vexed, but I wanted to see her so badly that — I must have been — I was waiting up there at midnight — I was only little.[8]

By 1910 Selina Cooper had made such an impressive mark on the suffrage movement that she was chosen (the only working class woman) to go on a twenty one member deputation to Asquith at Downing Street, along with Mrs Fawcett, Clementina Black, Bertha Mason, Eleanor Rathbone, Ethel Snowden, Isabella Ford, and Helena Swanwick. She was introduced as 'Mrs Cooper, Textile Worker', and was one of the four suffragists to make a speech.

Sarah Reddish and Sarah Dickenson were also sometimes 'borrowed' by the National Union in London, though on a more occasional basis than Selina Cooper, as their responsibilities in Bolton and in Manchester limited their activities further afield. (Also, they were perhaps not such able public speakers as Selina Cooper.) On one occasion it was recorded that £22 7s 4d was paid for 'fares and hotel expenses, also fee to Miss Reddish in connection with organizing in London', and on another Eva Gore-Booth wrote to Edith Palliser that 'there is a great deal that can be done. But to do it, it will be necessary for us to keep a Trade Union member of our Committee in London for two or three months. What do you feel your Committee can do towards the expense of this work?'[9] Possibly Sarah Dickenson, who attended various London trade union meetings, went down on this occasion.

The arrangement worked very conveniently for the National Union for, as a London-based organization, it lacked the industrial contacts the radical suffragists had so patiently built up. In fact Mrs Fawcett could become positively devious in trying to utilize these contacts to the best possible advantage of her campaign. In 1911, when the pit brow lasses' right to work became a political issue once again, she wrote to one of the London organizers to ask, 'Do you think you could get any of these pit brow women for your At Home on the 31st?' A few days later she sent a more conspiratorial warning. 'You must throw your fly over Miss Roper *very* carefully. It is all important to make the request for the loan of the pit brow girls *through* her for the 31st.'[10]

In turn these arrangements guaranteed the Lancashire women a national platform for their views. And the fact that working women, whether on a national or local scale, were playing a significant role in the suffrage campaign had immense repercussions on those working women's own lives. Whether they were among the handful of women who were paid wages in return for the work they did, or whether they squeezed women's suffrage activity into their weekends and spare evenings as best they could, their commitment was not something undertaken lightly. For the first time on a large scale, working class women became active in a major political battle.

Yet women as far as English law was concerned still lived in a twilight zone. Outside the home, justice was still administered by all-male courts, and inside the home a husband still had substantial rights over his wife's children, her property and her person. In terms of Edwardian values, a wife who left home, even to go to a political meeting for a few hours, could find herself up against a tirade of opposition, even from men who claimed to hold progressive views on everything else. 'The idea only slowly gains ground that she has the right to dispose of any of her time and thoughts outside the home,' wrote one suffragist Guildswoman. 'Even a co-operator has said, "My wife? What does she want with meetings? Let her stay at home and wash my moleskin trousers!" '

The very idea of women's suffrage offended deeply against accepted Edwardian ideas on motherhood and family life. 'It had long been doubtful whether a married woman is altogether a person,' the same writer commented. 'And we always think of a taxpayer as a dignified householder on whom the collector calls, and not as a mere drinker of cheap tea and eater of sultana pudding.'[11] The heckling that suffrage speakers provoked showed how threatening was the idea of votes for women to the ideal of domestic peace and order. 'Go home and wash the pots', 'Go whoam an mind yer babbies', people would jeer. 'Wot about the old man's kippers?'[12]

In some cases a wife who took even a passing interest in women's suffrage could cause violent domestic rows. One husband publicly slapped his wife's face when he found she had gone along to a meeting. Another woman, who had joined the WSPU in Manchester, described how husbands' antagonism was often the most forceful check on women's activity.

> Now, a lot of women in the rank-and-file, they didn't go to prison. We did quite a lot of things that we should have gone to prison for, had we been found out, but they – the trouble was in their own homes. So you can understand it. Their husbands didn't agree with them, in nine cases out of ten. Well, my – speaking for myself – my husband smashed my – broke my badge, and tore my card up ... And it took me a long, long time to get him to see my way, and to understand it.[13]

Even for women whose husbands did not react so harshly, there was often a muted but equally effective opposition to face. Families were so used to relying on the wife and mother to provide clean clothes, hot meals and fresh bread day in and day out, that they fiercely resented even an occasional outside interest, as Hannah Mitchell could readily testify:

> No cause can be won between dinner and tea, and most of us who were married had to work with one hand tied behind us, so to speak. Public disapproval can be faced and borne, but domestic unhappiness, the price many of us paid for our opinions and activities, was a very bitter thing.

Again, Hannah Mitchell is bitterly lucid about what happened when the magistrate sentenced herself, Adela Pankhurst and another woman to three days in Strangeways for interrupting a Liberal rally. To her great annoyance her husband turned up and paid her fine so that she could go home. 'He knew that we did not wish our fines to be paid, and was quite in sympathy with the militant campaign, but men are not so singleminded as women are ... Most of us who were married found that 'Votes for Women' were of less interest to our husbands than their own dinners. They simply could not understand why we made such a fuss about it.'[14]

Other suffragettes lacked Hannah Mitchell's iron resolve especially those who were mothers of large families. One member of the Preston WSPU, Mrs Towler, was imprisoned in Holloway after storming the House of Commons. Her husband was a tackler in one of the weaving sheds and they had four sons: before she went down to Westminster she spent a week baking for her family, and left enough food to keep the five of them going for a fortnight. The women were sentenced to six weeks in solitary confinement in Holloway, but once the first two weeks were up Mrs Towler became extremely distressed at the thought of her family going hungry. In the end, her agitation became so great that Mrs Pethwick-Lawrence was asked to come and bail her out. Mrs Towler went back to Preston and lit her oven.[15]

Middle class women could always rely on servants to provide their families with regular meals and look after the children. Working class women had no such safety net, and their absence from home, however brief, revealed how vital was their contribution to the family economy. In the cotton towns, there was an added factor to consider: nearly every unmarried woman and many married ones went out to work, very often in a cotton mill owned by a Liberal Party supporter who would not look kindly on this kind of insubordination among his employees. Ethel Brierley described what happened when Annie Kenney came campaigning near her mill in Lees. She was on her way back from the outside toilet when she saw her addressing a crowd of people.

> I had to go through one reeling room to get to my own, so they all knew . . . So I went to my work and carried on, and somebody went out; they went out to find [Annie Kenney] and they brought her back to the reeling room. I never saw her. I never went. She was in the next room . . . Well, it was Tuesday. And John Rhodes must have been away. I was quiet. But somebody told him in the morning. Oh, he was an ardent Liberal. Ooh, he had them all down in that little office, I can see − a lot of women there. I was the youngest. And he said if he could find who brought her in, they'd get their cards immediately. But nobody would give anybody away.[16]

Other employers were less gentlemanly than John Rhodes and decided to take action against insubordinate workers. A woman who worked in one of the small wool mills in Dobcross in Saddleworth described what happened the day a group of suffrage speakers visited her mill: her boss refused to let them go back to work after the meeting and since they were on piece work, this badly affected their wages.

> I can see them now, up back of that mill . . . with these big hats on and long trailing skirts. And us workers, you know, we − then boss fetched us in. We copped it for going out. When we went back us work, us shuttles had gone. They took shuttles off and this made us pay.[17]

Sometimes it was not only the employers who demanded retribution. Many weavers were still Liberals at heart, and did not look kindly on attacks on the Government. Jenny Jackson, a weaver in Preston, belonged to the same WSPU branch as Mrs Towler; she too was arrested and sentenced to seven days in Holloway. The news of her release travelled back to Preston faster than she did. When the other workers saw her walking towards the mill gate, they formed themselves into two lines and spat at her as she walked between them. In the end the antagonism became intolerable and she had to leave and look for a job elsewhere.[18]

Suffragists remained resolutely non-militant and became increasingly critical of the way WSPU policy demanded a carefully-orchestrated publicity machine. Helena Swanwick despised what she saw as their courting of martyrdom and faking of persecution solely so that the world would take notice of them. Teresa Billington-Grieg, after her brief spell in the WSPU, became one of the fiercest opponents of militancy:

> I do not believe in the modern militant suffrage movement. I have believed in it, worked in it, suffered in it, and rejoiced in it, and I have been disillusioned . . . What I condemn in militant tactics is the small pettiness, the crooked course, the double shuffle between revolution and injured innocence, the playing for effects and not for results.[19]

Suffragists like Selina Cooper soon lost all patience with the escalating violence, as well. Her Guild branch had sent a letter of solidarity after the Free Trade Hall incident, and she and her friends in Nelson ILP signed the manifesto in protest against the early suffragette imprisonment. But as militancy developed into arson, she felt she had no option but to turn her back completely on the WSPU — although she still greatly admired the courage of individual suffragettes like Mrs Pankhurst and Sylvia.

Suffragists were never imprisoned, but nonetheless faced considerable violence at meetings where hostile crowds seldom distinguished between militants and non-militants. Helena Swanwick once went to address a meeting on the Market Square at Macclesfield, an unfortunate choice of venue for missiles were ready at hand. Covered in eggs, fruit and vegetables, she had to abandon the meeting and retreat to a nearby pub to sluice herself down with buckets of water.[20]

A working class wife, whether a housewife or a wage-earner as well, had to consider seriously what becoming a suffragist speaker entailed, for any injury to her could cause upheaval in her family. Ethel Derbyshire was in just such a dilemma, pulled both ways by her family and by her politics. Married in 1903, she soon had three young children to look after, and her daughter described her problems:

> She did speaking for the movement in Blackburn on the market . . . They used to have speakers on the market-place, and the ILP had taken it for a meeting, you see . . . And they would drag her off. Well, of course, the other members, they would get round her and that; and they used to have to really guard her or else she would have been hurt. And she did it quite a few times and then she said she realized if she did get hurt, what would happen to her three young children. You see, there was me and two brothers then. And she said, well, in spite of what she believed in, she'd have to keep quiet a bit.[21]

Suffragists who did a lot of speaking had to learn to cope with heckling and rough handling, and few women were given more practice in this than Selina Cooper.

She went to Hull and she had to get up very early in the morning . . . she used to chalk the flags, you see. And she chalked the flags for this meeting. And all these men — there was auction of fish on — and they met her, to her alarm. She usually got antagonism. Well, they met her and *escorted* her to this dock, and she thought there was something fishy about this. Fishy, yes! Well, they keep live fish in tanks for hotels. Anyhow, they took my mother, and they said, 'We've got a platform ready for you, Mrs Cooper.' They knew her name 'cos it was all on — My mother was a strong woman . . . five foot seven . . . and broad built. And they took her on, and she thought, 'There's something funny about this!' And she started speaking, and, it started — the lid started coming up. And she put her legs astride to sort of hold it, and there were bass in it, live bass . . . And anyhow, she stood it. They clapped her like mad when she finished 'cos she stuck on it![22]

In some ways radical suffragists like Selina Cooper were liable to even greater social disapproval than the suffragettes. Suffragettes might slap policemen and break windows, but they had long narrowed their demands down to the vote and nothing but the vote. The radical suffragists still saw enfranchisement as just a part — though a very important part — of a far wider feminist and socialist programme. In small cotton towns they were quite likely to be harrassed for their subversive views.

Elementary school teachers like Alice Collinge were particularly vulnerable to hostility, for their salaries came out of public funds. After a short-lived flirtation with the early WSPU, Alice Collinge came under the influence of the wise Sarah Reddish. Never happy with militancy, she turned instead to the Bolton Women Textile Worker's Representation Committee, along with Cissy Foley and Clara Staton.[23]

At the same time she was still organist for the Bolton Labour Church, and was involved in local progressive women's groups which she used to address. One of her ex-pupils described how a school teacher had to be as discreet as possible about unconventional beliefs. 'People were against those things those days. A lot of them were against them — though my father wasn't . . . She didn't exactly tell us [that she was a suffragist], but I know my father and her used to talk together quite a lot, about getting the world a better place . . . especially for women.'[24]

Alice Collinge was also a minor poet and playwright, and in one of her short plays she presents a vivid illustration of the nature of the local opposition suffragists had to confront. Her heroine, Hilda Townley, delivers a public lecture advocating equal pay and equal educational opportunities for women. The next day she is visited by the town dignatories, outraged by her attempts to overturn the apple cart. One, Miss Wisely, tries to persuade her that it is women's duty to get married:

> I am not discussing educated women, Madam. I am thinking essentially of the lower classes ... They were the ones who will go astray. (Shakes her head.) And bad women make bad men, you know ... In short, Madam, I want my own sex to remain in subordination to the male. It is a law of nature, and woe to the ones who try to break the law ... [25]

Alice Collinge's progressive attitudes did eventually cost her her job. However the bone of contention was not, as it happened, her work with the radical suffragists but her general political perspective, notably her refusal to accept the child labour system that elementary schools condoned. When the School Inspector heard that she was not waking up the half-timers who dozed off in her class, and had stated that she would rather starve than wake them up, she was given the sack; without a good testimonial, she found it very hard to get another elementary school post.[26] Cissy Foley was more fortunate: she was not sacked and, even had she been, an experienced jack frame tenter like her would have had little difficulty finding a job in a nearby mill.

Considerable physical demands were made of the radical suffragists. For instance, the foot-slogging canvassing of signatures for petitions which had begun on May Day 1900 continued right through the decade. Later the National Union began to organize mass processions: the first, in February 1907, became known as the Mud March, as three or four thousand women had to battle their way bravely through the London rain with their banners and their bands. In June the following year the radical suffragists organized a demonstration in Manchester of two thousand working women demanding the vote to 'protect their labour, improve their wages and defend their industrial and trade union interests'.[27] They also staged subsequent demonstrations in Trafalgar Square in 1908 and 1910 and these offered women like Alice Collinge their first taste of large-scale public meetings. 'The memory of the one and only time I was to speak at Trafalgar Square, gives me amusement now-a-days,' she wrote. 'I was frightfully nervous, and prayed that the meeting would finish before my turn came, which it did. All the women made history that particular day, but me.'[28]

Unlike the London-orientated WSPU, the National Union could

always count on massive support the length and breadth of the country. In 1913 it decided to show the strength of its support outside the maelstrom of London politics by organizing a massive pilgrimage that would converge on the capital from all corners of Britain, and present a petition signed by 80,000 women demanding the vote. To thousands of members in the mushrooming suffrage societies the pilgrimage entailed considerable personal commitment and physical stamina. Few Lancashire women could spare the time to walk the two hundred miles down to London, and Selina Cooper for one joined the pilgrims once they eventually reached London. The only woman from her suffrage society who walked the whole distance was Emily Murgatroyd. 'It took her about a fortnight. And they got hospitality ...,' Mary Cooper explained, '... and blisters on their feet ... she was a real character, and very active physically.'

Emily Murgatroyd's weaver's wages — then about 23s — were badly needed at home, and her family must have felt the loss of a breadwinner's earnings while she was away on the pilgrimage. 'I had to save up money to leave with my mother,' she said, 'because she couldn't manage to get along without it. When I went away on suffrage work I always left a pound at home.'[29] Married women coming back from demonstrations or pilgrimages knew that the weekly wash waited for them. 'Working housewives,' commented Hannah Mitchell, 'faced with this accumulation of tasks, often resolved never to leave home again.'

Hannah Mitchell became occasional organizer for the WSPU for a short while, but found that the 'exciting days and sleepless nights' begun to take their toll on her health and she suffered a nervous breakdown. What deeply hurt her was that 'none of the Pankhursts had shown the slightest interest in my illness, not even a letter of sympathy ... I did not realize that in a great battle the individual does not count and stopping to pick up the wounded delays the fight.'[30] In this respect the National Union seems to have been a more considerate employer than the WSPU. Certainly in the case of Selina Cooper they provided exactly the kind of practical help she needed. They not only paid her a small salary, but — far more unusual — provided her, while Mary was young, with a living-in housekeeper (usually a friend of the family) realizing that if they did not do this they might lose one of their most talented speakers. 'We always had a maid,' Mary Cooper said, 'somebody to help. They lived equally with us.' One of the housekeepers was Mrs Holt, who worked as the cook at the Co-op restaurant in Nelson. 'She was my mother's friend, you see. And when she was without a home, she came to live here.' When Mary was older and could cope on her own with the housekeeping, Selina Cooper would invent games based on her suffrage journeys:

> When she used to go away for a week or a fortnight, we used to have a map on the wall, of England. I used to play with the kids at finding names, and that sort of thing. We used to play games about these places – and underneath this map she used to put me a menu down, what I'd to have for dinner. I'd to go out for dinner to get it. I was at school. I'd to go – I could cook a little bit, but not much, and I'd to go to such-and-such a shop on the Monday and another on the Tuesday. It went through a fortnight, all down the back – and what shopping I'd to do.[31]

Like Mary Cooper, Doris Chew had been used as a small child to her mother's demanding political life, though the two mothers coped with their absences in different ways. Ada Nield Chew worked for the Women's Trade Union League from 1900 to 1908, and gave them occasional assistance over the next few years. Doris Chew is still slightly mystified as to how her family coped during these early years. All she can recall is that her mother 'left me behind once, and then apparently I gave the impression that I never expected her to come back. So she decided that in future I had to go too. I didn't go to school till I was seven, so between two and seven I trailed round everywhere with her.'[32]

Just as Mary Cooper got to know the people in the local Board of Guardians' office, so Doris Chew sometimes found herself left in the care of unknown families:

> She always had hospitality, and I suppose it was an understood thing that if people gave her hospitality, they had to give it to me too. And I was left in the house while she went out and did her organizing and speaking. I wasn't taken round to meetings or anything like that. I have just disjointed memories of meeting other children, and people's things I envied like a beautiful theatre or a toy shop.[33]

Even working class women who could not give the same kind of commitment as Selina Cooper or Ada Nield Chew to the National Union (Ada Nield Chew became an organizer in 1911) could contribute to forming its policy. It valued its reputation for regional democracy, and kept well oiled the machinery whereby members of far flung suffrage societies could voice their views. From 1909-10, the National Union reorganized itself into fifteen regional federations – one was Manchester and District – each of which was subdivided into constituency-based groups. (So Selina Cooper's Nelson and Colne

Suffrage Committee was renamed after the constituency, and became known as the Clitheroe branch of the National Union; while Selina Cooper was away working, other people from Nelson acted as Secretary, though Robert Cooper still kept the accounts.)

By 1911 there were over three hundred branches and by the eve of the First World War the National Union could call upon a massive membership of 30,000 women. Each branch was able to send resolutions to headquarters,[34] and developed along lines chosen by its members. The Clitheroe Society was still made up exclusively of working class women and its links were always with local trade unions, the Guild and the ILP. In Oldham, the Suffrage Society was dominated by the wealthy Lees family of Werneth Park and tended to take a conservative view, canvassing merely for 'Votes for Women Householders'.[35] Ruth Dewhurst, who had formed the Oldham Suffrage Committee in 1904 under the guidance of the radical suffragists then in the North of England Society, seemed to have a low opinion of the Lees's politics, and instead joined the Lancashire Women Textile Workers' Representation Committee. The pattern in Bolton was similar: a respectable suffrage society had been formed in March 1908 and had a middle class membership. From the beginning it invited Sarah Reddish to join its committee; but she seems to have taken no part in their meetings and to have preferred to operate through the Bolton Women Textile Workers' Representation Committee which she had built up herself. On one occasion she wrote to the Suffrage Society, asking for its help in the campaign to protect the jobs of nearby pitbrow lasses, but otherwise the two groups seem to have co-existed quite separately. [36] The Altrincham Society in north Cheshire had an even more genteel approach to politics than Oldham and Bolton, and devoted much of its time to private performance of suffrage plays and tableaux for fund-raising purposes. Unfortunately, more is recorded about groups like these than about the groups in weaving constituencies like Darwen and Accrington.[37]

Working women in the cotton towns joined their suffrage societies in large numbers, but outside Lancashire this pattern tended to be less marked. At a national level, middle class women heavily outnumbered women like Selina Cooper or Ada Nield Chew. Eleanor Rathbone, Isabella Ford and Margaret Ashton had the time and money to sit on endless committees and run the business affairs. Sometimes this led to friction, as Ada Nield Chew's daughter described:

You have to remember that my mother was doing this work, not only because she believed in it, but because she wanted the money . . .

She was an introvert and she was a very proud woman. I told you, the National Union was run mostly by women — well, it was run by — full stop — middle class women. And she liked them, and she admired them, and she respected them. But she thought that a few of them looked down on her because she had to be paid for what she did and she resented that very much.[38]

It would have been impossible to run an organization in Edwardian England which cut across social divisions, in which there was no class snobbery of this kind. What is remarkable about the National Union is that, even though the bulk of its membership was middle class, the opinions of Selina Cooper, Sarah Dickenson, Sarah Reddish and Ada Nield Chew — all women with years of experience in the labour movement — were so respected.

The contrast between the National Union and the WSPU is dramatic. To begin with, at its peak the WSPU only had eighty eight branches of which no less than thirty four were in London.[39] Once the Pankhursts moved down to London in 1906, decisions tended to emanate from the centre outwards. Regional offices were maintained and Annie Kenney, for instance, was based in the West of England, Mary Gawthorpe, from the Leeds ILP, in Manchester (with extra offices in Preston and Rochdale.)[40] But they had little power, as Elizabeth Dean, who joined the Manchester WSPU in about 1911, explained:

When the women's suffrage movement was formed by the Pankhursts, it was really — what would you put it? — more middle class. They took decisions in London — and the carry-on that went on in London was really among the committee, you know. We was left to do any irritating things we could think about, on our own.[41]

Its main activities, co-ordinated by eighteen year-old Alice Milne (who had been left in charge when the Pankhursts left, and who had sometimes to be bailed out and cheered up periodically by the more experienced Mary Gawthorpe) consisted of dispatching speakers to heckle Liberal leaders, arranging welcomes for the flying visits from recently released suffragettes (notably Annie Kenney, by now quite a celebrity), and organizing rather mundane fund-raising schemes to finance the London activities. Poor Alice Milne was rushed off her feet, as the diary she kept in 1906 suggests:

All last week was a horror. Heavy rain. Jumble sale — no tables — last minute rush among institutions and S[econd] H[and] furniture shop. Got tables at last from the cleaner of a ragged school — had to carry them themselves (an

225

accident – dropping one table on a toe delayed them . . .).

Mass of goods – most unsáleable – 'words fail me!' But the great unwashed came trooping in when the doors were opened – we realized £5 in coppers! Close up somehow – dreadfully tired . . . All the rest of the week was equally horrible.[42]

In Manchester most of the WSPU members were educated middle class women, often university-trained school teachers, neither very rich nor very poor.[43] Of the rank-and-file WSPU membership in the cotton towns little is known. Quite possibly any suffragette activity within quite a wide radius was centred on the Manchester group. Nothing is known of Mary Gawthorpe's base in Rochdale, but luckily a biography of the woman who ran the Preston WSPU has recently been written. Edith Rigby, wife of a respected local doctor, was an eccentric and forceful lady who had sufficient stamina to survive all the brick-bats hurled at her by outraged Preston neighbours once they learned she had become a suffragette (and, later, learned that she had burnt down a millionaire's bungalow).

From the beginning Edith Rigby ran her WSPU branch with autocratic fervour. She pressurized various working women she knew into joining. One was Beth Hesmondhalgh, a winder of over twenty years experience in one of the Preston mills, whom Edith Rigby had met at an ILP meeting. 'She was so determined, she even tried to get round my husband to persuade me . . . When Mrs Rigby wanted you to undertake anything unpleasant or dangerous, she had a way of making you feel that *she* was doing *you* a favour!' 'The meetings were usually held in the Rigbys' house, where Edith Rigby would sit cross-legged on a Persian mat, smoking endless cigars. At five minutes to nine, she would always stand up, whatever the stage of the meeting, and say "Well, ladies, it's time for the doctor's supper. I must go . . . Good-night and thank you".[44] The members of the Preston WSPU – among them Beth Hesmondhalgh, Mrs Towler, Jenny Jackson – occasionally went down to London to take part in suffragette meetings or demonstrations, but never helped shape WSPU policy.

Again one of the vital differences between the WSPU and the National Union emerges: the WSPU never had an industrial base for its campaign, while the National Union Lancashire operation was firmly rooted in the demands of the disenfranchised textile workers. All the radical suffragists (with the obvious exception of Esther Roper, Eva Gore-Booth, Mrs Haworth, Mrs Thomasson and one or two others) had long personal experience of mill and factory work, and it was this that shaped their demand for womanhood suffrage. The WSPU, on the other hand, grew out of a critique of the ILP and the Labour Representation Committee; the Pankhursts' roots were in political parties rather than in trade unions or the cotton industry. Annie Kenney had, of course, spent some fifteen years in the carding room at Woodend Mill before being swept up by the Pankhursts, and many of her speeches referred to her working class perspective on suffrage.[45] Yet her involvement in the Card Room and Blowing Room Association was only a fleeting one and, despite occasionally dressing up in clogs and shawl for London demonstrations, she soon slipped gracefully into Christabel's 'aristocracy of the suffragettes'. When she referred to herself and her fellow suffragette, Lady Constance Lytton, she blithely remarked that she had not known class prejudice, but 'sex barriers meet me at every turn'. Just as the Preston mill workers were under Edith Rigby's thumb, so Annie Kenney was largely at Christabel's beck and call. When Christabel was exiled in Paris, it was the faithful Annie Kenney who, despite constant sea-sickness, crossed the channel each time to relay Christabel's instructions back to London.

The WSPU failed to recruit women textile workers and, after Christabel arrived in London in mid-1906, saw little real need to. They did make a few rather arbitrary stabs in that direction, but it was never part of a sustained campaign. Alice Milne noted in her diary in September 1906 that the WSPU used the peg of a strike of some Bolton weavers on which to hang a local campaign. 'Wildly exuberant crowd of weavers formed — emotional talk of women being the slaves of slaves and all pledged to work for Brotherhood of man along with Sisterhood of woman.'[46] Yet little came of it and Alice Collinge, listed that year as their Bolton contact, soon left to join the radical suffragists.[47] Similarly, Jennie Baines, a WSPU member from Stockport who worked closely with Alice Milne, went up to Rossendale to harrass the anti-suffrage MP; she was able to quote some facts and figures about the large number of women workers in the constituency, but in the end could only vaguely assure the women 'that our union is fighting for them.'[48]

The suffragettes also lacked a firm mass base outside London, and had little sustained contact with organized women workers. Once they were caught up in the campaign, they tended to spend a considerable time in London, rather than working in and around the area they grew up in. They were largely young and unmarried, and their mobility was limited by as few personal ties as possible. In every way, they had a very different life style from the radical suffragists, about half of whom were married and many of whom had children. Of the nineteen committee members of the Lancashire Women Textile Workers' Representation Committee listed in 1910, Sarah Reddish, Esther Roper, Eva Gore-Booth, Cissy Foley, Louisa Smith, Nellie Keenan, Isabel Forsyth, Katherine Rowton and Mary Carr from Hyde were single, but the remaining nine were married; and nearly all of them (Eva Gore-Booth is an obvious exception) worked and lived in the area in which they had grown up.[49]

The suffragettes could much more easily shrug off moral codes they dismissed as repressive or fuddy-duddy, while the radical suffragists had to temper their behaviour to local expectations. Like the Guildswomen, their frame of reference was working class family life and community politics. It was no good running a Moral Crusade, as Christabel did in 1913, and advocating 'votes for women and chastity for men', if the men you were accusing of being diseased lived down your street or worked next to you in the mill.[50] Teresa Billington-Grieg, liberated from the moral strictures of Blackburn's Catholic community, was free to publish her advanced ideas, and on one occasion in the early 1900s, caused great consternation when she opened a debate on marriage at the Manchester University Settlement; her speech, she recalled, 'was as advanced as any at that time . . . I denounced the promise of the wife to "obey" as being utterly immoral and originating in slavery' — at which point a disconcerted matron hurried a young couple out of earshot of such subversive ideas.[51] The Women's Co-operative Guild did, for instance, advocate more liberal divorce laws, but speakers who denounced the whole idea of marriage so brazenly would have got fairly short shrift from Guildswomen in Nelson or Bolton, Darwen or Accrington.

Free love — advocated by 'new young women' like Teresa Billington — was unrealistic for many when birth control information was still unobtainable for the vast majority of working class women.[52] For instance, in Manchester Humphrey Roe (who later married Marie Stopes) and Margaret Ashton tried to found a birth control clinic for working women just before the First World War; he offered one hospital £1,000 a year for five years (plus £12,000 on his death) to open such a clinic, but the offer was turned down in the end as it would have cost the hospital considerable public support.[53]

In fact, there was also a large body of opinion — even in the cotton towns — that argued fiercely against mothers going out to work at all, and married suffragists came in for their fair share of this criticism, especially if they occasionally had to travel away from home on National Union business. Ada Nield Chew solved the problem by taking Doris with her. 'Mind you, as one woman said to me, it wouldn't have worked if she'd had more than one child. Which is almost certainly true', Doris Chew said. 'You couldn't cart a family around — two or three, even.'[54] For one reason or another, Selina Cooper and Ada Nield Chew only had one child; Margaret Aldersley, on the other hand, had four and her family and neighbours took a dim view of trips across to Yorkshire or up to Scotland. They felt it was wrong to be continually leaving her home and be 'flying about the country'. In the end this censure and the rough reception she got at public meetings forced her to give up working for the National Union (though she still remained a member of the Clitheroe Suffrage Society).[55]

The radical suffragists always worked quite closely with sympathetic men — whether it was socialists like Thorley Smith or Keir Hardie, Philip Snowden, or long-standing sympathizers like Reverend Steinthal or trade unionists like William Williamson or Allan Gee — and nowhere in their writings or speeches is there any of the man-hating sentiments sometimes found in the later WSPU. Esther Roper would draw her brother in to help in campaigns, a Mr, Mrs and Miss Kershaw were all members of the Clitheroe Society, and, most importantly, Robert Cooper was wholly in sympathy with his wife's views. He kept the account book for the Society, even shared a speaking platform with his wife at a Brierfield meeting, was active in the Men's League for Women's Suffrage, and went down with Selina and Mary to the big National Union procession in 1911. Without this approval and backing, Selina Cooper's work would have been impossible. Mary also fully sympathized with her mother's political aims; she would sometimes go along to meetings with her and as soon as she was old enough, subscribed to the Society's funds. People used to say she was neglected as a child, but Mary knew that in many ways she was better looked after than some of the children of the local weavers: she had dozens of relations living nearby whose homes were always open to her, and when she was younger, Mrs Holt or somebody else she knew was always there to look after her. The only hardship was missing her mother when she was away, for they were always extremely close friends.

Despite the care with which Selina Cooper provided for Mary, one of the harshest critics was her own mother-in-law; she lived in the neighbourhood, and used to devise crafty schemes to tie Selina Cooper

XIII

The debate with the Labour Party

Once the suffragists started demanding votes for women more forcefully, the question of adult suffrage, which had been allowed to lie fallow since the 1884 Reform Act, quickly re-emerged as a controversial issue. For nearly twenty years trade unionists and socialists had let the idea of full adult suffrage lapse, content that the great majority of skilled, unionized working class men now had the vote.

Yet as soon as Helen Silcock and Allen Gee raised the issue of women's suffrage at the TUC Congresses in 1901 and 1902, an adult suffrage resolution was hastily drafted to defeat it. Then, in 1905 when the Engineers' delegate and Selina Cooper proposed a women's suffrage resolution, Harry Quelch and some trade unionists immediately intervened with a rival adult suffrage motion. No sooner had the WSPU and the radical suffragists begun to draw public attention to the urgency of their demand, than an Adult Suffrage Society was formed, led by the trade unionist Margaret Bondfield, who publicly said she 'deprecated votes for women as the hobby of disappointed old maids whom no one had wanted to marry'.[1]

From then on the adult suffragists, who included not only Margaret Bondfield, Quelch and Hyndman, but also Arthur Henderson (Labour MP since 1903)[2] were always able to command a majority. Labour's suspicion that a limited franchise bill would merely strengthen propertied interests ran so deep that the appeals of Selina Cooper or

231

Ben Turner had limited impact. Labour's great hope of changing society to benefit working people lay largely in the number of Labour MPs returned to Westminster, so any constitutional change which might conceivably benefit the established parties at the expense of Labour was quickly pounced on and rejected.

To Arthur Henderson and Margaret Bondfield the argument seemed clear cut: there must be opposition to any bill that was not in the Labour Party's interests. Their black and white point of view annoyed suffragists and suffragettes alike, because, they felt, it chose to ignore the practical mechanics of party politics. Neither a Liberal nor a Tory Government was at all likely to support a measure so wildly revolutionary as full adult suffrage; likewise complete manhood suffrage would be opposed on class grounds by the Tories and some Liberals and, even if it came about, it would push back the cause of women's suffrage for decades. They were equally annoyed by the way in which adult suffragists seemed to channel all their energies into blocking women's suffrage proposals, rather than pushing forward their *own* demands. The Adult Suffrage Society, Keir Hardie wrote caustically, 'holds no meetings, issues no literature . . . It is never heard of, save when it emerges to oppose the Women's Enfranchisement Bill. Its policy is that of the dog in the manger.'[3]

Labour's opposition to women's suffrage — partly very logical, partly a little hypocritical — dragged on through the 1900s. Both camps vehemently claimed to speak for the mass of women, whether wage earners themselves or the wives of working men, and working class women were constantly exhorted to take one side or the other in the arguments.

For women who had long experience of working in the labour movement — the Guild, the League or trade unions — it presented an agonizing dilemma. Many of the radical suffragists could appreciate both sides of the argument, and increasingly found themselves caught in an embarrassing no-man's-land between the extremes of Christabel Pankhurst and those of Harry Quelch. Throughout the decade argument was met by counter argument, accusations of 'sex prejudice' met by accusations of 'class prejudice'. The situation was constantly changing and individuals found themselves swopping sides in mid stream. This complex situation can best be understood in terms of how particular women came to terms with the dilemma.

At the turn of the century, Helen Silcock had been an outstanding suffragist, pleading on behalf of the disenfranchised Wigan weavers on both Westminster deputations and at two TUC Congresses. Yet from 1902-3 she dropped all contact with the radical suffragists; she had nothing to do with their new Lancashire Women Textile Workers' Representation Committee (though ironically they chose her constituency to field their first candidate) and seems not to have helped in Thorley Smith's election campaign. At the earliest opportunity, she joined Margaret Bondfield's Adult Suffrage Society.

Why had Helen Silcock made this *volte face*? The reasons seem complex. We have seen earlier how at the two Congresses she had demonstrated how willing she was to take an unpopular line in face of massive opposition; how the second time her motion was rejected she must have begun to entertain doubts about the rightness of women's suffrage and to feel that she was perhaps betraying her own class. She was already heavily involved in Wigan politics, especially as a member of the local Trades Council, and so had close contact with many adult suffragists. All the factors that undermined Thorley Smith's candidacy would have confirmed any doubts she already had about women's suffrage: Wigan was essentially a coal town not a cotton town, and the tradition of independent working women did not flourish strongly there; the Miners were virulent opponents of women's suffrage (her own father had been a member of the Miners for over fifty years) and were strongly represented on the Trades Council; and her membership of the Social Democratic Federation, so strong in Wigan, must have encouraged doubts about women's suffrage.

Helen Silcock's whole life was bound up by the people in these political factions: they were among her closest friends. The rather bizarre way in which the *Women's Trade Union Review* reported her wedding in 1902 confirms this, for it reads more like a political conference than a social event:

> Our congratulations to Miss Helen Silcock on her marriage to Mr Fairhurst, a prominent Trade Unionist in Wigan, are none the less hearty for being tardy. It was an interesting wedding. Delegates from the Wigan Trades Council, and Social Democratic Federation, from the Southport Women's Club, and last but not least, from the Women's Union, of which Miss Silcock has been President for many years, were present.[4]

When the radical suffragists came to support Thorley Smith in 1906, Helen Silcock, by then an influential woman, seems to have taken no part for or against his campaign. Although she was by then a member of the Adult Suffrage Society she must have felt sorely torn between her old and new loyalties, and concluded sadly at that point that her only tenable position was on the sidelines.

Selina Cooper, equally enmeshed in socialist politics and a one-time member of the Social Democratic Federation, never wavered from the women's suffrage convictions she had developed as a winder in the 1890s. Perhaps part of the explanation for her consistency lies in the independence of the mill women in Nelson where both the ILP and Guild branch were actively pro-suffrage. Her personal involvement with the ILP both locally and nationally must have helped sustain her commitment, even in the face of Labour Party opposition. Mary Cooper has vivid memories of a constant stream of penniless socialist speakers who were given hospitality by her parents:

> Ramsey MacDonald stayed here, Snowden and Keir Hardie, and they just stayed overnight. We had an ILP club, and they used to speak up there, and my mother used to put them up overnight. And I can always remember sleeping anyway. You know, we'd only two beds. We'd no bath, no wash basin; we mucked in, we mucked in, you see. And of course in those days MacDonald and Snowden and that, they roughed it too, because they were one of the people.[5]

Men like these encouraged Selina Cooper to keep on pressing for women's suffrage, and at the 1907 Labour Party Conference, she was back again as an ILP delegate, seconding the women's suffrage motion. (The Conference was held in Belfast and as a gesture of solidarity with Irish independence she wore an emerald green dress that Harriette Beanland had made for her.[6]) Hardie made a strong speech in support but once again Quelch's adult suffrage amendment won the day, this time by an overwhelming majority — 605,000 votes to 268,000.

Selina Cooper and Keir Hardie had been roundly defeated. For Hardie this was a tragic blow to so much that he stood for and he warned the Conference delegates that he would consider resigning from the party.[7] It was an equally heavy disappointment for Selina Cooper, and she decided to withdraw from Labour Party Conferences to devote herself to National Union campaigns.

Yet in all her suffrage work, Selina Cooper always held fast to her faith in the ILP brand of socialism. Like other radical suffragists, she never forgot that votes for women was just one aspect of a much wider political campaign. Yet, much of her National Union work took her deep into the heart of respectable suburban England, where the role of women was so different from that of the weaving towns she knew so well, and she often perplexed and angered middle class audiences by her forthright, uncompromising opinions.

On one occasion she worked with Emilie Gardner, the Birmingham based National Union organizer, who afterwards told Selina Cooper that 'I'd rather work with you than anybody ... you have so much influence into the red regions of socialism.' She badly wanted to become one of Selina Cooper's close friends, but there was just one problem. 'I always feel frightened that your dreadful jack-in-the-box "class war" feelings will pop up!'[8]

On another occasion Selina Cooper went down to speak at Tunbridge Wells, and received a similar letter from a suffragist she met there, urging her

> not to let that class-hatred and bitterness come into your heart again ... *None of us can help society being broken up into classes, and therefore if we cannot help it, why hate each other for it, but rather let us hold out hands of fellowship when and where we can, and be willing to work shoulder to shoulder for the good of all ... It is *love* not hate that makes the world go round ... Let us try and find out where we can all help each other regardless of class, as at the Suffrage meeting on Thursday.*[9]

Such appeals must have sounded a little hollow to Selina Cooper, with all she had seen as a Poor Law Guardian. Sometimes, according to her daughter, even stronger blandishments were offered to persuade her to abandon Labour for a purely suffrage platform.

> A lot of these rich women had been offering my mother bribes to come over to them — saying what — she had a lovely voice ... She spoke, no notes usually, and she was quick witted at replying, and that sort of thing. And there were letters saying, 'Oh, do stop with us. You could do well on our side.' ... And my mother used to say to them — I remember, I used to write her letters later, and I can remember her answering one, 'I may have a good voice, and I may be a good orator, but my power would finish if I came over.'[10]

Helen Silcock moved from women's suffrage to adult suffrage; Selina Cooper remained a lifelong women's suffragist; but Ada Nield Chew gradually moved from supporting adult suffrage in the early 1900s, to believing ardently in women's suffrage by about 1910. Precisely how her views changed from the days of her fight with Christabel in the *Clarion* to becoming a National Union organizer in 1911 is not recorded, and can only be guessed from the more general shifts in Labour opinion that were taking place at the time.

Along with other like-minded women connected with the ILP and the Women's Trade Union League, Ada Nield Chew became closely involved in the Women's Labour League from its foundation in 1906.[11] Later, when a branch was formed in Rochdale, she was elected

Secretary.

From the beginning the Women's Labour League found itself in an embarrassing cleft stick over women's suffrage. Under its President, Margaret MacDonald, wife of the Labour Party leader, the League committed itself to work for the Party and to canvass for all Labour candidates at elections. Yet this loyalty to husbands and brothers clashed with Labour's decision to reject women's suffrage in preference to adult suffrage, and many of the members objected to the fact that the League too had opted for adult suffrage. For instance, its executive included Mary Gawthorpe and Edith Rigby, both of whom cared passionately about votes for women and became deeply involved in the WSPU's militant programme. They resigned from the League, as did others — including Ethel Snowden and Teresa Billington-Greig — who became impatient with any Labour organization that did not commit itself to votes for women without delay.[12]

Charlotte Despard, one of the most respected members of the Women's Freedom League, did not resign from the Women's Labour League, but must have caused ructions within League circles because she pilloried adult suffrage publicly. Members of the Adult Suffrage Society, she said, were 'not merely halfhearted and without any real hope of success, but were in many cases actually dishonest in their alleged desire to extend the franchise to women'. Ada Nield Chew stayed with the Women's Labour League as well but followed the example of women like Mrs Despard in gradually losing patience with adult suffragists; before long she too was standing up at League Conferences and arguing that it was not up to them to modify their demand for women's suffrage to suit the Liberal Cabinet.[13]

At the same time, Ada Nield Chew seems to have drifted away from the Women's Trade Union League and into circles that took a more positive stand on votes for women. One of the most important influences on Labour women at this time was Charlotte Perkins Gilman, an American socialist writer. 'She did come actually to England on a speaking tour,' Doris Chew recalled, 'and she came to Rochdale, and my mother thought a great deal of her ideas ... She believed that women would achieve independence by co-operation, co-operative looking after children, co-operative meals, and so on.'[14] In particular, Gilman was able to reconcile the seemingly conflicting demands of socialism and women's suffrage in a way that must have caught Ada Nield Chew's imagination.

Said the Socialist to the Suffragist:
   'My cause is greater than yours!
You only work for a Special Class,
We for the gain of the General Mass,
   Which every good ensures!'

Said the Suffragist to the Socialist:
   'You underrate my Cause!
While women remain a Subject Class,
You never can move the General Mass,
   With your Economic Laws!'

'A lifted world lifts women up,'
   The Socialist explained.
'You cannot lift the world at all
While half of it is kept so small,'
   The Suffragist maintained.

The world awoke, and tartly spoke:
   'Your work is all the same:
Work together or work apart,
Work, each of you, with all your heart —
   Just get into the game!'[15]

So by 1911 Ada Nield Chew joined up with the radical suffragists. To them the Labour Party's rejection of women's suffrage seemed a treacherous rejection of the thousands of disenfranchised women who had supported Labour candidates like Shackleton. In 1907 Eva Gore-Booth (who appears to have been delegated by the others to be largely responsible for written propaganda, and who did indeed give an eloquence to their pamphlets) wrote a passionate critique of the way Selina Cooper's resolution had been rejected at the Belfast Conference:

Strangely enough, when the Labour Representation movement began to make itself felt in Lancashire, it was by the votes of women that it stood or fell . . . Among the Lancashire working women there is a strong inherent sense of commercial honesty and personal independence, and it is no exaggeration to say that among the more progressive workers there has grown up a deep feeling of bitterness and disappointment, a feeling which culminated this year when the Labour Party, led away by a theoretic inclination for the very stale red-herring of immediate complete and entire adult suffrage, refused to fulfil their written pledge and press forward a measure for the enfranchisement of women.[16]

The radical suffragists decided to have one final stab at changing the Labour Party's mind; Eva Gore-Booth, as a delegate from Sarah Dickenson's tiny Association of Machine, Electrical and Other Women Workers, attended the 1908 Labour Party Conference in Hull. Ben

237

Turner from the Yorkshire wool workers union (and, with Allen Gee, a far more valuable ally than any of the Lancashire labour leaders[17]) proposed the women's suffrage motion, but was immediately challenged by the perennial Quelch amendment, this time enlivened by disparaging references to the 'Merry Andrew antics' of the suffragettes. Eva Gore-Booth stood up and made an impassioned plea on behalf of the five million working women 'who have to go out the same as a man goes out on Monday mornings to their work for the same number of hours, but at the end of the week they come home with far less wages . . . I ask you to give your vote in the Conference for the very poorest of the poor, the poorest of your own class.'[18]

But Ben Turner and Eva Gore-Booth were as thoroughly routed as Selina Cooper and Keir Hardie had been the year before. Quelch's amendment once again won the day, this time by an even larger majority. For the radical suffragists this merely confirmed the chasm that divided them from mainstream Labour opinion.

Women's suffrage was not the only reason for the antagonism: it extended into a much wider debate about the whole position of working women. The radical suffragists had always based their demand for suffrage on the contribution working women — especially in textiles — made to the wealth of the country; despite this, they said, women workers were still paid less than men, and still had their work conditions controlled by a Parliament that was not elected by or accountable to them. Once they were armed with the vote, they argued — perhaps rather naively — their pay and conditions would no longer be so much lower than men's.

Here they stirred up another hornets' nest of controversy. Labour took the idea of the 'family wage' very seriously, feeling that an adult man should earn sufficient to keep his wife and children. The corollary of this was, of course, that women had less claim than men to a decent wage packet and to a job. The controversy exploded once the Liberals came to power in 1906, elected largely on their promise to introduce badly-needed social and economic reforms. One of the most pressing problems was unemployment, and the Liberals cast around for possible solutions — and decided that working wives could conveniently be squeezed out. Why should a married woman take a job from a man who had his whole family to support? In this, the initiative was largely taken by John Burns, onetime member of the Social Democratic Federation, but a Liberal MP since 1892. In 1906 he was given a seat in the new Cabinet as President of the Local Government Board. His own marriage was a conventional one and he was a firm believer in limiting married women's work in factories and workshops.[19] Many women socialists agreed with him; under socialism, Ethel Snowden wrote, 'married women with children will not work in the factory; at least not until the children are out of their hands. They will not wish to do so, for they will be free and their children will claim them.'[20] This argument made little sense to the radical suffragists who had grown up accepting that married women would work, and who were much influenced by the ideas of Blatchford and Charlotte Perkins Gilman that co-operative solutions to childcare were the ideal, and preferable to forcing women back into the home. They were particularly incensed when Shackleton started to demand a legal ban on married women's work, especially since some of them must have recalled that he himself had had to live on his wife's earnings for seventeen weeks when he was out of work in the 1880s.[21] Eva Gore-Booth drafted a penny pamphlet, published by the Women's Trade and Labour Council, called *Women's Right to Work*, which violently attacked Mr Shackleton

> whose reason for existing in a House of Commons is presumably his connection with a Trade Union composed of a majority of women, openly daring to declare that his members if they are married should not be allowed by law to work. In the event of a re-arrangement of work between employers and employed, are the 74,000 married women in the cotton trade likely to get their interests fought for, and their end held up by, Mr Shackleton?[22]

Despite pressing unemployment the idea of such legislation was never taken any further. More practical was a proposal aimed at restricting all women's work in certain trades — including pit-brow lasses and chain-makers — and to prohibit women from working after 8 pm by widening the categories of work governed by the Factory and Workshops Act. Banning evening work particularly hit barmaids' jobs, for pubs often stayed open after midnight. From 1907 the radical suffragists campaigned to defend the barmaids' 'right to work'.

In spring 1908 they were given an excellent opportunity to publicize both the barmaids' cause and their opposition to the Liberal legislation. A prominent Cabinet Minister, Winston Churchill, was standing at a by-election in north-west Manchester. Eva Gore-Booth's sister, Constance Markievicz, arrived for the campaign and lent it a certain untypical panache; for once the suffragists seemed to have ousted the suffragettes from the limelight, but without resorting to any kind of violence. The *Manchester Guardian* reported how:

A coach of the olden times was driven about Manchester yesterday to
advertise the political agitation on behalf of the barmaids. It was drawn by
four white horses, and the 'whip' was the Countess Markievicz, sister of Eva
Gore-Booth. In all parts of the city the coach and its passengers excited
general interest, and in the North-west division especially, the cause of the
barmaids was made known not only by demonstration, but by speeches and
personal interviews and distribution of literature.[23]

So popular did the coach become that when it arrived in Stevenson
Square two days later there was such a crowd of people it could not get
through, and the WSPU lorry, which had managed to get to the centre,
was shoved back again.[24] (Churchill lost the election and the ardently
Liberal *Manchester Guardian* complained about the 'little interests' —
and the powerful brewers — that had worked against their candidate.)

The radical suffragists — like the earlier nineteenth century feminists
— opposed all legislation that put any restrictions upon women's right
to work. But unlike their predecessors, their demands were essentially
practical, and stemmed from their own experiences as working women.
Tactically though, they were rather clumsy, and their campaign only
alienated them still further from mainstream Labour opinion. The
radical suffragists supported the barmaids as a way to improve working
women's wages and conditions. Unfortunately many local Labour
supporters did not see it in this light. To them it was a spit in the eye of
the temperance values they held so deep. Temperance and feminism
were often supported as part and parcel of the same campaign (though
not of course to the extent that this was so in America). Margaret
MacDonald, wife of the Party leader, even insisted that women were
only employed as barmaids 'as decoys to increase the sale of drink and
to make bars places of social resort'.[25] In Blackburn, Ethel Snowden,
as wife of the local MP, was involved in a suffragist temperance
campaign, with the aim of abolishing barmaids altogether. One of the
strongest sources of support for Thorley Smith had been the Wigan
temperance group, and, certainly in terms of numbers, the British
Women's Temperance Association was one of the most influential
suffrage supporters. In their characteristic enthusiasm to support one
small group of women workers the radical suffragists had managed to
alienate a large number of valuable Labour supporters.

More importantly, the radical suffragists acted tactlessly towards the
Women's Trade Union League leadership and hence many male trade
unionists. Mary Macarthur, now Secretary of the League and herself an
adult suffragist, took fierce personal exception to their opposition to

factory legislation. After one meeting the radical suffragists organized in London, she wrote a furious letter to the *Daily News* to make it clear that the League had 'toiled for more than a generation' for such protective laws, and did not intend having its work sniped at by a small group of provincial feminists:

> It seems to me that just as there can be no greater argument for women's suffrage than the life work of a woman like Mrs Sidney Webb [who had once signed an anti-suffrage petition], so there is nothing more calculated to delay its achievement than the propaganda of that small body, of which Miss Eva Gore-Both and Miss Roper are the chief exponents.[26]

She looked no more kindly on the way in which the radical suffragists fostered women-only unions. At a conference of women workers held in Manchester in 1907, Sarah Dickenson proudly described how the four thousand women (including over a thousand weavers) were members of small women's unions affiliated to the Women's Trade and Labour Council. Four of the unions she went on, had been so successful that they now employed a full-time Secretary (two of them probably Nellie Keenan for the Salford Weavers, Violet Grundy for the Ancoats Winders; Isabel Forsyth for the Bookbinders became full-time secretary the following year). In some cases wages had been increased by as much as 3s a week, and many of the members, she said, were 'prepared to push forward their claims to political rights through their union'.[27] She was immediately attacked by Mary Macarthur, who rounded on her for teaching women 'to clamour for the Parliamentary vote' before they had learned to take full part in their trade union; she maintained it was 'sex antagonism' to organize men and women into separate unions. Sarah Dickenson replied quite coolly that she had no idea of organizing separate unions for the sexes, but she rather agreed with the idea that it was useful for women to organize by themselves at first, and then for them to move on into a general trade union.

Sarah Dickenson might have won the skirmish, but Mary Macarthur was better placed to win the war. Among her powerful allies was David Shackleton, by now President of the Northern Counties Weavers' Amalgamated Association, vice-chairman of the Parliamentary Labour Party, Treasurer of the Women's Trade Union League, and a member of the powerful Parliamentary Committee of the TUC. He too was irritated by the radical suffragists' pin-prick attacks on his massive dignity, and during a debate on a women's suffrage bill in the Commons in 1907 he included an oblique dig at their propaganda. Women cotton workers 'might have been told by people who did not understand factory life that their wages would be increased [by women's suffrage], but no leader of the textile industries had told them anything of the kind'.[28] (He then added that he would vote against the bill in its next reading, on the grounds that it would merely enfranchise propertied women.)

Whatever the subject — protective legislation, working wives, women's right to work, all-women unions, or women's suffrage — the radical suffragists now always took a purist line with scant regard for Labour's political priorities. Labour saw its immediate strategy as winning seats in the Commons, combating poverty and unemployment, and supporting progressive Liberal reforms like labour exchanges and old age pensions. As the Labour Party refined its programme down to these key issues, the radical suffragists found they were increasingly on the wrong side of the line. Within a few short years the radical suffragists were now effectively occupying a political wilderness of their own.

Part of the reason for this lay in the tremendous growth of the Labour Party; part lay in the alienating effect of WSPU militancy; and part lay in the radical suffragists' unique regional strength — no other group of working women could match their political muscle, or would dare to press its own demands irrespective of what the Labour establishment thought.

Yet the radical suffragists were never completely without friends. There were always allies on the other side of the Pennines; and there was always the Women's Co-operative Guild. The Guild had also taken exception to John Burns' proposals about married women's work,[29] like the radical suffragists, the Guild still hoped that trade unionists, if approached with the right, carefully-worded proposal, would give their valuable backing to women's suffrage. They mulled this over and in October 1907 a letter from the Women's Trade and Labour Council was circulated to local trades councils, signed by Eva Gore-Booth, Sarah Dickenson, Sarah Reddish and Margaret Llewelyn Davies:

In view of the feeling among certain Trade Unionists against any partial measure on Women's Suffrage short of actual womanhood suffrage, we venture to ask you to consider the following proposed policy. We believe that there are a great many people who would honestly wish to further the cause of Women's Enfranchisement for the sake of the heavy industrial grievances of working women, if they could do so in a manner that they felt to be absolutely democratic. If this represents your feelings on the subject, we venture to ask you to pass a Resolution urging the Labour Party to take action next Session by proposing an amendment . . . that would be supported by

Adult Suffragists and Women Suffragists alike.[30]

It is not recorded how this conciliatory proposal was received, (though at least one council — Rawtenstall — voted in support and this may have provided Ben Turner and Eva Gore-Both with a little badly needed trade union support at the Labour Party Conference three months later.) However, after their subsequent defeat at the hands of Quelch, the radical suffragists, the Guild and other supporters decided to switch their focus from labour leaders to Asquith himself. The new Prime Minister was already prevaricating over women's suffrage. A letter urging him to stop wasting time was sent in September 1908 signed by an impressively wide range of pressure groups, including the Guild, the Women's Trade and Labour Council, the Lancashire Women Textile Workers' Representation Committee, the North of England Society, Margaret Ashton's group of Liberal women and the Women's Labour League.[31]

Asquith remained unimpressed. The more he was pressured, the more he found crafty ways to avoid giving the required legislation government backing to ensure its smooth passage through Westminster. Even the public outcry against hunger-striking and the forced feeding of imprisoned suffragettes failed to move him. Besides, the Liberal Government was having trouble riding various other political storms. It was increasingly difficult to evade the demand of Irish MPs for Home Rule for Ireland; Labour was outraged by the House of Lords' Osborne Judgement that made it illegal for trade unions to give financial support to Labour candidates at elections, and the demand for far-reaching social and economic reform ran at fever pitch. Then in April 1909 Lloyd George, as Chancellor of the Exchequer, introduced his 'People's Budget', designed to increase tax on wealth and property. After seven months tumultuous debate, it was thrown out of the House of Lords. The Liberals had to go back to the country, and a General Election focused on the burning question of the Budget and the power of the Lords was called for January 1910.

Just before polling began, Asquith made a public pledge that if, as seemed likely, the Liberals were returned, the Government would look sympathetically on women's suffrage. The National Union, trusting that Liberal promises would at last bear fruit, decided to play a low-key role in the election; the WSPU, although denouncing Asquith's pledge as worthless, contented itself during the election run-up with merely holding public meetings to draw votes away from the Liberals. Not so the radical suffragists. This was the first election since their near success at Wigan in 1906. They did not want to waste this rare opportunity to field a second suffrage candidate. This time they chose a constituency right in the heart of the cotton weaving belt, where the number of working women was amongst the highest in the country — Rossendale. Although this gave them a great advantage, other factors weighed heavily against them. Of these, the greatest hindrance was their isolation from the Labour Party. Unlike at Wigan, no Labour politician sent messages of solidarity: neither the Rossendale Labour Council nor local trade unions gave them support. Indeed, Liberal traditions still had such a strong hold on Rossendale that the Labour council had never even considered fielding a Labour candidate, being content with two-party elections. Rossendale was also a stronghold of Non-conformist temperance; (when a Liberal club was opened at Waterfoot, the audience broke out into cheering when they heard that no alcohol was to be sold on the premises) but the radical suffragists had alienated this potential support that they had relied on in Wigan.[32]

Nor did they receive any support from the National Union, which seemed to steer clear of the campaign and even dispatched Selina Cooper to the nearby Darwen constituency rather than to Rossendale.[33] So, completely on their own, the radical suffragists formed themselves into the Rossendale Suffrage Election Committee and, by stretching the limited funds to their utmost of the Industrial and Professional Women's Suffrage Society and the Lancashire Women Textile Workers' Representation Committee, somehow managed to collect the £500 necessary to run the campaign. £150 of this came from their candidate; in their straitened circumstances his largesse must have helped persuade the radical suffragists that he was their man. Otherwise he was as unlikely a candidate as their original Wigan man had been. His name was Arthur Bulley, he ran his own firm of Liverpool cotton brokers and was a member of both the Social Democratic Federation and the Fabian Society. He had no known connections with Rossendale and was hardly the sort of man to woo the weavers away from their Liberal habits.[34]

Even though the suffragist's chances of winning the seat were slim, Rossendale was a sensible choice. The sitting MP was Lewis Harcourt, a member of the Liberal Cabinet, a man who was completely out of sympathy with women's suffrage. He was a professional politician whom it would be extremely difficult to dislodge. Still, the radical suffragists, heartened by the 8,000 signatures they had collected locally in 1906, wrote cheerfully of their chances in the *Common Cause*:

> The strength of our position is that ordinary people are with us — and by ordinary people in an election I do not mean the politicians who belong to party organizations, and are loyal to their own side, and look upon the election as a game of football, and would never dream of considering the merits of a new idea. But the ordinary men (as the miners, for instance, in Wigan) know the difficulties of women in the industrial world, and the sharpness of their struggle to earn a bare pittance . . .[35]

Around Christmas 1909, a dozen suffragists travelled up to Rossendale to open the campaign. Some of them had been working together now for about ten years — Sarah Reddish, Sarah Dickenson, Katherine Rowton, Mrs Green, Esther Roper, Eva Gore-Booth and — when she could still manage it — Selina Cooper. A loyal brother and sister were roped in — Constance Markievicz and Reginald Roper. Others were slightly more recent supporters: Alice Collinge and other members of the Bolton Women Textile Workers' Representation Committee, probably Cissy Foley and Clara Staton; Sarah Whittaker from Accrington, and Miss M.A. Wroe from the Industrial and Professional Women's Suffrage Society.[36]

Bulley's campaign opened with a meeting in the Bacup Mechanics' Hall; it was in men's interests to enfranchise women, the candidate said, because if women had the power to enforce better wages it would improve things for men workers as well. A committee room was opened in Rawtenstall and dinner hour meetings were held every day at millgates in all the little Rossendale villages — Crawshawbooth, Cloughfoot, Waterfoot, Haslingden — with meetings in the town squares at night.[37] 'What days those were,' wrote Alice Collinge, 'standing in the market places lit up by pitch torches, and braving all kinds of weather. How we all entered heart and soul into the fray.'[38] 'It has been necessary to increase the number of dinner-hour meetings' boasted one report in the *Common Cause*, 'as we receive constant requests from mills where the workers want to hear the suffragists.'[39]

Such isolated pockets of enthusiasm were deceptive. The cards were heavily stacked against them. The General Election was not, in the eyes of the majority of voters, anything to do with women's suffrage: it was to do with Lloyd George and the House of Lords. The *Rossendale Echo* gave Bulley minimal coverage and was essentially pro-Harcourt. The *Rossendale Free Press* reprinted the National Union manifesto for some reason, but otherwise completely ignored Bulley and pulled out all stops to boost Harcourt. The twelve radical suffragists tried to race around the sprawling constituency — twenty eight square miles — in the one motor car at their disposal (Sarah Dickenson had a driving licence), but their campaign was doomed. The Liberals had stuck up posters announcing that 'A Vote for Bulley is a vote for the House of Lords' and had made women's suffrage seem totally irrelevant to the election.[40] Bulley polled a pitiful 639 votes and came bottom of the poll.

On a national scale, the General Election was not a success for the Liberals who lost their majority, and the balance of power was now held by eighty four Irish MPs and forty two Labour members. In the light of this and of Asquith's pre-election suffrage promise, a pro-suffrage Conciliation Committee was formed of fifty four MPs of all parties — including six Labour men. It was backed by the National Union and by the WSPU, which promptly declared a truce on anti-Government militancy. The Conciliation Committee decided to sponsor a women's suffrage bill sufficiently non-controversial that it would get widespread backing; to ensure the vital Tory support, it was drafted on narrow property lines to enfranchise only one million women. David Shackleton, who had included 'adult suffrage for women as well as men' in his recent election address, was by now held in considerable esteem by the Government; he was a safe choice to sponsor the bill. When he introduced the Second Reading in July 1910 he spoke in terms that the radical suffragists had been using for some years; he had been accused, he said, of talking 'about the thin end of the wedge. I wonder what kind of a cheer I should get . . . if I tried the thick end of the wedge. First of all, I should be fitted for a lunatic asylum. My reason for trying the thin end of the wedge is that I believe in the principle, and, once you get in the thin end, experience justifies extension of it as years go by.'

The debate lasted two days but, without government backing, the bill was doomed like all its predecessors; so was the Second Conciliation Bill, introduced the next year, 1911; the Government even introduced a manhood suffrage bill that in itself would not have given votes to a single woman — though this too was withdrawn. By the end of 1911 anger at Asquith's chicanery was becoming intense; the WSPU responded with an outbreak of mass window-breaking. Labour supporters, whose strongest objections to previous suffrage bills had been that they increased the power of propertied women, were furious that the Conciliation Committee had courted the Tories and proposed a restricted women's franchise, only to have it thrown out for lack of firm government support.

The Guild too was losing patience with supporting bills which would only enfranchise a tiny minority of Guildswomen — but were even so always rejected. In 1909 the Guild Executive (though not necessarily the local branches) decided to affiliate to a new group called the People's Suffrage Federation, of which Margaret Llewelyn Davies was Secretary.[41]

The Federation had attracted the support of some well-placed, influential politicians, often adult suffragists, including Margaret Bondfield, Arthur Henderson, Mary Macarthur and a sprinkling of progressive Liberals. Federation members decided that they *must* get Labour Party backing for women's suffrage, otherwise the two main parties would continue playing their time-wasting games in the Commons for ever, and possibly even pass another manhood suffrage bill that did not touch on women. At the 1912 Labour Party Conference, chaired by the sympathetic Ben Turner, Arthur Henderson pushed through a resolution that, although supporting adult suffrage, the Labour Party in Parliament must oppose any franchise bill that did not include women.[42]

The effect of the Henderson resolution — like the Wilkinson resolution of 1904 — was to give vital Labour backing to suffrage campaigns. Labour and suffrage were reunited after a separation of about seven or eight years. For women like Mrs Despard, Ada Nield Chew and Selina Cooper it gave tremendous hope and encouragement. The reconciliation, so long awaited, began to have other vital repercussions as well. Mrs Fawcett and her colleagues had always tried to campaign for suffrage on non-party lines, but now even they began to entertain doubts about their own political neutrality.[43] When they heard of Labour's declaration, they finally changed their minds. In May 1912 the National Union decided to 'strengthen any party in the House of Commons which adopts women's suffrage as part of its official programme'. 'Our change of policy was in effect a declaration of war against the official Liberal Party,' Mrs Fawcett wrote, 'and of support of the Labour Party, which was the only party which had made women's suffrage part of its programme.'

A special Election Fighting Fund was set up to help Labour candidates in by-elections. The National Union now employed sixty one organizers who, according to Mrs Fawcett, were chosen 'to carry out our Election Fighting Fund work from amongst our members whose personal sympathies were with the Labour Party'.[44] This was a marvellous opportunity for the radical suffragists. 'Labour women were very much sought after at that time,' Doris Chew, who was fourteen at the time, recalled, 'because they could appeal to the ordinary working man or woman — working man mainly, the ones with the votes.'[45]

In Lancashire most of the National Union work was undertaken by Ada Nield Chew, Margaret Aldersley and Selina Cooper, and they were soon appearing at by-elections in the region — Holmfirth in the West Riding, Hanley in the Potteries, Crewe, Keighley and Accrington.

Ada Nield Chew had been appointed as Rossendale organizer in 1911, but in July 1912 she went back to Crewe — once again. As part of the by-election campaign, she opened suffrage shops in Crewe High Street and other constituency towns. Here, she found she had to vie with Sylvia Pankhurst and dramatic WSPU literature, written in Paris and full of stories of hunger strikers and forced feeding, but she was still able to turn public attention to the real needs of working women.[46]

In October 1913 Selina Cooper and her friend from the Board of Guardians Margaret Aldersley campaigned at the Keighley by-election, just over the moors from Nelson, to mount a propaganda campaign.[47] They started speaking at the market cross in the middle of Haworth, one of the villages in the constituency, but, as Mary Cooper recounted, they soon came under fire:

> Well, they threw rotten eggs and tomatoes and all sorts of things . . . They kept coming back into this cafe where they were sheltering . . . and then Mrs Aldersley went out and came back crying — oh, covered with egg and tomatoes and — and so my mother — she's slow to rouse, but when my mother was roused I was scared stiff of her. She was right slow to rouse; my father was quick-tempered. Anyhow, my mother went out, and she stood on this cross, and she said, 'I'm stopping here, whatever you throw, so go and fetch all the stuff you've got to throw, because,' she says, 'I'm going to speak to you, I've come here to speak. And,' she says, 'this blooming village would never have been known about but for three women — the Brontes.'[48]

The National Union and the Labour Party organized a suffrage campaign, also during October, in Accrington. The sitting MP was Harold Baker, Financial Secretary to the Home Office, who the year before had moved the rejection of the Women's Franchise Bill. The campaign opened with a mass meeting in Accrington Town Hall; the impressive roll call of speakers encompassed suffragists who had been fighting for votes for women since the 1880s as well as Labour striplings whose political careers lay ahead of them. Isabella Ford,

Margaret Ashton, Helena Swanwick, Selina Cooper, Ada Nield Chew, Fenner (later Lord) Brockway, and Albert Smith (Clitheroe's new MP, since Shackleton went to work as senior labour advisor to the Home Secretary, Winston Churchill, at the end of 1910). On another occasion the youthful Ellen Wilkinson, who became a Labour Cabinet Minister in the 1940s, spoke. Unsurprisingly, speakers like these could easily fill Accrington's Empire Picture Palace with an audience of a thousand supporters.[49] Mrs Tozer, wife of the Vicar of Heywood, set up suffrage shops in Accrington, Church and Rishton for publicity and fund-raising. It was 'a week full of "crowded hours of glorious life"', Ada Nield Chew wrote.[50]

Over the next ten months before war broke out radical suffragists travelled the length and breadth of the country to fight by-elections for the National Union. In December Ada Nield Chew and Margaret Aldersley covered the South Lanark election, along with Ellen Wilkinson and Fenner Brockway. The following month Ada Nield Chew, this time with Selina Cooper, was in the north-west Durham constituency, in February she was at Leith Burgs and in May in north east Derbyshire.[51]

At the same time as the by-election campaigns were being fought, the organizers also helped persuade trade unions, trades councils, labour representation committees and even the TUC itself to adopt resolutions backing Labour's decision.[52] The renewed friendship between suffrage and labour was a real vindication of the radical suffragists' policy, and it gave all activists a fillip. The days of doubts and vacillation were over. Helen Silcock, for instance, committed herself once again to women's suffrage and early in 1914 became Secretary of the Wigan Suffrage Society.[53] Up in Colne the local ILP sponsored a joint meeting with the Clitheroe Suffrage Society and invited Harriette Beanland to come and speak at it.[54] Then, about a month before war broke out a joint women's suffrage and Labour demonstration was held in Manchester.[55]

These two and a half years were extremely fruitful, busy ones for the radical suffragists. Even so, they were not without their drawbacks. Although suffragists who supported Labour were in great demand in Lancashire, they were no longer in the policy-making position they had been earlier when they had been working solely through the Lancashire Women Textile Workers' Representation Committee. They obviously refused to compromise over major issues, but in many ways they must have had to toe the National Union line since it was paying their salaries.

Another problem was that there were many suffragists and socialists who resented the new friendship pact. In Bolton, for example, the pro-Liberal Suffrage Society was quite put out by the National Union pact with Labour, and complained that local societies like theirs had not been given sufficient time to consider the change.[56] Another source of local opposition came from the Bolton Spinners' Association, which thirty years before had supported the strike against the three women spinners. At the 1914 Labour Party Conference, John Battle, a spinner, said that he had 'no substantial grounds for believing women as a body wanted the vote', and that the members of the United Textile Factory Workers' Association whom he represented, mostly women, had refused (he claimed) to send him to a meeting of Bolton Trades Council in favour of women's suffrage.[57]

The friendship between suffrage and labour was also marred by antagonism from the WSPU. It is an irony that, as suffragists had slowly moved nearer to the Labour Party, so suffragettes had moved away. In September 1912, Christabel announced from Paris a new policy: since the Labour Party supported the Liberal Government, its candidates were to be opposed and its speakers heckled as if they had been Cabinet Ministers. Suffragettes even interrupted the 1914 ILP conference and tried to shout down Keir Hardie. Isabella Ford was on the platform with Hardie and sent Mrs Fawcett this eye witness account of the event. 'The militant section forms but a *fraction* of the women's movement', she reported Hardie as saying; 'and the National Union of Women's Suffrage Societies is carrying on, as the Labour Party carries on . . .' she went on:

> He mentioned . . . that the WSPU persisted in opposing the ILP who had stuck to the women's movement. He said how the Labour Party was not a Women's Suffrage Party — only — and he repeated again that they could accept no enfranchisement for men that did not include women. (cheers).
> The women were put out with quiet care and no rudeness. We all watched anxiously and the WSPU will *lie* when they say otherwise . . . You see they had to be put out — no speeches were possible and MacDonald was ill . . . and couldn't stand it all — no more could Snowden — and Hardie was quite done up . . .[58]

Despite the patient efforts of Isabella Ford, Selina Cooper and many other ILP members, the Labour Party only finally adopted women's suffrage two and a half years before war broke out. In a sense, the reconciliation between feminism and Labour came too late to have the radical effects that the early pioneers had hoped for. By 1912 the

Labour Party was becoming a party machine, committed to Parliamentary gradualism and competing with Liberals and Tories for the right to form a government. But it was also the major — in some ways, the *only* — party of progress and social reform; it was — directly and indirectly — the party that over the next forty years would construct much of what is today's welfare state.

Yet even by 1912 Keir Hardie's generation of ILP idealists and visionaries were heavily outnumbered by traditionally-minded trade unions and trades councils as well as political opportunists. It was also a question of the finance necessary to be politically effective. Trade unions had funds: individuals did not. The Labour Party was left without effective pressure from women within its own ranks on suffrage or the wider women's issues; the ideas of real equality both at work and in the home that the radical suffragists had dreamed of, were effectively put aside until the 1960s and 70s.

By 1912 the Pankhursts' choice of tactics had certainly made women's suffrage a live issue both in Parliament and throughout the country; but they never attracted widespread public support. The mass movement that the radical suffragists had hoped to build had been hampered by suffragette militancy, by the long breach with Labour, and by the weakness of the position of women workers elsewhere relative to those in Lancashire. Teresa Billington-Grieg had the foresight at this time to see what had been lost for future generations of women. 'Votes for women we must have, and many other things for women; but votes for women over-hurried and at any price may cost us too dear ... A slower, bigger and more outspoken movement alone would have had any chance to appeal to the women who are industrially enslaved.'[59]

XIV

What did you do in the Great War?

When the First World War broke out on 4 August 1914, it completely altered the course of suffrage politics. Christabel Pankhurst decided to come back from Paris and assess the situation; she was unlikely to be in any danger of arrest, since on 7 August the Home Secretary announced the release of all suffragette prisoners who would give an undertaking to refrain from illegal activities, and on 10th even this condition was waived. Christabel announced the Pankhurst position on the war: 'This was national militancy. As Suffragettes we could not be pacifists at any price. Mother and I declared support of our country. We declared an armistice with the Government and suspended militancy for the duration of the war.'[1]

Not all the WSPU supported them, but Christabel and her mother together with their most loyal followers, including Annie Kenney, offered their services to the government, and embarked on a speaking campaign in support of the war effort. Mrs Pankhurst called for conscription for men, and for women to replace them in the munitions factories. The message included industrial peace: 'We held gigantic meetings all over the country,' wrote Annie Kenney blithely. 'Both men and women munitions workers were appealed to, and the dangers of a munition strike, a coal strike, and a dockyard strike were explained . . . We called it "the Anti-Bolshevist campaign".'[2]

The National Union was less clear on its attitude to the war; it was, wrote Mrs Fawcett, 'a time of no little perplexity and anguish of mind to nearly all of us.'[3] Realizing that war was imminent, it held a large peace meeting in London on the very day hostilities began. But then, since war could not be averted, its leaders consulted the 500 local societies to decide what action should be taken. Eventually they settled on forms of work intended to lessen the inevitable suffering. National Union members established Red Cross Centres, canteens for soldiers, and even a small workshop to teach women acetylene welding for aircraft work.

But although Mrs Fawcett and most of the membership were agreed on this policy, many of the executive and leaders of local societies were against it, preferring to take a more positive pacifist line. In the spring of 1915 matters came to a head. There was a split, and all the national officers (including Helena Swanwick) except Mrs Fawcett and the treasurer resigned, and formed with others the Women's International League for Peace and Freedom.

Both the Fawcett and Swanwick factions of the suffragist movement, like the WSPU, gave up their work for the vote during the war. The only groups to carry on the agitation were the Women's Freedom League and Sylvia Pankhurst's recently formed East London Federation (although the latter became increasingly involved in community work such as running a nursery and a cost-price canteen). Most feminists, whichever camp they belonged to, felt at first that the War overshadowed their struggle too completely for them to carry on any effective propaganda. 'Many of us,' Mrs Fawcett wrote, 'believed that the great catastrophe of the world war would greatly hamper and retard the movement to which we had dedicated our lives. It only very gradually dawned upon us that the first results of the war would be the emancipation of women in our own and many other countries.'[4]

To begin with women were not regarded as having much to do with the war effort, apart from knitting socks and mufflers for the troops. But as the continued slaughter of the Western Front brought an insatiable demand for soldiers, women were called in to replace men in all sorts of traditionally male occupations; they became bus drivers, window cleaners, chimney sweeps and farm workers. Most importantly, they were needed in the engineering and munitions factories, on which the outcome of the war depended. In the wartime emergency, the male unions had to agree to women doing jobs from which they had previously been excluded, but they were able to insist that the 'dilutees' should only be used upon war work, not ordinary production, and that the men should get their jobs back when peace came. But once women were doing what had previously been skilled male work, male superiority took a severe shaking. Robert Roberts remembered that his father,

> in his cups was wont to boast that, at the lathe, he had to manipulate a micrometer and work to limits of one thousandth of an inch. We were much impressed, until one evening in 1917 a teenage sister running a capstan in the iron works remarked indifferently that she, too, used a 'mike' to even finer limits. There was, she said, 'nothing to it'. The old man fell silent. Thus did status crumble![5]

Even when doing men's work, women rarely got men's pay. But all the same their wages went up appreciably, so that by 1918 'munitionettes', as they were called earned well over £2 a week, while other women factory workers got at least 25s.[6] The men's trade unions had to take them seriously at last, and the number of unionized women rose by 160 per cent (compared with 45 per cent of men) to about 1,086,000.[7] Public opinion was astonished by the efforts women were making; the sheer hard work they had done both in the home and outside it in the pre-war years was ignored or discounted.

The one pre-war industry in which women had always worked in large numbers and were adequately paid was Lancashire cotton. But with war, this situation changed abruptly. The cotton trade depended very heavily on importing raw cotton and exporting woven goods, and the war completely disrupted the shipping patterns the industry had previously relied on. The cotton trade slumped, unemployment soared and within a few months nearly 60,000 members of the Weavers' Association were out of work. Gradually the industry began to pick up; men volunteering for the army helped the labour problem, and the demand for cloth for soldiers' kit bags or for aeroplane wings kept mills busy.

But before long the Lancashire cotton industry was plagued by other problems. As more and more men were called up, a male labour shortage grew increasingly acute. Some mills closed down completely for lack of workers — especially of big and little piecers. Others began to take women into hallowed areas of the mill like the mule spinning room (though not without a staunch fight put up by the Spinners' Association and the *Cotton Factory Times*). Generally, the First World War signalled the beginnings of the decline of the Lancashire cotton industry. Its confidence in its divine right to the world's cotton market began to crumble especially when, in 1917, the Government allowed India to increase the duty on its cotton imports from 3½ per cent to 7½ per cent. The *Cotton Factory Times* called it an 'insidious betrayal' but nevertheless gradually realized that the writing was on the wall.[8]

Some Lancashire women moved away from mill life to work in the booming munitions factories. Those who remained in the cotton mills did not share in the general improvement in women's wages and were badly hit by war-time inflation. All the new openings for women — nursing, munitions, office work — suddenly made mill life, with all the petty humiliations of fining, bullying and often atrocious working conditions, seem an increasingly unattractive proposition.

For years before the war the Lancashire radical suffragists had argued that because women textile workers, and especially those in the cotton mills, made a vital contribution to the national economy, they should have a right to join in electing the government. Now that women's work was everywhere recognized as vital to the war effort, this very same argument began to appear in some curious places. Asquith, always the most determined opponent of women's suffrage, told the House of Commons,

> They fill our munition factories; they have aided in the most effective way in the prosecution of the war. . . . .What is more, . . . they say, when the war comes to an end, and when those abnormal . . . conditions have to be revised, and when the process of industrial reconstruction has to be set on foot, have not the women a special claim to be heard on the many questions which will arise directly affecting their interests?[9]

It is difficult to assess exactly why women finally got the vote in 1918. The long years of agitation by suffragists and suffragettes had certainly pushed the question to the forefront. But the changed conditions of the war years undoubtedly shook up old ideas and prejudices, about women's position, as about so much else, and made it easier for the Coalition Government to accept a measure that had divided the Liberal Cabinet before 1914.

Even so, the National Union, still keeping a watchful eye on possible legislation, was worried in case there should be an attempt to revise the electoral laws to give the vote to men in the forces while denying it to women. For it was obvious that the pre-1914 electoral register was now useless, since one of its qualifications was twelve months' unbroken residence in one place which soldiers at the Front could not satisfy. Eventually the Government handed the problem over to a Speaker's Conference, which produced various recommendations to broaden the franchise, including a proposal for some measure of women's suffrage. The Government then introduced its Bill, giving the vote to all adult men, with a clause extending the franchise to all women over thirty. (This arbitrary age-bar was so that women, who comprised the majority of the population, but whose political allegiances were feared to be fickle and unstable, would not dominate the electorate.) It was ironic that, having been denied the vote when the suffrage campaigns were at their height, women should eventually be given it when activity had virtually stopped. There was a further irony, that long after the militants had determined on nothing less than a government-sponsored measure and when the national societies, both militant and non-militant, had unceasingly pressed for a limited admission to the franchise, women should receive their emancipation by a free vote on a minor clause at the tail end of an adult suffrage bill.

What did the Lancashire radical suffragists do while suffrage activities were largely suspended during the war? To answer that, it is necessary to look at the socialist movement. It was hopelessly fragmented; both Blatchford and Hyndman supported the war enthusiastically, believing that patriotism came before internationalism. The ILP was the only group that came out against the war, and then not without some dissension. Yet its views were sufficiently provocative for the police to raid the *Labour Leader's* Salford office in 1915. In the same year Keir Hardie died, having seen the destruction of his hopes of international working class action to stop the war, and his hopes for women's suffrage postponed, first by the Liberal Government and then by the war.

Many members of the ILP shared Hannah Mitchell's opinion that 'War in the main is a struggle for power, territory or trade, to be fought by the workers, who are always the losers.'[10] Her nineteen-year-old son, who had grown up to share her views, refused to fight. Men like him were helped by the No Conscription Fellowship, founded by ILP members, which also acted as a pressure group on the Government. Women, not liable to conscription themselves, took a considerable part in its work, along with other anti-war organizations. Hannah Mitchell belonged to both the No Conscription Fellowship, and also the Women's International League for Peace and Freedom, in which Ellen Wilkinson and Helena Swanwick were particularly active. Ethel Derbyshire, in the Blackburn ILP, used to speak at pacifist meetings, reciting anti-war poems. Her daughter, aged seven or eight at the time, remembers local opposition to the war:

> I've been at the ILP rooms. They used to have dances of a Saturday night, and so many of the boys had got their calling-up papers and wouldn't go; and they

knew that the military police were coming for them at such a time and they would be arrested. So they used to all be there at the dance, and they used to come for them, quite young boys, eighteen, nineteen, seventeen, and they'd wait, and they'd sing the Red Flag, when they went . . . [11]

Selina Cooper was also fiercely opposed to the war and became involved, along with other Nelson pacifists, in Helena Swanwick's Women's International League for Peace and Freedom.[12] She was recommended, probably on the strength of her Guardian experience, as someone who could serve on the local Munitions Tribunal to deal with minor 'breaches of discipline' among women workers. At first she refused, not wanting to have anything to do with the war, but changed her mind in the end, telling Mary that 'they've no voice if we sulk'. Somehow, she also managed to find time to sit on the local Relief Committees in Nelson and to organize a Nelson Maternity Centre.[13]

Ada Nield Chew was equally active. She was elected Rochdale Trades Council representative on the Mayor's Central Relief Committee and was closely involved in local schemes to give free meals to nursing and expectant mothers and children under three. She wrote regular articles in the *Common Cause* and the *Cotton Factory Times* pleading the case of working class women and urging the authorities to take advantage of the wartime situation to improve their conditions. An ardent pacifist, she utterly opposed the war and argued, quite logically, that the suffragists who supported the war were behaving far less consistently than the militant suffragettes who now supported militarism.

> The militant section of the movement . . . would without doubt place itself in the trenches quite cheerfully, if allowed. It is now . . . demanding, with all its usual pomp and circumstance of banner and procession, its share in the war. This is an entirely logical attitude and strictly in line with its attitude before the war. It always glorified the power of the primitive knock on the nose in preference to the more humane appeal to reason. . . . What of the others? . . . The non-militants − so-called − though bitterly repudiating militancy for women, are as ardent in their support of militancy for men as their more consistent and logical militant sisters.[14]

All the radical suffragists were pacifists, rejecting war as consistently as they had rejected the Pankhursts' militancy. Esther Roper and Eva Gore-Booth had moved to London in 1913 because Eva's delicate health could no longer tolerate the damp Manchester climate; they were, in their own words, 'extreme pacifists' and almost as soon as war was declared they began relief work among German women, children and old men living in England. In 1915 they joined the Women's Peace

Crusade and travelled the country speaking in support of a negotiated peace to end the war. 'In 1916,' Esther Roper wrote, 'we also worked for the No-Conscription Fellowship . . . Many of our dear friends were imprisoned for refusing Military Service. Many were court-martialled, constantly tried by tribunals, or deprived of posts. . . .'.[15] And from 1916 they suffered terrible anxiety about Constance Markievicz; one of the leaders of the Dublin Easter Rising, she was sentenced to death, and her sister and Esther Roper hurried over to Ireland. She was reprieved but spent several years in prison before being released when Irish independence was eventually granted.

After the war, when the vote was won, the two friends retired to a quiet life in Hampstead where they continued to work 'for the welfare of women workers'; but Eva Gore-Booth was now too ill for active campaigning and died in 1926.[16] Christabel and Mrs Pankhurst also gave up speaking on feminist platforms; Mrs Pankhurst travelled across Canada denouncing the twin evils of venereal disease and unchastity; she returned to England to join the Conservative Party, eventually dying in 1928 while nursing the solidly Labour constituency of Whitechapel. The later part of Christabel's career was even more bizarre. She took up the cause of the Second Coming of Christ, which the deteriorating situation in the 1920s and 1930s led her to believe was imminent, and died in California in 1958, a Dame Commander of the British Empire. Adela, who had emigrated to Australia, turned from socialism and was eventually interned for her fascist sympathies in the Second World War. Sylvia Pankhurst, the only one of her family not to break with its earlier political faith, ended up in Ethiopia as a determined champion of the right of African countries to govern themselves.[17] And Christabel's most devoted follower, Annie Kenney, never returned to Lancashire but instead devoted herself to the then popular cult of theosophy.

Unlike the WSPU, the National Union did not disintegrate as soon as women over thirty had won the vote. Selina Cooper's Clitheroe Society, for instance, only finally disbanded after seventeen years of hard fighting, in 1921. The war of course must have hit the members — about thirty altogether — quite severely; a fortnight after war broke out they donated 10s to a Nelson Distress Fund, and when the Society finally disbanded its funds totalled a meagre £1 5s 2d.[18] The National Union itself changed its name in 1919 to the National Union of Societies for Equal Citizenship. Mrs Fawcett, who had been involved in the struggle since 1867, retired, and her place was taken by Eleanor

Rathbone. Its demands were the wide ones that groups like the Guild and the radical suffragists had long made and campaigned for, often with considerable impact: equal pay, divorce law reform, equal guardianship rights over their children for women and men, and equal voting rights for all adult women.

Some of these were now enacted. The Maternity and Child Welfare Act of 1918 enabled clinics to be set up. The 1919 Sex Disqualification (Removal) Act allowed women to take up any civil or judicial post that was open to men — like MPs, barristers or magistrates. Later the Matrimonial Causes Act of 1923 allowed a wife to divorce her husband on grounds of adultery — an important step in demolishing the Victorian double standard.

Two reforms that dealt with more controversial areas had to wait longer. One was birth control, and the story of that struggle has been vividly retold in the biographies and autobiographies of Dora Russell, Marie Stopes and Stella Browne.[19] The other, child allowances, championed by Eleanor Rathbone, was an issue that divided socialists and feminists alike. It divided Selina Cooper from Ada Nield Chew, and Eleanor Rathbone from Mrs Fawcett (who regarded the idea as 'creeping socialism' and predicted it would 'destroy the fabric of family life'.)

Eleanor Rathbone, then Secretary of the Liverpool Suffrage Society, developed the bones of her scheme in the 1900s, and synthesized it in the 1920s in her book *The Disinherited Family: a plea for the endowment of the family*. Her premise was that the 'family wage' did not take into account the number of children a male breadwinner had to support nor indeed whether he was a good husband and father. How much better, she suggested, if the mother could rely on a regular sum to allow her to feed and clothe her children. Her ideas got an unfriendly reception in the cotton towns where married women were used to going out to work and valued their independence. The idea of being 'paid to stay at home and look after the children' seemed to many of them retrogressive and anti-feminist.[20]

Ada Nield Chew was one of those who strongly disapproved. A far better way of tackling the question of child care was through communal arrangements, she said. If 'babies were cared for during the hours the mothers were at work by trained mothers in special baby homes (quite near by), the Lancashire married woman would lead the van in the intelligent progress of her sex and class'.[21] Child allowances should be combated by all enlightened women, she went on:

More than all should women discourage the fostering of the ideal of the domestic tabby-cat-woman as that to which all womanhood should aspire . . . The children must be cared for, and women must care for them. But not by paying poor women to be mothers. Women must be financially independent of men. But not by paying poor women to be wives. Marriage and motherhood should not be for sale. They should be dissociated from what is for sale — domestic drudgery.[22]

Selina Cooper, on the other hand, was a strong believer in giving mothers a guaranteed weekly allowance of their own. She had worked closely with Eleanor Rathbone as a National Union organizer in 1905-6 and now she joined her in the campaign for family allowances. 'She went speaking, all for nothing, just her expenses, all over Lancashire and Yorkshire', Mary Cooper recalled.[23] She also remained committed to the ILP and to the Labour Party (although she grew critical of the Labour Party in the 1930s because she felt that they did not take a strong enough line against Hitler and fascism, her own views hardening after an investigative visit to Nazi Germany in 1934).

Ethel Derbyshire remained in the ILP all her life, which she felt came close to her own socialist beliefs, but she refused to join the Labour Party. Hannah Mitchell took the same stance, on feminist grounds — that she did not like the Party's constituency Women's Sections. She was not, she protested, 'prepared to be a camp follower, or a member of what seemed to me a permanent Social Committee, or Official cake-maker to the Labour Party'.[24] As an ILP nominee she stood as a town councillor and, once elected, was able to push for several reforms to benefit women — among which she was proudest of the public wash-house erected in her ward. Selina Cooper also stood for her local council but was not elected, probably because there was still a strong prejudice against voting for women. Generally it was difficult in the 1920s and 30s to persuade women to come forward to take up the rights which had been fought for so courageously. There had been such an exclusive concentration on getting the vote — largely because of the Pankhursts' emphasis — that once it had been won feminist enthusiasm died away. The Women's Co-operative Guild, such a staunch campaigner for working women before the war, never regained its early political commitment; its members grew older and few younger ones joined them. The Women's Institute Movement, on the other hand, could boast a membership of quarter of a million by 1925; led by titled women it welcomed both suffragists and anti-suffragists to its ranks and soon developed a conservative Jam-and-Jerusalem image.

The sheer range and diversity of the inequalities that still existed may have discouraged many; the Bolton Women's Citizen's Association, for instance, tried to sustain its note of earnest optimism but had to admit it had 'struggled on through some very depressing years, at times almost seeming to beat the air'.[25] One of its earliest members, Sarah Reddish, was now in her seventies; she was forced by illness to give up her many public campaigns some time before her death in 1928.

Other radical suffragists a generation younger than Sarah Reddish eagerly took up their new opportunities. Cissy Foley, who had been able to leave the mill and become a nurse during the war, took charge of Bolton's first voluntary child clinic, known as the 'Babies' Welcome', and helped children grow up in conditions healthier and pleasanter than she herself had known.[26] Alice Collinge became an English tutor to the Bolton branch of the Workers' Educational Association, and was active in the Lancashire Authors' Association.[27]

Sarah Dickenson became women's organizer for the Manchester and Salford Trades and Labour Council when the two women's councils were amalgamated in 1918; she remained a delegate to the Council until 1930, representing the tiny Union of Machine, Electrical and other Women Workers. In 1923 she became a JP, after the Trades Council had urged that there should be more Labour magistrates — especially women — appointed to the bench.[28] She was joined three years later by Hannah Mitchell, and the two of them found plenty of work for feminists. Hannah Mitchell vividly recalled the 'unhappy marriages with all their attendant misery and hopeless future, wretched women and desperate men and, worst of all, unhappy children . . . Hardened girls come to seek justice for themselves and their helpless babies.'[29]

Selina Cooper was also appointed as a magistrate and became particularly concerned with cases involving battered wives. But in Burnley between the wars the major problem was the plight of the local cotton workers, something she knew only too well, for her husband Robert was out of work for a long time. She found herself in constant conflict with her predominantly conservative colleagues, for she invariably took the side of the workers and unions. The conflict came to a head in 1931-2 when the Burnley weavers protested against a scheme to increase their work load to eight looms without an increase in pay. She was present at a 'more looms' demonstration in the market place, which turned violent after police horses were called in. When the demonstrators were brought up in court, Selina Cooper's mill-owning colleagues insisted that as a fellow demonstrator she should leave the bench, to which she retorted, 'Well, I'll have to obey the magistrate's order, but I'm stopping here to give a statement to the press, when it's all finished,' which she did, setting out the other side of the case.[30]

Still living in the small terraced house from which she had organized the original Nelson and Colne Suffrage Society in 1904, she was readily accessible to local people. She was one of them. Mary Cooper described how 'they'd say to my mother, "We go to other magistrates, they keep us in the lobby, or . . . out in the rain." No wonder they worshipped her. They'd come here, always come here, for wanting things doing. And they come yet, and she's been dead thirty years, and they come here, wanting me to help them.'[31]

In many ways Selina Cooper typified the group of Lancashire working women described as 'radical suffragists'. The majority of them fought for far wider reforms than the vote both before and after the war, and always retained close links with the unions, the Guilds and the ILP branches from which they sprang. Yet none of them went into national politics. They had little interest in the political machinery of Whitehall and Westminster, preferring to use their influence in the cotton towns where their strength had always lain. Other women reacted differently once they had the vote. Margaret Bondfield from the Adult Suffrage Society became a Labour MP and in 1929 the first woman Cabinet minister. Ellen Wilkinson, who had appeared at Accrington and South Lanark in 1913, became an MP, was closely involved in the Jarrow march in the 1930s and entered the Cabinet after the War. Ironically none of the suffragettes who stood for election in 1918 — Christabel, Mrs Pethwick-Lawrence and Mrs How Martyn — was elected, and the only woman who was — Constance Markievicz — refused to take her seat as a Sinn Feiner.

The radical suffragists had directed their campaign towards a unique group of women. From 1884, when the Weavers' Amalgamation was formed, until the First World War, the Lancashire cotton workers were by far the highest paid and best organized of all working class women. The pride they took in their work and in their status as skilled workers led them to demand the vote for themselves. But from the outbreak of war, all this changed. Automatic looms and the decline of mule spinning in favour of ring machines gradually eroded their status as skilled workers. The cotton industry went into a decline from which it never recovered. First the German market was lost, and exports to India, always Lancashire's principle customer began to drop drastically from 3,000 million yards in 1913 to 300 million in 1938,[32] as India was able to impose her own tariffs on imported goods. Alice Foley, by now an official of the Bolton Weavers, met Gandhi when he visited Lancashire in response to appeals from the cotton workers and saw how he 'was genuinely moved by what he had seen and heard . . . but gently reminded us that *his* people had been on the edge of starvation since time immemorial.'[33]

Lancashire could no longer export goods in vast quantities all over the world. The industry went into a decline, unemployment soared and wages fell. Relative to other women workers in the newer industries, Lancashire women, caught in a downward spiral, never recovered their earlier position. Yet for thirty years, they had been the vanguard of working women in Britain. The radical suffragists had been their mouthpiece; from a position of unique industrial strength they had fought for a whole range of feminist demands which would affect women in all aspects of their lives. Their campaign was unpopular to many at the time and was dismissed by both the Labour Party and by the suffragettes. Few of their demands were realized in their own lifetimes: only now is a first child entitled to a family allowance, thirty years after Selina Cooper's death; equal pay for women has only recently been included in legislation, and then only in a diluted form. Yet the greatest vindication of the radical suffragists is that the political issues over which they themselves risked such unpopularity are the very issues being raised again by the wave of feminism which succeeded them.

— THE END —

FOOTNOTES

INTRODUCTION

1. *Reformers' Year Book,* 1907, edited by Pethwick-Lawrence, F.W., and Edwards, J., p 152
2. Pankhurst, E., *My Own Story,* Eveleigh Nash, London 1914, was in fact ghosted by an American, Rheta Childe Door, as part of a campaign to raise money and support in America. Pankhurst, C., *Unshackled,* Hutchinson, London 1959, was published posthumously. Pankhurst, E.S., *The Life of Emmeline Pankhurst,* T. Werner Laurie, London 1935, relied heavily for its early chapters on *My Own Story.* For full details see bibliography
3. See Rosen, A., *Rise Up, Women!* Routledge & Kegan Paul, London 1974. Raeburn, A., *The Militant Suffragettes,* Michael Joseph, London 1973. Neale, R.S., *Class and Ideology in the Nineteenth Century,* Routledge & Kegan Paul, London 1972. Mackenzie, M., *Shoulder to Shoulder,* Penguin, London 1975
4. Fawcett, M.G., *Women's Suffrage,* T.C. & E.C. Jack, London 1911. Fawcett, M.G., *The Women's Victory - and After,* Sidgwick and Jackson, London 1920. Fawcett, M.G., *What I Remember,* Fisher Unwin, London 1924
5. Strachey, R., *The Cause,* Virago, London 1978, pp 200 & 289. See also Strachey, R., *Millicent Garrett Fawcett,* John Murray, London 1931
6. The exceptions are the *Englishwoman's Review,* a women's rights journal; the *Women's Trade Union Review,* though it had no direct interest in women's suffrage; the *Clarion* which generally adopted an adult suffragist line, but gave space to women suffragists; and Eva Gore-Booth's suffrage quarterly, *Women's Labour News,* of which no known copies survive
7. Interview recorded by authors, March 1976
8. Interview recorded by authors, June 1976
9. Interview recorded by authors, March 1976
10. *Women's Trade Union Review,* July 1902
11. For further discussion see Liddington, J., 'Working Class Women in the North West II'. *Oral History* Vol 5, No 2; Liddington, J., 'Rediscovering Suffrage History', *History Workshop Journal,* No 4, autumn 1977

CHAPTER ONE   WHO WERE THE RADICAL SUFFRAGISTS?

1. NESWS, *Annual Report* 1905
2. Interview recorded by authors, March 1976; NESWS *Annual Report* 1901; indirect speech has been transcribed as direct speech
3. Interview recorded by authors, May 1977
4. *Reformers' Year Book,* 1906, p 152 including photograph
5. Davies, M.L., *The Women's Co-operative Guild,* Women's Co-operative Guild, Kirkby Lonsdale, Westmorland 1904, p 31
6. *Manchester Guardian,* 19.3.1901
7. See article by Frow, E. & R., and Bellamy, J., in *Dictionary of Labour Biography*

8. Foley, A., *A Bolton Childhood,* Manchester University Press & North-Western District of WEA, Manchester 1973, p 45
9. Interview recorded by authors, October 1976
10. Interview recorded by authors, March 1976
11. *Women's Trade Union Review,* 11.11.1904
12. *Common Cause,* 27.2.1914
13. Gore-Booth, E., *Women Workers and Parliamentary Representation,* Textile Tracts No 1, Lancashire Women Textile Workers' Representation Committee, no date
14. NESWS, *Annual Report* 1903
15. Ramsay MacDonald to Selina Cooper, undated letter
16. Pankhurst, C., *Unshackled,* p 67
17. Pankhurst, E., *My Own Story,* p 57
18. *Wigan Observer,* 6.1.1906

CHAPTER TWO   DAILY LIFE FOR WORKING WOMEN

1. See, for example, Davies, M.L., *Life As We Have Known It,* Virago 1977
2. Pollitt, H., *Serving My Time,* Lawrence & Wishart, London 1940, p 19
3. Davies, M.L., *The Women's Co-operative Guild,* p 153
4. See Rowbotham, S., *Hidden From History,* Pluto, London 1973
5. Interview recorded by authors, May 1977
6. Mitchell, H.M., *The Hard Way Up,* Virago, London 1977, pp 101-2. See also *Maternity: Letters from working women* collected by the Women's Co-operative Guild, Virago, London 1978
7. Higgs, H., 'Workmen's Budgets', *Royal Statistical Society Journal,* June 1893, pp 269-70; Bell, Mrs H., *At the Works,* Edward Arnold, London 1907, p 182
8. Foley, A., *A Bolton Childhood,* pp 19-20 & 45
9. See, for instance, Greenwood, W., *There Was A Time,* Jonathan Cape, London 1967, pp 68-9
10. Mitchell, H., *The Hard Way Up,* p 123
11. Pollitt, H., *Serving My Time,* pp 26-7
12. Clynes, J.R., *Memoirs 1869-1924,* Hutchinson, London 1937
13. Interview recorded by authors, October 1976
14. Davies, M.L., *The Women's Co-operative Guild,* p 128; the occasion was a debate on half-timers at the 1894 Women's Co-operative Guild Annual Congress
15. For further discussion of half-timers and working class education, see Frow, E. & R., *The Half-time System in Education,* Morten, Manchester 1970, and Simon, B., *Education and the Labour Movement 1870-1920,* Lawrence & Wishart, London 1965
16. Foley, A., *A Bolton Childhood,* p 31
17. Roberts, R., *A Ragged Schooling,* Manchester University Press, Manchester 1976, p 5; see also Sharpe, S., *Just Like a Girl,* Penguin, London 1976, for further discussion of working class girls' education
18. Interview recorded by authors, June 1976
19. Interview in the *Guardian,* 14.7.1976
20. Manchester & Salford Women's Trade Union Council, *Annual Report* 1903
21. The statistics are taken from a paper given by Frances Ashwell, one of the Secretaries to the Women's Trade Union Council, on 'Conditions of Women's Wages in Manchester' which was reported in the *Monthly Herald,* July 1897.

The *Herald* was the local Co-operative paper and was particularly interested because the Women's Co-operative Guild had taken part in the survey. See also the Women's Trade Union Council, *Annual Report* 1899

22. Quoted in Ramelson, M., *The Petticoat Rebellion,* Lawrence & Wishart, London 1967, p 103

23. *Women's Suffrage Journal,* October 1884 & November 1887.Indirect speech has been transcribed as direct speech

24. *Women's Trade Union Review,* October 1903. Information on the northern organizers is taken largely from the *Review;* Boone, G., *The Women's Trade Union Leagues in Great Britain and in the United States of America,* Columbia University Press, 1942, does not refer to them, and is largely based for this period on Hamilton, M.A., *Mary Macarthur: A Biographical Sketch,* Leonard Parsons, London 1925, which does not attempt to give a portrait of the League as a whole

25. Manchester and Salford Women's Trade Union Council, *Annual Report* 1895. For a fuller account of the Council, see Frow, E. & R., *To Make That Future - Now!* Morten, Manchester 1977

26. See for example Taylor, J.T., *The Jubilee History of the Oldham Industrial Co-operative Society Ltd 1850-1900*

27. Lawrence, D.H., *Sons and Lovers.* Penguin, London 1977, p 68

28. Rigby, T., *History of Bury Co-operative Society*, Crompton, Bury 1905, p 71

29. Interview recorded by authors, June 1976

30. Davies, M.L., *The Women's Co-operative Guild,* p 33

31. Engels, F., Preface to the 1892 English edition of *The Conditions of the Working Class in England,* Granada, London 1969, p 31

32. Rowbotham, S., *Hidden from History,* p 61

33. *Women's Trade Union Review,* October 1894

34. See Morton, A.L., & Tate, G., *The British Labour Movement,* Lawrence & Wishart, London 1956, p 165; for further information on the SDF and feminism see Rowbotham, S., *Hidden from History,* chs 13 & 16

35. See Tsuzuki, C., *H.M. Hyndman and British Socialism,* Oxford University Press, Oxford, 1961 p 979; Clegg, H.A., Fox, A., & Thompson, A.F., *A History of British Trade Unions Since 1889,* Clarendon Press, Oxford 1964, p 298; Bealey, F., & Pelling, H., *Labour & Politics 1900-1906,* Macmillan, London 1958, p 102

36. *Crewe Chronicle,* 2.6.1894

37. Billington-Grieg papers, Fawcett Library, 'Social and Feminist Awakening' File

38. Mitchell, H., *The Hard Way Up,* p 96

CHAPTER THREE   NINETEENTH CENTURY LANCASHIRE

1. Pollitt, H., *Serving My Time,* p 18

2. Lloyd, A.L., *Folk Song in England,* Lawrence & Wishart, London 1967, p 303

3. Marx, K., *Capital,* Vol 1

4. See Neff, W., *Victorian Working Women,* Frank Cass & Co., London 1966

5. Gaskell, E.C., *North and South,* Penguin, London 1970, p 110

6. Quoted by Neff, W., *Victorian Working Women,* p 34

7. See Gardiner, J., 'Women's Work in the Industrial Revolution' in *Conditions*

of Illusion, Feminist Books, Leeds 1974, pp 247-50; also Anderson, M; *Family Structure in Nineteenth Century Lancashire,* Cambridge University Press, 1971

8. Drake, B., *Women in Trade Unions,* Labour Research Department and Allen & Unwin, London 1920, pp 3-4; Turner, H.A., *Trade Union Growth, Structure & Policy. A Comparative Study of the Cotton Unions,* Allen & Unwin, London 1962, p 95

9. 'A Report of the Proceedings of a Delegate Meeting, of the Operative Spinners of England, Ireland and Scotland, Assembled at Ramsay, Isle of Man on Sunday December 5th, 1829, and Three Following Days'

10. Quoted by Chapman, S.J., *The Lancashire Cotton Industry: A Study in Economic Development,* University of Manchester Press, Manchester 1904, p 214

11. *The Times* 19.4.1834; Bennett, A., *Oldham Trades and Labour Council Centenary 1867-1967* notes that the 'Ancient Virgins' was an early card-room society, although no other labour historian seems to have made this connection

12. Turner, H.A., *Trade Union Growth, Structure and Policy,* pp 107 & 144-5. See chapter 5 of this book for detailed discussion of weavers' union. *Preston Guardian* 19.11.1853 & 10.12.1853; we are grateful to Dermot Healy for noting these references

13. See Davidoff, L., L'Esperance, J., and Newby, H., 'Landscape with Figures: Home and Community in English Society' in *The Rights and Wrongs of Women,* Penguin, London 1976, p 155.

14. *Cotton Factory Times,* 14.8.1891

15. As the Lancashire cotton industry blossomed, so that of India dramatically declined. 'Dacca, which was once the Manchester of India, has fallen off from a very flourishing town to a very poor and small one', reported one colonial official in 1840; 'The distress there has been very great indeed'. Quoted in Griffiths, P., *The British Impact on India,* Macdonald, London 1952. See also Hobsbawm, E.J., *Industry and Empire,* Penguin, London 1969, pp 58 & 143; Kuczynski, J., *Labour Conditions Under Industrial Capitalism,* Barnes & Noble, New York 1972, Part II p 25

16. Charles Macara, 1906, quoted by Clarke, P., *Lancashire and the New Liberalism,* Cambridge University Press 1971, p 76

17. Peroni, R., *Industrial Lancashire,* Nelson, London 1976, p 34

18. Webb, B., *My Apprenticeship,* Penguin, London 1938, p 177

19. Luty, M., *My Life Has Sparkled,* unpublished typescript, p 13; see also, Luty, M., *A Penniless Globetrotter,* Accrington 1937, pp 9-37

20. Luty, M., *A Penniless Globetrotter,* pp 37-9

21. By 1851, Lancashire farmers were complaining that they could not get women to single their turnips, and the higher wages demanded by men nearly doubled the cost of getting the crop in; see Samuel, R., *Village Life and Labour,* Routledge & Kegan Paul, London 1975, p 13

22. Bradley, H., *And Miss Carter Wore Pink,* Jonathan Cape, London 1971, p 3; Helen Bradley was born in 1900

23. Interview recorded by authors, July 1976

24. Interview recorded by authors, July 1976

25. Hyndman, H.M., *Further Reminiscences,* Macmillan, London 1912, pp 61-2

26. Interview recorded by authors, September 1976

27. 1901 Census; figures are for women over ten years old, and 'married women'

includes widows. 33.8 per cent of married women in Burnley, 37.9 per cent in Blackburn and 30.5 per cent in Preston were classified as occupied

28. Interview recorded by authors, June 1976
29. See Chapman, S.J., *The Lancashire Cotton Industry*
30. Interview recorded by authors, June 1976
31. See Tennant, M., 'Infantile Mortality' in Swanwick, H.M., (ed) *Women in Industry from Seven Points of View*, Duckworth, London 1908
32. Hutchins, B., 'Statistics of Women's Life and Employment', *Royal Statistical Society Journal*, June 1909
33. Davies, M.L., *The Women's Co-operative Guild*, p 133
34. Foley, A., *A Bolton Childhood*, p 50
35. Manchester Polytechnic, Manchester Studies Unit, Interview No 15, pp 2-3
36. Essex University Oral History Archive; interview recorded by Thelma Crook, 1969
37. For detailed analysis of the controversy over women's work at the pit top see John, A.V., 'The Lancashire Pit Brow Lasses' in North West Group for the Study of Labour History *Bulletin* No 3. Census figures for Wigan: 63.7 per cent of unmarried and 10.5 per cent of married women worked
38. Engels, F., *Conditions of the Working Class in England* p 76
39. See Hobsbawm, E.J., *Industry and Empire*, ch 7; Briggs, A., *Victorian Cities*, Collins, London 1963, Ch 3
40. Tomlinson, W., *Byeways of Manchester Life*, Butterworth & Nodal, Manchester 1887, p 102
41. Chapman, S.J., *The Lancashire Cotton Industry*, p 160; in Manchester and Salford three-quarters of the cotton workers were women
42. Greenwood, W., *There Was a Time*, p 40
43. See Hammond, J.L. and B., *The Skilled Labourer*, Longmans, London 1919; Drake, B., *Women in Trade Unions*, p 4
44. *The Times*, 19.4.1834
45. Frow, E. & R., *To Make That Future - Now!* notes that, of the 20,000 or more strikers, some must have been women, but they are lost in the general term 'cotton operatives'
46. Garnett, J., & Mead, D., *Struggles of the Lancashire Cotton Workers*, unpublished typescript, Working Class Movement Library
47. Thompson, E.P., *The Making of the English Working Class*, Penguin, London 1968, pp 454 & 788
48. *Votes for Women*, October 1907, 'Battle of Peterloo' by Pankhurst, E.S.
49. Percival, P., *Failsworth Folk and Failsworth Memories*, Manchester 1901
50. *Northern Star* 2.2.1839. See also Thompson, D., 'Women and Nineteenth Century Radical Politics: A Lost Dimension' in *The Rights and Wrongs of Women*

CHAPTER FOUR   WOMEN'S SUFFRAGE IN MANCHESTER

1. Example used by Caroline Norton in her attempt to win the right to custody of her own children - see Strachey, R., *The Cause*, Virago, London 1978, p 37
2. Strachey, R., *The Cause*, p 223
3. *Punch*, 10.5.1884, quoted in Rover, C., *The Punch Book of Women's Rights*, Hutchinson, London 1967, p 66

4. Nightingale, F., 'Cassandra', appended to Strachey, R., *The Cause*, p 405
5. See Neff, W., *Victorian Working Women*, pp 157-8
6. Strachey, R., *The Cause*, p 60-2
7. See Strachey, R., *The Cause*, p 101
8. Strachey, R., *The Cause*, pp 103-4
9. See Fulford, R., *Votes for Women*, Faber & Faber, London 1958, p 43
10. Fawcett, M.G., *What I Remember*, p 64
11. There is some controversy over whether London or Manchester formed the first suffrage society; this in part hinges on whether the group that met in Manchester on 11 January 1867 immediately constituted itself into a Society or worked as a committee for the first eight months. Certainly a provisional London suffrage committee was formed in April 1866 to organize the petition; it became the London National Society for Women's Suffrage in July 1867
12. Pankhurst, E.S., *The Suffragette Movement*, Virago, London 1977, p 10. See also Briggs, A., *Victorian Cities*, ch 3
13. See, for instance, *Manchester Guardian* 9.10.1856 for a report of the opening of the permanent Free Trade Hall, 1856
14. Fulford, R., *Votes for Women*, p 32
15. See Pankhurst, E.S., *The Suffragette Movement*, p 29
16. However, she did grow up in an atmosphere of Manchester Liberalism; her sister recalled how 'the stormy discussions connected with the Anti-Corn Law League were reproduced in miniature in our juvenile circle,' and that there was 'excitement' over the Chartists; see Blackburn, H., *Women's Suffrage*, Williams & Norgate, London 1902, p 28
17. Blackburn, H., *Women's Suffrage*, p 42
18. Quoted by Rosen, A., *Rise Up, Women!* p 8
19. *Oldham Chronicle* 9.6.1962
20. Strachey, R., *The Cause*, p 118
21. Quoted in Blackburn, H., *Women's Suffrage* p 110
22. Blackburn, H., *Women's Suffrage* pp 148-153; because of the confusing nature of the municipal franchise, it is difficult to estimate accurately the number of working class women who were eligible to vote
23. *Women's Suffrage Journal* April 1886
24. For Isabella Ford, see Pankhurst, E.S., *The Suffragette Movement* pp 177-8, and Rowbotham, S., *Hidden from History* pp 54 & 62. Very little research has so far been done analysing membership of local suffrage societies, though some idea can be gained from the amounts paid by individuals and recorded in subscription lists
25. Apart from Dr. Pankhurst's great admiration for the Chartist leader Ernest Jones, there were no known connections between working class Chartist traditions and the new group of middle class suffragists
26. Letter written early in 1869, quoted in Strachey, R., *The Cause*, p 117
27. In fact the Women's Liberal Federation was divided over women's suffrage, and in 1893 a breakaway Women's Liberal Association was formed with specifically pro-suffrage aims; they only gave their support to those Liberal MPs who agreed with them. Mrs. Pankhurst was one of the Association's early members; see Strachey, R., *The Cause* p 279, and Pankhurst, E.S., *The Life of Emmeline Pankhurst* pp 31-2
28. See the cartoon in *Comus,* October 1877, reproduced in Strachey, R., *The Cause*

269

29.   Pankhurst, E.S., *The Suffragette Movement* p 57
30.   Pankhurst, E.S., *The Suffragette Movement* p 90
31.   Pankhurst, E.S., *Life of Emmeline Pankhurst* p 29
32.   *Englishwoman's Review* 15.1.1893; according to a letter dated December
      1892 she was a nominee of the McLaren family; see Fawcett papers
33.   Stocks, M., *My Commonplace Book,* Peter Davies, London 1970, p 71
34.   Swanwick, H.M., *I Have Been Young,* Gollancz, London 1935, pp 185-7
35.   This seems to be the first major reference to women's industrial position by
      suffrage societies, though there were of course earlier examples of individual
      suffragists campaigning for the rights of working women
36.   See *Englishwoman's Review* 15.7.1893; Blackburn, H., *Women's Suffrage*
      pp 195-201; Mason, B., *The Story of the Women's Suffrage Movement,*
      Sheridan and Hughes, Manchester 1912, pp 69-70
37.   Pankhurst, S., *The Suffragette Movement,* p 116
38.   Manchester University Graduates' Register
39.   Stocks, M.D., *Fifty Years in Every Street,* University of Manchester Press,
      Manchester 1945, pp 6, 35, 69. The only record of Esther Roper's life in
      Manchester was the window she donated to the Settlement in memory of
      Eva Gore-Booth, but the building is now derelict
40.   NESWS *Annual Reports* 1899, 1900, 1902
41.   MNSWS *Annual Reports* 1894-5
42.   There is no direct evidence of Annie Heaton's job, but one of the few meet-
      ings she is known to have addressed was the Burnley Women Winders on
      17.10.1900
43.   MNSWS *Annual Report* 1894
44.   Women's Trade Union League *Annual Report* 1893
45.   In the early 1880s there were nearly 1,000 names in Lydia Becker's account
      book, and their contributions amounted to £1,000 to £1,500 a year. By the
      time Esther Roper took over as Secretary, subscriptions had declined to
      under £200 from a mere handful of supporters. Within two years she had
      virtually doubled this, though the increase hardly kept pace with her
      ambitious programme and was still well below the level in the Becker hey-
      day. MNSWS *Annual Reports* 1894 & 1895; the records for 1896-99 are
      lost, and the *Englishwoman's Review* provides the only reliable account of
      these years
46.   Roper, E., (ed) *Poems of Eva Gore-Booth,* Longmans, London 1929, p 9
47.   Pankhurst, E.S., *The Suffragette Movement,* p 164
48.   Marreco, A., *The Rebel Countess,* Weidenfeld and Nicholson, London 1967,
      pp 9, 62-4
49.   Billington-Grieg, T., 'Social and Feminist Awakening' file, Billington-Grieg
      papers
50.   Roper, E., (ed) *Poems of Eva Gore-Booth,* p 11
51.   Mrs Green was one of the most active NESWS speakers for about fifteen
      years and was a member of the Beswick branch of the Women's Co-operative
      Guild; see biographical note at end
52.   Roper, E., (ed) *Poems of Eva Gore-Booth,* pp 13-4 Eva Gore-Booth was
      heavily involved in the Settlement; she ran reading classes at the Ancoats
      Brotherhood on Sunday mornings, as well as an 'Ancoats Elizabethan Society'
      which provided occasional entertainment at the Women's Trade Council
      meetings

53. Manchester and Salford Women's Trade Union Council, *Annual Report* 1903
54. Roper, E., (ed) *Poems of Eva Gore-Booth,* p 12; there are no known surviving copies of this paper

CHAPTER FIVE   WEAVERS AND WINDERS

1. Turner, H.A., *Trade Union Growth, Structure and Policy*, pp 24-5
2. See Tippett, L.H.C., *A Portrait of the Lancashire Textile Industry,* Oxford University Press, Oxford 1969, ch 3 for a clear description of the processes
3. Gaskell, E.C., *North and South,* p 146
4. Pankhurst, E.S., *The Suffragette,* Sturgis & Walton, New York, 1911, pp 19-20
5. Pollitt, H., *Serving My Time,* p 28
6. Kenney, A., *Memories of a Militant,* Edward Arnold, London 1924, pp 16 & 19
7. Foley, A., *A Bolton Childhood,* p 47
8. Essex University Oral History Archive
9. All wage rates are 1906 figures and are based largely on 'The Statistics of Wages in the Nineteenth Century: the Cotton Industry', by George Henry Wood, *Journal of the Royal Statistical Society,* June 1910, vol LXXIII, part VI
10. Comparative wage rates for 1906 from Clegg, H.A., Fox, A., & Thompson, A.F., *A History of British Trade Unions Since 1889,* pp 480-2
11. *Oldham Standard,* September 1890, quoted by Bennett, A., *Oldham Trades and Labour Council Centenary 1867-1967*
12. Clynes, J.R., *Memoirs,* p 74
13. See also Bennett, A., *Oldham Trades and Labour Council Centenary 1867-1967,* Turner, H.A., *Trade Union Growth, Structure and Policy,* and Drake, B., *Women in Trade Unions*
14. Compare the way in which her union experience has been glorified in Pankhurst, C., *Unshackled,* p 45; *Votes for Women,* October 1907; Kenney, A., *Memories of a Militant,* pp 31-2, 41
15. Kenney, R., *Westering,* J.M. Dent, London 1939, pp 20-21
16. Drake, B., *Women in Trade Unions,* p 23; *Women's Suffrage Journal* February 1887. The Women's Trade Union League did not intervene on the side of the women workers, for fear of alienating trade union support; they realized they could only advise trade unionists against these restrictive rulings if the women themselves were strong enough to demand equal pay with the men and so remove the threat of undercutting. By the 1880s the League was very wary of alienating the big male unions. However Lydia Becker had no such reservation and gave the women piecers her full support in her *Journal*
17. Drake, B., *Women in Trade Unions,* p 125, notes that in a couple of non-union mills there were women working as spinners on old-fashioned mules. Turner, H.A., *Trade Union Growth, Structure and Policy,* p 143, notes that in the 1890s a few unions around Oldham did accept women into their piecers' union, but that this was never encouraged by the mule spinners. Certainly in the Bolton area, and possibly elsewhere, the tradition of women

piecers seems to have continued virtually uninterrupted until mule spinning was finally superceded by ring spinning. A wider oral survey would be necessary to discover the attitudes of women spinners and piecers to these cotton mill conventions

18. Roberts, R., *The Classic Slum,* University of Manchester Press, Manchester 1971, p 20
19. Ring spinners who were included in the Cardroom Associations during the 1900s may have been among the audiences addressed by the various suffrage speakers. Also, the pro-suffrage Manchester and Salford Women's Trade Council included a 'Ring Spinners' Union' in the 1900s
20. Interview recorded by the authors, May 1977
21. See Essex University Oral History Archive
22. Fields, G., *Sing As We Go,* World Distributors, London 1962, p 28
23. Interview recorded by authors, September 1976
24. Foley, A., *A Bolton Childhood,* p 58; of course such celebrations were not exclusive to the winding room
25. Interview recorded by authors, September 1976
26. Adult women weavers comprised 23.1 per cent; girls added a further 5.3 per cent
27. Foley, A., *A Bolton Childhood,* p 52
28. *Oldham Chronicle* 31.7.1893
29. See for instance Davies, M.L., (ed) *Life as We Have Known It,* p 102
30. Greenwood, W., *There Was A Time,* p 67
31. Foley, A., *A Bolton Childhood,* pp 51-2
32. *Oldham Evening Express,* 24.6.1889
33. Drake, B., *Women in Trade Unions,* makes the case that equal pay prevailed in the Lancashire weaving sheds. However, twenty years earlier, two other Fabian historians, Sidney and Beatrice Webb, in *Industrial Democracy,* London 1897 p 501, had described how although 'the piecework list of prices, to which all workers must conform, applies to men and women alike ... It is interesting to observe that the maintenance of a Standard Rate has resulted in a real, though unobtrusive, segregation. There is no attempt to discriminate between women's work and men's work as such. . . But, taking the cotton-weaving trade as a whole, the great majority of the women will be found engaged on the comparatively light work paid at the lower rates. On the other hand, a majority of the men will be found practically monopolizing the heavy trade, priced at higher rates per yard, and resulting in larger weekly earnings'
34. Foley, A., *A Bolton Childhood,* p 64; see also Chew, A.N., 'All in a Day's Work', *The Englishwoman,* July 1912, reprinted in Pike, R.E., *Human Documents of the Lloyd George Era,* Allen & Unwin, London 1972. Drake, B., *Women in Trade Unions* p 121 noted that women were never encouraged to become tacklers, and this promotional bar seems to have been one of the major differences between men and women weavers
35. Oldham Weavers' Association Executive Council minutes, 1904 & 5
36. See Bornat, J., 'Home and Work: A New Context for Trade Union History', *Oral History* Vol 5, No 2, for a discussion of how these factors affected women workers in the West Riding
37. Interview recorded by authors, July 1976; it would be interesting to find out how the women in the 1880s, the first generation to join cotton unions in

massive numbers, decided to become members

38. Foley, A., *A Bolton Childhood*, p 64
39. *Women's Trade Union Review,* October 1894
40. For further details about Helen Silcock, see *Reformers' Year Book* 1906. There is no direct evidence that she was a member of the Wigan SDF, but she seems to have been in very close contact with it; see Chapter thirteen. For the Wigan Weavers' Association and its difficulties, see Hopwood, E., *The Lancashire Weavers' Story,* Manchester 1969, p 45
41. *Women's Trade Union Review* January 1897 and January 1899. The woman who spoke at the 1898 TUC was listed as a 'Miss Silcox' but this is surely a misprint
42. Oldham Weavers' and Winders' Council minutes, 1896-1901
43. *Cotton Factory Times,* 9.7.1920
44. Mrs. Aldersley's precise trade is not recorded; she was a textile worker in Burnley, so weaving is most likely
45. For a detailed account of the changes in the cotton unions' position on labour representation, see Clarke P., *Lancashire and the new Liberalism,* Cambridge University Press, 1971, pp 90-95
46. Gore-Booth, E., 'The Women's Suffrage Movement Among Trade Unionists' in Villiers, B., (ed) *The Case for Women's Suffrage,* T. Fisher Unwin, London 1907, p 61
47. Interview with Selina Cooper, the *Queen* 17.4.1909

CHAPTER SIX   JOBS OUTSIDE THE MILL

1. Swanwick, H.M., *I Have Been Young,* pp 150-1
2. Census returns, Lancashire 1901
3. Davies, C.S., *North Country Bred,* Routledge & Kegan Paul, London 1963, p 61
4. Interview recorded by authors, June 1976
5. Billington-Grieg papers, unsorted MSS in 'Materials for Memoirs' and 'Mrs. Billington-Grieg's Writings' boxes. It is difficult to discover precisely when and where she was a pupil teacher
6. See typed autobiographical essay in *Bolton Evening News* Library. Simon, B., *Education and the Labour Movement,* Lawrence & Wishart, London 1965 notes that the scheme was for boys and girls from fourteen to eighteen
7. *Bolton Evening News* 2.6.1931
8. For the Equal Pay League, see Pierotti, A.M., *The Story of the National Union of Teachers,* National Union of Women Teachers, 1963, pp 1-2. On equal pay see Tropp, A., *The School Teachers,* Heinemann, London 1957, pp 157-8, 214-6
9. *Wigan Observer* 7.10.1911; we are grateful to Angela John for noting this report
10. Interview recorded by authors, March 1976
11. See article by Frow, E. & R., and Bellamy, J., in *Dictionary of Labour Biography*
12. *Crewe Chronicle* 30.6.1894
13. *Common Cause* 17.10.1913
14. *Crewe Chronicle* 5.5.1894. The precedents for this political strategy of

anonymous campaigning include, for instance, J.R. Clynes's series of protest letters to an Oldham paper in the 1880s, signed 'Piecer'

15. *Crewe Chronicle* 19.5.1894; see also Mitchell, H., *The Hard Way Up*, pp 71-4
16. *Clarion* 10.2.1894; *Crewe Chronicle* 26.5.1894
17. Chaloner, W.H., *The Social and Economic Developments of Crewe*, Manchester University Press, Manchester 1950, p 166
18. *Crewe Chronicle* 2.6.1894
19. *Clarion* 30.6.1894
20. *Crewe Chronicle* 18.8.1894
21. *Common Cause* 9.4.1914
22. *Common Cause* 9.4.1914; *Crewe Chronicle* 25.8.1894 & 1.9.1894
23. Roper, E., (ed) *Poems of Eva Gore-Booth*, pp 13-4
24. From these small beginnings in various parts of the country, the tailoresses' cause made substantial progress, until in 1900 they were admitted by the Tailors' Society into a new Female Section

CHAPTER SEVEN POLITICAL APPRENTICESHIP

1. *Crewe Chronicle* 5.5.1894
2. Luty, M., *A Penniless Globetrotter*, p 40
3. Essex University Oral History Archive
4. Foley, A., *A Bolton Childhood*, p 8
5. Foley, A., *A Bolton Childhood*, p 10
6. Foley, A., *A Bolton Childhood*, pp 44-5
7. Foley, A., *A Bolton Childhood*, p 44
8. Interview recorded by authors, July 1976
9. Billington-Greig papers, 'Social and Feminist Awakening' file
10. Simon, B., *Education and the Labour Movement*, pp 86-92
11. Interview recorded by the authors, May 1977; St. John's Ambulance invitation, dated 20.11.1895
12. Luty, M., *My Life Has Sparkled*, p 16
13. Interview recorded by authors, July 1976
14. Interview recorded by authors, June 1976
15. Interview recorded by authors, March 1976
16. Foley, A., *A Bolton Childhood*, p 25. Free libraries, provided by local councils, were also opening at this time
17. Interview recorded by authors, July 1976
18. Davies, M.K., *Life as We Have Known It*, pp 120-1; Mrs. Woodward's account
19. Foley, A., *A Bolton Childhood*, p 46
20. Billington-Greig papers, 'Mrs Billington-Grieg's Writings' file; Teresa Billington was born in 1877, so this would be about 1890
21. Foley, A., *A Bolton Childhood*, p 46
22. For another account of a local Labour Church, see Mitchell, H., *The Hard Way Up*, pp 116-21
23. Typed autobiographical essay in *Bolton Evening News* library
24. Undated pamphlet in Manchester Central Reference Library, published by the Labour Church Union, Bradford
25. Foley, A., *A Bolton Childhood*, p 68
26. Blatchford, R., *Merrie England*, Clarion, London 1893, reprinted 1976, p 91

27.   Kenney, R., *Westering,* pp 20-1
28.   *Clarion,* 24.8.1906
29.   Fincher, J., *The Clarion Movement,* M.A. Thesis, Manchester University, 1971.
      'Our Women's Letter' was originally run by Eleanor Keeling, and later by
      'Julia Dawson', the pen-name of Mrs. Đ.J. Myddleton-Worrall. Julia Dawson
      also wrote in the *Women's Trade Union Review*
30.   *Clarion* 23.6.1894
31.   Dangle's article, *Clarion* 26.5.1894; Enid Stacy's reply, *Clarion* 26.5.1894
32.   Kenney, R., *Westering,* p 25
33.   Blatchford, R., *Merrie England,* p 3. An Oldham spinner would earn about
      10s a week more than the average man, but Blatchford was trying to show
      that even a skilled worker did not earn enough for a comfortable life
34.   Blatchford, R., *Merrie England,* p 17
35.   Blatchford, R., *Merrie England,* p 20
36.   Kenney, A., *Memories of a Militant,* p 115
37.   *Monthly Herald,* April 1898
38.   Foley, A., *A Bolton Childhood,* p 72
39.   Unpublished typescript, Foley papers
40.   Groom, T., *National Clarion Cycling Club 1894-1944,* Jubilee Souvenir,
      National Clarion Cycling Club, Halifax 1944. The lease of the Knutsford
      club house expired in 1902, so it was transferred to Handforth, just north of
      Wilmslow
41.   Groom, T., *National Clarion Cycling Club 1894-1944*
42.   Interview recorded by the authors, September 1976. In the late 1890s
      Selina and Robert Cooper were involved in a similar project, setting up the
      first Holiday Fellowship hostel at Keld, Yorkshire
43.   Foley, A., *A Bolton Childhood,* p 72. For a vivid account of Clarion
      activities, see Davies, C.S., *North Country Bred,* ch 11
44.   Pankhurst, E.S., *The Suffragette Movement,* p 140

CHAPTER EIGHT   WOMEN AND SOCIALISM

1.   MNSWS *Annual Report* 1894-5; the ILP Annual Reports give details of the
      Suffrage debates
2.   *Clarion* 12.1.1896
3.   Pankhurst, E.S., *The Suffragette Movement,* p 127
4.   *Clarion* 11.7.1896
5.   Interview recorded by authors, June 1976. Manchester Polytechnic, Man-
      chester Studies Unit, interview recorded March 1975; Elsie Plant's descrip-
      tion of speaking was at a slightly later date, but mirrors the experience of
      earlier ILP women
6.   *Crewe Chronicle* 19.5.1894 & 2.6.1894
7.   *Socialist Leader* 24.11.1973; NESWS *Annual Report* 1905
8.   *Labour Leader* 18.7.1903
9.   Mitchell, H., *The Hard Way Up,* p 126
10.   *Clarion* 29.8.1896
11.   Pankhurst, E.S., *The Suffragette Movement* pp 127-8
12.   *Labour Prophet* February 1894
13.   MNSWS *Annual Report* 1895. Enid Stacy also spoke at the first annual

meeting of the NUWSS in Manchester in 1898; she joined Esther Roper in a suffrage deputation of women graduates to Westminster in 1903, and her early death was noted sadly by Esther Roper in her 1903 *Annual Report*

14. Stacy, E., 'A Century of Women's Rights' in Carpenter, E., (ed) *Forecasts of the Coming Century,* Labour Press, Manchester 1897, pp 86-101

15. In discussing protective legislation, Enid Stacy refers to the women chainmakers in the Black Country, discussed in chapter 2. She says that it is the duty of women in jobs like that 'to submit to regulations which will help the more easy and speedy transition to a time when an unfettered choice will be a *reality* in industry'

16. MacMillan, M., *The Life of Rachel MacMillan,* Dent, London 1927, p 85

17. *Bolton Evening News* 6.3.1946 noted that Alice Collinge was 'won over to the Labour Party' by Philip Snowden. Other ILP women, including Hannah Mitchell and Teresa Billington, were drawn into the early WSPU, as the Pankhursts recruited almost entirely among the ILP at first

18 *Clarion* 29.2.1896

19. *Clarion* 30.5.1896

20. Interview recorded by authors, March 1976

21. *Clarion* 4.7.1896

22. *Clarion* 5.9.1896

23. Mitchell, H., *The Hard Way Up,* pp 107-8

24. WTUL *Annual Report* 1899. Miss Mayo was also an occasional League organizer

25. WTUL *Review* January 1899

26. WTUL *Review* January 1903

27. WTUL *Review* October 1905; a strong branch was then formed

28. Davies, M.L., *The Women's Co-operative Guild,* pp 61-2

29. *Queen* 17.4.1909

30. Interview recorded by authors, May 1977

31. Born 1850 in Westleigh, between Bolton and Wigan

32. Compare, for instance, Mr. Benson in Thompson, P., *The Edwardians,* Weidenfeld and Nicholson, London 1975, pp 123-134, who was also from Bolton

33. *Monthly Herald* May 1898

34. Davies, M.L., *The Women's Co-operative Guild,* p 28

35. Davies, M.L., (ed) *Life as We Have Known It,* p 133

36. Her father had spoken publicly in favour of including women on the board from the first elections in the 1870

37. There were however some objections from fellow socialists because she was middle class. Bather, L., *Manchester and Salford Trades Council,* Ph.D., Manchester 1956, pp 139-49

38. The details of the qualifications of the municipal franchise are complex and were often changed from act to act. For the ways in which working class women might qualify see Rover, C., *Women's Suffrage and Party Politics in Britain 1866-1914,* Routledge & Kegan Paul, London 1967

39. Davies, M.L., *The Women's Co-operative Guild,* p 135

40. Pankhurst, E.S., *The Suffragette Movement,* pp 131-2

41. *Bolton Journal* 24.2.1928

42. Guardian election poster, Manchester Central Reference Library

43. For Selina Cooper's period as a Guardian, see *Nelson Leader* 25.5.1901,

16.9.1901, 5.1.1902, quoted by Firth, P., *Socialism and the Origins of the Labour Party in Nelson and District 1890-1906*, M.A., Manchester 1975, pp 48-50

44. Interview recorded by authors, March 1976
45. See Gaffin, J., 'Women and Co-operation' in Middleton, L., (ed), *Women in the Labour Movement*
46. *Englishwoman's Review* 16.10.1893
47. *Co-operative News* 27.3.1897
48. See *Englishwoman's Review*
49. *Englishwoman's Review* 15.10.1897
50. *Monthly Herald* May 1898

CHAPTER NINE   TEXTILE WORKERS AND THE SUFFRAGE CAMPAIGN

1. The only evidence that Sarah Dickenson was interested in women's suffrage in the 1890s is that she first met Eva Gore-Booth at Esther Roper's office - that is, the NESWS office; this would have been 1897 or 1898
2. Gore-Booth, E., 'The Women's Suffrage Movement among Trade Unionists', in *The Case for Women's Suffrage*
3. Reprinted in the *Englishwoman's Review* 15.4.1901
4. *Manchester Guardian* 2.5.1900
5. NESWS *Annual Report* 1899 notes 'Mrs Hodgson Bayfield, the Society's agent.' It is likely she was an active Guildswoman for the *Monthly Herald* May 1898 noted that a Miss Hodgson spoke at a Guild meeting on 'The Equalization of the Marriage Laws', and she may have married in the interim. During the first year for which the NESWS listed its meetings, Mrs. Bayfield addressed no fewer than five Guild meetings
6. NESWS *Annual Report* 1899; the suffragists interviewed the four candidates, including Winston Churchill who was unsympathetic
7. The details of payment are unclear, but may well have been made on a per day basis
8. Webb, C., *The Woman with the Basket,* Women's Co-operative Guild, Manchester 1927, pp 200-1; it is not clear whether the Mrs Green in the Guild was the same Mrs Green who was employed as a petition worker, but it is extremely likely
9. *Englishwoman's Review* 15.4.1902
10. WTUL *Review* April 1900. Sarah Reddish worked with Helen Silcock in March, two months before the campaign began
11. NESWS *Annual Report* 1900
12. *Manchester Guardian* 19.3.1901
13. NESWS *Annual Report* 1901
14. *Englishwoman's Review* 15.4.1901
15. *Englishwoman's Review* 15.4.1902
16. *Clarion* 15.9.1900
17. *Englishwoman's Review* 15.10.1901
18. *Women's Suffrage Journal* October 1884
19. The Franchise Committee was probably a sub-committee of the powerful Parliamentary Committee
20. *Englishwoman's Review* 15.10.1901
21. *Women's Suffrage Journal* October 1884

22. *Clarion* 19.9.1902 and *Englishwoman's Review* 15.10.1902. Helen Fairhurst was nominated to the Parliamentary Committee, but was not successful

23. *Mr Keir Hardie MP on Women's Suffrage*, Central Society for Women's Suffrage 1902

24. *Englishwoman's Review* 15.4.1902. The speeches were published by the Central Society for Women's Suffrage, as *Working Women on Women's Suffrage*, 1902. We were unable to locate this pamphlet until a copy was discovered in Amsterdam

25. *Clarion* 6.6.1902

26. Nash, R., 'The Co-operator and the Citizen' in *The Case for Women's Suffrage*, p 71

27. *Nelson Chronicle* 24.1.1902

28. See *Dictionary of Labour Biography;* also, Clark, P.F., *Lancashire and the New Liberalism*, pp 85-95, and Bealey, F., and Pelling, H., *Labour and Politics* pp 98-101

29. *Women's Suffrage Record* October 1903, quoted by Rosen, A., *Rise Up, Women!* p 20

30. *Clarion* 18.7.1902

31. *Nelson Chronicle* 18.7.1902

32. *Nelson Chronicle* 18.7.1902

33. *Clarion* 15.8.1902 ·

34. NESWS *Annual Report* 1902

35. NESWS *Annual Report* 1903

36. *Clarion* 31.10.1902

37. See Drake, B., *Women in Trade Unions*, pp 61-2

38. Interviews recorded by authors, March and June 1976

39. For the SDF link, see Thomas Foster to Selina Cooper, letter dated 14.1.1907, asking her advice on how 'to propagate socialism among our women folk' and inviting her to speak at an SDF Discussion Class. For the ILP, see *Manifesto to the Women's Social and Political Union*, undated. For the Nelson Guild, see chapter ten. For subscriptions, see *Clitheroe Branch of the National Union of Women's Suffrage Societies: Treasurer's Book*

40. Interview recorded by authors, June 1976

41. What is perhaps distinctive about Selina Cooper's suffrage group is that it included very few middle class women, and that it ran continuously from 1904 to 1921. Far more detailed local research is needed for an overall pattern to emerge, but see chapter twelve

42. Mrs Green had been less active in 1902, the year when she was Guild President

43. NESWS *Annual Reports* 1903 & 1904. *Clarion* 5.9.1902 & 17.10.1902

44. The pattern of support in the West Riding demands further local research; committees affiliated to the NESWS had been formed at Sowerby Bridge, Colne Valley, Keighley, Halifax, Wakefield, Elland and Normanton

45. *Labour Leader* 1903

46. Neither the radical suffragists' precise motives nor the exact date has been recorded

47. The only detailed membership record is in *Joint Report of Women's Suffrage Work*, William Morris Press, Manchester 1911. It lists nineteen Committee Members, over a hundred donors and subscribers, and funds of over £600

48. *Bolton Journal* 14.2.1913
49. NESWS *Annual Report* 1903
50. *Clarion* 16.10.1903
51. Printed letter from Esther Roper, 27.6.1904
52. The date Cissy Foley joined is not recorded, though her younger sister noted she was involved by 1905
53. The *Preston Co-operative Record*, 1905
54. NESWS *Annual Report* 1905

CHAPTER TEN THE PANKHURSTS IN MANCHESTER

1. Pankhurst, E.S., *The Suffragette Movement*, p 135
2. Hyndman, H.M., *Further Reminiscences*, Macmillan, London 1912, p 290
3. Pankhurst, E.S., *The Life of Emmeline Pankhurst*, p 43
4. Pankhurst, E.S., *The Suffragette Movement*, p 157
5. See also *Clarion*, 1.8.1902
6. Compare Pankhurst, E., *My Own Story*, p 35. Manchester Central ILP minutes 6.10.1903; these are the only Manchester ILP records that are preserved, though we have now been able to read the ILP Conference Reports for these years
7. Manchester Central ILP minutes 4.9.1906
8. Pankhurst, C., *Unshackled*, p 40
9. Swanwick, H.M., *I Have Been Young*, p 188
10. Pankhurst, E.S., *The Suffragette Movement;* p 164
11. It is interesting to compare Christabel's achievement with that of Philippa Fawcett, Mrs Fawcett's daughter. In 1890 she was placed 'above the senior wrangler' in the Cambridge University Mathematical Tripos. However, she could not take her degree and Cambridge did not capitulate to its women students until the 1920s when it compromised and agreed to award them 'titular degrees'
12. Hyndman, H.M., *Further Reminiscences*, p 291
13. Pankhurst, C., *Unshackled*, p 43
14. Pankhurst, C., *Unshackled*, p 42
15. Pankhurst, E.S., *The Suffragette Movement*, p 165
16. Pankhurst, C., *Unshackled*, p 41
17. Quoted in Thompson, L., *The Enthusiasts*, Gollancz, London 1971, p 136; the diary entry is undated; however Pankhurst, E.S., *The Life of Emmeline Pankhurst*, p 47 suggests the episode took place before the WSPU was formed
18. *Labour Leader* 14.3.1903; *Clarion* 13.3.1903
19. *Labour Leader* 23.5.1903 & 30.5.1903; see also Clarke, P.F., *Lancashire and the New Liberalism*, p 319. The NESWS *Annual Report*, 1903, does not mention the episode or even the by-election, and it would be interesting to know who 'her friends' were. Possibly Christabel took unilateral action at Preston; she had just issued a penny pamphlet, 'The Parliamentary Vote for Women'
20. *ILP News*, August 1903
21. Billington-Grieg, T., 'Women's Freedom League' file
22. There is no contemporary record of Mrs. Pankhurst's own thinking and motives at this point
23. Other possible factors were the mounting unemployment in the cotton

industry, and the episode of the exclusion of women from the ILP branch based at Pankhurst Hall. See Rosen, A., *Rise Up, Women!*, p 29, and Pankhurst, E.S., *The Suffragette Movement*, p 167

24. Pankhurst, E.S., *The Suffragette Movement*, p 168; see also Pankhurst, C., *Unshackled*, p 43-4, which implies Christabel formed the WSPU with her mother. Sylvia, not in Manchester at the time, does not give an eye-witness account, and Manchester Central ILP minutes suggest Christabel may well have been party to her mother's plans early in October; she joined the branch 6.10.1903 and was present at the meeting a fortnight later when women's suffrage was debated

25. Pankhurst, C., *Unshackled*, p 43. An undated interview with Helen Harker *(Daily Mail* cutting, Eccles Library suffrage collection) noted 'I was No. 1 member to be enrolled by Mrs Pankhurst in Manchester.' The names of remaining founder members seem lost, though a letter in *Clarion* 21.5.1905 signed by nine ILP women, including Christabel and Teresa Billington, might indicate the names of some of the others

26. Pankhurst, E.S., *The Suffragette Movement*, p 187
27. Pankhurst, C., *Unshackled*, p 44
28. *Labour Leader*, 31.10.1906
29. *Clarion* 1.1.1904 also noted that the WSPU had issued a bright yellow pamphlet as their 'Woman's Charter'
30. Pankhurst, E.S., *The Suffragette Movement*, p 168
31. *Labour Leader* 14.11.1903
32. Manchester and Salford Women's Trades Union Council, *Annual Report* 1904. Frow, E. & R., *To Make That Future - Now!* pp 51-2. No records of the new Council have survived. Christabel Pankhurst presumably resigned at the same time
33. *Labour Leader* 16.4.1904 & 23.4.1904
34. Rowbotham, S., *Hidden from History*, p 83.
35. The surveys were also weakened by the fact they weren't carried out nationally, or even in all ILP branches, but only in those sympathetic to women's suffrage, such as Manchester Central
36. *Clarion* 23.9.1904
37. *Clarion* 16.12.1904. We are grateful to Edward Teague for drawing our attention to this correspondence
38. *Clarion* 30.12.1904
39. *Clarion* 30.12.1904; also 8,000 women in the Scottish Co-operative Women's Guild
40. *Clarion* 6.1.1905
41. *Clarion* 13.1.1905
42. *Clarion* 10.2.1905 & 17.2.1905
43. Other correspondents who took part included Rachel Scott, Teresa Billington and Mrs. Pankhurst
44. Labour Representation Committee, Annual Conference Report, 1905; indirect speech has been transcribed as direct speech. See also Cross, C., *Philip Snowden,* Barrie and Rockliff, London 1966, Snowden to Selina Cooper, letter dated 24.1.1905
45. *Clarion* 20.1.1905
46. *Clarion* 3.2.1905
47. Pankhurst, C., *Unshackled*, p 47; *Labour Leader* 19.5.1905, quoted by

Rosen, A., *Rise Up, Women!* p 38. NESWS *Annual Report* 1905 merely noted that the Bill was talked out; Pankhurst, E.S., *The Suffragette Movement* p 182 notes that NUWSS members did not take part in the lobbying, so it is not known whether any radical suffragists were present

48. Precisely why Christabel concentrated so exclusively on Trades Council meetings is not known; however, she may have noted that they were becoming an increasingly significant factor in LRC deliberations, and that they included more socialists than most unions
49. *Labour Leader* 18.7.1903
50. Pankhurst, E.S., *The Suffragette Movement,* pp 185-6 and 208. Precisely how Annie Kenney was drawn into the WSPU is not known; see Kenney, A., *Memories of a Militant,* p 27; Pankhurst, C., *Unshackled,* p 44; Pankhurst E.S., *The Suffragette Movement,* p 186; and NESWS *Annual Reports* 1904 & 5. Her connections with the Oldham ILP are also unclear, though Sylvia notes she was a member of the local ILP choir
51. Pankhurst, E.S., *The Suffragette Movement,* pp 186-7
52. A more detailed description of this well known incident can be found in Pankhurst, C., *Unshackled;* Mackenzie, M., *Shoulder to Shoulder;* Neale R.S., *Class and Ideology in the Nineteenth Century,* Routledge & Kegan Paul London 1972, pp 154-9
53. *Manchester Guardian,* 14.10.1905; compare Kenney, A., *Memoirs of a Militant,* p 37
54. *Manchester Guardian* 16.10.1905
55. Manchester Central ILP, minutes 18.10.1905
56. *Manchester Evening News* 21.10.1905; see also Pankhurst, C., *Unshackled,* p 54, and Pankhurst, E.S., *The Suffragette Movement,* p 191
57. Poster in Local History Library, Manchester. Pankhurst, C., *Unshackled* p 55 makes only brief mention of Teresa Billington's achievement here
58. *Manchester Guardian* 21.10.1905; also *Manchester Evening Chronicle* 20.10.1905, quoted by Mackenzie, M., *Shoulder to Shoulder*

CHAPTER ELEVEN   THE SUFFRAGE MOVEMENTS SPLIT

1. Billington-Grieg, T., 'Social and Feminist Awakening' file
2. Billington-Grieg, T., 'Social and Feminist Awakening' file
3. *Manchester Guardian:* 16.10.1905
4. Margaret Ashton to Mrs. Fawcett, letter dated 16.1.1906, Suffrage MSS Manchester Central Library
5. Pankhurst, E.S., *The Suffragette Movement,* p 195-6
6. NESWS *Annual Report* 1908
7. Swanwick, H.M., *I Have Been Young,* pp 183-201
8. NESWS *Annual Report* 1905; National Industrial and Professional Women's Suffrage Society, subscription list, 1911
9. Brown, D., *The Labour Movement in Wigan 1874-1967,* M.A. Thesis, Liverpool, 1969
10. *Wigan Observer:* 6.1.1906
11. *Wigan Observer:* 3.1.1906
12. *Wigan Observer:* 10.1.1906
13. Roper, E., (ed) *The Poems of Eva Gore-Booth*
14. *Wigan Observer:* 20.1.1906. The elections results were: Sir F.S. Powell, Bart.:

3,573; Thorley Smith: 2,205; Colonel Woods: 1,900 Fulford, R., *Votes for Women,* p 92

15. Billington-Grieg, T., 'Women's Freedom League' file; also Manchester Central ILP minutes 19.9.1905

16. Rosen, A., *Rise Up, Women!* p 60

17. *Reformers' Year Book* 1907

18. Nash, R., 'Co-operator and Citizen' in *The Case for Women's Suffrage,* p 72; Pankhurst, E.S., *The Suffragette Movement,* p 196. Neither account refers to the radical suffragist groups, but it is highly unlikely they did not sign, as their relationship with the Guild was so cordial

19. Ramsay MacDonald to Selina Cooper, undated letter. The letter must have been written sometime between Easter 1905 and Easter 1907. Pankhurst, E.S., *The Suffragette Movement* p 203 notes that the postmen's delegate voted wrongly and the margin was really larger

20. Montefiore, D., *From a Victorian to a Modern,* E. Archer, London 1927, pp 46-7; also, Pankhurst, E.S., *The Suffragette Movement,* p 211

21. *Reformers' Year Book* 1907 p 146; Montefiore, D., *From A Victorian to a Modern,* p 54. Possibly a petition from 85,000 Lancashire women cotton operatives was handed to the Prime Minister on this occasion; Selina Cooper had the billhead of a 'Woman's Franchise Petition', on to which this information was later added in handwriting, but this might possibly be a confusion with a later petition

22. *Clarion:* 1.6.1906

23. Pankhurst, E.S., *The Suffragette Movement,* photograph opposite p 212, (Longman edition, 1931) Keir Hardie speaking, Trafalgar Square, May 19, 1906. What part the radical suffragists played at this meeting is not recorded, but note Eva Gore-Booth to Edith Palliser, letter dated 19.11.1906, in Industrial Suffrage File

24. Arthur Ponsonby (on behalf of Campbell-Bannerman) to Selina Cooper, letter dated 14.6.1906, thanking her for sending a copy of the Nelson Society's resolution. This is the only record of any such letters, but it is unlikely Nelson took this initiative independent of the rest of Lancashire

25. Rosen, A., *Rise Up, Women!* p 70

26. Supplement to the *Co-operative News* 30.6.1906

27. *Clarion:* 24.8.1906

28. Eva Gore-Booth to Mrs. Fawcett, 25.10.1906, on Lancashire Women Textile Workers' Representation Committee notepaper

29. Eva Gore-Booth to Edith Palliser, letter dated November 1906, Industrial Suffrage File. Also, *Englishwoman's Review* 16.7.1900

30. However the National Union Annual Report 1907, notes a London conference 8.2.1907 attended by the NUWSS, WSPU, ILP and the three radical suffragist organizations

31. Pankhurst, C., *Unshackled,* pp 66-7

32. Alice Milne's Diary, 22.10.1906, as copied by Teresa Billington-Grieg

33. Billington-Grieg, T., *The Militant Suffrage Movement,* Frank Palmer, London 191? pp 75-6

34. Mary Gawthorpe, a leading figure in the Leeds ILP, began to support Smillie, until reprimanded by the WSPU

35. Loose letter in Manchester Central ILP minute book to F. Toulmin, 28.8.1906; Manchester Central ILP minutes 4.9.1906; Billington-Grieg, T., 'Politics and Suffrage' file - her anger is directed towards the Pankhursts rather than to the ILP

36. *Manifesto to the Women's Social and Political Union,* undated, copy in Manchester Central Library
37. *Clarion:* 2.11.1906
38. Manchester Central ILP minutes 19.3.1907
39. Pankhurst, E.S., *The Suffragette Movement,* p. 264; Billington-Grieg, T., *The Militant Suffrage Movement,* p 77
40. Billington-Grieg, T., 'Politics and Suffrage' file
41. Billington-Grieg, T., *The Militant Suffrage Movement,* p 13

CHAPTER TWELVE   WORKING WOMEN AS SUFFRAGISTS

1. *Joint Report of Women's Suffrage Work*
2. NUWSS *Annual Report* 1907
3. *Queen* 17.4.1909
4. Executive Committee of London Society, minutes 4.10.1906 (Helena Swanwick went on to found the *Common Cause* in 1909 which became the leading suffragist journal)
5. Selina Cooper to Mary Cooper, postcard dated 7.11.1906
6. Bertrand Russell to Selina Cooper, letter dated May 1907; NUWSS *Annual Report* 1907
7. NUWSS *Annual Report* 1908; she worked with Margaret Ashton, Helena Swanwick, Mrs Fawcett and Miss Abadam
8. Interview recorded by authors, May 1977
9. Eva Gore-Booth to Edith Palliser, letter dated 19.11.1906, Industrial Suffrage file
10. Mrs Fawcett to Miss Strachey, card dated 21.10.1911, Industrial Suffrage file
11. Nash, R., 'Co-operator and Citizen' in Villiers, B., (ed) *The Case for Women's Suffrage*
12. Stocks, M., *My Commonplace Book,* p 73; Mitchell, H., *The Hard Way Up,* pp 153 & 159
13. Interview recorded by the Manchester Studies Unit, Manchester Polytechnic, October 1974
14. Mitchell, H., *The Hard Way Up,* p 130-149
15. Hesketh, P., *My Aunt Edith,* P. Davies, London 1966, pp 52-4; see also Raeburn, A., *Militant Suffragettes,* Michael Joseph, London 1973, pp 246-8, about Mrs. Higginson, also from Preston
16. Interview recorded by authors, July 1976; Annie Kenney was probably campaigning for Victor Grayson, a socialist pro-suffrage candidate for Colne Valley, but the incident would have had similar repercussions had she been campaigning purely for women's suffrage
17. Interview recorded by authors, May 1976
18. Hesketh, P., *My Aunt Edith,* pp 41, 50-2
19. Billington-Grieg, T., *The Militant Suffrage Movement,* Frank Palmer, London 1911, pp 24
20. Swanwick, H., *I Have Been Young,* p 199
21. Interview recorded by authors, September 1976; Ethel Derbyshire was subsequently awarded a ribbon bearing National Union colours
22. Interview recorded by authors, March 1976

23. Collinge, A., typed autobiographical essay in *Bolton Evening News* library; *Reformers' Year Book* 1907 lists ten contact addresses for the WSPU, of which eight are in Lancashire and include Hannah Mitchell for Ashton, Mrs Duxbury for Blackburn, and Alice Collinge for Bolton; Alice Collinge notes that 'soon after' this she left to join Sarah Reddish

24. Interview by authors, October 1976; letter to authors from Harry Wood, 28.10.1976

25. Collinge, A., 'Bayton' pub. in *Her Way and Three Other Plays,* Arthur H. Stockwell, London n.d.

26. Letter to authors from Christine Hanscombe, 10.12.1976. It would be interesting to know how much Alice Collinge was influenced by Edward Carpenter, who spoke at the Bolton Labour Church, and with whom she shared an enthusiasm for Walt Whitman and a simple country-based way of life

27. See Leech, C., *The Feminist Movement in Manchester 1903-14,* M.A., Manchester 1971, p 37

28. Collinge, A., typed autobiographical essay; she gives no date for this demonstration

29. *Burnley Express and News* 26.3.1968. Interview recorded by authors, May 1977

30. Mitchell, H., *The Hard Way Up,* p 170

31. Interview recorded by authors, March 1976

32. Interview recorded by authors, March 1976; during 1902 Ada Nield Chew was actually living in the Potteries, though this was discontinued as the League found it too expensive, WTUL *Annual Report* 1903

33. Interview recorded by authors, March 1976

34. For instance, Mrs Fawcett to Selina Cooper, letter dated 13.6.1917; and Margaret Ashton to Selina Cooper, letter dated 24.11.1915

35. *Common Cause* 30.3.1911; one of its members, Mary Higgs, wrote *Glimpses into the Abyss,* see *Suffrage Annual and Women's Who's Who,* London 1913

36. Haslam, Mrs, *Women's Suffrage in Bolton 1908-20,* p 8; also Bolton Suffrage Society Minute Books, 12.1.1909 & 8.9.1911

37. *Common Cause* 25.5.1909 & 10.12.1909. It would be interesting to know more about Sarah Whittaker, for instance

38. Interview recorded by authors, March 1976

39. Fulford, R., *Votes for Women,* p 149

40. Rosen, A., *Rise Up, Women!* p 115

41. Interview recorded by authors, July 1976

42. Alice Milne's diary, 17.10.1906, as copied by Teresa Billington-Grieg

43. See Leech, C., *The Feminist Movement in Manchester 1903-14,* pp 14-6; Smethurst, J.B., 'The Suffrage Movement in Eccles' in *Lectures 1971-2,* Eccles and District History Society; *Englishwoman's Review* 15.10.1904

44. Hesketh, P., *My Aunt Edith,* pp 31-40, 51, 70, 141. The details of Edith Rigby's membership of the ILP are confused, but she seems to have resigned about 1907

45. For instance, *Manchester Guardian* 3.10.1905, 'Women and the Unemployment Act'

46. Alice Milne's diary, 19.9.1906, as copied by Teresa Billington-Grieg

47. The suffragette incursion seems to have caused local irritation; see *Bolton Evening News* 29.8.1906

48. *Votes for Women* 9.7.1908, 17.8.1908, 10.9.1908

49. *Joint Report of Women's Suffrage Work;* and contrast Rosen, A., *Rise Up, Women!* p 210

50. See Rosen, A., *Rise Up, Women!* ch 17

51. Billington-Grieg, T., 'Social and Feminist Awakening' file

52. The degree to which birth control information was available in the cotton towns demands further research, as does the link between family size and married women's full-time, relatively well paid work. It seems birth control was already discussed in progressive circles, for as early as 1896 Julia Dawson was supplying 'Malthusian books' to *Clarion* readers, but the demand was so great that after dispatching 400 copies free, she had to ask 1d and 6d for the pamphlets; *Clarion* 25.1.1896
    See also McLaren, A., 'Women's Work and the Regulation of Family Size', *History Workshop Journal* No 4, Autumn 1977, which discusses the use among Lancashire textile families of abortion as a form of birth control

53. Maude, A., *Life of Marie Stopes,* Williams and Norgate, London 1924, p 124

54. Interview recorded by authors, March 1976; *Clarion* 6.10.1905 notes David Shackleton's opposition to working mothers

55. Information from Margaret Aldersley's niece; unfortunately there is little documentary evidence available

56. Interview recorded by authors, May 1977

CHAPTER THIRTEEN   THE DEBATE WITH THE LABOUR PARTY

1. Pankhurst, E.S., *The Suffragette Movement,* p 178, Bondfield, M., *A Life's Work,* Hutchinson, London 1949, p 82

2. See also Ramelson, M., *The Petticoat Rebellion* p 154 for Ramsay MacDonald

3. Pankhurst, E.S., *The Suffragette Movement,* p 245

4. WTUL *Review* July 1902

5. Interview recorded by authors, March 1976

6. Interview recorded by authors, May 1977

7. See Pankhurst, E.S., *The Suffragette Movement,* p 246

8. Emilie Gardner to Selina Cooper, letter dated 21.6.1908

9. Susan Power to Selina Cooper, letter dated 28.10.1906

10. Interview recorded by authors, March 1976; it is possible such offers emanated from the WSPU

11. *Clarion* 29.6.1906

12. Rendel, M., 'The Contribution of the Women's Labour League to the winning of the Franchise' in Middleton, L., (ed) *Women in the Labour Movement,* Croom Helm 1977; also *Reformers' Year Book* 1907; Snowden, E., *The Woman Socialist,* London 1907, p 19; MacDonald, R., *Margaret Ethel MacDonald, A Memoir,* Hodder & Stoughton, London 1912, p 202. Edith Rigby's relationship with the League is unclear.

13. Noted by Rendel, M., in 'The Contribution of the Women's Labour League to the winning of the Franchise' in Middleton, L., (ed), *Women in the Labour Movement,* p 73

14. Interview recorded by authors, March 1976; see also *Clarion* 19.9.1896

15. Gilman, C.P., 'The Socialist and the Suffragist' in *Suffrage Songs and Verses,* Charlton, New York 1911 (middle two stanzas omitted)

16. Gore-Booth, E., 'The Women's Suffrage Movement among Trade Unionists' in Villiers, B. (ed), *The Case for Women's Suffrage*

17. Turner, B., *About Myself*, Cayme Press, London 1930, p 53 and ch 24. William Wilkinson had died in 1906

18. Labour Party Conference Report 1908

19. Grubb, A.P. *From Candle Factory to British Cabinet*, Edwin Dalton, London 1908, pp 246-50.

20. Snowden, E., *The Woman Socialist*, p 81

21. *Dictionary of Labour Biography*

22. Gore-Booth, E., *Women's Right to Work*, Manchester & Salford Women's Trade & Labour Council, Manchester n.d., pp 4-5

23. *Manchester Guardian* 22.4.1908

24. *Manchester Guardian* 24.4.1908

25. MacDonald, R., *Margaret Ethel MacDonald, A Memoir*, p 169

26. *Daily News* 8.7.1909, Industrial Suffrage file, Fawcett Library

27. National Union of Women Workers, conference paper, Manchester, October 1907

28. *Hansard*, vol CLXX pp 1102-1163, Dickenson's Women's Enfranchisement Bill, 8.3.1907

29. *Englishwoman's Review* 15.4.1908

30. Letters to Preston Trades Council, and Rawtenstall Trades and Labour Council, dated 3.10.1907

31. Rendel, M., 'The Contribution of the Women's Labour League to the winning of the Franchise' in Middleton, L. (ed), *Women in the Labour Movement*, pp 63-6

32. Clarke, P., *Lancashire and the new Liberalism*, pp 35 & 120. 4th Annual Report of the Rossendale Labour Council, and the Minutes of Rawtenstall Trades and Labour Council, February 1910

33. NUWSS *Annual Report* 1910

34. *Common Cause* 25.11.1909, 9.12.1909, 16.12.1909, 23.12.1909; the original candidate, Malcolm Mitchell, was Honorary Secretary of the Men's League for Women's Suffrage. The only evidence of any Labour support for Bulley is a 'Copy of Letter to Women's Suffrage Candidate', dated 5.1.1910 from the Liverpool Labour Representation Committee

35. *Common Cause* 25.11.1909

36. *Common Cause* 20.1.1910

37. *Common Cause* 30.12.1909, 6.1.1910, 13.1.1910

38. Typed autobiographical essay, *Bolton Evening News* Library

39. *Common Cause* 20.1.1910

40. *Common Cause* 27.1.1910; *Rossendale Echo* 12.1.1910; *Rossendale Free Press* 1.1.1910

41. *Common Cause* 25.11.1909; Clarke, P., *Lancashire and the New Liberalism*, pp 158-9

42. Fulford, R., *Votes for Women*, p 213; Ramelson, M., *The Petticoat Rebellion* pp 158-9

43. Fawcett, G.M., *What I Remember*, p 65

44. Fawcett, G.M., *The Women's Victory — and After*, pp 29-37

45. Interview recorded by authors, March 1976

46. Pankhurst, E.S., *The Suffragette Movement* pp 396-9; Sylvia does not refer to Ada Nield Chew, but merely asserts — implausibly —that the WSPU was more popular with Labour Party workers than the NUSWS's suffragists

47. *Manchester Guardian* 31.10.1913
48. Interview recorded by authors, March 1976
49. Contrast Pankhurst, E.S., *The Suffragette Movement*, p 485 that 'the NUWSS never captured the interest of the multitude. It was so staid, so willing to wait, so incorrigibly leisurely'
50. *Common Cause* 31.10.1913; *Manchester Guardian* 21.10.1913, 24.10.1913, 27.10.1913
51. *Common Cause* 12.12.1913, 16.1.1914, 6.2.1914, 20.2.1914, 15.5.1914
52. *Manchester Guardian* 30.10.1913
53. *Common Cause* 6.2.1914
54. *Common Cause* 6.2.1914
55. *Common Cause* 3.7.1914
56. Bolton Suffrage Society, Minutes, 10.5.1912 & 25.2.1913
57. Labour Party Conference Report 1914
58. Isabella Ford to Mrs Fawcett, letter dated 14.4.1914, Industrial Suffrage file, Fawcett Library
59. Billington-Greig, T., *The Militant Suffrage Movement*, pp 3 & 154

CHAPTER FOURTEEN   WHAT DID YOU DO IN THE GREAT WAR?

1. Pankhurst, C., *Unshackled*, p 288
2. Fawcett, M.G., *Memories of a Militant*, p 282
3. Fawcett, M.G., *The Women's Victory – and After*, pp 87-8
4. Fawcett, M.G., *The Women's Victory – and After*, p 87
5. Roberts, R., *The Classic Slum*, pp 198-9
6. Marwick, A., *The Deluge*, Macmillan, London 1965, p 94
7. Drake, B., *Women in Trade Unions*, p 111; this figure does not include teachers
8. Hopwood, E., *The Lancashire Weavers' Story*, pp 81-2; Hutchins, B.L., *Women in Modern Industry*, G. Bell and Sons, London 1915, p 240; *Cotton Factory Times* 9.3.1917
9. Quoted by Fawcett, M.G., *The Women's Victory – and After*, p 133
10. Mitchell, H., *The Hard Way Up*, p 183
11. Interview recorded by authors, September 1976
12. Helena Swanwick to Selina Cooper, letter dated 20.9.1917
13. Interview recorded by authors, June 1976. W.H. Beveridge to Selina Cooper, letter dated March 1916
14. See *Cotton Factory Times*
15. Roper, E., (ed), *Prison letters of Countess Marcievicz*, Longman's, London 1934, pp 103-4, Gore-Booth, E., *The Tribunal*, National Labour Press, London, n.d.
16. Roper, E., (ed), *Poems of Eva Gore-Booth*, p 28
17. Mitchell, D., *The Fighting Pankhursts*, Jonathan Cape, London 1967, gives a fuller account
18. *Clitheroe Branch of the National Union of Women's Suffrage Societies: Treasurer's Book*, entry dated 18.8.1914
19. Russell, D., *The Tamarisk Tree*, Virago, London 1977; Rowbotham, S., *A New World for Women*, Pluto Press, London 1977; Maude A., *Life of Marie Stopes*, William and Norgate, London 1924

20.   Rathbone, E., *The Disinherited Family*, E. Arnold, London 1924, p 245
21.   *Common Cause* 6.3.1914
22.   *Common Cause* 27.2.1914
23.   Interview recorded by authors, March 1976
24.   Mitchell, H., *The Hard Way Up*, p 189
25.   Bolton Women's Citizen's Association, *Annual Report*, 1925
26.   Foley, A., *A Bolton Childhood*, p 80
27.   *Bolton Evening News* 6.3.1946
28.   See Frow, E. & R., and Bellamy, J., *Dictionary of Labour Biography*
29.   Mitchell, H., *The Hard Way Up*, p 229
30.   Interview recorded by authors, March 1976
31.   Interview recorded by authors, March 1976
32.   Hopwood, E., *The Lancashire Weavers' Story*, p 143
33.   Foley, A., *A Bolton Childhood*, p 90

BIOGRAPHIES

ALDERSLEY, Margaret
c.1852-c.1940
from Burnley; married;
3 daughters, one son
c.1910 PLG; Nelson & Clitheroe
Suffrage Society; Textile Comm
c.1912 organizer for NUWSS
1913 Keighley & S. Lanark by-
elections for NUWSS
c.1922-6 Australia

ATKINSON, Mary
from Brierfield; married
c.1910 Textile Comm
c.1912 member of Clitheroe
Suffrage Society

BAYFIELD, Mrs Hodgson
from Chorlton, probably active
W Co-op G. By 1899 NESWS
organizer
1900 starts textile workers' petition
campaign, Blackburn
1902 Chelsea Town Hall meeting
1906 resigns NESWS due to illness
1912 Whalley Range & Chorlton
Constituency organization committee of NESWS

BEANLAND, Harriette
from Nelson; tailoress
Nelson ILP
1904 PLG Nelson, as Nelson Lab Rep
Comm candidate
c1906 signs ILP manifesto supporting
suffragettes

Clitheroe Suffrage Society; Ind &
Prof

CHEW, Ada Nield
28.1.1870-27.12.1945
Born Ada Nield, Staffordshire
9 brothers, 3 sisters
1881 leaves school
1894 tailoress; 'Factory Girl'
campaign in *Crewe Chronicle*
1894 PLG, Nantwich
c.1894 Crewe ILP:
1896 Clarion van
1897 marries George Chew, ex-
weaver
1898 daughter, Doris
1900-8 organizer for WTUL
1906 W Lab L. Rochdale
1908-11 works part-time for WTUL
1911-14 organizer for NUWSS, based
in Rossendale
1912-14 Crewe, Holmfirth, S Lanark,
N W Durham, Leith Burgs etc by-
elections for NUWSS
1914 Rochdale Trades Council
representative on Mayor's Central
Relief Committee
1915 Secretary, Rochdale Suffrage
Society. Contributed articles to
*Crewe Chronicle, Women's Trade
Union Review, Clarion, Common
Cause, Englishwoman, Cotton
Factory Times, Rochdale Observer*
etc

COLLINGE, Alice
1873-28.8.1957
Childhood: Rawtenstall
c.1885-91 pupil-teacher Newchurch-in-
Rossendale
Teaches at St Matthew's School, Bolton
Organist, Bolton Labour Church
Vegetarian
c.1906 President, Bolton WSPU
c.1907 Bolton Women's Textile
Workers' Representation Comm
c.1910 local collector for Textile
Comm
1910 Rossendale election campaign
1920-1 English tutor, Bolton WEA
Lancashire Authors' Association
Publications include *Her Way and
Three Other Plays*, & a book of
poems

COOPER, Selina Jane
1864 - Nov 1946
born Selina Coombe, Callington, Cornwall

1876 half-timer in cotton mill; 1889
becomes winder in Brierfield
1890s joins Nelson ILP and SDF
1893 on winders' union committee
1896 married Robert Cooper, post-
office worker & later weaver
1890s joins SDF and ILP, by 1898 active
in W Co-op G
1900 daughter, Mary
1901-7 PLG Nelson (1904 as
Nelson Lab Rep Comm candidate)
1901 & 2 textile workers' deputations to Westminster
1903 Textile Comm
1904 Secretary, Nelson & Colne
(later Clitheroe) Suffrage Comm
1905 Lab Rep Comm Conference
1906-14 organizer for NUWSS
1907 Labour Party Conference
1907 Wimbledon by-election;
campaigns for Bertrand Russell
1910 Rossendale election campaign
Darwen constituency for NUWSS
1910 deputation to Asquith
1911 organizes local section of
NUWSS pilgrimage to London
1912-14 Keighley, N W Durham,
etc by-elections for NUWSS
1913 organises local section of NUWSS
pilgrimage to London
1915 organizes Maternity Centre
in Nelson
1924 borough magistrate
1934 visits Nazi Germany for Women
Against War & Fascism
1938 Vice-chairman, Burnley Guardians'
Committee
1940 Chairman, Burnley Guardians'
Committee
Also, member of Lancashire Health
Insurance Appeals Committee, member
of National Co-operative Health
Insurance Committee, member of
Nelson Education Committee etc

DERBYSHIRE, Ethel
14.6.1879 - 1976
Born Fen district, Cambridgeshire
Youngest of 14 children
1886 family moves to Blackburn
1889 half-timer in cotton mill in
weaving shed; becomes a winder
Blackburn Socialist Sunday School
Spiritualist Church
1891 joins Blackburn Weavers'
Association
1903 marries Billy Derbyshire;

1 daughter, 2 sons
Closely connected with Blackburn
ILP; open air speaking for women's
suffrage; recites anti-war poems at
pacifist meetings

DEWHURST, Ruth
from Oldham; married
1904 Secretary, Oldham Suffrage
Committee
c1910 Textile Comm

DICKENSON, Sarah
28.3.1868 - 26.12.1954
Born Salford; 3 brothers, 2 sisters
c.1879 starts work, probably as
half-time weaver's tenter in
Howarth's Mill, Salford
1889 Secretary, Manchester &
Salford Association of Machine,
Electrical & other Women Workers
1895 Co-Secretary of Manchester &
Salford Women's Trade Council
1895 marries William Dickenson,
enameller
1901 textile workers' deputation to
Westminster
1903 Textile Comm
1904 Secretary, Manchester
Suffrage Committee
1904 Co-Secretary of Trade & Lab
1910 Rossendale election campaign
1918 Trades Council women's
organizer
1923 Magistrate
c.1939, MBE for her service to
Manchester

FOLEY, Catherine (Cissy)
1879-c.1945
from Bolton; 3 brothers, 2 sisters
from c.1892 jack frame tenter in
spinning mill
Committee member, Bolton Card
Room Association
Bolton Labour Church
mid-1900s Textile Comm
c.1914 nurse
c.1918 runs Bolton's first voluntary
Child Clinic
1920s marries

FORSYTH, Isabel
Aged 13, starts work in a printing
firm
1896-1942 Secretary, Manchester
and Salford Society of Women
Employed in the Bookbinding and

Printing Trades
1908 full-time Secretary of this
union
By 1910 Textile Comm; Trade &
Lab

GORE-BOOTH, Eva Selena
1870-1926
Childhood: County Sligo, Ireland
1896 meets Esther Roper in Italy
1897 first book of poetry published
By 1897 moves to the Roper household, Manchester, and soon
becomes a NESWS speaker
By 1900 involved in Manchester
University Settlement
By 1899 on NESWS executive
1900 Co-Secretary of Manchester
& Salford Women's Trade Council
1903 Textile Comm
1906 Wigan campaign
1908 Barmaids' campaign
1910 Rossendale campaign
1913 leaves Manchester because of ill-
health
1915-6 Women's Peace Crusade
1916 No Conscription Fellowship
Publications include *Women's Labour
News* (which she edited), *The Egyptian
Pillar, The Agate Lamp* and other books
of poems; *Women's Right to Work,
Women Workers & Parliamentary
Representation*, articles in the
Common Cause etc.

GREEN, Mrs
Beswick W Co-op Guild; W Co-op
Guild Central Committee
from 1894 Deputy Chairman, Gorton
NNSWS sub-committee
1901 NESWS petition worker
1901 campaign in West Riding for
textile workers' petition
1902 probably W Co-op G President
1910 Rossendale campaign

GRUNDY, Violet
from Ancoats; winder
Secretary Union of Patent Co-op
Winders, Hank and Bobbin Winders,
Gassers, Doublers & Reelers
By 1910 Textile Comm; Trade & Lab

HAWORTH, Mrs
1902 Graduates' suffrage deputation to
Westminster
from c.1906 Ind & Prof (Treasurer)
member of Accrington Suffrage
Society

HEATON, Annie
from Burnley; mill worker
1893 works for WTUL
1894 Special Appeal organizer
1901 textile workers' deputation to
Westminster

HIGGINBOTHAM, Miss
c.1877 starts work in cotton mill,
probably in Hyde
1902 textile workers' deputation to
Westminster
1904 Secretary, Hyde Suffrage
Committee

KEENAN, Nellie
from Salford; weaver
from 1902 Treasurer (later Secretary)
Salford Power-Loom Weavers'
Association
from c.1904 Textile Comm
1904 Trade & Lab (Treasurer)
from c.1906 Ind & Prof

MURGATROYD, Emily
1877-c.1970
from Brierfield; from c.1887 weaver
Active in Nelson Weavers' Association
Member of Clitheroe Suffrage Society
1913 walks to London on NUWSS
pilgrimage

MYERS, Mrs
from Nelson
c.1909 Secretary, Clitheroe Suffrage
Society

PEARCE, Mrs
from Bolton; probably cotton worker
Bolton ILP
1901 textile workers' deputation to
Westminster

REDDISH, Sarah
1850-1928
from 1861 silk out-worker, later
worked as winder and roller-coverer in
a cotton mill
1886-1901 President, Bolton W Co-op
Guild
1889-91 & 1895-98 W Co-op Guild
Central Committee
1893-5 regional organizer for W Co-op
Guild in north of England
1896 or 7 Clarion Van
1897 President W Co-op Guild
1899 WTUL organizer
1900 elected to Bolton School Board
1900 petition worker for NESWS
1901 deputation of textile workers to
Westminster

1903 Textile Comm
to 1904 NESWS organizer
1905-21 Bolton PLG
c.1906 Ind & Prof
c.1910 visited Belgium & brought back
ideas to start a Bolton School for
Mothers
1910 Rossendale campaign
from 1911 President of Manchester &
Salford Women's Trade Society,
1919-20 organized Bolton Women's
Citizens' Association
Also, on the Distress Committee, the
Insurance Act Local Committee,
governor of Bolton Girls' High School
etc.
Publications include *Women & County
& Borough Councils: A Claim for
Eligibility.*

ROPER, Esther Gertrude
4.8.1868 - April 1938
Born Wilmslow, Cheshire
1891 Graduates from Owens College,
Manchester
1893-1905 Secretary of MNSWS (later,
NESWS)
1894 organizes Special Appeal
campaign among working women
1895 Manchester University Settlement Committee
1901 & 2 textile workers' deputation
to Westminster
1902 graduates' deputation to
Westminster
1903 Textile Comm
1906 Wigan campaign
from c.1906 Ind & Prof
1908 Barmaids' campaign
1910 Rossendale campaign
1913 leaves Manchester with Eva
Gore-Booth
1915-6 Women's Peace Crusade
1916 No Conscription Fellowship
Publications include
*The Cotton Trade Unions & the
Enfranchisement of Women*,
articles in *Common Cause*,
textbooks on Renaissance Italy;
Introduction to *The Prison
Letters of Constance Markievicz* and
The Poems of Eva Gore-Booth

ROWLETTE, Miss
1904 Textile workers' campaign in
Yorkshire
1906 to mid-Glamorgan for NUWSS
with Selina Cooper & Ethel Snowden

ROWTON, Katherine
1900 petition worker for NESWS
1901 textile workers' deputation to
Westminster
1900s PLG, Manchester
to 1903 organizer for NESWS
by 1910 Textile Comm
1910 Rossendale campaign

SHIMBLES, Miss
from Nelson; trade unionist
(probably a weaver); member of the
Clitheroe Suffrage Society

SHUTTLEWORTH, Florence
from Brierfield
Nelson ILP
member of Clitheroe Suffrage Society

SILCOCK, Helen
1866 - 19?
Childhood: Newcastle
9 brothers and sisters
1881 starts work in a Wigan cotton
mill
1890 joins the newly-founded Wigan
Weavers' Association
1892 elected to Wigan Weavers'
committee
1894 elected unanimously as Wigan
Weavers' President
1890s probably joins Wigan SDF
from 1890s member of Wigan Trades
Council executive
1897 WTUL pay her union salary
1901 & 1902 textile workers'
deputation to Westminster
1901 & 1902 raises women's suffrage
at TUC
1902 marries Mr Fairhurst, a Wigan
trade unionist

by 1906 member, Adult Suffrage
Society
1914 Secretary, Wigan Suffrage
Society

SMITH, Louisa
from Manchester, machinist
c.1900 meets Eva Gore-Booth at
Manchester University Settlement
Probably member of Manchester
Tailoresses' Union
by 1910 Textile Comm

STATON, Clara
from 1904 Secretary, Bolton Suffrage
Committee
by 1910 Textile Comm

THOMASSON, Mrs
from c.1906 Ind & Prof; donates £210
to its funds

TOZER, Mrs
Wife of Vicar of Heywood
1910 Rossendale campaign

WHITTAKER, Sara
1904 Secretary, Accrington Suffrage
Committee
by 1910 Textile Comm
1910 Rossendale campaign

WINBOLT, Mrs
from Stockport area
from c.1870 silk handloom weaver
1880s converted to women's suffrage
by Lydia Becker
1894 Special Appeal organizer for
MNSWS
1902 textile workers' deputation to
Westminster

WROE, Miss M.A.
by 1910 Ind & Prof
1910 Rossendale campaign

BIBLIOGRAPHY

BOOKS BY SUFFRAGISTS AND THEIR CONTEMPORARIES

Billington-Grieg, T., *The Militant Suffrage Movement,* Frank Palmer, London 1911
Blackburn, H., *Women's Suffrage,* Williams and Norgate, London 1902
Blatchford, R., *Merrie England,* Clarion, London 1893
Carpenter, E. (ed), *Forecasts of the Coming Century,* Labour Press, Manchester 1897
Carpenter, E., *Love's Coming of Age,* Allen and Unwin, London 1896
Chapman, S.J., *The Lancashire Cotton Industry: A Study in Economic Development,* University of Manchester Press, Manchester 1904
Collinge, A., *Her Way and Three Other Plays,* Arthur Stockwell, London n.d.
Davies, M.L., (ed), *Life as We Have Known It,* Virago, London 1977
Davies, M.L., (ed), *Maternity,* Virago, London 1978

Davies, M.L., *The Women's Co-operative Guild 1883-1904*, Women's Co-operative Guild, Kirkby Lonsdale, Westmorland 1904

Drake, B., *Women in Trade Unions*, Labour Research Department and Allen & Unwin, London 1920

Fawcett, M.G., *Women's Suffrage*, T.A. & E.C. Jack, London 1911

Fawcett, M.G., *The Women's Victory – and After*, Sidgwick and Jackson, London 1920

Fawcett, M.G., *What I Remember*, T. Fisher Unwin, London 1924

Hutchins, B.L., *Women in Modern Industry*, G. Bell & Sons, London 1915

MacDonald, J.R., *Margaret Ethel MacDonald. A Memoir*, Hodder & Stoughton, London 1912

Mason, B., *The Story of the Women's Suffrage Movement*, Sherraton and Hughes, Manchester 1912

Pankhurst, E.S., *The Suffragette*, Sturgis and Walton, New York 1911

Pethwick Lawrence, F.W., & Edwards, J. (eds), *The Reformers' Year Books*, London 1901-9

Roper, E. (ed), *Poems of Eva Gore-Booth*, Longmans, London 1929

Roper, E. (ed), *Prison Letters of Countess Markievicz*, Longmans, London 1934

Suffrage Annual & Women's Who's Who, Stanley Paul & Co., London 1913

Swanwick, H.M., *Women in Industry from Seven Points of View*, Duckworth, London 1908

Taylor, J.T., *The Jubilee History of the Oldham Industrial Co-operative Society Limited 1850-1900*, Manchester 1900

Tomlinson, W., *Bye-ways of Manchester Life*, Butterworth & Nodal, Manchester 1887

Villiers, B., (ed), *The Case for Women's Suffrage*, T. Fisher Unwin, London 1907

Wallis, L., *Life and Letters of Caroline Martyn*, Labour Leader Publishing Department, London & Glasgow 1898

Webb, S. & B., *Industrial Democracy*, Longmans Green, London 1897

AUTOBIOGRAPHIES

Bondfield, M., *A Life's Work*, Hutchinson, London 1949

Clynes, J.R., *Memoirs 1869-1924*, vol 1, Hutchinson, London 1937

Collinge, A., Unpublished typed autobiographical essay, *Bolton Evening News* library

Davies, C.S., *North Country Bred*, Routledge & Kegan Paul, London 1963

Foley, A., *A Bolton Childhood*, Manchester University Extra-Mural Department & North-Western District of WEA, Manchester 1973

Greenwood, W., *There Was a Time*, Jonathan Cape, London 1967

Hyndman, H.M., *Further Reminiscences*, Macmillan, London 1912

Kenney, A., *Memories of a Militant*, Edward Arnold, London 1924

Kenney, R., *Westering*, J.M. Dent, London 1939

Luty, M., *A Penniless Globetrotter*, Wardleworth, Accrington 1937

Luty, M., *My Life has Sparkled*, unpublished typescript, n.d., Rawtenstall Public Library

Mitchell, H., *The Hard Way Up*, Virago, London 1977

Pankhurst, C., *Unshackled*, Hutchinson, London 1959

Pankhurst, E., *My Own Story*, Eveleigh Nash, London 1914

Pollitt, H., *Serving My Time*, Lawrence & Wishart, London 1940

Roberts, R., *The Classic Slum*, Manchester University Press, Manchester 1971

Roberts, R., *A Ragged Schooling*, Manchester University Press, Manchester 1976

Stocks, M., *My Commonplace Book*, Peter Davies, London 1970

Swanwick, H.M., *I Have Been Young*, Victor Gollancz; London 1935

OTHER BOOKS

Anderson, M., *Family Structure in Nineteenth Century Lancashire*, Cambridge

University Press, Cambridge 1971

Bealey, F., and Pelling, H., *Labour and Politics,* Macmillan, London 1958

Bennett, A., *Oldham Trades and Labour Council Centenary 1867-1967*

Boone, G., *The Women's Trade Union Leagues in Great Britain and the United States of America,* Columbia University Press, 1942

Bradley, H., *And Miss Carter Wore Pink,* Jonathan Cape, London 1971

Briggs, A., *Victorian Cities,* Collins, London 1963

Bussey, G., & Tims, M., *Women's International League for Peace and Freedom 1915-1965. A Record of 50 Years' Work,* Allen & Unwin, London 1965

Catling, H., *The Spinning Mule,* David and Charles, Newton Abbott 1970

Chaloner, W.H., *The Social and Economic Development of Crewe 1780-1923,* Manchester University Press, Manchester 1950

Clarke, P.F., *Lancashire and the New Liberalism,* Cambridge University Press, Cambridge 1971

Clegg, H.A., Fox, A., & Thompson, A.F., *A History of British Trade Unions Since 1889,* Clarendon Press, Oxford 1964

Cole, G.D.H., & Postgate, R., *The Common People,* Methuen, London 1938

Cross, C., *Philip Snowden,* Barrie & Rockliff, London 1966

Frow, E. & R., *The Half Time System in Education,* Morten, Manchester 1970

Frow, E. & R., *To Make That Future — Now!* Morten, Manchester 1976

Fulford, R., *Votes for Women,* Faber & Faber, London 1958

Groom, T., *National Clarion Cycling Club 1894-1944. The Fifty-year Story of the Club,* National Clarion Cycling Club, Halifax 1944

Hamilton, M.A., *Mary Macarthur,* Leonard Parsons, London 1925

Hesketh, P., *My Aunt Edith,* Peter Davies, London 1966

Hobsbawm, E.J., *Industry and Empire,* Weidenfeld & Nicholson, London 1968

Hopwood, E., *The Lancashire Weavers' Story,* Amalgamated Weavers' Association, Manchester 1969

Kamm, J., *Rapiers and Battleaxes,* Allen & Unwin, London 1966

Kuczynski, J., *A Short History of Labour Conditions under Industrial Capitalism in Great Britain and the Empire,* Barnes & Noble, New York 1972

Lloyd, A., *Folk Song in England,* Lawrence & Wishart, London 1967

Mackenzie, M., *Shoulder to Shoulder,* Penguin, London 1975

Mahon, J., *Harry Pollitt. A Biography,* Lawrence & Wishart, London 1976

Marreco, A., *The Rebel Countess,* Weidenfeld & Nicholson, London 1967

Marwick, A., *The Deluge,* Macmillan, London 1965

McMillan, M., *The Life of Rachel McMillan,* Dent, London 1927

Middleton, L. (ed), *Women in the Labour Movement,* Croom Helm, London 1977

Mitchell, D., *The Fighting Pankhursts,* Jonathan Cape, London 1967

Morgan, K.O., *Keir Hardie,* Weidenfeld & Nicholson, London 1975

Morton, A.L., & Tate, G., *The British Labour Movement,* Lawrence & Wishart, London 1956

Neale, R.S., *Class and Ideology in the Nineteenth Century,* Routledge & Kegan Paul, London 1972

Neff, W.F., *Victorian Working Women,* Frank Cass & Co., London, 1966

Pankhurst, E.S., *The Suffragette Movement,* Virago, London 1977

Pankhurst, E.S., *The Life of Emmeline Pankhurst,* T. Werner Laurie, London 1935

Pelling, H., *The Origins of the Labour Party,* Oxford University Press, Oxford 1965

Peroni, R., *Industrial Lancashire,* Nelson, London 1976

Pike, E.R., *Human Documents of the Lloyd George Era,* Allen & Unwin, London 1972

Raeburn, A., *The Militant Suffragettes,* Michael Joseph, London 1973

Ramelson, M., *The Petticoat Rebellion,* Lawrence & Wishart, London 1967

Rosen, A., *Rise Up, Women!* Routledge & Kegan Paul, London 1974

Rover, C., *Women's Suffrage and Party Politics in Britain, 1866-1914,* Routledge & Kegan Paul, London 1967

Rowbotham, S., *Hidden from History,* Pluto, London 1973

Samuel, R., (ed) *Village Life and Labour,* Routledge & Kegan Paul, London 1975

Saville, J., and Bellamy, J., *Dictionary of Labour Biography,* Vols I & II, 1972 and 1974

Simon, B., *Education and the Labour Movement 1870-1920,* Lawrence & Wishart London 1965

Stewart, W., *Keir Hardie,* ILP, London 1921

Stocks, M., *Fifty Years in Every Street,* Manchester University Press, Manchester 1945

Strachey, R., *The Cause,* Virago, London 1978

Strachey, R., *Millicent Garrett Fawcett,* John Murray, London 1931

Thompson, E.P., *The Making of the English Working Class,* Penguin, London 1969

Thompson, L., *The Enthusiasts,* Gollancz, London 1971

Thompson, P., *The Edwardians: the Remaking of British Society,* Weidenfeld and Nicholson, London 1975

Tippett, L.H.C., *A Portrait of the Lancashire Textile Industry,* Oxford University Press, Oxford 1969

Tsuzuki, C., *H.M. Hyndman and British Socialism,* Oxford University Press, Oxford 1961

Turner, H.A., *Trade Union Growth, Structure and Policy. A Comparative Study of the Cotton Unions,* Allen & Unwin, London 1962

Webb, C., *The Woman with the Basket,* Women's Co-operative Guild, Manchester 1927

PAMPHLETS BY SUFFRAGISTS AND THEIR CONTEMPORARIES

Gore-Booth, E., *The Tribunal,* National Labour Press, London n.d., probably c. 1916

Gore-Booth, E., *Women's Right to Work,* Manchester & Salford Women's Trades and Labour Council, Manchester, n.d., probably 1908-9

Gore-Booth, E., *Women Workers and Parliamentary Representation,* Lancashire and Cheshire Women Textile and other Workers' Representation Committee, n.d., probably c. 1904

Hardie, K., *Mr Keir Hardie MP on Women's Suffrage,* Central Society for Women's Suffrage, 1902

Joint Report of Women's Suffrage Work, William Morris Press, Manchester 1911

Manifesto to the Women's Social and Political Union, signed by ILP women members, n.d. but probably 1906

Woollerton, A., *The Labour Movement in Manchester and Salford,* City of Manchester ILP, Manchester 1907

UNPUBLISHED THESES

Bather, L., *Manchester and Salford Trades Council from 1880,* Ph.D., Manchester 1956

Brown, D., *The Labour Movement in Wigan 1874-1967,* M.A., Liverpool 1969

Bryan, S.M., *The Women's Suffrage Question in the Manchester Area 1890-1906,* M.A., Manchester 1977

Fincher, J.A., *The Clarion Movement,* M.A., Manchester 1971

Firth, P., *Socialism and the Origins of the Labour Party in Nelson and District 1890-1906,* M.A., Manchester 1975

Garnett, J., & Mead, D., *Struggles of the Lancashire Cotton Workers.* Copy in the Working Class Movement Library

Leech, C.E., *The Feminist Movement in Manchester 1903-1914,* M.A., Manchester 1971

MINUTES AND ANNUAL REPORTS

Bolton Women's Citizen Association: *Annual Report;* Bolton Women's Local Government Society: *Minute Books;* Bolton Women's Suffrage Society: *Minute Books* and *Annual Reports;* Labour Representation Committee (later, Labour Party) *Annual Conference Reports;* Manchester Central ILP: *Minute Books;* Manchester National Society for Women's Suffrage: *Annual Reports;* Manchester, Salford and District Women's Trade Union Council: *Annual Reports;* National Union of Women's Suffrage Societies: *Annual Reports;* National Union of Women Workers: *Report of Annual Conference, 1907;* North of England Society for Women's Suffrage: *Annual Reports;* Oldham Weaver's and Winders' Council: *Minutes;* Women's Trade Union League: *Annual Reports.*

OTHER ARCHIVES

Billington-Grieg papers, Fawcett Library; Cooper papers, Lancashire Record Office, Preston (collection DDX 1137); Foley papers, Bolton Public Library; Industrial Suffrage file, Fawcett Library; Suffrage papers, London Museum; Suffrage papers, Manchester Central Reference Library archives.

NEWSPAPERS AND MAGAZINES

Blackburn Labour Journal; Bolton Journal; Bolton Evening News; Burnley Express & News; Clarion; Common Cause; Co-operative News; Cotton Factory Times; Crewe Chronicle; Englishwoman's Review; History Workshop Journal; Labour Leader; Labour Prophet; Manchester Evening News; Manchester Guardian; Monthly Herald; Nelson Chronicle; Northern Star; Oldham Chronicle; Oldham Standard; Oral History Journal; Preston Co-operative Record; Rossendale Echo; Rossendale Free Press; Royal Statistical Society Journal; Socialist Leader; Votes for Women; Wigan and District Advertiser; Women's Suffrage Journal; Women's Trade Union Review.

INDEX

297

graduates' deputation, 77
Green, Mrs, 81, 145, 149, 162, 245
Greenwood, Walter, 61, 94
Grey, Sir Edward, MP, 189, 191
Grundy, Violet, 93, 179, 197, 241

Harcourt, Rt Hon, Lewis MP, 244-5
half-timers, 34, 221
Hardie, Keir, 44-5, 152-3; & women's
  suffrage, 123, 125, 180, 188, 192,
  232, 234; & radical suffragists, 162,
  165-6, 174, 199, 229; &
  Pankhursts, 167-8, 171-2, 174, 190,
  208, 250; and also, 120, 124, 157,
  234, 256
Harker, Helen, 175, 190-2
Harker, John, 15, 190
Hard Way Up, The, 15; see also,
  Hannah Mitchell
Haslingden, 158, 245
Haworth, 248
Haworth, Mrs Alfred, 197
Heaton, Annie, 78, 79, 93, 144, 147-8
Henderson, Arthur, MP, 231-2, 247
Heptonstall, 25
Hesmondhalgh, Beth, 226
Higginbotham, Miss, 153
Hodge, John, 173
Holt, Mrs, 222, 229
hosiery workers, 47, 162
housekeeping money, 32, 39-40
housework, 30-1, 140
Huddersfield, 149, 151, 207
Hull, 191, 220
Hyde, 153, 158, 228
Hyndman, H.M., 43-4, 56-7, 98, 167,
  170, 256

ILP News, 174
Independent Labour Party, 44-5, 79; &
  women, 45, 82, 120, 125-201; &
  radical suffragists, 15, 131-2, 146,
  152; & Pankhursts, 167-9, 188,
  190-2, 200, 207-8, 250-1; at 1905
  Labour Conference, 184-6; at 1907
  Labour Conference, 234; pacifism,
  256
infant mortality, 58; see also, childcare
India, 54, 60, 262-3
Ireland, 80, 243, 246, 258, 262
Isle of Man, 51, 74

Jackson, Jenny, 218, 226
Juggins, Mr, 37
Justice, 44, 98

Keenan, Nellie, 99, 143, 159, 165,
  178-9, 182, 195, 197, 228, 241

Keighley, 248
Kenney, Annie, in card room, 56, 86,
  89; & WSPU, 12, 189-192, 200,
  205-6, 218, 225, 227; First World
  War & after, 252, 258; see also 120
Kenney, Rowland, 56, 89, 118-9, 120
Kershaw family, 229
Knutsford, 123, 196, 213

Labour Churches, 117-8, 129, 146
Labour Gazette, 59
Labour Leader, 162, 173, 176, 179,
  181, 188, 256
Labour Party, & women's suffrage,
  231-2, 242, 244, 246; Annual
  Conferences & suffrage, 14; 1906,
  201; 1907, 234; 1908, 237-8; 1912,
  247; 1914, 250; pact with NUWSS,
  247-250
Labour Prophet, 129
Labour Representation Committee,
  formed, 45; & unions, 99, 126,
  154-7; & WSPU, 173-4; Annual
  Conferences, 1903, 173; 1904,
  159-60; 1905, 184-6; and also,
  138-9, 151, 152, 163
Ladies' Discussion Circle, 67
Lancashire & Cheshire Women
  Textile & other Workers'
  Representation Committee,
  formed, 163-4; & Wigan campaign,
  164-5, 197-200; growth of, 165-6,
  196-7; campaigns, 206, 243, 244;
  and also, 175, 180, 212, 249; see
  also, radical suffragists
Lancashire and Cheshire Union of
  Women's Liberal Associations, 194
Lancaster, 58
Laurel Bank Mill, 99
Lawrence, D.H, 40
Leeds, 73, 80, 106, 126, 135, 153,
  160, 181, 225
Lees, 55-6, 89, 96, 218
Lees family, 224
Leicester, 134, 177, 187
Leicestershire, 160
Levenshulme, 71, 142
libraries, 35, 116
Link, The, 42
Liverpool, 105, 177, 184, 186, 214,
  244, 259
Liverpool Women Textile Workers'
  Committee, 166
Lloyd George, Rt Hon. David, MP,
  243, 245
looms, see weavers
Lostock strike, 90
Love's Coming of Age, 121-2

300

Luty, Mary, 54-5, 112, 115

Macarthur, Mary, 240-1, 247
Macclesfield, 219
Macdonald, George, 80
MacDonald, James Ramsay, 27, 45, 126, 201, 234, 250
MacDonald, Margaret, 236, 240
McMillan, Margaret, 118, 120, 131, 135, 153, 207-8
McMurdo, Catherine, 62
Manchester, & cotton industry, 60-1; radicalism in, 62; liberalism in, 68-9, 130; & Independent Labour Party, 127, 128, 137, 167-9, 175, 190-2, 207-8; and also, 102, 103, 104, 118, 133, 136, 142, 166, 171, 214, 223, 225, 228, 239-40, 241, 249
Manchester & Salford Association of Machine, Electrical & other Women Workers, 39, 237, 261
Manchester & Salford Society of Women Employed in the Bookbinding & Printing Trades, 39, 241
Manchester & Salford Trades Council, 38, 175, 190, 261
Manchester & Salford Women's Trade & Labour Council, 179-80, 190-2, 197, 239, 241, 243
Manchester & Salford Women's Trade Union Council, 15, 39, 82, 110, 143-4, 159, 162, 171, 178-9
Manchester Central ILP branch, 171, 175, 188, 190, 207-8
Manchester Guardian, 16, 72, 156, 178, 190, 194, 239, 240
Manchester Labour Press, 121, 130
Manchester Ladies Literary Society, 70
Manchester National Society for Women's Suffrage, 69-82; formed, 69; activities, 71-3; decline, 75; & Special Appeal, 78-9; renamed, 82
Manchester University, *see* Owens College
manhood suffrage, 63, 141, 180, 186, 232
Markievicz, Constance, 81, 239-240, 245, 258, 262
Marland, Annie, 38, 43, 79, 88-9, 97, 98, 106, 134
marriage and suffrage activity, 216-7
married women's work, 36, 49-51, 58-61, 228, 238-9
married women's legal rights, 65, 68, 74-5, 216-7, 259
Married Women's Property Committee,

Martyn, Caroline, 129, 134
Marx, Eleanor, 43, 100
Marx, Karl, 48, 115
Mason, Bertha, 79, 215
matchgirls' strike, 42
Mawdsley, James, 43
Maxwell, Lily, 71
May Day, 44, 143
Mayo, Miss, 134
Men's League for Women's Suffrage, 229
Merrie England, 120-1, 122; *see also*, Blatchford, Robert
Methodism, *see* religion
Middlesborough, 32
Middleton, 34
militancy, attitudes to, 203-6, 209-210, 211, 218-9
Mill, John Stuart, 67-8, 71, 140, 202
Milne, Alice, 206, 225, 227
Mills, Mrs, 191
miners, 45, 60, 97, 99, 198-9, 207, 214
Mitchell, Hannah, 15, 33, 138, 140, 188, 189-90, 222, 260-1; quoted, 16, 31-2, 46, 134, 217, 222, 256
Montefiore, Dora, 199, 200, 202
Monthly Herald, 122
Morris, William, 75, 116, 126
Mossley, 88
Mud March, 221
munitions workers, 253-5
Murgatroyd, Emily, 99, 161, 222

nail-makers, *see* chain-makers
National Association for the Promotion of Social Science, 70
National Industrial & Professional Women's Suffrage Society, 197, 212, 244, 245
National Liberal Federation, 141
National Society for Women's Suffrage, 68
National Union of Societies for Equal Citizenship, 258-9
National Union of Teachers, 104-5
National Union of Women's Suffrage Societies, formed, 75, 82; links with radical suffragists, 191, 212-6, 247-9; employs Lancashire organizers, 213-5, 222-5, 235, 247-9; attitude to militancy, 194-5, 209; campaigns, 221, 223; compared to WSPU, 224-9; & First World War, 252-8; *and also*, 13, 187, 202, 243-4
Nelson, 21, 58, 110, 138-40, 147; Women's Co-operative Guild, 136, 147, 161, 180, 191, 219, 234;

301

socialism in, 44, 126, 138-40, 155, 161, 219, 234, 257; & women's suffrage, 157, 158, 234

Nelson and Colne Suffrage Committee, 147, 160-1, 223

Nelson Chronicle, 155

Nield, Ada, *see* Chew, Ada Nield

Nightingale, Florence, 65

No Conscription Fellowship, 256

Non-conformism, *see* religion

North and South, 49, 85

Northern Star, 119

North of England Society for Women's Suffrage, formed 82; early activity, 82, 99; textile workers' campaign, 143-166; & radical suffragists, 157, 162-3, 243; radical suffragists resign, 193-7; *and also* 131, 167, 177, 187, 191

Northern Counties Amalgamated Association of Weavers, Winders & Warpers, *see* Weavers' Association

nursing, 112, 261

Oldham spinners, 51, 59, 121; card room workers, 52, 87, 88, 89; 1834 riot, 61-2; weavers, 48, 94, 95, 96, 98; co-op, 115; Trades Council, 87; & women's suffrage, 145, 160, 177, 190, 224

Openshaw, 142

oral history, 18, 160; *see also*, documentary records, scarcity of

Osborne Judgement, 243

Owens College, 77, 115, 170

Oxford, 42, 115

pacifism, 254, 256-8

Palliser, Edith, 82, 206, 213, 214, 215

Pankhurst, Adela, 172, 205, 217, 258

Pankhurst, Christabel, youth, 169-70; & radical suffragists, 156, 170-4, 178-9; & Labour, 172-7, 179, 183.4, 207-8, 250-1; & WSPU, 174-7. 188-192, 201, 203, 206-210, 227-9; resigns from NESWS, 193-7; tactics, 209-210; First World War & after, 252, 258, 262; *and also*, 11, 12, 28, 124

Pankhurst, Emmeline, childhood, 74; marriage, 74; attitude to women's suffrage, 74-5; 78, 156, 165, 167-9, 172, 186; & ILP, 79, 127, 137, 167-9, 184, 186, 208; as Poor Law Guardian, 137, 167-8; & WSPU, 174-7, 187, 190-1, 200-1, 202, 204-5, 210; First World War & after, 252, 258; *and also* 121, 219

Pankhurst Hall, 116

Pankhurst, Harry, 172

Pankhurst, Dr. Richard, active in Manchester, 69, 71, 74, 78, 124; & ILP, 79, 116, 127, 167; death, 168

Pankhurst, Sylvia, 124, 171, 200, 210, 219, 248, 253, 258; quoted, 12, 68, 80, 73, 86, 129, 167-8, 170-1, 188

Parliamentary Labour Party, 243

pawnbrokers, 33

Pearce, Mrs, 147-8

People's Suffrage Federation, 247

Peterloo, 62

Petticoat Rebellion, The, 24

Pethwick-Lawrences, 200, 205, 208, 210, 217, 262

piecers, 89-90

pit-brow lasses, 60, 215-6, 239

Plant, Elsie, 116, 128

Platt brothers, 54, 88

Pollitt, Harry, 30, 86

Pollitt, Mrs, 30, 47

Poor Law Guardians, 33, 88; women as, 137-140, 154, 161, 235

Potteries, 38, 58, 135, 162, 181

Powell, Sir Francis, 199

Preston, weavers, 53, 94, 146, 218; WSPU, 217, 218, 226; *and also*, 58, 62, 173, 225

Primrose League, 45, 73

printers, 39, 197

Private Members' Bills, 70, 157-8, 180, Rollit's, 76, 140; Crooks' 165, 187; Bamford Slack's, 187; Dickinson's, 241; *see also*, Conciliation Bills

pupil teachers, 103-4

Queen's College, 66

'Queen's Gardens' lecture, 53

Quelch, Harry, 44, 98; & women's suffrage, 185-6, 201, 234, 238

Radcliffe, 148

radical suffragists, 15, 18, 20-9, 42, 125, 131, 143-66, 197-206, 211-230; & WSPU, 176-7, 190-2, 195-7, 203; resign from NESWS, 193-7; & Labour Party, 231-7; & right-to-work campaign, 237-242; & Rossendale campaign, 243-6; First World War & after, 256-263

Railway Servants Union, 152, 154

Rathbone, Eleanor, 214, 215

Ramelson, Marian, 14

Ramsbottom, Mrs, 145

Rawtenstall, 104, 242

Reddish, Sarah, starts work, 93; Clarion Van, 134; Women's Trade Union League, 134-5, 144, 146; Women's Trade Union League,

304